REGNUM STUDIES IN GLOBAL CHRISTIANITY

Jesus and the Incarnation

Reflections of Christians from Islamic Contexts

REGNUM STUDIES IN GLOBAL CHRISTIANITY

(Previously GLOBAL THEOLOGICAL VOICES series)

Series Preface

In the latter part of the twentieth century the world witnessed significant changes in global Christian dynamics. Take for example the significant growth of Christianity in some of the poorest countries of the world. Not only have numbers increased, but the emphasis of their engagement has expanded to include ministry to a wider socio-cultural context than had previously been the case. The *Regnum Studies in Global Christianity* series explores the issues with which the global church struggles, focusing in particular on ministry rooted in Africa, Asia, Latin America and Eastern Europe.

Not only does the series make available studies that will help the global church learn from past and present, it provides a platform for provocative and prophetic voices to speak to the future of Christianity. The editors and the publisher pray particularly that the series will grow as a public space, where the voices of church leaders from the majority world will contribute out of wisdom drawn from experience and reflection, thus shaping a healthy future for the global church. To this end, the editors invite theological seminaries and universities from around the world to submit relevant scholarly dissertations for possible publication in the series. Through this, it is hoped that the series will provide a forum for South-to-South as well as South-to-North dialogues.

Series Editors

REGNUM STUDIES IN GLOBAL CHRISTIANITY

Jesus and the Incarnation

Reflections of Christians from Islamic Contexts

Edited by

David Emmanuel Singh

First published 2011 by Regnum Books International

Regnum is an imprint of the Oxford Centre for Mission Studies
St. Philip and St. James Church
Woodstock Road
Oxford, OX2 6HR, UK
www.ocms.ac.uk/regnum

09 08 07 06 05 04 03 8 7 6 5 4 3 2 1

British Library Cataloguing in Publication Data
A catalogue record for this book is available from the British Library

ISBN - 978-1-506478-04-3

Typeset by RBI and Words by Design
Cover design by Words by Design
Cover shows a detail of The Nativity by Taddeo Gaddi with an image of the Qur'an

The financial assistance of Robin and Nancy Wainwright of Middle East Fellowship towards this publication is gratefully acknowledged.

Distributed by 1517 Media in the US and Canada

Contents

PART IV: DIALOGUE AND WITNESS

Foreword

J. Dudley Woodberry

Dr J. Dudley Woodberry is Dean Emeritus and Senior Professor of Islamic Studies at the School of Intercultural Studies, Fuller Theological Seminary, USA

A Persian carpet depicting Jesus and Mary hung on the wall in front of us when my wife and I visited a missionary colleague a few days ago.[1] It illustrates both the potential and the problems that the authors of these essays face as they discuss the Incarnation in Muslim contexts.

Near the top of the carpet was the Qur'anic statement "That is Jesus, the son of Mary" (19:34), indicating that the carpet was intended as a depiction of the Jesus of the Qur'an with all the affirmation and denials that it contains with respect to the Biblical record. The visual art in turn illustrates the Qur'anic record: angels that had taken part in the annunciation (Q 3:42), Mary with her arms crossed in front of her indicating purity (Q 19:20, 27-29), and the young Jesus comforting her.

Around the border is a sensitive Persian poem which builds upon the account in the 19th surah entitled Mary and shows the emotional bond in popular piety with Mary and Jesus. Starting with Mary's service in the temple, according to Muslim tradition, it depicts her pain and shame in childbirth, and the divine care for her. Then she points to Jesus as the source of life and security for people in trouble.[2]

The lines of the poem are interspersed with images of the Qajar kings, who ruled Iran during the 19th and early 20th centuries, thus linking Persian culture with the Qur'anic Jesus and Mary. The difference of style within the patterns indicates that the making of the carpet was a family endeavour. As in all traditional knotted-pile carpets, each of the thousands of pieces of wool that make up the pattern is tied to the underlying strands by a hand-made knot, so it cannot unravel like knitting. Thus the carpet illustrates how the Jesus of the Qur'an is bound to the hearts and minds of Muslims by religion, art, poetry, ethnic culture, and family by daily knots throughout their lives.

In order to ascertain the challenges for the writers of the following chapters on the Incarnation, we shall highlight some of the issues in the Biblical and Qur'anic sources. When we turn to the Gospels, we see that the response of the Jewish establishment to some of the claims of Jesus was similar to that of some subsequent Muslims. When Jesus walked in the temple in the portico of

---

[1] Joyce Davenport, who served with her husband Harold in Iraq and Lebanon.

[2] I received help in the Persian translation from a former student Yvette Bearce.

Solomon, where the al-Aqsa mosque is today, the Jews took up stones to stone him, saying:

> [We] are going to stone you…for blaspheming, because you, though only a human being, are making yourself God.
>
> Jesus answered,
>
> Can you say that the one who the Father has sanctified and sent into the world is blaspheming because I said, "I am God's son"? (Jn. 10:23, 31, 33, 36)

Thus we need to ascertain what is meant by the Biblical terms ascribed to Jesus and compare these with Qur'anic understandings of them. First, does this title "Son of God," which is used of Adam (Lk. 3:38), David's successor (2 Sam. 7:14), and the anointed king (Ps. 2:7), mean not deity itself but rather one with a special relationship to God as his representative? Thus we need to see what it means when applied to Jesus. The high priest apparently understood it to mean the Messiah when he asked, "Are you the Christ, the son of the Blessed One?" (Mk 14:61). It is used for Jesus by the voice from heaven after his baptism and the coming of the Spirit "This is my beloved son with whom I am well pleased" (Matt. 3:17; Mk. 1:11; Lk. 3:22). Thus in the pattern of Psalm 2:7, the term appears to indicate his anointing by the Spirit as a king. John in turn says, "The Word became flesh and lived among us, and we have seen his glory, the glory of the Father's only son (or as of a father's only son), full of grace and truth" (Jn. 1:14). Therefore, for John the word "son" means the Word made flesh who communicates God's word.

The Qur'an, however, repudiates the claim that God had a son, on the grounds of the oneness of God (4:171; 19:34-35). Both passages use the term *walad*, which designates a physical son, rather than *ibn*, a term that can have a metaphorical meaning more in keeping with the Biblical use of the title "son" for Jesus. A carnal perspective on "sonship" is found in Surah 6:101: "How can He [God] have a son when He has no consort?" Surah 5:116 even seems to suggest that some Christians, at least, may venerate Jesus and Mary as gods: "God will say: 'O Jesus…did you say to people, 'Worship me and my mother as gods beside God?' He will say…'Never could I say what I have no right [to say]'." The qur'anic reference to Lat, Uzza, and Manat (52:19-20) is understood in Muslim tradition to designate idols that were considered to be daughters of God, and reflects the disdain which the Qur'an came to have of any reference to God having a child. The Qur'an concludes, "They blaspheme who say 'God is Christ the son of Mary," and it gives as evidence that they had human needs: "They both had to eat food" (5:72, 75).

The next topics relevant to the Incarnation, which appear in the scriptures of both faiths, are the titles the "Word of God" and the "Spirit of God," though in both scriptures, God is shrouded in mystery. In the Hebrew scriptures, God is present both in his Word and in his Spirit starting with the creation story:

> In the beginning when God created the heavens and the earth, the earth was a formless void and darkness covered the face of the deep, while the spirit of God swept over the face of the waters. Then God said: "Let there be light" (Gen. 1:1-3).

In the New Testament we have complementary Christologies based both on God's Word and God's Spirit respectively. The first is discussed in John 1:1, 14:

> In the beginning was the Word and the Word was with God and the Word was God....
>
> And the Word became flesh and lived among us, and we have seen his glory, the glory of the Father's only Son (or as of a father's only son), full of grace and truth.

The Word made flesh as God's son reveals God's glory and makes the Father known (1:14-18). Yet John also exposes an underlying Spirit Christology. The Spirit descends on Jesus at his baptism and in turn he baptizes with the Holy Spirit (Jn. 6:33).

The synoptic Gospels emphasize the Spirit Christology with an underlying Word Christology. At Jesus' baptism, the Spirit descends on him and the voice from heaven declares him to be the Son of God (Matt. 3:13-17; Mk. 6:9-11; Lk. 3:21-22). He is thus the Messiah, the anointed one. In Capernaum, he announces, "The Spirit of the Lord is upon me, because he has anointed me to preach good news..." (Lk. 1:18-19).[3]

Turning to the Qur'an, we see Jesus described both as the Word of God and the Spirit of God (5:110; 37:171; 40:68; 66:12). As in Matthew 1:18 when Mary is found to be with child from the Holy Spirit, God, in Surah 21:91, declares, "We breathed into her our spirit." Other verses also ascribe "a word of God" or a "word from God" to him such as Surah 3:45: "God announces to you the good news/gospel (*yubashiruki*) of a word from him; his name will be Messiah, Jesus, son of Mary." The points of contact are suggestive, yet Surah 4:171 limits these to Jesus only being an apostle, God's Word, and a Spirit from him.

When my wife and I saw the Persian carpet with the words, "That is Jesus, son of Mary," we were told that it was originally one of a pair, but our friend has never seen the other carpet. The essays in this volume may be envisioned as a start in replacing the missing carpet of the pair. Using as many of the existing

---

[3] For a more complete discussion of the Son of God and the Word and Spirit Christologies see Colin Brown, "Trinity and Incarnation: In Search of Contemporary Orthodoxy," *Ex Auditu* 7(1991): 83-100.

patterns and dyes as possible, we might add to the previous title "That is Jesus, the son of Mary," the ascription "the Word and Spirit of God" which both of our scriptures also affirm. In place of the picture of the boy Jesus comforting Mary, there might be another of the mature Jesus assuring Mary, that even from the cross, John will care for her (Jn, 19:26). Replacing the Persian poem around the border might be the prophetic words of Isaiah that Jesus read in the synagogue of his hometown of Nazareth: "The Spirit of the Lord is upon me and He has anointed me to bring good news…proclaim release…the recovery of sight...to proclaim the year of the Lord's favour" (Lk. 4:18-19; Isa. 61:1-2). Then, interspersed with these words, where the Qajar kings were pictured, can be portrayed those to whom Jesus ministered, with emphasis on those, such as the blind who received sight, that are also mentioned in the Qur'an. As day by day, we tie the knots with our Muslim co-workers, to bring out these patterns, perhaps we may together get a glimpse of "the glory of God in the face of Jesus Christ."

PART I: INTRODUCTION

‘The Word Made Flesh’: Community, Dialogue and Witness

David Emmanuel Singh

Dr. David Emmanuel Singh is Research Tutor at the Oxford Centre for Mission Studies, UK

This is the second in the series of three books. The first, *Jesus and the Cross*, published in 2009, was well received by theological students, teachers and generally Christians living in Muslim contexts. This book on Jesus and the Incarnation aspires to achieve the same level of interest among similar audiences.[1] The readership is expected to be varied but particularly theological students and, here, those specialising in the theology of religions and ordinary Christians wanting to hear different Christian voices on one of the most intractable ‘problems’ in the Christian theology of religions, namely, the Incarnation. For this reason, the book includes papers written by a variety of Christian authors representing a range of approaches and contexts. The approaches include exegetical/hermeneutical, empirical socio-anthropological, philosophical, historical, biographical and missional

The attempt here is to allow these voices to speak for themselves from within the context of a broader structure centred on the notions of ‘the Word made Flesh’ and ‘the Word made Book’. The fundamental concern is not to interrogate the particular intellectual positions of the contributing authors but to allow the varied discourse on a central pillar of Christian faith, the Incarnation, to be available to the readers who can choose from this elements they deem to be useful for their witness and dialogue with Muslims and/or their continuing learning about Christian relations with Muslims. In other words, this is not a statement representing any particular intellectual position apart from the most general one which is the centrality of the Word made flesh as confessed by Christians and attested to by Christian history. It attempts to do so by organising the discourse around the discussion on the Word which is to be the basis for a sense of community, not as an end in itself but as a means to the performance of Christian witness and dialogue with Muslims.

[1] The last book in this series, *Jesus and the Resurrection,* is forthcoming.

The Word

In Christianity, the notion of 'the Word' remains inseparable from the historic Christian witness to the Incarnation and Jesus Christ. This is especially where Christians part ways with Muslims. Where Christians and Muslims can meet is in considering the pre-existing Word. For this reason, I think, it is a promising concept to explore here.

Most modern scholars agree that Athanasius of Alexandria (ca. 293-373) represented the 'orthodox' Christian position. His *De incarnatione verbe dei* is one of the earliest works on 'the Word made Flesh' where he speaks of the incarnation as the solution to a divine dilemma.[2] Aquinas' 'treatise on the most Holy Trinity' addressed the question of the origin of 'the divine persons.' The logos is one who 'proceeds' in God Himself and has being in Him. There is no other Word that derives from here. This Word became flesh.[3] In Islam the notion of *al-lawh al- mahfuz* (lit. 'The Guarded Tablet') is as central a notion as the logos of Christianity. The difference appears to be in that whereas the Christian notion of the Word is personal, the Muslim Word is understood almost in the Aristotelian sense of 'substance'.[4] What seems comparable between Christians and Muslims is the idea that what was part of God becomes something/somebody. In Christianity, the logos appeared in the form of the person of Jesus Christ while in Islam it was the eternal Qur'an which appeared in the form of the physical Qur'an. The dogmatic starting points of Christian and Muslim witnesses, therefore, are: 'The Word made Person/Flesh' and 'the Word made Book'.

In practice and in doctrine, the idea of the Word as Book has been shared by many Christians to nearly the same degree as Muslims. Grafton's paper, on the ancient Arab Christianity and Van Dyke's translation of the Bible into Arabic, is a fine example.[5] Arabic Christianity has existed for centuries alongside the dominant religion of Islam and has typically evolved a distinctive identity that reflects not just Arabic culture but the superimposing reality of Islam. 'The Word made Book', Grafton argues is one expression of this association. This means that many Christian Arabs have the same sort of understanding of revelation and the Scriptures as the majority around them. The Bible to them would be the Word of God in a similar sense as the Qur'an for Muslims.

In practice too, Christians have widely held the Scriptures to be 'the Word.' Ignatius of Antioch, also called Theophorus (ca. 35-117), was an early Church Father and Patriarch of Antioch. Like the Apostles, he is known for a good number of letters to churches under his care.[6] One of these was to 'the Philadelphians' from a town in an area now in Turkey. It was a significant centre

---

[2] Athanasius 1996:31ff.

[3] Thomas Aquinas 1947:268ff.

[4] Glasse 2002:275. Compare with the Islamic philosophical notion of *al-jawhar*.

[5] See Grafton's paper.

[6] See Kleist 1946.

of early Christianity. In his letter to the Philadelphians, St. Ignatius sought to address what he saw as a serious error in the doctrines of the Book and Jesus. Some people were found popularising the notion that if something was absent in 'the ancient scriptures' (Hebrew scriptures) it was not worth believing in. They were particularly referring to the Gospel of Jesus and the argument was that since the Gospel was not in the ancient scriptures, it could not be right and, hence, not worth believing. Obviously, this was seen to be a cause of insidious disunity. St. Ignatius' answer to this was not through the re-reading of the ancient scriptures to prove that the Gospel was present there but to challenge the Philadelphians not to focus on the Book but on the person of Jesus. The Book was from God who is Spirit, but it was the person of Jesus who was the true incarnation of the Spirit. 'The archives ought not to be preferred to the Spirit.'[7]

The Hebrew-Christian canon was formed through different processes in history and in a particular cultural milieu. Both positive and negative examples have been cited of its influence upon those who lived by it. The positive impact, it can be argued, was linked to the consequences of certain developments in the Church. Protestantism introduced the notion of the 'liberty of examination and discussion'. There was the Spirit of God behind the scriptures. The Church was accountable for the way in which it arrogated the right to be the single interpreter of the scripture, which was supreme over the Church. The Spirit superseded the scripture. God alone was the sovereign and the scriptures were under him. Each believer had their liberated conscience in direct contact with the scripture. Thus, the order they conceived for the great Protestant liberation was: the Spirit, the scriptures, and human conscience.[8]

However, the notion of liberty was not entirely natural in some contexts.[9] The Protestant access to the Bible meant in some contexts that certain types of people, such as the 'witches' were excommunicated. So convinced was Martin Luther (1483-1546) of the ban against witchcraft and the excommunication of the witches that it was recommended that witches be 'put to death without mercy and without regard to legal niceties.'[10] John Calvin (1509-1564) shared the belief in the witches having a pact with the devil. His demonology was founded on the scriptures[11] and this had the same authority as the inviolable church dogma. The Biblically supported demonology, therefore, was in these cases, the basis for the justification of the persecution of witches.[12] The reformers sought freedom for Christians but this freedom was not absolute. Even for Calvin, Christian freedom or freedom of conscience was not the same as

---

[7] *Philadelphia* VIII.
[8] Wylie 2002:649-650.
[9] Donaldson 2009:118.
[10] See Smith 2008:234.
[11] E.g. Eph. 6.11-12 and the Old Testament examples come from the narrative of Samuel and Saul and his sermons on Deut 18.10-12. See Kors and Peters 2001 and Calvin 1988.
[12] Kors and Peters 2001.

individual autonomy.[13] It meant being subject to the will of God (revealed in the Word of God). The Word of God needed interpretation and the will of God needed an agency to draw it from the Word. The reformers themselves acted as the primary interpreters of the Word with exceptional cases of passionate excesses as in the examples above.

The Word we speak of is not the Book but the person of Christ. This poses some problem for Christian theologians of Islam. How does one relate with Muslims if it is assumed that unlike Christianity, there is no notion of 'the Word as Person' in Islam? In speaking of the Incarnation of the Word in John's Gospel Grams engages with Hick.[14] We know Hick has been a supporter of oral and written dialogue with Muslims. In replacing the Person of Jesus with a transcendental reality, Hick dispenses with the traditional centrality of Christology in Christian Muslim dialogue. This dovetails perfectly with the traditional Islamic rejection of the incarnation of Jesus. Grams endorses an opposite view, that the Qur'an denies the incarnation of Jesus. On the positive side, his argument is that there is promise in using John's 'concrete' theologizing.[15] He speaks of the Word's incarnation in creation, in the Mosaic Law, and in Jesus as offering particular instances of the revelations of God. The person of the Word has the capacity to 'translate' itself to become manifest and through ceasing to remain hidden in transcendence. God's compassion through the Incarnation of the Word thus becomes self-giving, sacrificial, and transformative. Jesus' Incarnation was therefore a form of translation. As Walls affirms, 'Incarnation is translation'.[16] If, therefore, it is argued, the Incarnation is an instance of the divinity translating into humanity, its appropriation in different cultures and periods must allow for a degree of diversity.[17] The sum of the argument, therefore, is that the concreteness of the Incarnation needs to be acknowledged but not in a rigid and mono-cultural sense; the Incarnation would be meaningless and have no transformative power without the possibility of translation.

Azumah, like Grams, agrees with the view that the doctrine of the Incarnation is central to Christianity but has been viewed with suspicion and rejected in Islam.[18] However, Azumah goes further than Grams because he expands on the key sub-theme of translation. The sphere of the notion of translation for him can be expanded to allow a view of the interesting comparative discussion in Islam and Christianity. Christian orthodoxy (needless to say after a long struggle) has come to view scriptural and cultural translation as an integral part of orthodoxy. Islamic orthodoxy would appear to most, in comparison, doggedly opposed to

[13] See Kaplan 2007:24.
[14] See Grams' paper.
[15] See Hick and Meltzer 1989.
[16] Walls 1996:27-28.
[17] Walls 1996:27-28.
[18] See Azumah's paper.

translation (especially scriptural translation). This 'change of gear', proposed by Azumah, promises some movement in engagement beyond the traditional impasse on Christology-centred dialogue and witness. Thus, both Grams and Azumah start with assuming that Christology is absent in Islam. The former presses ahead with locating an alternative for engagement through emphasizing the 'concrete dimension' of the Incarnation and the latter refocuses attention on the broader cultural meaning of translation for a comparative exposition. Both are creative in their proposals and persuasive in their arguments but does Christian witness/dialogue have no possibility of enagaging Muslims at the deeper level of Christology?

Firstly, one needs to clarify that Christian engagement with Muslims at the level of theology/Christology is not simply a matter of historical interest or a matter relating to the past. A number of well known theologians of our time, Cragg, Hick and Kung, have all been engaging with Muslims, with Christology at the very heart of the dialogue.[19] That is to say, even if there are strong historical and other reasons to suggest that on the issue of Christology/theology there can be no meeting between Christians and Muslims; one must not give up on it, as Hick does. There is no Christianity without Christology. The reality is that it cannot in any context of dialogue or witness be ignored.

Secondly, not only have Muslims been writing on dialogue with Christianity involving the Incarnation, but also they have been demonstrating a diversity of perspectives based on their deeper understanding of the other and their own traditions. Siddiqui, writing on Mahmoud Ayoub, suggests, for example, that the Qur'an for him contains an unambiguous Christology where Jesus Christ is seen as one 'fortified with the Holy Spirit'.[20] Ayoub's commitment to dialogue was rooted in his early association with Christians and his doctoral work completed under W.C. Smith,[21] and there have been many like him in recent times.[22] Perhaps, as Christians, we ought to look wider for the evidence of Muslim Christologies which then can be promising starting points for deeper inter-faith conversations.

Thirdly, some question the notion that the history of dialogue shows that exercises in dialogue on Christology (especially if it is assumed to be absent in Islam/the Qur'an) are futile and that one should not, therefore, engage with Muslims. Cragg touches on it in his typically crisp and tightly argued paper: '*Incarnatus non est*: The Qur'an and Christology'.[23] Cragg is asking whether the Qur'an totally rejects the Christian notion of Incarnation as the Word made flesh.

---

[19] See his discussion of the 9th century Christian thinking on Christology for Muslims in Beaumont 2005:xxi.

[20] Siddiqui 1997:107.

[21] See Siddiqui 1997:97-109 and Ayoub 1978.

[22] For example, Hasan Askari, Khurshid Ahmad, Muhammad Talbi, and Sayyid Hossein Nasr.

[23] See Cragg's paper.

If one looked closely enough one would see that the Qur'an and Muhammad were closer to the notion of 'the Christhood of Jesus' than has been accepted by both Christians and Muslims. That Islam does have a Christology has not been in question. The fundamental difference in the Christian and Islamic Christologies, according to many, has been that for Christians, Christology is primarily in the domain of the ontological whereas for Muslims it has been in the functional sense of *masih*, the anointed one. The task of Jesus in the Qur'an is, therefore, assumed to be functional i.e., to bring the Word of God for the guidance of humanity. However, Cragg argues that Christians and Muslims need to move forward beyond this point. There is room for Christological dialogue not only in this pragmatic sense but also in the deeply theological and ontological senses.

If one examines the actual Islamic piety surrounding Muhammad, for example, one realizes that he has a much larger place in Islam than simply that of a 'messenger' or an 'employee of God'. His name appears next to God on many inscriptions on mosques and he is considered by many to be the 'living carrier' of the Word of God. Muhammad enjoys a closer relation with God like no one else. The Qur'an and Muhammad have a closer connection than one thinks as the third person passes into the second person 'discourse with Muhammad' in it when God addresses Muhammad and not just speaks through him![24] The Qur'an in such intensely personal addresses demonstrates space for a deep sense of intimacy and familiarity of Muhammad with the divine agency; his work as a prophet is not disengaged from him as a person possessing a passionate longing for God and care for humanity (especially in the Meccan phase); he is not simply seen by the Qur'an as an instrument, but someone who has intrinsic worth and connection with God. Cragg's approach here will likely provide an additional insight into a widely held assumption subscribed to by Grams and Azumah papers.

The Qur'an is held sacred by a living people of faith. This raises the question of whether 'non-Muslims' have the 'right' to read and interpret it. Marshall has argued for this right on the grounds of the Muslim claim that the Qur'an is universal in its relevance.[25] Indeed as Cragg tells us, the Qur'an is, despite difficulties involving internal cohesion, order and chronology, one of the more 'urgently consulted' books outside the academies.[26] Marshall's argument for non-Muslim access seems limited to its use in academic contexts. Cragg seems to have a more ambivalent approach to the Qur'an. In a lecture at the University of Gloucestershire, Cragg supported Montgomery Watt's position on Muhammad by distinguishing Muhammad 'in Mecca' and 'in Medina' (prophet and statesman) expressing his wish for Muslims to recover the 'Meccan dimensions of Islam'. [27] There is, according to him, something in the 'Meccan verses' which

[24] See, for example, Surah 96 and 74.
[25] Marshall 1999.
[26] Cragg 2005:11-12.
[27] 'Sufism in Britain' 13 April 2010.

is akin to Hebrew prophecy. The rationale for this level of Christian appreciation for the Qur'an in Cragg's thinking may have the objective of realising better relations with Muslims but it is does not exclude Christian witness/dialogue. Zahniser takes this idea to a completely different level in arguing for reasons why Christians can/should use the Qur'an.[28] Many Christian will clearly have difficulties in Zahniser's position on the 'sympathy of scriptures' to this level of its appropriation in Christian contexts. Some, like Cragg would not be averse to the idea of the Qur'an 'containing' the Word, not least those from the Meccan phase. Indeed, some converts to Christianity (as in our examples in this volume) would testify too that their reading of the Qur'an led them to Jesus, the Word in flesh! However, by any standard, Zahniser's is a radical approach and his recommendations are hard for most Christians to accept. It must also be said here, firstly, that the 'sympathy of scriptures' should not be disengaged from its context in witness/dialogue; secondly, 'sympathy' should be properly understood in the context of the history of interactions between Christians, Jews and 'pagan Arabs'. One must also realise that Muhammad's self-perception as a prophet was modelled on the Judeo-Christian tradition;[29] and thirdly, it should be understood also in the context of the experience of the converts who testify to having searched for Jesus, the Word in flesh having been introduced to Jesus in the Qur'an.[30]

Community

The Qur'anic 'salvation history' encompasses Judaism and Christianity. Christians and Jews are considered 'the people of the Book' for their close historical contact in Arabia, prior to the advent of Islam. Hence, similarities between them are to be expected. Muslims are charged not to 'dispute' with Christians unless there are some among them who 'act unjustly'. Muslims are also mandated by the Qur'an to treat them as part of the larger community of the people of the Book because, 'We believe in that which has been revealed to us and revealed to you, and our God and your God is One, and to Him do we submit'.[31] There are of course contradictory verses like Surah 5.51, but if understood in the light of Surah 29.46, these are likely focussing on those who 'act unjustly' and not all Christians and Jews. No community can be expected to be entirely uniform not even a community that possesses the Book. The fact is that there is always a remnant even among those who have gone far astray: '…a party of the people of the Book stand for the right, they recite the verses of God during the hours of the night, prostrating themselves in prayer. They believe in God and the Last Day…and they hasten in (all) good works; and they are among

[28] See Zahniser's paper.
[29] See Singh 2008.
[30] See papers below.
[31] Surah 29.46.

the righteous. And whatever good they do, nothing will be rejected of them; for God knows well those who do right.'[32]

This general sense of broader ecumenicity notwithstanding, Islam makes a clear evolutionary distinction between the former books and their peoples and the Qur'an/Muslims. This sort of evolutionary understanding of revelation has been evidently employed by Muslim scholars to reconcile contradictions within the Qur'an. The principle of *naskh* (abrogation), for instance, originated in the Islamic disciplines of *tafsir* (Qur'anic interpretation) and *fiqh* (jurisprudence). When there was contradiction in legal rulings, a chronologically prior verse or tradition upon which a ruling in question was based was understood to have been superseded by a later one. Based on this idea of chronologically successive sources, a revised ruling could be given without any sense of violating the authority of the source. In terms of religion, Islam is all-encompassing. It sees the history of religions as a linear story of human failures and divine interventions. This history also has an underlying teleological purpose of leading to the Qur'an, Muhammad and Islam. With the appearance of the final religion, the grounds for the need for previous religions were diminished. Religions which were chronologically prior were thus in this sense 'abrogated'. This did not mean that the old was entirely replaced by the new – this was expected but not coercively demanded. The Qur'an allowed for the coexistence and continuance of the old religions provided those following these 'rejected evil and believed in God.'[33]

One cannot miss the apparent similarities. Not only do two of the world's oldest surviving cultures, Hebrew/Jewish and Arab, seem to share a number of prophets, these prophets seem to be central to their peoples' salvation histories. Their sacred histories are punctuated by the stories of habitual disobedience and the consequent divine interventions by the means of the Word (prophetic and written). In the Hebrew/Jewish tradition, prophets have been understood to belong to 'major' and 'minor' categories and in the Arab/Islamic tradition into the categories of those with the book and those without. There is neither intrinsic hierarchy between the major and the minor prophets of the OT, nor the prophets with and the prophets without books in the Qur'an. Their fundamental task is to warn, guide, challenge, and invite the peoples back to obedience and faithfulness to God. Although there are fundamental differences about the nature of 'the Book' among Christians and Muslims, the similarities we have alluded to could be a basis for a sense of community. There is potential here for a broader functional *oikomene* and the reading of the Qur'an as suggested above may help with dialogue and witness in this context.

[32] Surah 3.113-115.

[33] Surah 2.256: 'There is no compulsion in religion, for the right way is clear from the wrong way. Whoever therefore rejects the forces of evil and believes in God, he has taken hold of a support most unfailing, which shall never give way, for God is All-Hearing and All-Knowing.'

However, the similarities have a deeper dimension in Abraham, the very quintescence of obedient faith in God: 'Now the Lord had said unto Abram, Get thee our of they country...unto a land that...'[34] This is followed by some unequivocal and unconditional promises to Abraham: 'I will show you', 'I will make of thee..', 'I will bless thee,' I will make great...', I will bless...' and I will curse....'[35] This was the start of what promised to be the communities of God – separate but not in any necessary conflict.[36] Both blessed by God in good measure, even Ishmael: 'I will surely bless him', I will make him fruitful', I will greatly increase his numbers...', I will make him into a great nation.' According to another translation, 'As for Ishmael, I will bless him also...'[37] Hence, conflict is not the necessary corollory of the parting of ways of the divinely blessed Isaac and Ishmael. Their parting need not have ever exluded the encompassing grace and compassion of the God of Abraham. However, this is not the reality of the situation.

But at the heart of their sacred books, and the communities these engendered, is an awareness of the need for association and intimacy. The Book itself however can also bind and limit the real personal experience. It can become an end in itself and, hence, revered for its holiness and obeyed for its 'divinity.' Its letter can legislate but it cannot embrace the depth of emotions and the quirkiness that defines persons. A community that is formed and shaped by the power of the spoken/written Word and the agency of the divinely appointed prophets, lives by the shared understanding of this Word and the memory of the prophetic example. It attempts to live by the letter of the Word and awaits the deeper knowledge of and intimacy with God to advance as a people of God. The community awaits a movement into the realm of direct experience of the Word in person. This is where the paths converge and there is the greatest potential for community.

Shi'ism has a natural propensity for person rather than word-centricism. Ali's proximity to the Prophet and his own ability at direct awareness of the world beyond (as per Muslim witness) may have been contributing factors. Here, the people of the Word in person have a natural ally because the Shi'ites can transcend that which is written, owing to 'Ali's direct familial memory of the prophet of Mecca.[38] The prophecy of Muhammad in Yathrib (Medina) creatively engaged with the unfolding of history in the City of the Prophet. The idea of 'prophetic statesmanship' may sound paradoxical but it was inevitable. As the Arab communal spirituality, which saw itself in relation to the Hebrew tradition, evolved into a religion, it dissociated itself from its broader association with the

---

[34] Genesis 12.1ff.

[35] Genesis 12.1ff.

[36] 'Parting of ways'; see Cragg 2004

[37] New Living Translation.

[38] See Watt 1953 and 1956 for the the stories of Muhammad in Mecca and Madina. Muhammad in Mecca was a persecuted prophet and the revelation here suggests an oracular style similar to the OT prophets, whereas Muhammad in Madina was a statesman and the tone of the Qur'anic content changes in style in the phase of his prophecy.

Hebrews. As I have argued elsewhere, much of the current Muslim use of Biblical material may appear to be explicitly polemical but this was not always the case. The particular passages Muslim polemics are drawn from, among others, occur in Isaiah and Deuteronomy. These are used for their assumed connection with the earliest parts of Surat 96 and 74. The parallel narrative expositions of these Qur'anic passages in canonical traditions and the earliest Sirat suggests a relational, not a polemical, tone that involves the issue of Muhammad's identity as a prophet like Moses. Addressing the issue of Muhammad's prophetic identity, early on, was inextricably linked to the Jewish and Christian traditions of Moses. A change from a relational to polemical approach was likely due to the early post-Meccan developments in Islam and may be explained, at least partly, as a later 're-reading' of an earlier tradition.[39]

Meeting and intersecting of similarly shaped and related 'cultures,' like the Muslim, Christian and Jewish, further enhanced the need for a more secure and de-limited experience. Theologies, creeds and the exchange of polemics played their part but the suffering prophet of Mecca did not ever pass away in the experience many Muslims. He remained ever-present through the sacred memories of the sufferings and martyrdoms in Shi'ism. The experiential impact of the Muharram rituals, among the Dawoodi Bohra community, offers an instance of this phenomenon. It also offers a fresh perspective for Christian reflection on Jesus and the Incarnation. McVicker argues that there exists an inherent multi-sensory communication when the women of this community participate in these rituals. These women experience the Karbala narrative through their bodily senses and human inter-connectedness, and the resulting affective resonance triggers physical, psychological, social, emotional, and soteriological effects. Observing the women's devotion reveals, according to McVicker, the importance of the multi-sensory communication of the message of the Incarnation.[40]

Sufism or Islamic Mysticism claims to be rooted in the experience of the Prophet in Mecca. The earliest traditions support the idea that the visions resulting in the revelations Muhammad received were real encounters with the angel of revelation, Jibril (Gabriel). These did not come suddenly to a 'man of the world' but to someone deeply engaged in the worship of God and meditation upon him. The experience of being endowed with knowledge preceded the reading of it. The Prophet was commanded to read something he had been given but he was not aware of.[41] This simple early spirituality of the Prophet lies at the heart of Sufism. As expected, changes occurred within Sufism too as it became increasingly intellectualised, not least with the introduction of Neoplatonic philosophy but this did not change the essential character of its inward person-

---

[39] For more on early Islam, which saw itself in relation to Christianity and Judaism of its time (and not in opposition to it), see Singh 2008.

[40] See McVicker's paper.

[41] Surah 96.1-5.

centricism. Philosophy gave a new lease of life through lending a new non-concrete language and its use lent a gradually incremental sense of identity and a broader acceptance but not without a struggle.

The notion of intimacy has been present in Islam, therefore, as Cragg too has argued. Like Cragg, most Christians living in Islamic contexts would potentially see this as an opportunity for closer relations for a genuine and heartfelt witness and dialogue towards the apprehension of the fullness of the Word in the Incarnation of Jesus Christ. Some, like Bennett (inspired by his encounter with Bangaladeshi Islam) see in the particular aspects of Sufism (as in the Sufi experience of 'the indwelling of God') not just 'common grounds' for Christian witness to the fulness of God's Incarnation in Jesus Christ, but instead a 'parallel path' to the one in the Christian faith.[42] This is where many Christians would 'part ways' with Bennett. However, rather than dismissing Bennett's position as liberal and relativist, Christians on the side of Cragg, must not only be aware of it but must also engage with it. This is the reason for including Bennett's reflections here.

There are possibilities for a sense of 'community for witness/dialogue' with Muslims, not just at the emotional/spiritual level, but also at the intellectual/philosophical level. The creation of a sense of community alone can facilitate the conditions for fruitful dialogue and witness. Not engaging with Muslim neighbours is not an option for Christians; this is the way forward. The intellectual Sufism of someone as illustrious as Ibn 'Arabi (1165-1240) can be given here as a case of an intellectual Sufi contribution to our discussion. Ibn 'Arabi argues that the Christian testimony to an Incarnational Christology is entirely trustworthy. Jesus' being and his role was (and continues to be) exceptional and unparalleled. Jesus was brought into being extraordinarily by the sole agency of the 'divine substance.' This state of being was not simply spiritually substantive; it was personal in possessing the attributes of mercy, love, compassion, knowledge etc. – the Word became flesh. Here was/is the *logos*, the Word of Islam as Jefffrey alludes to in the introduction to his translation of Ibn 'Arabi's *Shajarat al kawn* (the Tree of the Universe).[43] The factuality of the procession of the Word[44] has two sides: one facing God in Himself and the other facing the universe as yet to be created through his command, *kun*, 'be'. This is the Good News for all that the God who creates by his mere command is also characterised by his 'personal beauty' (*jamal*) – his personal characteristics which endear and connect him to humanity. Humanity is invited to an intimate association with the Creator. Undoubtedly, there is even in traditional Islam, a Christology but it is not as fully evolved as it is in intellectual Sufism. Traditional Islam largely operates at the concrete level and understandably thinks of the Christology in the functional-pragmatic sense. Clearly, the potential for dialogue

---

[42] See Bennett's paper.
[43] See the introduction to the translation in Ibn 'Arabi 1959.
[44] See Aquinas 1947:268ff.

with Christians here is limited. The ontological sense expounded in intellectual Sufism corresponds to a degree to Christianity's own historic version. One could approach the 'problem of Christology' from the point of view of Ibn 'Arabi where Jesus' unique being in history and his 'special substance' give him the exalted position of being 'the Universal Spirit'. He is given the status of being a special instance of the coming into being of this Spirit. This Jesus, according to Ibn 'Arabi, can be the reason for the human potential to grasp and obey the will of God as a single community.[45]

However, such a rationale for a sense of community is clearly too abstract. The Protestant Christian, who attempts at contextualisation in the Central Asian Islamic society, provides, as Penner shows, a more concrete instance of the actual efforts of Christians longing for a more encompassing sense of community. This need for community based on faith is not strange as it arises from post-Soviet Central Asia where faiths survived against all the odds. There is among those engaged in the contextualisation of the Gospel an expectation that Muslims will reciprocate.[46] Peyrouse, we might point out, has gone further than Penner in investigating the particular case of Islam and Orthodox Christianity in post-Soviet Central Asia with a view to understanding the reasons for their move towards partnership.[47] He argues that since the collapse of the Soviet empire, there has been a definite movement toward closer ties between Central Asian Muslims and Orthodox Christians. Their aim has been to jointly counter the Protestant and Arab missions, which seek to sweep up, not just the masses, but also to influence the state. The point is that in Central Asian states, Orthodox Christianity and indigenous Islam share a common cultural and national identity. Another work shows that the phenomenon of 'cultural tensions' between Muslim and Christian in Central Asia has been of relatively recent origin. The reality is that the Muslim-Christian presence here dates back hundreds of years. It was a long stretch of time in which they evolved their uniquely shared culture. More than any other, it is the experience of the Soviet empire that drew them closer together and helped forge a shared cultural identity. The influx of Muslim and Christian missionaries, it is suggested, upsets this balance and, hence, their efforts at countering these by coming closer together as a single front.[48] To some, this may raise pertinent questions about the role of missions in Central Asia. Are these missions, well intentioned as they are, really serving the interests of the Kingdom of God? Many believe that the ancient Christianity (and Islam) of Central Asia should have a chance of continued peace and to further a culturally acceptable means of dialogue and witness. How this leads to a natural flourishing of witness and dialogue between them would be an interesting case for a separate study.

---

[45] See Singh's paper.
[46] See Penner's paper.
[47] Peyrouse 2008.
[48] van Goder 2008.

Dialogue and Witness

The terms dialogue and witness are not exactly synonymous but they are close in meaning. A 'witness' is someone who possesses direct sensory knowledge of something; an expression of which seeks to certify something deemed to be significant by the believer. For example, if one believes Jesus is the Word made flesh, based on the emotional and intellectual apprehension of this proposition, one would naturally make an outward expression to certify this truth. If such an expression happens naturally and spontaneously in a community, it is expressed as a personal witness and not as a dogma. It would not be out of place for a discussion to ensue. The goal would not be polemical (exposing weaknesses), apologetic (defence) or juridical (seeking to prove that the other is wrong) or legislative (absolutize an experiential truth or a historical testimony). The aim of the witness would be to 'certify' the truth through personal testimony, allowing space for others to make their responses. This network of witnesses, operating within the context of an acknowledged community, is the ideal sort of dialogue. What happens here is an extension of one's living relationship with the Person of Jesus as *da'wa* and is to Muslims, a way of submitting to the will of Allah, revealed in the Qur'an. One's witness-dialogue cannot be formulaic or dogmatic here because it rests on the living relationships - both 'vertical' and 'horizontal'.

However, the reality is however that many Christians resent the very notion of dialogue. Our collective memory of the effects of the pluralist theology of religions has had a significant role to play here. It does not need to be so because the idea of dialogue in religious or faith settings is hardly new. Although its appeal among many Christians, not least among Evangelicals in the West, has waned, dialogue is increasingly becoming a significant means for Muslims wanting to relate with Christians as 'the People of the Book' (*ahl al-kitab*). Peace TV programmes are an illustration of this, as are other efforts like Muslim Dialogue aimed purely at promoting 'dialogue, tolerance and understanding'.[49] Sayyid Muhammad Khatami's work too is significant, as this represents a wide spectrum of Shia Muslims wanting to dialogue with Christians and promote civil society institutions which can, it is suggested, make it possible.[50]

Christians need to seize this opportunity and reciprocate because the logic for dialogue and its practice have been rooted in the Christian history of relations with other faiths. For many Christians, dialogue was a natural and uncontrived means of witnessing. Stanley Jones, for example, did not fear dialogue would lead to the dilution and relativisation of the Christian faith. To Jones, dialogue was putting his 'faith out' before others, who were human and friends first before they were Hindus or Muslims. His witness to the living person of Jesus placed the narrative of his experience in the 'public domain'. This allowed others the chance to engage with it on their terms and, for him, a chance to deal with the

---

[49] Muslim Dialogue 2010.
[50] Khatami 2000.

compliments, 'scars' and 'doubts' etc. in all honesty before God and before fellow humans. Jones famously said that he did so because he could not, 'live in a paradise if it turns out to be a fool's paradise'. At over 80, as he reflected back on the experience of his practice of witness as dialogue, he did not have any regrets.[51] Cragg, in a lecture in Oxford, argued that academic centres in the 1930s subscribed to a dogmatically neutral approach to religions.[52] This approach reflects the priorities of dynamic witness – dynamic both because it is based on the refreshing relationship with the living Word and is expressed in a manner that permits discourse. It demonstrates a trust in God and an appreciation for His immense generosity.

Nevertheless, there is a problem here for the Christian theologians of Islam, not least for those who presume there is in Islam no notion of 'the Word as Person.' How is dialogue-witness possible in such a context? Being influenced by this presumption, some theologians strongly advise not to bring theology and, particularly, the notion of Jesus Christ, into a dialogue. Sperber, for example, argues against it because theological dialogues have been historically futile.[53] A case in point is in the story of the Muslim rule over the largely Christian Middle East. Early Christianity faced many challenges against their belief in the Incarnation – the Word becoming flesh. Firstly, it appeared to them that the sacred texts of Islam made no room for the Incarnation. This belief was based on the obviously repeated denial of the Christian belief in Jesus being the Son of God. To the Muslim mind, the idea of God begetting a son was blasphemous. Early Christians argued that there was no biological sense in the Father-Son imagery. It was the divine Word that became flesh. Secondly, Muslims argued that Christ was human and not divine and that the Christian idea of the Incarnation was a mis-representation of this truth. The divinity of Christ was defended by Christians with reference to the scriptures, and by analogies proposing the value for humans of a personal revelation of God. Thirdly, Muslims held that any supposed union between the human and divine in Christ would adversely affect the divinity. Christians replied that the human actions in Christ did not weaken the divinity, by referring to the union of the soul and body in humans, in which the soul is untainted by the influence of the body, to argue that the humanity of Christ need not damage the divinity.

Given the long history of such arguments and counter-arguments, some argue, therefore, that one should not engage in addressing the lack of sincere and heartfelt dialogue.[54] But we live in a world where not having a dialogue is not an option; it is a necessity. Many argue that in the context of new realities, the old methods of polemics and one-sided proclamations must make way for creative

[51] See Jones 1928:20.
[52] Cragg 2009.
[53] See Sperber 2000:99.
[54] See Beaumont's paper.

forms of conversation and debate.[55] The Christian witness needs to shed its association with power and the Christian faith needs to be allowed time for translation into the dominant local culture, so it can then meaningfully converse with the context in the true spirit of the Incarnation of Jesus Christ. If Christology remains a stumbling block, part of the problem lies in the way Christians often converse with Muslims about Christ, not as friends and neighbours, but as agents from distant planets. Their methods can be mechanistic and impersonal, more informed by their particular choice of theological orthodoxies than by their direct relationships with the living Christ and Muslims. Perhaps there is a need for Christians to look for newer and context-specific incarnational models. Hamran Ambrie of Indonesia is one such example.[56] Instead of the classic conciliar formulations of theology, Ambrie uses the term, 'Trinity of Powers' and called the incarnate Christ a 'Divine Man', whereas the invisible Christ was the 'Person of Divine Power'. Notwithstanding the controversy, his is not simply an experiment or a method or an approach but an actual life lived in communion with Muslims. This story of dialogue and witness is closer to what Christianity is really about: Christianity is not about the absolute transcendence and oneness of God but rather about the 'communion of life and love'. The doctrine of the Trinity demands this approach not as an option but as a way of life.[57]

Proximity with Muslims on the ground, in contexts where Christians incarnationally share the same physical space as their Muslim neighbours, should enable Christians, with the mind of Christ, to see things mere visitors would miss. What I have in mind are, not only the stories of people like John Subhan,[58] but also many less illustrious and local stories of those who, at great risk to their life and safety, claimed to have had the direct awareness of the Jesus of the Injil, not in opposition to but in communion with the Qur'an. What this requires is love and respect for Muslims, not as objects of mission or potential converts, but as fellows. The Incarnation of Jesus is a model for the operation of this sort of love. It requires one to be born or be re-born into a culture which has its own range of expressions from the popular to the intellectual.[59] For those who are thus reborn, it appears that the Qur'an is not just a book of revelation but a source of spiritual guidance and a means of meeting with Jesus.[60] The evidence for the legitimacy for the use of the Qur'an to point to the Biblical message comes for Christians from the Biblical writers who were familiar with the sacred and secular literature of their time; they borrowed words, ideas etc. from these sources sometimes without adaptation; and this did not involve the approval of everything in the original. As the story from Indonesia shows, the Qur'an can lead Muslims to

[55] See for an example of such an effort from the Muslims quarters, Peace TV.
[56] See Culver's paper.
[57] See Jukko 2007:119.
[58] See 'Introduction' by Singh in Subhan 2010.
[59] See Parshall's paper.
[60] See Riddell et al.

Jesus. Muhammad can also be seen by some, as leading Muslims back to this Jesus and his message. The Gospel can also be seen by some Muslims to be containing the true and detailed contents of the Qur'an about Jesus.

The Gospel of John reminds us that Jesus is not simply the son of a carpenter from the nondescript town of Nazareth. John starts from the 'beginning', i.e. 'before all things'. Before everything began, there was the Word in a deep and mysterious communion with God himself.[61] This Word became flesh. His words and deeds reflected his communion of being with God as when he healed the sick, raised the dead and was resurrected from the dead and also when he said, 'my Father and I are always working' and 'My Father and I are one' and 'I am....'[62] The mystery of God was revealed in Jesus but this revelation remains somewhat veiled. The invitation of Jesus is not to a place and relationship of stasis, but to an exciting journey of ever-growing revelations of the mystery of God in Christ. The discipleship of Jesus, one hopes, does not cease on this side of eternity, it continues throughout eternity. As Vanier suggests, the object of this journey is not simply to achieve salvation or eternity with Christ, for that would be too static a life, but is to seek 'nourishment'. This is a journey of growth, wisdom, liberation, and understanding.[63] Will there not be a place here for how the revelation of Jesus in the Qur'an is leading Muslims to a journey of discovery of their own? Are there no meeting grounds along the way around Jesus and/or his reality (the Word), he who 'was at the beginning with God'?

The presence of theologies, other than the Christian, poses a serious problem for Christian theologians. How does one explain these in relation to the historic Christian witness to the salvific purpose of God in Christ? The Christian attempts at addressing this question have led to several different answers and theological positions. The range of Christian theological positions are well known and, hence, do not require a re-exposition. Many categorize Lesslie Newbigin (1909-1998), a Scottish missionary and Bishop of the Madras Diocese of the Church of South India, in the so-called 'exclusivist camp'. Abraham argues rightly that classifying Newbigin thus is simplistic.[64] Newbgin's writings were born out of his rich cross-cultural experience as well as his sharp critical insights as a missionary. He deserves a fresh look. Central to his Christology is the humble creaturely acknowledgement of mystery. Our knowledge of Christ does not exhaust his Person. There is a difference between the reality of Jesus (as he really is) and the actuality of Jesus (as he is known). This difference and the acknowledgement of the mystery in the being of Jesus must be the very foundation of Christian life and the rationale for an open and honest dialogue with Islam. The objective of this dialogue is the journey in search of the mystery of 'Jesus' reality'. Happy reading!

---

61 See John 1:1-18.
62 John 5:17; 10:30; 14:6-7.
63 Vanier 2004:116ff.
64 See Abraham.

PART II: THE WORD

Incarnatus non est: The Qur'an and Christology

Kenneth Cragg

Bishop Kenneth Cragg, a former Bishop of Jerusalem, is a Fellow of Jesus College, Oxford

It is widely assumed that the Qur'an and Islam have a total veto on the Christian faith in the Incarnation, the Gospel of 'the Word made flesh', and it is well to take that anathema seriously, since it lies at the heart of any inter-theology between the mosque and the church

Yet, we do well to give ourselves pause in exempting Islam from a due recokoning, on its part, with why Christology plays so large a place in Christianity. The Qur'an and its whole meaning about the person of Muhammad – his very biography in its *tanzil* – bring it closer to the Christhood of Jesus than is commonly supposed.

A distinction in the term 'Christology' is first necessary. In Christian usage, it has to do with ontology, with the being of God, as intended by the credal phrase 'of one substance with the Father.' It has to do there with the metaphysics required in all theology. Insofar as Muslims use the term 'Christology', they would only have in mind the *masih* status with which 'Isa is endowed in every mention of his name in the Qur'an ('Isa ibn Maryam al-Masih). This has to do with his being 'anointed' in the honoured sequence of the messengers *(al-rasul, al-mubashshirun, al-mundhirun)* and penultimate to Muhammad, *khat al-nabuwwa* (the seal of prophets). As Fazlur Rahman was bold to say of the whole Qur'an, this task was entirely 'functional.'[1] It lay strictly in the bringing of 'words,' whereby *hud,* or 'guidance,' was granted to humankind. So, there was room for 'Christology' but in this pragmatic sense of an envoy with words.

Even so, it is important to note how deeply this divine agency in the exclusive realm of words, this 'transcribation' of a literal text, involved the living person of the unique messenger. It is there in the very *shahadah* itself: *Muhammad rasul Allah*, 'the apostle of Allah' – *mudaf wa mudaf ilahi,* as the grammarians say, joined thus with Allah in an intimate relation. In great mosques, or former mosques, like *Sancta Sophia (Hagia Sophia)*, we find two huge medallions carrying the names 'Allah' and 'Muhammad' set aloft for all to read. There is a vital, more than symbolic 'society' between the 'employer' and the 'employed' in the divine concern.

[1] See Rahman 1980 xi & 1-3. The Qur'an is no treatise about God and His nature: His existence, for the Qur'an is strictly functional. The aim of the Qur'an is man and his behaviour not God.

While it is true that this inter-association is strictly practical and is allowed in classical Islam no other quality,[2] it remains theologically intimate in being effectively realist. Muhammad enjoys a relation with Allah, such as no other human knew as such, as Allah bestowed on no one else. In this sense the Qur'an is effectuated in him and he, as *rasul,* in the Qur'an. Much of the scripture is 'third Person' text, as in the long narratives and in the affirmations as in *al-fatihah – la ilaha illa-allah.* But often it passes into 'second person' discourse with Muhammad as the 'addressee.' Take the questions directly put to him in Surah 95:

> Have We not made you to be open of heart?
>
> Have We not lifted from you the burden that was breaking your back? And have We not established your reputation?
>
> Truly with hardship there comes ease. So then, having found the burden gone, pursue your task. Make the Lord your heart's desire.

Thus, the text engages Muhammad with its content via mind and soul. Again, in Surah 93, we find it incorporating the very shape of the text into his own story:

> Did He not find you an orphan and gave you shelter?
>
> Did he not find you lost on your way and guided you?
>
> Did he not find you destitute and rnrich you? …so make the Lord your heart's desire.

In this way, Muhammad is invited into the very texture of the Book. It is as if his very biography is necessary to it.

The argument, here, is that this biography is necessary to its incidence. There is, therefore, a certain 'incarnation' here. Muslims would shrink from calling it such but the fact remains that such it is. The point is clearer still when we recall how *tanzil* had to happen *ala mukthin,* 'at intervals', so that it might be gathered into the sequences of days and months, of times and places, attention to which would come to be the mainspring of Hadith as the all-important clue *tafsir,* or exegesis. So Surah 76.23 has it:

> It is we who have communicated the Qur'an to you from above in gradual sequence. So await with patience what your Lord determines.

---

[2] As in the previous note but, nevertheless, entailing an agency which the humanity in the Prophet is engaged by the divine in the text. The Qur'an is understood 'as the very speech of Allah,' *kitabuhu* and *kalamuhu.* In this sense it might be said to be of 'a substance with Allah,' – the 'with' via that possessive 'of.'

This would be his answer to those scoffers who taunted him about having its 'revelations' all at once. What was the point of these suspect interludes in its 'descent' they asked? Muhammad had to be reassured as in 87.6:

> We will give you to speak the Qur'an and you will not forget – other than God has willed. He knows all that is in open evidence and all that is concealed. We will take you gently where rest will be yours.

All had to proceed in direct challenge to the pagan errors of the Quraish in his native Mecca. Surah 109 insists:

> Say, 'You who reject faith, I do not worship what you worship, nor do you worship what I worship. Never shall I be a worshipper of what you have worshipped not will you be worshippers of what I worship. To you your religion and to me mine.'

It was the stress of such confrontation that there are frequent[3] passages of consolation and summons to an appropriate patience.

> By the pen and the Scripture they set down In the grace of your Lord, you are not *jinn*-possessed. Truly yours is a rightful reward and you have in hand a great understanding. You will see – as they will too – which of you it is who is demented… so then, do not obey those who call it all lies. Were you to be ingratiating with them they would like it well and they would be the same with you.

The invocation of 'the pen' here in Surah 68 is significant, seeing that –via its calligraphy – Islam is so much a scribal faith having a 'scripture' which is *per se* the revelation.[4] More important still are the words *anta 'ala khuluqin 'azim,* here translated, 'You have in hand a great undertaking,' but could equally well be rendered, 'You are of a tremendous character.' The *khuluq* here is both the task and the task-achiever. There could be no clearer clue to how the two are one, the message-brought and the message-bringer.

It was vital for both these aspect that the Qur'an's meaning be squarely related to its Meccan setting. Hence, no doubt, the vivid recital in Surah 100 of the dawn raiding and bitter feuds among the tribes:

---

[3] It is intriguing to note, how in recent times, this sharply rejectionist passage, disallowing all converse with the pagans, is happily invoked by those who call for dialogue. Then the sense is held to be *eirenis*, a counsel of co-existent systems. At least – given this mindset – the last clause is capable of this reading, 'To you your religion and to me mine.'

[4] It is this feature which makes it radically different from the New Testament where the primary revelation is the person, work and 'event' of Jesus as the Christ. From this, the Gospel and letters are derivative and secondary. There is no *tanzil* dictating the text. It comes via the mind-in-memory of the disciples and inside the process of faith-expansion in the Mediterranean world.

> By the snorting war-horses that strike fire with their hoofs as they storm forward at dawn, a single host in the midst of their dust-cloud: man is indeed ungrateful to his Lord. He Himself is the surest witness to the fact. Man is violent on his passion for wealth. Is he not aware that their Lord knows them through and through in that day when the tombs yield up their dead and all men's hidden thoughts are open knowledge?

The same care of the Qur'an for the exact *mise-en-scène* is evident in Surah 106's delineation of the Meccan caravans plying their trade northward or southward:

> Who gave the Quraysh their talents for the arts of peace, for trade and commerce, and for journeys south and north at proper seasons, and made their home inviolable in Makkah? Surely they, if any, should adore their Lord and listen to His Message of Unity and Truth.

It is evident enough in all these ways that the Qur'an is 'incarnational,' in that the content is weaved into the fabric of a narrative and bound up with the incidence of a history. We have neither the text without the story, nor the meaning without the incidence of an event. It is as if all is 'biographisised' around Muhammad and the twenty-three years of his career in prophethood. Why else the identifying of all the Surahs (save Surah 9) with either Mecca or Yathrib (the Medina to be)? Muhammad as its sole recipient enters into its gist as the human pivot on whose vocation to this history the whole is required to turn.

We find something of the same phenomenon when we turn to the previous messengers – Noah, Hud, Shu'aib, Salih, Abraham – on whose lives the text is told as commentary or elucidation. The most notable exemplar of this quality is Joseph/Yusuf, who has a whole Surah (12) to himself. He is indeed a messenger but he is much more. From his youthful 'dreaming,' via the bitter enmity of his brothers, he comes through the pit and the prison to the summit of near Pharonic power in Egypt to be 'Joseph the provider.'[5] The Bible and the Qur'an alike convey his significance in the story rather than in any mere words of his, save those where he tells his puzzled brethren, 'I am Joseph your brother…' That 'I am' is eloquent beyond language.

It is important, in this way, to see how so much, in both scriptures, is this 'lived,' and not merely 'uttered'. This is not to argue that Islam is bound to acknowledge what Christian faith has always confessed as the Incarnation of Christ. It is to say that the principle has to be accepted as present or latent in any 'revelation.' If the eternal is to enter into the temporal, there must be a point of entry where the universal has become the particular, the timeless the time-told. This will be the case whether we locate it in 'textuality' or in a 'personality.'

---

[5] That story is wonderfully told with embellishments carefully drawn from study and sojourn in the Nile Valley by Mann 1933/1978. Mann wrote, he said 'with a kind of autobiographical pensiveness,' during and beyond the rise of the Nazi regime.

That distinction explains how vitally different is the New Testament from the Qur'an. Its Gospels and Letters are not 'dictated' texts in a *tanzil*; they are inspired within a community which is itself the outcome of their meaning. There would have been no knowing scripture without a going church and no going church without a knowing faith. The text is derivative from what it tells. In Old Testament terms, there is the same sequence there. We can capture it in the phrase, 'the place of the Name.' What we have in the script is what the Hebrews knew in the event, notably in Exodus and Exile. This 'Name' quality of the former is in the pledge to Moses (when he sought some 'guarantee' about his calling), 'I will be there as whom there I will be.' (Exodus 3.10)[6] They would know the God of Exodus only in going through the journey and ever after they could have the assurance that 'He would ever be there as who there He was.' 'The place of the Name' was history. Later, on entry and monarchy in the land, it could be geographical, as in Solomon's great prayer, 'When we pray towards this place of which Thou has said, "My Name shall be there".' (1 Kings 8.29)

Is it not a radical extension of this theme – radical indeed but not discontinuous – when Christians learned their confession concerning a babe in a manger and a man on a Cross, that 'God has been there as who and how there He was'? Jesus in his story was the signature, the credential, of God. It is by this road that we have to understand his Incarnation. The Creed's *incarnatus est* was not the devising of rationality: it was the experience of faith, an experiential theology.

We might borrow the Arabic usage of the nominal sentence where a noun generates an adjective which must then be read as essentially defining it, as in *Allahu akbar.* Grammarians talk of *al-mudaf wa-l-mudaf ilaihi:* two 'annexed' together, the original and the predicate concerning it. The Father/Son inter-definition in Christian faith is exactly this way. Though uncongenial to Islam, the analogy of divine Fatherhood was welcome to the Hebrew mind from creation and nature, as in Malachi 1.6, 'If therefore I be a father, where is mine honour' and Psalm 103.13, 'Like as a father pities his children so the Lord pities those that fear Him.' In the New Testament this, from nature, deepens into the divine fatherly initiative of grace and redemption, so that 'Sonship' is realised where it is active in the enterprise of salvation. That enterprise distinctively tells – where it fulfils – the divine Fatherhood. Hence John 14.6, 'No one comes to the Father but by me.' This is not to be read as saying, 'No one comes to the Father but through me.' That would exclude Abraham and Moses and all the prophets. It would deny how Job came so desperately to Yahweh in his perplexity and pain. Yet the words are profoundly true, in that we only come to this fulness and finality of Fatherhood as accomplished in this Sonship. We have to realise how 'inclusive' is divine Fatherhood in the natural order if we are to understand the 'exclusivity' in such passages as John 14.6 and Acts 4.12. That quality is inherent in the very

---

6 This is the sense of his enquiring after 'the Name' when in theophany he is addressed from 'the burning bush' – still proudly on view at the Monastery on Mount Sinai.

quality of grace. For that 'Name' translates into 'Only the love that suffers is the power that reigns.' Only 'God in Christ' is 'God in the event of human remaking in love.' This kind of careful discrimination between what 'includes' and what 'excludes' is crucial in the contemporary task of inter-faith dialogue and/or comparative studies.

Knowing 'Sonship' this way as the undertaking of divine 'Fatherhood' requires us to note in such dialogue how far we are from the notion of 'adoption' or *ittikhadh* which the Qur'an postulates as being the culpable doctrine of Christianity. The Qur'anic references are many but all of them misread what it means. 'Adoption' was in fact repudiated in the New Testament as something beloved by Gnostic heresy.[7] For 'adoption' equals deification, in that it affirms a human 'elevated' arbitrarily to divine status. The Qur'an does well to repudiate this notion; it is only mistaken in thinking that the church held it. The direction of the Incarnation is all the other way. It tells of a *tanzil,* a divine condescension, a venture into human time and place and condition for a supremely transcendent end. This 'Word made flesh' had its antecedents in the Hebraic tradition in such passages as Exodus 3.7-8, 'I know their sorrows: I am come down to deliver,' and, even more pointedly, when Yaḥweh says in Isaiah 43.24, 'You made Me to serve with your sins.'

Here we encounter the great theme of divine liability to us humans, or divine vulnerability at our hands. Any thought of a 'suffering transcendence' would seem to be anathema to the Muslim mind. It smacks too much of 'paradox,' a usage in life which is unwelcome to the mind of Islam.[8] Yet is not divine 'risk' there – if not vulnerability – (are they not akin?) in Surah 2.30 and the reality of creation and human creaturehood put in charge of it. When the angels protest that this fickle creature will 'corrupt in the earth and shed blood (*yufsidu fiha was yasfik sl-dima'*) and no one can read history and think they were wrong – Allah, nevertheless, overrules them and proceeds with the risk He is manifestly undertaking. He tells the angels enigmatically *'alam ma la ta'lamun,* I known what to you is unknown,' i.e., 'I appreciate the risk entailed and I am taking it.' Is

[7] The view that was able to take on the myth of 'incarnation' despite their horror of 'enfleshment' and their 'enmity' to the body, by the doctrine that all was 'only in the realm of seeming, or apparentness.' Their name derives from the Greek verb, *dokeo,* 'to seem so,' or 'be apparent.' It is this idea and its corollaries which Surah 4.157 has in its *shubhihalahum,* where the hidden pronoun may be, either 'it,' i.e. 'crucifixion,' or 'he' that is Jesus/'Isa.

[8] There is, it would seem, no precise word for 'paradox' in Arabic. Islam anyway is not given to the idea of such as 'the courage of the fearful' or 'the eloquence of silence' or 'the truth of fiction.' In his introduction to Doughty's work (192) Lawrence (xx-xxiii) wrote of the Arab peoples, 'The desert inhabits considered opinions…the clear hardness of their beliefs. They are a certain people despising doubt, our modern crown of thorns. They are monopolists of revealed religion… The only refuge and rhythm of their being is in God.' Even so, Surah 8.41 is capable of the high analogy (akin to Christian usage in theology) of *ibn al-sabil,* 'the son of the path,' i.e. 'the habitual wayfarer.'

there something enigmatic about that statement? At least it is clear that Allah now has a stake in these humans whom He has made 'trustees' (not owners) of His good earth, by the free grant to them of *khilafah* (the Biblical 'dominion') as His *khulafa'* with a sub-sovereignity therein. This can only mean divine liability for what ensues on our part. He has willed, by this measure, to have His will turn on ours. Hence the crucial summons to *Islam,* to a willed conformity to what – still relating to Allah – has been entrusted to us. Is it not precisely this awesome vocation of our creature-hood that necessitated, for our guidance (*huda*) and 'reminder' (*dhikr),* the divine 'sending' of prophethood which was clear tribute to what we may call 'the privilege' of man. There would be no point sending messengers to puppets. Thus our 'mastery' is evidence of the 'mystery' – the marvel – of Allah's investment in us humans. In bestowing this privilege on us he has engaged Himself in liability for us, incurring a situation which turns on our amenability – or otherwise – to His will and His law.

There is a clear reference to this 'liability' to, in and for us in a passage in Surah 4.165 which tells of *rusulan wa mubashshirin wa mundhirin,* 'apostles, tidings-bringers and warners,' and continues, '…so that there could be no argument (no case) that humankind could bring against Allah after the messengers.'

Clearly, then, there would have been a case against God had these emissaries not been sent. Allah would then have been in default; culpably negligent of a duty incumbent on Him. Why so? Because then we humans would have been left in *jahiliyyah,* the 'state of wild ignorance' from which Islam rescues us.

This logic is very precious to the Christian mind for it allows us to ask whether we cannot have an expectation as to God's obligation which deals with our wrongness when His law has been denied and flouted. If, in line with 4.165, we are thinking thus of using 'He ought' in our theology, our thought about Allah, then how far can it, should it, reach?

We could see this question implicit in Islam's *bismillah,* telling of *al-rahman al-rahim,* if we take the progression there can be between the two terms. *Al-rahman* can be a substantive in its own right as a synonym for God, more often than is the case with *al-rahim.* Is not the former about the 'mercy' of Allah as a 'property,' denoting His innermost nature, while *al-rahim* denotes that quality in its actual exercise, or – in Christian phrasing, 'God does what He does that he may be who He is?' His doing fulfils His being; His identity is told in His action. This is the very heart of faith in the Incarnation, as that in which God 'fulfilled' Himself in our history. So then, when we think to use 'ought' about God, we have the warrant from Himself as being tested, on our part, by His own leave.

Something like this happens in Muslim devotion when the 'Divine Names,' *al-asma' al husna,* are used as descriptive of Allah, sufficient in themselves to stand alone as nouns: thus, *alrazzaq,* 'the bestower,' *al-wahhab,* 'the Giver,' *al-latif,* 'the Gently-kind.' What has been meant by *incarnatus est* is present here in that God is ready to be 'self-identified' in deeds, events, in the natural order. Why not also in the order of history as in *al-hakim,* 'the wise-ruling,' *al-ghufran,* 'the Forgiver'? To hold and use these Names is in no way derogatory, nor 'reductionist' of divine majesty. They do not contravene the directive, *kabbirhu takbiran,* 917.111, 'Make Him greatly great.' They fulfil it. We might be bold to say that the very pattern of divine 'naming,' with the adjectival becoming nounal is close to reading 'God in Christ' as thereby and therein 'the Christ in God.'

With all this in view, it is necessary to turn back to the Qur'an's allowance of 'adoption,' in which there was the fallacy of denouncing what Christian orthodoxy was never holding. The passages are frequent. Surah 2.116 has, 'They say, Allah has taken to Himself as son' and cries, 'Glorified be he…' 'He is the owner of all.' Surah 10.68 repeats the same charge and has the same rebuttal; likewise, 19.88-89, 21.26, with the preface, 'They say,' which – as we have seen – 'they do not say.' So that accusation is void. There seems to be a reference to the same 'false deifiers' in the words about making their God of their own desire in 45.23 and 72.3.[9]

This use of *ittikhadh,* thus to mean fabricating 'gods' out of human whim, is made in 4.125 of Abraham 'taking up' Allah as 'friend,' while in 18.4 those are 'warned' who say that Allah 'adopts a son.' So the verb is liable to have a good meaning as well as one that must be reproached. Is there not, for our contemporary world of the secular and its technology a larger relevance to this charge – as in 45.23 – of 'making to themselves a god of their desire' than it ever had in the pagan world of the Quraish? It was one thing for idolaters in their 'house of Rimmon' to bow down to images; it is quite another to 'worship' money on the Stock Exchange or take savage pride in one's suicide for Islam or be enslaved to the cult of violence. It is well to realise that the cult of violence can take these idolatrous forms, no less than the go-getting of lust and greed. For here, there is the supreme irony and paradox of 'go-making' via 'man-self-deluding.' How the irony is there in 17.40 where Muhammad taunts the Meccans: 'Has your Lord then marked you out (chosen) you by bestowing sons on you while He has adopted (*ittikhadha*) females for Himself from among the angels? Verily what a monstrous thing you say!'

Are we to think now that the pagans had a better sense of sexual equality or balance than the new faith? But the main point is the use of *ittikhadha* on Allah's part, so that it may have a positive and legitimate sense. In any event, the Qur'an's rebuke for the 'adoption' of Jesus into divine status, fails on two counts – it was never so in fact nor in faith.

It remains in this study of the Qur'an and Christology to turn to the positive meaning of belief as 'trust,' as frequently enjoined and prized in the Islamic scripture where the two words, *'alaika tawakkalt* occur seven times. It is noteworthy that the clauses, which open and close the great Christian hymn *te deum laudamus,* are also highly Islamic, 'We praise The O God, we acknowledge Thee to be the Lord… O Lord, in Thee have I trusted….'

---

9 cf. Surah 23.71, 25.43.

Even the order of emphasis is the same. The Latin is not – as it might be – *laudamus te,* 'we praise Thee.' The *te* pronoun precedes, in order to be emphatic. It is likewise with the Arabic of the *fatihah, iyyaka* (not *te*) *na'bud* – the comparable device of both languages to attain emphasis.

There are several who use these two words in the Qur'an. In 9.129, it is Muhammad, as in his gesture when the pagans turn away. In 10.71, they are what Noah says to his people. In 11.51, they are on the lips of the prophet Hud remonstrating with his tribe, while, in 11.88, it is the prophet Shu'aib. In 12.67, they are used by Jacob in sending his sons down to Egypt to buy corn from the Joseph whom they do not yet identify. In 13.20, it is again Muhammad, who is directed to entrust himself to Allah, when commissioned to preach. They are his again when, in 42.10, he is involved in altercation with opponents of his message.

Thus, there is a clear kinship in the words between Christian liturgy and Muslim devotion. It is only when we come in the *te deum* to 'the Father everlasting', that we are in trouble with Islam. The more we can note and employ vocabulary that can be common, the better placed are we for creative dialogue about our understanding of the same language.

Either way, the vital reality for faith, theology and life, is that the secret lies in trust and trust alone. Belief is a matter of the head – in that we 'love the Lord our God with all our minds' – but more of the heart. As Moses learned, when he sought one in Exodus 3.10ff., for the venture of liberation there is never a 'guarantee,' only the reliance that the heart places on the pledges of God. 'He that wills to know, let him do.' Paul saw it this way when he wrote to Timothy, 'I know whom (not what) I have believed...' (2 Tim. 1.12) '...and am persuaded He is able....' There follows then reciprocally the 'trust' which the Lord places in His apostolic recruits concerning the people and the truth 'committed to His charge.'

Such, then, is our confidence in the reality of divine Incarnation. We take out the *non* from *incarnatus est* and know that soundly interpreted, rightly stated and heartily confessed, it ought to find no crippling anathema from inside a lively Islamic theology. When the Creed speaks of 'the Son' as 'of one substance with the Father' it is by its understanding of divine Unity that it does so. The 'doing' of the incarnate enterprise is one with the 'being' of the Eternal. 'Where there is only a unity, there is no unity.' It is in Being who He is' that He does what he does alike in creation and in grace.

The Doctrine of the Incarnation supports the Christian Use of the Qur'an "for Example of Life and the Instruction of Manners": A Proposal

A.H. Mathias Zahniser

Rev. Dr. A. H. Mathias Zahniser is Scholar-in-Residence at Greenville College, Greenville, IL and Professor Emeritus of Christian Mission at Asbury Theological Seminary, Wilmore, KY

A trip to any major book shop in my North American context reveals that in this age of globalization, people from Muslim and Christian backgrounds are reading each other's scriptures. In other contexts, Christians from Muslim cultural contexts are shaping their Christian faith in a Muslim order, along the lines of Messianic Judaism.[1] Can Christians benefit from reading the Qur'an for examples of godly living and instruction in fruitful behaviour? Does the Qur'an not present itself as direct divine discourse to a later Prophet who fulfils and replaces the message of Jesus? How then can Christians inside or outside of Muslim culture benefit from its message? In this paper I am offering a Christian theological perspective that both recognizes the Qur'an's value for Christian discipleship and provides for a Christian evaluation of its contents. The hermeneutical key to my proposal is the Incarnation.

Incarnation as Divine Self-Disclosure

St. Athanasius (c. 296-373), who set out the first list of the books of the Christian canon in 367 and devoted his life to promoting and defending the Nicene Creed, clearly sees the Word-become-flesh as the revelation of God. The Incarnation solves a divine dilemma: even though God placed in humans the divine image, enabling them to know God, they made graven images of their own and worshipped the creation rather than the Creator; so in addition, God provided the works of creation as signs to lead humans to a knowledge of their Maker; then, a law was provided and prophets arose in the hope that humans would come to know the Father and the Father's Word. Since this plan also failed, the Word

[1] For a brief, lucid, and balanced summary of views on Muslim insider movements, see Cumming 2009. Brown 2007 offers a more detailed study. Chandler 2008 provides an example of an individual who has kept his Muslim culture and participates in his Muslim community, while maintaining a devout loyalty to Jesus as Saviour and Lord.

became flesh, not only to destroy the curses of death resulting from the fall, but to reveal definitively the Word, Wisdom, and Power of God (John 1:14-18).

> For this reason He did not offer the sacrifice on behalf of all immediately.... [F]or if He had surrendered His body to death and then raised it again at once He would have ceased to be an object of our senses. Instead of that, He stayed in His body and let Himself be seen in it, doing acts and giving signs which showed Him to be not only man, but also God the Word. There were thus two things... the Saviour did for us by becoming Man. He banished death from us and made us anew; and... became visible through His works and revealed Himself as the Word of the Father, the Ruler and King of the whole creation.[2]

According to Richard Bauckham, Professor of New Testament Studies at St. Mary's College, University of St. Andrews, Scotland, speaking about the dogma of the Incarnation, the Fathers were more successful in appropriating the banishing-death-and-making-us-new feature of New Testament Christology than they were in appropriating its other key feature: 'the revelation of the divine identity in the human life of Jesus and his cross.' This neglect he attributes to 'the shift to categories of divine nature and the Platonic definition of divine nature which the fathers took for granted.'[3] Bauckham's emphasis on the divine identity rather than on the divine nature more adequately illuminates the incarnational views of the New Testament writers within their Second Temple Jewish context. The focus on divine nature in the context of Greek philosophy yields statements about '*what* God is'; while a focus on divine identity results in talk about '*who* God is.'[4] Realizing that, according to the New Testament writers, Jesus participates in the identity of God gives proper attention to Jesus as the ultimate in divine self-disclosure. Let us look at one example from the many Bauckham cites.

Philippians 2:6-11 supports Bauckham's thesis that New Testament writers believed Jesus participated in the identity of God. The hymn includes the cola in the left column of the following table,[5] and their parallels from Isaiah 45, 52, and 53 appear in the right column:

Philippians 2:9-11	Isaiah 52-53 and 45
Therefore also God *exalted him to the highest place* (2:9)	"Therefore... (53:12) he shall be exalted and lifted up and shall be very high" (53:13)

[2] Athanasius 1957.

[3] Bauckham 1998:79. Bauckham incorporated this book in a subsequent expanded work, 2008: 59. Since the material is identical in both editions, I will cite both in subsequent notes.

[4] Bauckham 1998:78; 2008:58.

[5] Bauckham 1998:58-59; 2008:43.

and conferred on him the Name	
that is above every name, (2:9)	…For I am God, and there is no
so that at the name of Jesus	other (45:22).
every knee should bend, (2:10)	"To me every knee shall bow,
in heaven and on earth and under the earth,	
and every tongue should acknowledge that Jesus Christ is Lord,	every tongue shall swear" (45:23)
to the glory of God the Father (2:11)	

The matching cola indicate that what Isaiah says about God, the hymn says about Jesus. Bauckham comments on the significance of the way the allusions in Isaiah 52-53 cohere with those in Isaiah 45:

> Paul is reading Deutero-Isaiah 52-53 to mean that the career of the Servant of the Lord, his suffering, humiliation, death and exaltation, is the way in which the sovereignty of the one true God comes to be acknowledged by all the nations.[6]

Bauckham enlists the throne scenes in Revelation chapters 4 and 5[7] and the 'I am' statements of Jesus in the Gospel according to John, especially John 8:28, in support of his incarnational argument.[8]

Citing one of the great Incarnation verses, "we have seen his glory, the glory as of a father's only son" (John 1:14), Bauckham concludes succinctly and boldly, 'This glory is the visible manifestation of who God is….'[9] The revelation of the glory of the Lord represents an even wider theme of Second Isaiah, heralded by New Testament writers: 'Then the glory of the Lord shall be revealed, / and all flesh shall see it together'. (Isaiah 40:3)[10]

Clark Pinnock, Professor Emeritus of Systematic Theology at McMaster Divinity College, Hamilton, Ontario, cautions his readers not to look too narrowly at the Incarnation, asserting that the entire "representative journey of Jesus" in the Spirit from his birth to his ascension represents divine self-disclosure.[11] This definitive divine self-disclosure through Incarnation becomes for the Christian the ultimate criterion for discerning truth. As Jesus himself declared before Pilate, "For this I was born and for this I came into the world, to testify to the truth" (John 18:37b). As the Word become flesh, by which God's

---

[6] Bauckham 1998:58-59; 2008:43.

[7] Bauckham 1998:62-63; 2008:45-46.

[8] Bauckham 1998:65-66; 2008:47.

[9] Bauckham 1998:66; 2008:49.

[10] Parsons 2005:216 makes use of Bauckham's analysis in presenting a Christology contextualized for Muslim culture. He says the concept of divine humility has made it harder for Muslims than for Jews of the Second Temple period to accept New Testament Christology.

[11] Pinnock 1996:95, 102.

glory can be known, it makes all other words preliminary and all other divine discourse preparatory, even though they may be temporally later than the representative journey of Jesus in the Spirit.

A New Proposal

The Incarnation, understood in this way as revelation in personhood, opens the door for Christians to draw from God's revelation through Muhammad, truth, values and behaviour compatible with God's self-revelation in the Incarnation as portrayed in the New Testament. Once Jesus, who participates in God's identity, has definitively revealed God's nature, God's will, and God's way (John 14:6), Christians may legitimately view even subsequent divine revelation through this incarnational lens.

Even though the Qur'an, as divine revelation through Muhammad, is historically later than the representative journey of Jesus in the Spirit, it can be considered hermeneutically prior to that journey. Christians interpret even the Hebrew Scriptures included in their canon through the lens of the birth, life, teachings, death and resurrection of Jesus. Does the doctrine of the Incarnation not entail that they can also interpret the Qur'an through this same lens?

I am not, however, proposing that the Qur'an be added to the Christian canon. And I am not suggesting that it be bound with the Old and New Testaments in the Bible as the Apocrypha is by some Christian traditions. The Apocrypha, however, may offer an analogy for the relation of the Qur'an to Christian canonical scripture. St. Jerome (c. 340-420), the early church father and translator of the Latin Vulgate, held that the Church should read the Apocrypha "*for example of life and instruction of manners*," but not "to establish any doctrine."[12] Even the Protestant reformer Martin Luther (1483-1546) who objected to the Apocrypha's doctrines of the "salvific effects of works of mercy" (Tobit 4:8-11; Sirach 29:9-12) and "the intercession of the saints" (2 Maccabees 15:12-14) held that the books of the Apocrypha are both "useful and good to read."[13]

Realities that Deserve Attention

Employing the Qur'an as a source of models and instructions for living for Christians, especially those whose worldview and ethos Muslim culture has significantly influenced, faces some significant challenges: the Qur'an, though historically later than the New Testament, presents itself as the direct word of God *in the form of divine discourse*. The Qur'an challenges the New Testament

[12] From Article VI of the 'Articles of Religion of the Protestant Episcopal Church in the United States of America in 1801,' *Book of Common Prayer* 1977:868.

[13] DeSilva, 2006: 198. I am not saying Martin Luther would have approved of my proposal, only that he valued writings for Christians that he judged contained material incompatible with sound Biblical teaching.

witness to truths revealed by, or entailed in, the Incarnation. Qur'anic stories of Biblical characters and events differ from their counterparts in the Christian canon. Finally, what is the value of the Qur'an for Christian discipleship? In exploring these challenges, I am not trying to make an airtight argument for this proposal, but to provide breathing room for discussing it.

The Qur'an, though historically later than the New Testament, comes in the form of direct divine discourse

On several occasions a Muslim has asked me this question, "We Muslims honour Jesus; what do you Christians think about Muhammad?" Can Christians consider Muhammad a prophet? Can Christians consider Muhammad the seal of the prophets?[14] Did Muhammad receive divine revelation? Christian belief in the Incarnation as definitive and final revelation in personhood allows them to recognize Muhammad as a prophet of God and to recognize the Qur'an as prophetic discourse. It also allows Christians to recognize the Qur'an's limitations for representing definitive divine self-disclosure. It also frees Christians to benefit from the models and meanings in the Qur'an compatible with the New Testament witness.

I am writing this chapter in the season of Advent when some of the daily lectionary readings come from the eighth century prophet Amos. After delivering seven prophetic judgments in direct divine discourse against peoples surrounding them, this prophet from Judah turns to the people of Israel and prophesies against them for what amounts to 17 verses, beginning with the same introductory formula he used in his prophesies against their seven neighbouring peoples: "Thus says the Lord: For three transgressions of Israel and for four, I will not revoke the punishment…." (2:6-16). Except for a final prediction of the restoration of David's kingdom (9:11-15), the remainder of the book, though interspersed with some historical narrative, contains polemical and visionary direct prophetic discourse of warnings to Israel (3:1-9:10). The final prophecy against Israel opens with the following verse revealing the Lord's liberating involvement with peoples other than Israel:

> Are you not like the Ethiopians to me,
> O people of Israel? says the Lord.
> Did I not bring Israel up from the land of Egypt,
> and the Philistines from Caphtor
> and the Arameans from Kir? (9:7 NRSV).

God's redemptive engagement with people other than Israel takes on more flesh in the story of Peter's visit to Caesarea and the house of Cornelius, "a devout man who feared God," "gave alms generously," and "prayed constantly to God" (Acts 10:1-11:18). Peter learns that an angel from God had assured the

[14] Surah 33:40.

Roman centurion: "Cornelius…Your prayers and your alms have ascended as a memorial before God…." (10:3-4; 11:30-31).

Given these scriptural perspectives, Christians should not find God's speaking to prophets outside the Biblical tradition terribly odd.[15] Nevertheless, one of the major issues related to this project remains that the Qur'an comes to its receptors as prophetic discourse *in the divine voice*.

Theologically, the self-revelation of God in the *sunnah* of Jesus the Messiah, that is, his exemplary life, his authoritative teachings, and his representative death and resurrection in solidarity with both God and humanity, would be unnecessary as revelation were it possible for God to do with verbal discourse what can only be done by divine engagement. The full reality of what God intends for human experience and cosmic order can only be seen when it is lived out by the last Adam (i.e., Jesus; 1 Corinthians 15:45) in the way it could not have been lived out by the first Adam or by any subsequent "Adam" or "Eve."

Divine discourse to prophets accepts limitations imposed by local knowledge. This can be illustrated by two examples from the Qur'an itself. Even though the Qur'anic story of Dhu 'l-Qarnayn, possibly Alexander the Great, is narrated through the Prophet in divine discourse, it contains the following passage that assumes the great general could reach the place where the sun goes down:

> Verily, we established his power on earth, and we gave him the ways and the means to all ends. One way he followed until, when he reached the setting of the sun (*maghrib al-shams*), he found it set in a spring of murky water (*taghrubu fi 'ayn*[in] *hami'at*[in]). Near it he found a people: we said: 'O Zul-qarnain! Either punish them, or treat them with kindness.'[16]

The leading historians, and almost all the significant Qur'an commentators in the first two Muslim centuries, transmitted a second example of the limitations imposed on the Prophet by local knowledge. At a time of intense persecution of the followers of Muhammad in the fifth year of his mission in Mecca, Muhammad uttered the following revelation: 'Have you considered *dal-Lativine al-Lat, al-'Uzza* and *Manat*, the third, the other?',[17] followed by the following two verses recognizing the intercession of these three local deities, 'Indeed they are the high cranes/the high maidens, and indeed their intercession is to be

---

[15] The Lebanese Bishop Georges Khodr 1981:38, points to the book of Acts to show how the economy of the Spirit allows the apostles to see the work of God in the gentile and "pagan" world, even though those same apostles fault these same pagan people for their idolatry.

[16] Surah 18:84-86. A. Yusuf Ali's rendering of the meaning in English of the Qur'an supplies the citations in this chapter, unless otherwise noted (Qur'an 1946). Sometimes I leave out his parenthetical insertions. Muhammad A. S. Abdel Haleem renders verse 85 by adding an interpretive comment in brackets: "he found it [seemed to be] setting into a muddy spring" (Qur'an 2005).

[17] Surah 53:19-20.

desired.'[18] Some of these early exegetical traditions also report the verses later substituted for these verses: 'Would you have sons and for him daughters? That indeed would be a crooked division'.[19] According to some of these reports, Gabriel later apprised Muhammad of his error and recited the correct verses in place of those interjected by Satan. Other reports have Muhammad realizing the error himself. Verse 23 was then added:

> These are nothing but names you have devised—you and your forefathers—for which God has sent down no authority for them. They follow nothing but conjecture and what their own souls desire! Even though Guidance has already come to them from their Lord![20]

In spite of the early traditions supporting this story, two considerations have made rejection of its authenticity virtually a test of orthodoxy for modern Muslims.[21] First, it portrays the Prophet as—at least on one occasion—unable to discern the difference between divine and Satanic inspiration, a conclusion contrary to the established doctrine of divine protection of prophets from sin (*'ismat al-anbiya'*).[22] Second, it does not meet the test for reliable transmission used by the main collectors and evaluators of Islamic normative tradition. Some Muslim authorities say this narrative was transmitted before these standards were applied.[23] Scholars such as Frank Peters ask, according to Ahmad, whether it is possible to imagine such an "inauspicious" narrative being reported if it were not true.[24] My point is that the divine discourse is engaged with Muhammad and with his context. While Muhammad receives messages from God, he himself is engaged with the material; in order to communicate, prophetic discourse must participate in local knowledge.

Bishop Kenneth Cragg respects the discourse of the Qur'an. But he chides those Muslims who, in order to protect the Qur'an from any human engagement at all, believe in "a literal 'dictation' of this *kitab* ['book'] to a wholly passive Muhammad… so that it might be an 'immaculate' text, unaffected by the potential 'corruption' of an active human reception of it, via 'thoughts and intents

[18] Ahmad 2004:532; translation by Ahmad.

[19] Surah 53:21-22.

[20] My translation; see also 53:26-27.

[21] Ahmad 2004:531. At least one current very orthodox Muslim accepts the reports of this event, even though he would consider revelation (*wahy*) as I am interpreting it here merely the inspiration (*ilham*) of "poets, artists and saints" (Zaki, 1991: 43). In fact, Cragg, 1994:45-49, sees parallels between the inspiration of the poet William Blake and the revelatory experiences of Muhammad.

[22] Ahmad 2004:533-34.

[23] Ahmad 2004:534.

[24] Ahmad 2004:535; Peters, 1994: 161. The quotation is from Peters.

of the heart', never participatory in its contents, …based on the prescript: 'the more it is divine requires that it be ever the less human.'"[25]

According to Cragg:

> The source of this conviction may be admired—but not approved—as valid desire to be holding what is 'of God' as exclusively 'by God', or to have confidence in 'God's word' having no human agency, no human 'mix'. … To think Muhammad participatory in the incidence would cancel all 'Quranicity'. Faith would be left with a cracked bell or a forged cheque….[26]

Cragg reminds his readers that Muhammad had a heart (*qalb*), "the very wellspring of personal being."[27] The human dimension of the Qur'an as prophetic divine discourse resides in Muhammad's reception of the divine revelation that Gabriel brought down on his 'heart'.[28] This expression "can only mean that there was 'heartfeltness' in his experience of *tanzil* (sending down), a personal factor of feeling and ardour in the onset of *wahy*."[29] Only from Muhammad's heart, Cragg points out, does the message get to his ears and "on to" his lips.[30]

In other words even direct divine revelation is culturally relevant and humanly received and uttered. The Prophet participates even in the direct divine revelation of the Qur'an. The Arabic language must then convey it; a particular audience must attend to it; and it must interpret events and issues of intimate significance to them. All these purposes involve the human factor; but they are all, as Cragg insists, "'wherebys' of the eternal."[31]

Cragg's interpretation appears to me congruent with a Christian understanding of prophecy and helps Christians see that the Qur'an can be both words of God to Muhammad and helpful scripture for Christians, when seen through the lens of the New Testament.

---

[25] Cragg 2005:97. Zaki 1991:43, 47, takes this position, but not for the reason Cragg critiques. According to Zaki, because *anzala* ('he sent down,' i.e., 'revealed'; e.g., in Surah12:2" 'We sent it down') is a transitive form of the verb *nazala* ('he/it descended') and requires a direct object, something already existing is 'sent down.' Therefore, the Qur'an is in no sense the creation of Muhammad, but an object sent down, albeit seriatim (Surah 17:106). Zaki says, this precludes the possibility of error 'save in the course of subsequent transcription, due to the fallibility of the human medium, or the deficiencies of the Arabic script before [the Caliph] Hallaj's [r. 694-714] orthographic reforms.'

[26] Cragg, 2005: 97.

[27] Cragg, 2005: 96.

[28] Surah 2:97.

[29] Cragg, 2005: 98.

[30] Cragg, 2005: 98.

[31] Cragg, 2005: 97-98. See also K. Cragg, 1994, entirely devoted to this theme, and especially pages 13-24 and 43-53. Note also the repetition of the concept of "participation" in both Cragg, 2005 and 1994. Just as in Jesus the Messiah there is divine participation in a fully human journey, so in the Qur'an, according to Cragg, there is the human participation of Muhammad in the divine Word. This is my position as well.

The Qur'an challenges the New Testament witness to truth revealed by, or entailed in, the Incarnation

Strong denials of the Christian doctrines of the Incarnation and the Trinity in the Qur'an must surely give us pause in the pursuit of support for Christian use of the Qur'an for models and teaching in matters compatible with the New Testament witness.[32] Cragg's eloquent point about the Qur'anic revelation coming to the heart of Muhammad, who addresses a particular people in a language of their heart and within a specific cultural *context,* applies to this reality also. The Prophet of Islam came to convince Arabian polytheists that only one Ultimate Divine Being exists. The grammatical form of part of the *shahadah* makes this very clear. The *la* beginning the phrase *la ilaha,* 'there is no god,' indicated by the vowel (*fathah*) at its end, called *la li-nafyi 'l-jins*, negates the whole category or genus of deity, 'there is no god *at all* except God.' Muhammad was addressing people who were worshipping many gods. He was sensitive to *shirk*, associating other beings with the one God. When he saw anything akin to it, he sought the help of God.

The theology and practice of some Christians, known to Muhammad, may have come close to polytheism, and appeared to veer towards it, or were, if not theoretically, then functionally, deifying their leaders:

> They take their priests and their anchorites to be their lords in derogation of God, and Christ, the son of Mary; yet they were commanded to worship but One God: there is no god but He. Praise and glory to Him....[33]

The following verses from Surah 5 offer evidence that some of the Christians addressed may have believed—functionally, if not theoretically—in a 'family' Trinity of Jesus, Mary, and the Father.[34]

> In blasphemy indeed are those who say that God is Christ the son of Mary. Say: 'Who then hath the least power against God, if His Will were to destroy Christ the son of Mary, his mother, and... everyone that is on the earth?' (17)

> Christ, the son of Mary, was no more than a Messenger; many were the Messengers that passed away before him. His mother was a woman of truth. They had both to eat their (daily) food.... (75)

> God will say, "O Jesus, Son of Mary, didst thou say unto men, 'Worship me and my mother as gods in derogation of God'?" (116a).

---

[32] E.g., Surah 4:171; 5:17, 72,75, 116; 9:31; 61:6.

[33] Surah 9:31.

[34] Cuypers 2009:431-32 sees this rather as an argument *ad absurdum* against the *Theotokos* 'Mother of God' / 'God-bearer' doctrine of the Council of Ephesus (431) in order to show that if Jesus is divine then his mother had to be divine.

The concept of the Trinity as Father, Son, and Mother would give an entirely different cast to the doctrine of the Trinity, in the context of active Arabian polytheism, where people believed God had divine daughters.

In some mosques I have visited, I have been asked, 'Why do you believe Jesus is *a god*?' Yet, I have never heard a Christian say Jesus was 'a god' or that the Holy Spirit is 'a god'! There is only *the one God*. To say that Jesus, even in the days of his flesh, participates in the identity of God is different than positing him as a god alongside of God. The following Qur'anic formula gets closer to the view of Christians from earliest times to the present. It seems to suggest that Christians in Muhammad's experience had struggled over just how Jesus and the Holy Spirit related to each other and to God.

> [T]o Jesus, the son of Mary, We gave Clear (Signs), and strengthened him with the Holy Spirit. If God had so willed, succeeding generations would not have fought among each other, after Clear (Signs) had come to them, but they (chose) to wrangle, some believing and others rejecting....[35]

This is not to say that the Qur'an has no inaccurate interpretations of orthodox Christian doctrine, or that it does not object to it.[36] My point is that prophetic discourse engaged in polemic, though in the form of direct divine address, and interpreted as such by its prophet and receptors, is still contextualized for local knowledge and thus limited in the absolute quality of its truth. The fact that it needs to be interpreted in the light of the Incarnation does not deprive the Qur'an of benefit to Christian readers. The Qur'an, however, may also be addressing a local Christian witness that is itself compromised in its expression of truth and duty.

The Qur'anic call to armed conflict surely counts as one of the most obvious features in the Qur'an that exist in tension with the New Testament witness to the content and meaning of Jesus' participatory and representative journey of solidarity with God and humankind.[37] They contrast with the teachings of Jesus and his own witness as to the nature of his kingdom: 'My kingdom is not from this world. If my kingdom were from this world, my followers would be fighting to keep me from being handed over to the Jews. But as it is, my kingdom is not from here.'[38] The refusal of the early Christians to engage in war, or in any form of killing, is well-known.

The obvious parallel between the Qur'an and both the Old Testament and the Apocrypha in regard to divinely sanctioned war suggests that the Qur'an

---

35 Surah 2:253.

36 See, e.g., Surah 4:170-75, and my discussion of this thematic unit in light of the doublet 4:48 and 4:116 in Zahniser 1997:79-84.

37 E.g., Surah 4:71-104. See Haleem, 1999: chapter 5; and Aslan, 2006: chapter 4, for helpful Muslim discussions of war and peace in the Qur'an and Islam.

38 See John 18:36; see also Matthew 4:9-10; 5:9-11, 38-48; 10:16-33; Luke 4:5-8; 22:35-38.

interpreted by the *sunnah* of Jesus and the New Testament can be fruitful for Christian discipleship in spite of its position on armed conflict. For example, the Hebrew scriptures of the Christian canon require armed conflict and provide directives for carrying it out in God's name and on behalf of God's people (Deuteronomy 20:1-20); and the First Book of Maccabees describes how the God of Israel used the Jewish priest Mattathias and his five sons and a grandson to lead a successful war against the Seleucid Syrian oppressors of Israel.[39]

Qur'anic stories of Biblical characters and events differ from their counterparts in the Christian canon

Among its rich traditions about Moses, the Qur'an provides in Surah 18:60-82 a narrative not found in the Torah with a point of its own. Beginning abruptly, in the approximate middle of the Surah, the story begins with a dialogue: "Moses said to his servant, 'I will not rest until I reach the place where the two seas meet, even if it takes me years'" (60).[40] When Moses and his servant reach the junction of the two rivers, they discover they have forgotten their fish, preventing the servant from providing Moses with the meal he asks for. Retracing their steps in pursuit of the lost fish, they stumble onto 'one of God's servants' to whom God has shown mercy and taught knowledge. Moses promises to be the servant's student in exchange for 'some of the right guidance' the God-taught stranger has learned. The servant agrees, provided Moses will patiently refrain from questioning anything until the servant chooses to explain it.

Moses and the servant get into a boat. The servant shocks Moses by hacking a hole in the boat and sinking it. Moses chastises the servant for subjecting them to drowning. The servant upbraids Moses for forgetting the patience he promised. Next, they encounter a young boy whom God's servant immediately kills. Moses upbraids the servant, saying, 'Truly you have done a foul deed!' 'Did I not tell you,' says the servant, 'you would never be able to bear with me patiently?' A repentant Moses exclaims, 'If ever I question anything you do, banish me from your company—you have put up with enough from me.' When the two hungry travellers reach a town, they ask for food. But the people refuse them any sustenance. Nevertheless, the servant of God repairs a collapsed wall in their town. Again, impatient Moses questions the servant for doing this when the town had nothing for them to eat.

Here the exasperated servant gives up on Moses. But before they part, the servant explains his strange actions. The boat belonged to some needy people who made their living from the sea; the servant damaged it because he knew a king would soon come and sequester every serviceable craft. The slain youth's parents are people of faith, 'We feared that this son would grieve them by obstinate rebellion and ingratitude, so we desired their Lord to give them another

---

[39] E.g., 1 Maccabees 2:23-26, 42-48; 3:10-25; 5:21-23, 28-54; and 6:40-46. Harrington, 2006: 1477.

[40] Qur'an 2005.

child, better in purity and closer in affection.' The wall belonged to two destitute orphans and a treasure was buried beneath it. The Lord intended them to reach maturity and dig up the treasure. These are the things over which you were not able to be patient".[41]

An earlier verse typifies the Qur'an's frequent reference to itself, 'In this Qur'an We have presented every kind of example (*mathal*) for people, but the human is more contentious than any other creature'.[42] Then the Qur'an faults Muhammad's audience for over-confidence in knowledge and points out the audience's need for divine mercy.[43] The Moses story represents just such a Qur'anic example of over-confident knowledge.

Stories that supplement the accounts in the Old Testament also occur among the 14 or 15 books of the Apocrypha. The book of Esther adds six additional chapters to the canonical book of Esther. The book of Baruch and the Letter of Jeremiah, add to what we know from the book of Jeremiah. Although Baruch may be legendary, it exemplifies 'a relatively common practice during the late Second Temple period to compose edifying works that expanded the Biblical tradition.'[44] Baruch connects with Biblical Deuteronomy, Job, Jeremiah, Daniel, and Isaiah. Like the Qur'an, it adapts stories, poetry, and wisdom to its context.

Since the Moses story is a travel story, a travel story of 'the Two-horned One' follows.[45] Unlike the cautionary tale about Moses' over-confidence in knowledge, however, it focuses on judgment: rewards and punishment, to be meted out on the Last Day—another earlier theme.[46] The Surah then ends on this same eschatological note.[47]

This rather protracted story with its fascination and important moral makes a good transition to our final reality: people will ask this question.

The Value of the Qur'an for Christian Discipleship

Christians in general can benefit from reading the Qur'an. But especially those Christians shaped by Muslim culture, because they will have had extensive

[41] Surah 18:60-82. See Wheeler, 2002: 6-26 for an extended discussion of this story and its expansion in the commentaries; a shorter discussion is found in Schöck, 2003: 425-26.
[42] Surah 18:54. My modification of Haleem's translation in *Qur'an*, 2005.
[43] Surah 18:54-59.
[44] Newsom, 2006: 1452. The *Prayer of Azariah* and the *Song of the Three Jews*, and the narratives of *Susanna* and *Bel and the Dragon* represent components in the Latin and Greek versions of the canonical book of Daniel. *Azariah* allows the reader to enter into the experience of the three pious Jews who survived the fiery furnace; and *Susanna* and *Bel* reiterate the Jewish theme of the faithful Jewish hero or heroine even in persecution (Wills, 2006: 1470). First and Second Esdras, consisting of 4, 5, and 6 Ezra, offer supplements to canonical 2 Chronicles, Ezra, and Nehemiah.
[45] Surah 18:83-101.
[46] Surah 18:58-59.
[47] Surah 18:101-110.

exposure to the Qur'an and its impact on the cultural traditions of individuals, families, and communities. Being able to include the Qur'an in their edifying reading, interpreted in compatibility with the New Testament, can be very constructive for the formation of disciples of Jesus and, in the case of Christians formed or influenced by Muslim culture, the continuity of their identity.

Kenneth E. Nolin spent decades living among Muslims, studying the Qur'an with them and sharing with Christians what he learned. As a result of his 'interscriptural adventure,'[48] he identifies a number of unique contributions of Islam to Christianity: a deep and abiding reverence for God, a sense of thanksgiving for the bounties of God, a deep sense of the presence of God, a compelling sense of Muslim brother and sisterhood, and the illuminating contrast between the concepts of *kufr*, 'unbelief,' and its opposite, *shukr*, 'thankfulness.'[49] The most important of these contributions, according to Nolin, is a deep and abiding reverence for God.[50] A good example of this is the opening Surah of the Qur'an, recited seventeen times a day by Muslims who observe the five times of prayer. It ascribes to God mercy, lordship, guidance, and blessing.[51] A book of readings from the Qur'an selected by Kenneth Cragg includes, in addition to the seven verses of Surah 1, 85 verses devoted to God's praise.[52]

The Qur'an places a high value on community. For example, its admonition of believers to charge each other to behave acceptably and to avoid disapproved behaviour (*al-amr bi-l-ma'ruf wa-l-nahy 'an al-munkar*) contributes to excellent community life.[53] As a communally approved and practiced habit, it can encourage constructive behavior without causing the stigma of "judgmentalism." Christians, leaders and lay people alike, can use the Qur'an overtly to support this communal solidarity.

The Qur'an's firm commitment to justice and equality of all persons also contributes to communal solidarity. The Qur'an even upbraids Muhammad for paying attention to an important tribal leader he was trying to lead to Islam, while ignoring a poor blind man. The blind man, according to the Qur'an, 'came to thee striving earnestly, and with fear; of him wast thou unmindful'.[54]

The Qur'an provides insights into the development of Christian positions on issues impinging upon individuals and societies in general. In the area of economics, it provides 'a series of values, guidelines and rules which serve as a basis for developing appropriate economic systems and institutions for Muslim

[48] Nolin, 1993: 115.

[49] Nolin, 1993: 105-111. Nolin follows these unique contributions with three Christian contributions to Islam from the Bible: a sense of assurance; a new impetus for right living and service to humanity; and an awareness of the pervasive and insidious nature of human wrong (Nolin, 1993: 111-14).

[50] Nolin, 1993: 107-08.

[51] Surah 1:1-7.

[52] Cragg, 1988: 84-92.

[53] Surah 3:110.

[54] Surah 80:8-10.

communities.'[55] For example, the Qur'an speaks confidently regarding the eschewing of interest—especially where it becomes the cause of people moving more deeply into debt—and of enriching the few at the expense of the many. Islamic banking has grown out of this conviction and provides a check against unregulated capitalism as well as against state controlled socialism.

The Qur'an's edifying stories, graphic descriptions, and pointed injunctions contribute to the improvement of personal character and inter-personal morals and manners. A popular rendering in English of Abu Hamid Muhammad al-Ghazali's (d. 1111) *Al-khuluq al-hasan* (Good Moral Character and Conduct) by Aslam Abdullah cites support from the Qur'an for such morals and manners as self-improvement and realization; truth and honesty; pledges and promises; sincerity; generosity and benevolence; patience; etiquette in conversation; tolerance and pardon; and avoiding rancour and enmity.[56] For example, this verse encourages sincerity:

> O ye who believe! Cancel not your charity by reminders of your generosity or by injury, like those who spend their substance to be seen of men, but believe neither in God nor in the Last Day. They are in Parable like a hard barren rock, on which is a little soil; on it falls heavy rain, which leaves it a bare stone...[57]

In gathering these representative Qur'anic contributions to Christian instruction in manners and examples for living, I do not mean that no such resources exist in the Christian canon. But especially those with a unique Islamic character and compatible with the New Testament's wide-ranging witness will be especially supportive to Christians who have been shaped by Islamic religion and culture, and may be helpful to other Christian readers as well.

The Christian Reading of the Qur'an: An Inter-scriptural Adventure

Some Christian traditions, for nearly two millennia, have considered the Apocrypha or Deuterocanonical Books of the Bible an important source 'for example of life and instruction of manners.' Protestants usually do not see the need for extra scriptural books, though I have personally found them—including the Qur'an—illuminating. I do not mean to suggest that the Bible is not fully adequate for 'teaching, reproof, correction, and training in righteousness' (2 Timothy 3:16); but the Qur'an can add dimensions to the repertoire of

---

[55] Saeed 2002: 5-9.

[56] Abdullah 1997. According to Muzammil Siddiqi, who introduces the volume, al-Ghazali's *Al-khuluq al-hasan* "occupies the second most important place in Islamic teachings" (Abdullah, 1997: vii).

[57] Surah 2:264. Good works in Christianity, while not alone salvific, are necessarily involved in redemption. Both the New Testament and the Qur'an tie faith and works together (James 2:18; Surah 37:109-11). See Zahniser 2009: 227-34.

information and inspiration for Christians, especially those shaped by Muslim religious culture.

The ultimate divine self-disclosure in the Incarnation enables the Qur'an, though subsequent to the Bible, to prepare the way for its witness. Does the Word made flesh not render all words secondary (John 1:14)? Yet I believe that what Martin Luther said about the books of the Apocrypha, can also be said of the Qur'an: There is much in it 'useful and good to read.' Christians may find the reading of the Qur'an an inter-scriptural adventure edifying "for example of life and instruction in manners" when interpreted through the lens of the Word made flesh according to the New Testament witness.

Revealing Divine Identity: The Incarnation of the Word in John's Gospel

Rollin G. Grams

Rollin G. Grams is an Associate Professor of New Testament at Gordon-Conwell Theological Seminary and a theological educator serving internationally with United World Mission

Introduction

The present topic, the incarnation of Jesus Christ, is one of the major points at which Christianity and Islam divide. As Kenneth Cragg has stated:[1]

> I suppose it would be right to say that the central controversy between Islam and Christianity has to do with the distancing or otherwise between the divine and the human. It is this which pervades all the themes of revelation, prophetic vocation, the ways of divine mercy, the categories of law and love, the degree of *Kenosis* in creation itself on God's part, and the question of Jesus and the Cross.

Badru Kateregga agrees:[2]

> This is the point where Muslims and Christians painfully part company. The issue is deeply theological and anthropological. The Christian view of incarnation seems to compromise God's transcendence and sovereignty while at the same time exalting a mere man to God-like status. By denying the incarnation, Islam is really affirming both the transcendence of God *and* the rightful status of man as the servant and *khalifa* of God on earth.

The present essay examines this divide between Muslims and Christians over the Incarnation by looking at how this teaching is understood in the canonical Gospel of John nearly four centuries before its articulation at the Council of Chalcedon in 451 CE. The arguments here advanced are (1) that Islam is in agreement with John at a number of points in what is said about God and (2) John offers an even more profound understanding of God in what he says about Jesus. The essay begins by arguing that the dialogue set up here with John's Gospel and Islam needs to begin with this theological discussion, not with an historical debate, so as to appreciate what is being said about God.

---

[1] Cragg 1980:xiv.

[2] Kateregga 1980:132.

The Historical Versus Theological Dialogue

One approach to a consideration of the Christology in John's Gospel - a discussion typical of twentieth century scholarship - focuses on this Gospel's historicity. This approach enquires into what can be said of the historical Jesus in John's Gospel. Is he more a literary character, in John's narrative, or an actual historical figure, that really spoke and acted as he is depicted? Does the Gospel of John represent a development in the last decade of the 1st century CE of a high Christology that the church earlier in the 1st century did not have (including a doctrine of the Incarnation)?

One scholar, John Hick, has built his reputation on denouncing the Incarnation as well as the historicity of John's Gospel, which is often thought to have been written at the end of the 1st century CE. Hick argues that the theological conviction of the Incarnation developed in the late first century Church in response to consternation over Christ's supposed failure to return in the expected time and in the context of Greco-Roman polytheism.[3] His argument may be received as an attack on orthodoxy, but in a lecture to the Iranian Institute of Philosophy, he sees it as a way to build a bridge in dialogue with Islam: if one can eliminate the doctrine of the Incarnation from Christianity, then Christianity and Islam will have less to divide them.[4]

This essay will not, however, focus on the question of the historical veracity of John's Gospel. Relevant arguments on John's historicity and his not deviating from early Christian teaching may be found elsewhere.[5] The plausibility of Jesus' divinity within the historical and theological context of Jewish monotheism has been argued well by scholars such as Richard Bauckham.[6] John's high Christology, moreover, fits well with the early Christian worship of Jesus.[7] There are, moreover, strong indications that a theology of Incarnation existed well before the end of the 1st century CE and that a high

---

[3] Hick 1993/2005:4-5. Arguments that the early Church reached a 'crisis of a delayed return of Christ,' and that this crisis led to theological and ecclesiastical changes in the late 1st century, hinge on proving that the Church expected Christ to return promptly and that His not appearing resulted in a crisis. Such arguments abounded in the mid-20th century, but there is very little evidence in their favour. There is, e.g., nothing like IV Ezra's agonizing examination of the Jews' situation before God after their failed war against Rome in AD 66-73. That was a true crisis with theological implications. On the contrary, Jesus Himself indicated that He was inaugurating a world-wide mission that was not something to be accomplished in a short interval (see, among many such arguments, Grams 2008). Jesus also said that nobody knows the hour of His return (Mk. 13.32).

[4] Hick 2009.

[5] A few recent works that make this point might be suggested for further reading on the historicity of John's Gospel: Blomberg 2001, Keener 2003, and especially Bauckham 2006.

[6] See, e.g., Bauckham 1998.

[7] See, e.g., Hurtado 2003 and Hurtado 2005.

Christology did not evolve as responses to crises in the Church in the middle to late first century.[8]

Instead, this essay will seek to understand John's Incarnation theology. It, therefore, offers a presentation of Incarnation theology in a more 21st century dialogue, where the theology of this canonical book can engage alternative theologies without thinking that every theological discussion must be set on ice until historical questions are answered. Thus the question posed will not be, 'Does John's Incarnation theology go back to the historical Jesus' but 'What does John's Incarnation theology add to our understanding of God?' In this way, dialogue with Islam will not be conducted through revision of Christian theology via a modernist historical reconstruction. It will rather be conducted by exploring the theological challenge that canonical Christianity makes in such a dialogue.

Qur'anic and Johannine Affirmations about God

The Qur'an affirms that God is compassionate, merciful, and forgiving. He 'is most compassionate towards man, a dispenser of grace.[9] He is not only 'full of compassion and mercy towards the believers';[10] but also towards all humankind.[11] God has, moreover, 'willed upon Himself the law of grace and mercy'.[12] He is a 'bestower of mercy',[13] and so it makes sense to pray for forgiveness and mercy from Him.[14] His mercy is 'life-giving'.[15] At the same time, God 'causes to suffer whomever He wills, and bestows His mercy on whomever He wills'. Also, those who deny 'the truth of God's messages' have equally abandoned all hope of His grace and mercy.[16]

The Qur'an also states that God forgives sinners who pray for forgiveness, cease to sin knowingly, who believe, and who do righteous deeds.[17] 'He is much-

---

[8] On this point, consider the arguments of Moule 1977. Moule argues against the likes of Boers 1970 p. 450 ff. Boers, following Bousset, states that 'the fundamental problem of a Christology of the NT...was that the view of Jesus found in NT Christology was not historically true of Jesus himself' (p. 452). The most articulate evolutionary perspective to 1st century Christology came three years after Moule with Dunn 1989. A number of scholars have argued against such evolutionary approaches to New Testament Christology. In addition to Moule might be listed Oscar Cullmann, Martin Hengel, Richard Bauckham, Larry Hurtado, Seyoon Kim, and Gordon Fee. See the discussion of these views in Fee 2007p.10 ff.

[9] Surah 2.143; cf. 2.207; 3.30; 9.117; cf. 9.128; 22.65. In this essay, English quotations from the Qur'an are from Asad 2009.

[10] Surah16.7; cf. 16.47.

[11] Surah 24.20; 57.9; 59.10.

[12] Surah 6.12; cf. 6.54.

[13] Surah 16.119; 23.109, 118.

[14] Surah 2.286; 4.26f; 7.23, 149, 155; 9.15, 27, 117, 118, 128; 11.47; 27.46.

[15] Surah 12.87.

[16] Surah 29.21and 23.

[17] See Surah 3.135; 57.28; 11.11; 22.50; 35.7.

forgiving to those who turn unto Him again and again'.[18] He loves, forgives, and dispenses grace to the one who loves Him and who follows the Prophet.[19] Yet, as the One, to whom all in heaven and earth belongs, 'He forgives whom He wills, and He chastises whom He wills'.[20] One person whom God does not forgive is he or she who ascribes divinity to anyone other than God.[21]

In so describing God, the Qur'an affirms the key revelation of God to Moses on Mt. Sinai in Exodus 34.6-7:

> The LORD passed before him, and proclaimed, "The LORD, the LORD, a God merciful and gracious, slow to anger, and abounding in steadfast love and faithfulness, keeping steadfast love for the thousandth generation, forgiving iniquity and transgression and sin, yet by no means clearing the guilty, but visiting the iniquity of the parents upon the children and the children's children, to the third and the fourth generation."[22]

The New Testament affirms the same view of God: He is infinitely patient and forgiving, gracious, merciful, and loving, and yet He will also one day judge sinners. There are, however, two ways in which the New Testament takes this view of God a little further, and both can be found in 1 John 4.10: 'In this is love, not that we loved God but that he loved us and sent his Son to be the atoning sacrifice for our sins.'

The two new perspectives are (1) that God's love is not just a response to repentance but also precedes it, and (2) God's love is seen in His sending His Son as a sin offering for our sins. John captures these points in the simple statement that 'God is love' (1 Jn. 4.8). In the second claim, the Incarnation and cross of Jesus are affirmed as a single act of God's love. Because God's sending His Son is in order that He might make a sin offering for our sins as the Lamb of God (Jn. 1.29), the Incarnation and cross both reveal God's love and accomplish salvation. This point is made in a remarkable way in John's Gospel, as this essay will shortly demonstrate.

The Qur'an, however, rejects Christian teaching about Jesus' divine identity, Incarnation, and saving death. Even so, there is some agreement about what is affirmed concerning God. The Incarnation could, for example, be misunderstood along Graeco-Roman lines in terms of a god having intercourse with a woman and begetting a son, such as the story of Hercules' origin from Zeus and Alcmene.[23] From an Islamic and Christian point of view, such a notion fails on

---

[18] Surah 17.25.

[19] Surah 3.31.

[20] Surah 3.129; 48.14.

[21] Surah 4.48; 116; 9.113; 60.12; 33.73; 44.42.

[22] Here and elsewhere, the translation used for the Bible is the New Revised Standard Version.

[23] There is, however, no connection between the Christian doctrine of the Incarnation and anything else in the historical-cultural context. Harnack argued over a hundred years ago.

several counts: (1) God has no consort; (2) God did not beget a son; (3) Jesus' birth was miraculous; (4) Jesus was not partly divine and partly human; (5) there is only one God; and (6) divine power and authority has no limitations.

As far as the Qur'an is concerned, these points are made in passages such as the following:[24]

> Said she [Mary]: "O my Sustainer! How can I have a son when no man has ever touched me?" [The angel] answered: "Thus it is: God creates what He wills when He wills a thing to be, He but says unto it, 'Be' - and it is.
>
> Indeed, the truth denies they who say, "Behold, God is the Christ, son of Mary." Say: "And who could have prevailed with God in any way had it been His will to destroy the Christ, son of Mary, and his mother, and everyone who is on earth-all of them? For, God's is the dominion over the heavens and the earth and all that is between them; He creates what He wills: and God has the power to will anything!"
>
> ... the Originator of the heavens and the earth! How could it be that He should have a child without there ever having been a mate for Him - since it is He who has created everything, and He alone knows everything? Such is God, your Sustainer: there is no deity save Him, the Creator of everything: worship, then, Him alone -for it is He who has everything in His care.
>
> It is not conceivable that God should have taken unto Himself a son: limitless is He in His glory! When He wills a thing to be, He but says unto it "Be" -and it is! He begets not, and neither is He begotten.

The Gospel of John affirms the same points. The Qur'an departs from John's teaching about Jesus, of course, but the agreement should be noted. The six points noted above might be briefly examined with respect to John's Gospel.

Regarding points 1 and 2· Jesus being the 'Son' of God is not the result of God having a consort and begetting a Son (points 1 and 2). This is stated in the first three verses of the Gospel: 'In the beginning was the Word, and the Word was with God, and the Word was God. He was in the beginning with God. All things came into being through him, and without him not one thing came into being.' (Jn. 1.1-3) Jesus, as the Word of God, was with God 'in the beginning'. Thus Jesus was not 'begotten': His existence was as God's existence - eternal, prior to creation, and not separable from who God is. As Jesus says, 'So now,

---

that the doctrine of the Incarnation originated as Christianity took on Greek modes of thought (1897:218). But Dunn concludes his examination of possibilities by saying, '...we have found nothing in pre-Christian Judaism or the wider religious thought of the Hellenistic world which provides sufficient explanation of the origin of the doctrine of the Incarnation, no way of speaking about God, the gods, or intermediary beings which so far as we can tell would have given birth to this doctrine apart from Christianity' (1989:253).

[24] Surah 3.47; 5.17; 6.101-102 and 112.3.

Father, glorify me in your own presence with the glory that I had in your presence before the world existed.' (Jn.17.5). Since this was so, He was not part of creation but the One who created it. Orthodoxy settled this at the Council of Nicaea in 325 when it condemned Arianism for its teaching that Jesus was begotten in time. If one sets aside the dispute momentarily between Islam and Christianity over Jesus' divinity, the point of agreement can stand that Jesus is not 'Son' in any sense of being begotten by God as a parent begets a child.

Point 3: John writes, 'And the Word became flesh' (1.14) and 'John [the Baptist] testified to him and cried out, "This was he of whom I said, 'He who comes after me ranks ahead of me because he was before me'" (1.15). The story of Jesus' birth is lacking in John's Gospel, but the implications of Jn. 1.14-15 are that Jesus is pre-existent and therefore does not come to be through intercourse or birth. Rather, His humanity is understood as a 'tabernacling' (*eskēnōsen*) among humanity (1.14). The Qur'an sees Jesus' conception as a miraculous creation at the time of the Virgin Mary's conception. There are affinities with the story in Matthew and Luke in this view. It is not the view of Arius, who held that Jesus' *existence* had a beginning as the first creation before all the rest of creation. But the pre-existence of Jesus is what requires the notion of Jesus' Incarnation on either the Arian or Orthodox view over against that of Islam.

Point 4: Like the later Qur'an, John denies that Jesus was partly divine and partly human. Jesus' identity with God ('I and the Father, we are One,' Jn. 10.30; 'God the only and beloved child, the one in the Father's bosom,' Jn. 1.18)[25] is not compromised. Indeed, it is precisely because of Jesus' identity with God that He is able to reveal God so perfectly. He is the 'Word' (Jn. 1.1, 14), the One who makes God known (Jn. 1.18), the One on whom the angels of God ascend and descend in heavenly revelation (Jn. 1.18), and so, the Johannine Jesus says, the one who has seen Jesus has seen the Father (Jn. 14.9). The revelation of God in Jesus, therefore, solves the problem of how full divinity can be revealed fully in this limited and sinful world. So, over against the Qur'an, John affirms that Jesus is fully God and fully human.

This is a profound point in Christianity, for it affirms that God's revelation can be translated (or 'Incarnated'). David Shenk contrasts two incidents: that of a person converting to Islam being told that he must now learn Arabic to read the Qur'an and that of Shenk's parents, missionaries to the Zanaki people of Tanzania, for whom the scriptures were translated. The difference between Islam and Christianity, Shenk observes, is that, for the Muslim, 'the final revelation is the Word revealed as an Arabic book.' But 'within the Christian faith the Word has become flesh and lived among us' (so Jn. 1.14).[26] He continues, 'A core issue is that the Arabic Qur'an and the Shari'a that has developed around the Qur'an

---

[25] My translations.

[26] Shenk 2008:231; cf. Walls 1996:27.

requires a process of cultural Arabization for those who are becoming Muslims.'[27]

Point 5: Both Islam and the Gospel of John affirm monotheism. When Jesus says, 'I and the Father, we are one' (Jn. 10.30), He is affirming not only something about Himself that Judaism and, later, Islam rejects; He is also affirming something about God that all three religions affirm. He is affirming that God is One, and beside Him there is no other. Furthermore, when Jesus uses 'I AM' of himself in John's Gospel, he is using a reference that was used in the Old Testament to affirm monotheism (as we shall see below). Jesus' divine identity is decidedly not affirmed in John's Gospel by allowing a second deity; rather, Jesus' divine identity means that his identity is within the identity of the one God.

Point 6: Whatever is understood of the Incarnation, it is not a limitation of divine power and authority in John's Gospel. We find in John's Gospel that Jesus does whatever God does, although what he does is in perfect unity with the Father and not in any way independent: 'Jesus said to them, "Very truly, I tell you, the Son can do nothing on his own, but only what he sees the Father doing; for whatever the Father does, the Son does likewise' (Jn. 5.19). John seeks, rather, to demonstrate something more profound: Jesus' humanity holds the full revelation of God, not only His power and authority but also other dimensions of His identity such as His love, mercy, compassion, and forgiveness, as this essay next argues.

Incarnation in John: An Understanding of God

Ernst Käsemann failed to understand the emphasis John puts on the Incarnation. Käsemann argued that Jesus' feet never really touch the ground in John's Gospel, and he accused John of an essentially docetic Christology.[28] But the humanity of Jesus is emphasized throughout the Gospel,[29] whether he is celebrating a wedding feast, sitting tired by a well in Samaria, weeping at a friend's grave, or arranging for his mother's care as he is dying on the cross. John's theology is not docetic but incarnational.

But how does John present the Incarnation of Jesus? We could simply note that Jesus is presented as both human and divine in the Gospel and move directly to the later creeds that 'solve' the mystery of the Incarnation in terms of substance—a theology of being or ontology. Yet there is more to John's theology of the Incarnation. He draws out the relational and ethical significance of Jesus' Incarnation. This aspect of Jesus' Incarnation has significance not only for a dialogue with Islam but also for our own calling as Jesus' disciples in mission. In this functional Christology, too, we learn something profound about the identity

[27] Shenk 2008:241.
[28] Käsemann 1968.
[29] cf. Thompson 1993.

of God.[30] The Incarnation is not just a teaching about Christology, that is, that Jesus was pre-existent and so took on human nature. It is equally a teaching in John's Gospel about who God is. Indeed, this is perhaps the primary significance of Jesus' Incarnation in John's Gospel.

John draws out the Significance of Jesus' Incarnation in Three Important Ways

The first way in which John speaks of Jesus' Incarnation can be summed up in the term '*monogenēs*,' which he uses four times. The term should not be translated 'only begotten';[31] rather, it captures two thoughts: the one and only son, and the beloved son. An only child is especially dear to parents. Think of the sadness of Chinese parents in the 2008 earthquake that killed so many only children. Parents were left childless. A one and only child is a much beloved child. And so John uses this term to capture the idea, not only of Jesus' uniquely divine identity, but also Jesus' unique loving relationship with the Father. He is 'in the bosom of the Father.' Moreover, as we learn in the third use of '*monogenēs*,' this is a term that is used of Jesus' Incarnation and crucifixion. Jn. 3.16 states that God's love was revealed to the world in this way, that God sent His only and beloved Son to this sinful world of ours so that those who believe in Him might have eternal life (Jn. 3.16).

The term '*monogenēs*,' then, is also a term to explain Jesus' Incarnation. This is seen in a powerful way already in the prologue. The Johannine literature bears evidence of drawing out theological points with the use of numbers.[32] '*Monogenēs'* has the numerical value of 496, which is also the number of syllables in the prologue. And in the prologue, John describes the Incarnation of the *Logos* on three occasions: 'At Creation, when the Word of God brought life and light to all (1.4). At Sinai, when the Word of God was given through Moses as Law (1.17). In Jesus, when the Word of God became flesh, the only and beloved son of God, in whom the grace and truth of God was fully revealed (1.14, 16, 17).

A second way John describes the Incarnation is in terms of the revelation of God's identity on the cross. Martin Hengel points out that, for Irenaeus:

---

[30] The reader is referred to Thompson's excellent study of God in the fourth Gospel (2001).

[31] See the excellent discussion of how not to and how to translate this term in Keener 2003:410-416. Keener notes that 'only begotten' would make more sense were the term *monogennētos*, and he draws particular attention to Gen. 22.2, where God says to Abraham, 'Take your son, your only son Isaac, whom you love….' While the Greek term *monogenēs* is not found here in the Septuagint, Josephus does use the term in his discussion of this event in *Ant.* 1.222 (and he uses an additional term meaning 'much loved'). The emphasis does not fall on 'beggetting' but on 'only' and 'beloved'.

[32] Menken 1985; also Bauckham 2007:275ff.

> The Logos is identical with the God *who reveals himself* and takes on personal character by virtue of the fact that this Logos has truly become human in Jesus. In this way, Irenaeus...has recognized the salvation-historical character of the Prologue of John that culminates in incarnation.[33]

Still more than this is at work in John's theology of Incarnation. Not only does God reveal Himself, and not only does Jesus take on human character: Jesus' Incarnation in John's theology is a revelation of the essential being of God in sacrificial suffering. To discuss this point, more needs to be understood about John's use of numbers. As Mark Stibbe points out, John structures material into units of 7 or 3[34]:

7 discourses (3.16-21/4.5-27/5.19/47/6.27-58/7-8/10.1ff/14-17)

7 miracles/signs (2.1-11/4.46-54/5.1-15/6.1-15/6.16-21/9.1-7/11.1-44),

7 'I am' (egō eimi) sayings with predicative nominatives (6.35; 8.12; 10.7;

10.11; 11.25; 14.6; 15.1)

3 Passovers (2.13; 6.4; 13.1)

Pilate's 3 protests of Jesus' innocence (18.38; 19.4; 19.6)

3 equal passion sections (18 1-27; 18.28-19.16a; 19.16b-42).

To this list, we now add a discussion of the absolute 'I AM' sayings in John's Gospel. Richard Bauckham notes that Jesus uses the absolute identification 'I AM' of Himself on seven occasions in John. The Septuagint also uses the absolute 'I AM' seven times (Dt. 32.39; Is. 41.4; 43.10; plus the double '*egō eimi, egō eimi* in Is. 43.25; 45.18; 46.4; 51.12). The notion in the Old Testament, as the context of these passages shows, expresses God's oneness—there is no other god.[35] The absolute 'I AM' sayings bring to mind God's revelation of Himself to Moses in Exodus 3.14 (although the Septuagint does not have the absolute 'I AM' statement, despite the following NRSV translation): 'God said to Moses, 'I AM WHO I AM.' He said further, "Thus you shall say to the Israelites, 'I AM has sent me to you'.'"

The absolute use of 'I AM' is found in the Old Testament. For example, note the double usage of this statement inIsaiah: 'I, I am [Greek: 'I AM, I AM'] He who blots out your transgressions for my own sake, and I will not remember your sins' (Is. 43.25).

---

[33] Hengel 2008:265-294.
[34] Stibbe 1992.
[35] Bauckham 2007:243ff.

Jesus' use of the formula in John's Gospel indicates that Jesus is the true revelation of God, not just a revealer of God. The seven-fold use of the formula also indicates that Jesus is the full or complete revelation of God. He is the One on whom and in whom the glory of God is revealed: 'And [Jesus] said to [Nathaneal], "Very truly, I tell you, you will see heaven opened and the angels of God ascending and descending upon the Son of Man".' (Jn. 1.51)

In John's Gospel, another aspect of Jesus' revelation of God is found in three passages where Jesus speaks of His being 'raised up'. The Old Testament background for this saying appears to come from Is. 6.1; 52.13; 57.15, and possibly Ps. 110.1.[36] As Isaiah 52.13 states, the servant of God will be lifted up ('See, my servant shall prosper; he shall be exalted and lifted up, and shall be very high'), but the next chapter presents the servant's suffering and being crushed. John brings out both ideas through the double meaning of 'lifted up', i.e., on a cross and in exaltation.

The absolute 'I AM' sayings and the 'raised up' passages of Jesus intersect in the middle of each, at Jn. 8.28.[37] This arrangement forms a cross, which is most appropriate,[38] for in John's theology of the cross, to be 'raised up' is to be crucified *and* to be glorified (Jn. 12.32-34). Jesus' ultimate revelation of the glory of God takes place on the cross. This is illustrated in diagram on the following page.

The middle of both of these descriptions occurs in the exact same verse, Jn. 8.28: 'So Jesus said, whenever you see the Son of Man raised up, then know that I am, and I do nothing from myself, but I speak things as the Father has taught me.' Thus, the identity of God is revealed, not only in Jesus, but especially in Jesus' death on the cross. This point was a major theological statement in the 1st century. That God is compassionate, loving and forgiving, is something already revealed to Moses and all the Israelites at Mt. Sinai in Ex. 33-34. The Qur'an would later recognize this as well. What we now see is that divine compassion, love and forgiveness are revealed most fully in Jesus' death for us on the cross.

Two Johannine texts make the point on compassion and love: 'For God so loved the world that he gave his only Son, so that everyone who believes in him may not perish but may have eternal life;' (John 3:16) and on forgiveness: 'The next day [John the Baptist] saw Jesus coming toward him and declared, "Here is the Lamb of God who takes away the sin of the world!' (Jn. 1.29)

---

[36] See Bauckham 1998:49ff.; Jn. 12.38-41, e.g., has both Is. 53 and Is. 6 in view.
[37] Bauckham 1998:65.
[38] Whether John also thought of this arrangement as in the shape of a cross we will perhaps never know.

John 4:26 Jesus said to her, "**I am** he, the one who is speaking to you."[39]

John 6:20 But he said to them, "**It is I**; do not be afraid."

John 8:24 I told you that you would die in your sins, for you will die in your sins unless you believe that **I am** he."

John 3:14-15 [14] And just as Moses **lifted up** the serpent in the wilderness, so must the Son of Man be **lifted up**, [15] that whoever believes in him may have eternal life.

John 8:28 So Jesus said, "When you have **lifted up** the Son of Man, then you will realize that **I am** he, and that I do nothing on my own, but I speak these things as the Father instructed me.

John 12:32-34 [32] And I, when I am **lifted up** from the earth, will draw all people to myself." [33] He said this to indicate the kind of death he was to die. [34] The crowd answered him, "We have heard from the law that the Messiah remains forever. How can you say that the Son of Man must be **lifted up**? Who is this Son of Man?"

John 8:58 Jesus said to them, "Very truly, I tell you, before Abraham was, **I am**."

John 13:19 I tell you this now, before it occurs, so that when it does occur, you may believe that **I am** he.

John 18:5-6, 8 [5] They answered, "Jesus of Nazareth." Jesus replied, "**I am he**." Judas, who betrayed him, was standing with them. [6] When Jesus said to them, "**I am** he," they stepped back and fell to the ground.... [8] Jesus answered, "I told you that **I am** he. So if you are looking for me, let these men go."[40]

Divine Identity and the Cross in John's Gospel

---

[39] The English translation of the *New Revised Standard Version* does not capture the absolute uses of 'I am' in these verses. 'I am,' e.g., is here translated 'I am he.' The Greek, however, has only '*egō eimi*.'

[40] Note the threefold repetition of 'I AM' in this last passage.

Thirdly, John expresses Jesus' Incarnation in terms of servant love and unity. At the beginning of the upper room discourse, in Jn. 13, Jesus, the divine Son of God, washes his disciples' feet. He then gives them a new commandment: love one another (Jn. 13.34). At the end of the discourse (Jn. 17) is found Jesus' prayer of unity for his disciples. They are to become the community of love and unity from God that bears witness to the love and unity of God. They are brought into the love and unity that Jesus, the only and beloved Son, has with the Father. God, who revealed Himself as the God of compassion and love in Ex. 34, not only sends Jesus into the world out of His divine love, but also calls Jesus' disciples into a loving relationship with Him through Jesus. Jesus is the one through whom divine love flows in the community's relationships and in their relationship with God.

Conclusion: Divine Identity and the Word Made Flesh

The Gospel of John, as we have seen, claims that the glory of God, the 'I AM' of the burning bush, does not remain unknowable. It is revealed in the life and light of creation. It is revealed in the Law of Moses. And it is revealed most fully in the grace and truth of the Word that was made flesh and tabernacled among us. The moment, when this Word made flesh most fully revealed God's glory as the 'I AM,' came when the only and beloved Son was lifted up on the cross. Just here was divine love fully revealed and fully effective as compassion, mercy, and forgiveness.

In a speech seeking religious pluralism between world religions that was delivered to the Institute for the Islamic Culture and Thought in Tehran, John Hick sought a rather different perspective from that in the Gospel of John. He suggested that41 the ultimate reality is in itself beyond the scope of human description and understanding.... God in God's ultimate eternal self-existent being is ineffable, or as I would rather say, trans-categorial, beyond the scope of our human conceptual systems. And so we have a distinction of God in God's infinite self-existent being:

> God as humanly knowable.... So my hypothesis is that the world religions are oriented towards the same Ultimate Reality, which is however manifested within their different thought-worlds and forms of experience in different ways.... But the only stable and enduring basis for peace will come about when dialogue leads to a mutual acceptance of the world religions as different but equally valid relationships to the ultimate reality.

This Platonic perspective is the opposite from what we find in John's Gospel. Hick's approach is to affirm the unknowable and abstract as the ideal: God is an

[41] Hick 2005.

'ultimate reality'. He then denigrates the particular and concrete for being inadequate, erroneous, and incomplete. One might think of Plato's picture of the realm of particulars as shadows on a cave wall rather than the real thing itself (*Republic,* bk. 7). Moreover, Hick suggests, if we want a peaceful world, we have to find a way to get away from claims that our particular religious views are absolute.

John's claim, however, is that the God, who cannot be seen, is revealed in Jesus Christ, and the abstract characteristic of God as 'I AM' is revealed concretely in Jesus' 'lifting up' on the cross. In Jesus' Incarnation and death as God's sacrificial Lamb, God's loving, compassionate, and forgiving character, already announced in Ex. 34, is now fully revealed and effective for whoever in the world will believe that He has been sent by the Father (Jn. 5.38; 6.29; 11.42; 17.21).

What Hick forfeits in his opting for an understanding of God as some vague, ultimate reality, is the most significant revelation of God's identity in Jesus' Incarnation and crucifixion. What Islam forfeits in speaking of God's compassion, mercy and forgiveness without reference to the Incarnation and crucifixion of Jesus is an understanding of God's love as self-giving, sacrificial, and transformative.[42] It is not merely the mercy that the exalted One can show towards a repentant underling. As Richard Bauckham says in reference to Isaiah's theology:[43]

> ... God is not only the high and lofty one who reigns from his throne in the high and holy place; he also abases himself to the condition of the crushed and the lowly (Is. 57.15). And when the nations acknowledge his unique deity and turn to him for salvation, it is the Servant, humiliated and now exalted to sovereignty on the divine throne, whom they acknowledge.

John saw this fact about God's identity in the life and teaching of Jesus, the only and beloved Son of God, the I AM, and the incarnate Word of God, who revealed the identity of the Father as compassionate, merciful, and forgiving when He was 'lifted up' on the cross for our sins.

---

[42] I have argued elsewhere that the attempt to describe God with the abstract virtues of beneficence and mercy apart from the concreteness of the cross opens such virtues up to any interpretation and fails to appreciate the profound understanding that the cross offers. Cf. Grams 2008:157-166.

[43] Bauckham 1998:51.

Incarnation and Translation in Islam and Christianity

John Azumah

Rev. Dr. Johan Azumah is Director of the Centre for Islamic Studies and Christian-Muslim Relations and Lecturer of Islamic Studies

Incarnation and Translation in Christian and Islamic Thought

On the face of it, in terms of our topic, Islam and Christianity could not have had more contrasting standpoints. The term 'incarnate' derives from Latin *in* or *into* + *caro* (flesh) meaning 'being in flesh' or 'to become flesh'. In mainstream Christian teaching, the doctrine of Incarnation is about God, who is Spirit in essence, assuming the nature and form of a human being in the person of Jesus and coming to dwell amongst mankind in order to save humanity from the predicament of sin. Incarnation, as a Christian doctrine, seeks to walk a narrow line. On the one hand, Christians are committed to monotheism: there is only one God. However, from the accounts in the Bible, it is clear that Jesus' disciples, who were themselves devout monotheists, had the experience that in Jesus they were encountering God. It is this experience which is expressed in the Christian doctrine of the Incarnation.

The doctrine itself states that God, in one of the modes of his triune being and without in any way ceasing to be God, has revealed himself to mankind for their salvation by coming amongst them as a man in the person of Jesus who is held to be the incarnate Word or Son of God.[1] Although the term 'incarnation' itself is not found in the Bible, its clearest Biblical teaching is in the Prologue of the Gospel of John, where it states: 'In the beginning was the Word, the Word was with God, and the Word was God' then goes on to add that 'And the Word became flesh, and dwelt among us'. New Testament writers were fully convinced that this teaching is in consonance, indeed, fulfilment of Old Testament or the Hebrew Bible prophecies: "All this took place to fulfil what the Lord had said through the prophet: The Virgin will be with child and will give birth to a son, and they will call him 'Immanuel' — which means, 'God with us'" (Matthew 1:22-23).[2]

The Apostle Paul elaborates on the doctrine of the Incarnation in the very well known passage in Philippians 2:5-7: 'Your attitude should be the same as that of Christ Jesus: Who, being in very nature God, did not consider equality with God something to be grasped, but made himself nothing, taking the very

---

[1] See Hebblethwaite 1983.

[2] Cf. Isaiah 7:14.

nature of a servant, being made in human likeness.' The Christian doctrine of the Incarnation is, therefore, not about the deification of a human being but the condescension of God to humankind. In the Incarnation, as traditionally defined, the divine nature of the Son was joined but not mixed with human nature in one divine Person, Jesus Christ, who was both "truly God and truly man".

Debate on the Incarnation raged most especially during the first four centuries of Christianity. Divergent views rejected as heresies included Docetism, which taught that Jesus was a divine being that took on human appearance but not flesh; Arianism which held that Christ was a created being; and Nestorianism which maintained that the Son of God and the man, Jesus, shared the same body but retained two separate natures. The most widely accepted definitions of the Incarnation and the nature of Jesus were made by the early Christian Church at the First Council of Nicaea in 325, the Council of Ephesus in 431 and the Council of Chalcedon in 451. These councils declared that Jesus was both fully God: begotten from, but not created by the Father; and fully man: taking his flesh and human nature from the Virgin Mary. These two natures, human and divine, were hypostatically united into the one personhood of Jesus Christ. A much later divergent position is the doctrine of Oneness held by certain groups of Pentecostals who maintain that God is absolutely and indivisibly one and that He creates or manifests himself in the form of theophanies, Jesus being the last, best and most complete theophany of God. In the last century, liberal and modernist Protestant theologians have questioned the intelligibility as well as the centrality of the doctrine and considered it "mythical".[3]

The doctrine of the Incarnation, as a mainstream Christian belief, also helps give the Christian understanding of revelation its distinctiveness. This is aptly conveyed in the Epistle to the Hebrews 1:1-4:

> In the past God spoke to our forefathers through the prophets at many times and in various ways, but in these last days he has spoken to us by his Son, whom he appointed heir of all things, and through whom he made the universe. The Son is the radiance of God's glory and the exact representation of his being, sustaining all things by his powerful word.

In other words, Jesus is God's final ('in these last days) and ultimate self-disclosure of himself – "the exact representation" of God – who ever walked on the phase of the earth in human history.

And it is in the area of revelation that Islam and Christianity appear to chart different paths. Islam teaches that God does not reveal Himself but rather His will in the form of the Qur'an. As a result of the Islamic teaching, Muslim theologians have always viewed the doctrine of the Incarnation with suspicion and derision because it is seen as compromising divine transcendence and running the risk of committing the unpardonable sin of 'association', *shirk*, i.e. likening or

---

[3] See Hick 1977.

associating anything or anyone with God. Thus, even though the Qur'an records the virgin birth of Jesus and accords him titles such us 'Word of God' and 'Spirit of God', it strongly rejects the doctrine of Incarnation. In the words of the Qur'an, God neither begets nor is he begotten (Sura 112). Muslim authors normally use the term *hulul* ('infusion', of two spirits within one body) in reference to the Christian doctrine of the Incarnation. In the past, individual Sufis and sects have been accused for belief in *hulul* and branded heretical.

Having said that, Muslims have had their own internal controversies on the nature and status of the Qur'an as the Word of God, similar to the Christological controversies. The question that arose for Muslims was whether the Qur'an, as the speech of God, is created and, therefore, not eternal or uncreated and, therefore, eternal and divine. These controversies reached their peak during the 9th century. The Mu'tazila school, under the patronage of the ruling Caliph at the time, al-Ma'mun (d. 833 CE), held the view that the Qur'an was created while other leading scholars and schools of theology maintained that the Qur'an was the uncreated speech of God. In other words, the Qur'an, as the speech of God, shares in the divine attribute of eternity. Imam Abu al-Hasan al-Ash'ari (d. 936 CE), who can be said to be the St. Athanasius of Islam, championed the view that the Qur'an was uncreated, 'without asking how' (*bila kaif*) which won the day and remains the official Sunni Muslim view of the Qur'an. As with the Christological controversies, the *mihna*, as it came to be known, was about the nature of God as it was about the nature of revelation.

The official Sunni Muslim teaching on the Qur'an can be said to be in consonance with the first part of John's Prologue: 'In the beginning was the Word, the Word was with God, and the Word was God'. John 1:14, 'And the Word became flesh, and dwelt among us', i.e. the Incarnation, is the juncture at which Islamic and Christian teaching part company. A Muslim scholar, in a correspondence with a Christian colleague as far back as the 10th century, expressed this repugnance in the following words:

> In your error, your ignorance and your presumption in the face of God – Praise and Glory to Him – you still pretend that God came down from His Majesty, His Sovereighty, His Almighty Power, His Light, His Glory, His Force, His Greatness and His Power, even to the point of entering into the womb of a woman in suffocating grief, imperfection, in narrow and dark confines and in pain, that he stayed in her during nine months to come out as do all the sons of Adam, that he was then fed at her breast during two years, behaved as any child does and grew as any other child, year by year, crying, sleeping, eating, drinking, experiencing hunger and thirst during the whole of his life. Well then: who was ruling the heavens and the earth? Who was holding them? Who made laws for them? Who dictated the course of the sun, the moon, the stars, of the night, of the day, and of

the winds? Who created? Who gave life and death while Isa was in the womb of his mother and after he came into the world? Praise and Glory to God![4]

To quote Isma'il al-Faruqi, one of the most eloquent voices of orthodox Islam in the last century, 'God does not reveal Himself. He does not reveal Himself to anyone in any way. God reveals only His Will'.[5] This is because 'God, according to Muslim witness, is absolute and transcendent' and must always remain 'ontologically disparate' from the whole of creation including humankind', since it is impossible to have 'complete transcendence and self-revelation at the same time'.[6] In the Muslim mind, for Allah to have a child, He must have a spouse, which is beyond the nature of God. Yusuf Ali, one of the leading Qur'anic commentators of the last century, sums up the Islamic position in the following words:

> Begetting a son is a physical act depending on the need of men's animal nature. God Most High is independent of all needs, and it is derogatory to Him to attribute such an act to Him. It is merely a relic of pagan and anthropomorphic superstitions. Such an attribution to God of a material nature, and of the lower animal functions of sex is derogatory to the dignity and glory of God. The belief in God begetting a son is not a question of Words or of speculative thought. It is a stupendous blasphemy against God. It lowers God to the level of an animal.[7]

However, a highly regarded African Muslim mystic and scholar takes a different view. Amadou Hampate Ba (1900-1991), a revered Malian Muslim mystic, talks about what he calls 'the mysterious link between the Qur'anic name of Jesus and the name by which God has named Himself'. Ba uses numerology to calculate the numerical value of Allah and the title 'Messiah, son of Mary', exclusively given to Jesus in the Qur'an and concludes that:

> Whoever is enlightened by this secret stops being amazed when he hears that Jesus participates, in a certain way, in the Essence of the Divine Being. Are not the Word and the Spirit of a being inevitably a part of him? But, the two expressions "God's Word" and "the Spirit of God" were attributed to the Virgin Mary's son by the Qur'an itself …I could, without trouble, without prejudice or fear, set myself to listen to the Christian Path and to appreciate, for example, the depth of the Gospel according to John, notably in the first three verses of its prologue: "In the beginning was the Word, the Word was with God, the Word was God. He was in the beginning with God. All things came to be through him, without him nothing came to be".[8]

---

[4] Umar's Letter to Leo, cited in Gaudeul 2000:153.
[5] Al-Faruqi 1982:47.
[6] Kateregga & Shenk 1980:88.
[7] See Troll 1998:93-4.
[8] Cited from Gaudeul 2000:158-9.

The contrasting attitudes toward the doctrine of Incarnation are carried into the understanding of scriptural and cultural translation in Islam and Christianity. Language wise, Jesus spoke and taught in Aramaic but the New Testament was written in Greek. Thus, right at its inception, Christianity had no one sacred language. On the contrary, at the Pentecost experience in Acts chapter 2, the Holy Spirit caused the disciples to testify in "other tongues", i.e. languages other than their own, to the amazement of foreign visitors who were astonished to hear Galileans declare the wonders of God in their own native tongues. The Pentecost event for many, provides a clear Biblical case, indeed, imperative, for the place of the mother tongue and, therefore, scriptural translation in Christian mission.

Similarly, culturally, the Jewish factor never actually gained roots in Christianity, even though it started as a Jewish sect. Attempts by some Judaizers, also known in the New Testament as the 'circumcision party', to have Gentile converts observe the intricacies of Jewish rituals and law, were successfully thwarted by the outpouring of the Holy Spirit on uncircumcised Gentile believers (Acts 10:45), and Paul's insistence that 'Circumcision is nothing and uncircumcision is nothing. Keeping God's commands is what counts' (1 Corinthians 7:19 & Galatians 5:6; 6:15). The Council met in Jerusalem in Acts 15 and came up with a landmark decision that signalled the beginning of the process of freeing the Gospel from Jewish cultural clutches. Peter's address to the Council is very instructive:

> Brothers, you know that some time ago God made a choice among you that the Gentiles might hear from my lips the message of the gospel and believe. God, who knows the heart, showed that he accepted them by giving the Holy Spirit to them, just as he did to us. He made no distinction between us and them, for he purified their hearts by faith. Now then, why do you try to test God by putting on the necks of the disciples a yoke that neither we nor our fathers have been able to bear? No! We believe it is through the grace of our Lord Jesus that we are saved, just as they are.

Thus, the gospel was hatched, or rather freed, from its Jewish and Semitic cultural shell and set on a cross-cultural course. Similarly, geographically, Christianity has had no permanent centre. Jerusalem started of as the centre of Christianity, but then the centre of gravity quickly moved to places like Antioch, Alexandria, Rome, Constantinople, then Europe and North America and now to the Global South, Asia, Africa and Latin America. The cross-cultural development of Christianity is what accounts for Lamin Sanneh's view of Christian mission history as a "translation movement".

In Christianity, the doctrine of the Incarnation provides a theological warrant for translation. By his condescension to humanity and becoming flesh in the person of Jesus, God has demonstrated clearly that the Christian Gospel is not be quarantined in a particular culture or geographical location but translated or inculturated into every language and culture. Christian mission is not only about the Great Commission in Matthew 20:19-20, but also about John 20:21: 'As the Father has sent me, I am sending you.' And how did the Father send Jesus? The Father sent Jesus '*who, being in very nature God'*, to empty Himself, to take human form and the very nature of a slave, in order that He might save humankind. Hence Paul could also say; 'To the Jews I became like a Jew, to win the Jews. To those under the law I became like one under the law (though I myself am not under the law), so as to win those under the law' (1Cor. 9:20). All of these make translation a theological and Biblical imperative in Christianity.

Unlike Christianity, whose umbilical cord with its Semitic cultural cradle is all but severed, 'Islam is the spiritual base of Arab culture'.[9] To use the words of al-Faruqi, 'Islam did not come into existential being *ex nihilo*; nor did it ever create for itself a consciousness or spirit that was not Arab. Its original Arab spirit was never dislodged or even contested by the particular spirit of the ethnic groups that embraced Islam, as was to happen to Christianity after the Reformation'.[10] The Qur'an was revealed in the Arabic language, using such familiar Arab mediums as poetical prose, socio-religious expressions, symbolism and rituals.[11] Muslims treat Arabic, to use the words of a leading African Muslim scholar, A. Mazrui, as 'the language of God'.[12]

When it comes to scriptural translation, therefore, Islam upholds the universal adherence to a nontranslatable Arabic Qur'an. For much of the history of Islam, the authorities regarded translations as impious or even blasphemous. The Arabic nature of the Qur'an is repeated in several places in the Qur'an itself. "*Lo! We have revealed it, a Lecture in Arabic, that ye may understand*" (Sura 12:2).[13] Muslims have come to ascribe to Arabic the status of not just a language of revelation, but a revealed language and have developed the doctrine of the *ijaz*, 'inimitability' of the eloquence of the Qur'an. Thus developed a deeply rooted conviction, still holding sway, of an acceptable recitation of the Qur'an is possible only in Arabic. Only one out of the four Schools of Law, the Hanafi'i School of Law, allows for exceptions in this regard under special circumstances.[14]

It was during the last two centuries that Muslims started venturing into the task of translating the Qur'an in a major way. This was mainly as a reaction to what Yusuf Ali calls, 'the amount of mischief' done by non-Muslim and Christian missionary translations of the Muslim Holy Book.[15] Those Muslims, who ventured into translating the Qur'an, saw their task as a necessary evil and

---

[9] Hasan 1985:56.
[10] Al-Faruqi 1962:202.
[11] El-Awa 1973:177-80; Watt 1953:7ff; Wendell 1972:12-41.
[12] Mazrui 1987.
[13] Cf. 41:2-3; 12:2; 13:37; 20:113; 39:28; 41:2-3; 42:7; 43:3.
[14] Bobzin 2006:340ff.
[15] *The Qur'an* 1975: ix.

went at length to explain both the need and constraints of the exercise. To start with, in the main, Muslim translations of the Qur'an are entitled "The Meaning" or "Interpretation" and, in some cases, "The Interpretation of the Meaning" of the Qur'an. These caveats are intended to make the point that the translated versions are no substitutes for the Arabic Qur'an. The British convert to Islam, Marmaduke Pickthall's (1875-1936) comments in the foreword of his translation is instructive in this regard:

> It may be reasonably claimed that no holy Scripture can be fairly presented by one who disbelieves its inspiration and its message; and this is the first English translation of the Qur'an by an Englishman who is a Muslim. Some of the translations [in the past by non-Muslims] include commentation offensive to Muslims, and almost all employ a style of language which Muslims at once recognise as unworthy. The Qur'an cannot be translated. That is the belief of old-fashioned Sheykhs and the view of the present writer. The Book is here rendered almost literally and every effort has been made to choose befitting language. But the result is not the Glorious Qur'an, that inimitable symphony, the very sounds of which move men to tears and ecstasy. It is only an attempt to present the meaning of the Qur'an – and peradventure something of the charm – in English. It can never take the place of the Qur'an in Arabic, nor is it meant to do so.[16]

Translated versions of the Qur'an, therefore, have no spiritual, liturgical or devotional value. The Qur'an can only be recited in Arabic. The attitude that a translation of the Qur'an, in the true sense, is impossible is based on the argument that its wording is a miracle (*mu'djiza*) incapable of imitation by man. The concession, made early in Islamic history, was for the "translation" in the sense of a commentary of, rather than, the Qur'an itself.

Muslims have, therefore, generally regarded scriptural translation in Christianity as evidence of corruption in the Christian Bible. As early as the 995 CE, a prominent Muslim scholar by the name of Abd al-Jabbar, wrote a spirited polemic against Christianity, in which one of his main complaints was on the issue of scriptural translation in Christianity. Abd al-Jabbar saw it as the corruption, *tahrif*, of the message preached by Jesus. He claims:

> None of [the] gospels, is however in the language spoken by Christ and his disciples, i.e. Hebrew, the language of Abraham, God's Friend, and the other prophets, in which they spoke and in which God's books were revealed to them and to the rest of the children of Israel, and in which God addressed them. … Thus they turned to other languages not spoken by Christ and his disciples … such as the Romans, Syrians, Persians, Indians, Armenians and other barbarian speaking nations.[17]

[16] *The Glorious Qur'an* 2006.
[17] Cited in Sanneh 1989:218.

Culturally, the Arab factor still holds sway in Islam, despite the fact that less than 20% of the global Muslim population are Arabic-speaking. Some Muslims speak of Islam as, 'solely given in terms of Arab consciousness, necessarily informed in the Arabic tongue, necessarily figurized in Arab ethic and culture and necessarily embodied in the Arab stream of being'.[18] The emphasis on the "solely" and "necessarily" suggests that the Arab factor is absolute and non-negotiable as far as Islam is concerned. In other words, the Arabic language and culture cannot be divorced from Islam. The Call to Prayer has to be in Arabic and all Muslims have to pray in the direction of the *qibla*, i.e. towards Mecca, which remains Islam's holiest city and the centre of religious orientation. The annual pilgrimage cements the status of Mecca in particular, and Saudi Arabia in general, as the undisputed geographical centre (Holy Land) of Islam. Al-Faruqi spells out the full implications of the Arab factor in Islam for non-Arab converts in the following words:

> Converts to Islam [have] to learn an Arabic Qur'an; that is, ethically and religiously think in Arabic, and to think in terms of ideas of Arab consciousness. They [have] to emulate Arab conduct; that is to realize values whose ought-to-be's and ought-to-do's have been constructed as particulars of Arab personal and social life.[19]

There is, therefore, no way, some have explicitly argued, in which Islam can be separated from the Arab factor because 'Arab history is inseparable from the history of Islam and Arabic was the vehicle by which Islam was initially conveyed to different parts of the world'.[20] To separate Islam from the Arab factor would only lead in one direction, namely, decline and degeneration if not dissolution. To quote al-Faruqi once more, 'a Pakistani, a Nigerian or Croatian may possess [Islam] in a degree as high, or higher, than any Meccan, Syrian or Egyptian. But commitment to [Islam] of the many communities within this stream on the whole varies in one direction only: it becomes progressively weaker, just as the stream water becomes progressively shallower, the further it is removed from the principal bed of the stream'.[21] Thus, Islam, in effect, can only be found in its purest or fullest form in its original Arab cultural garb. All non-Arab cultures are potential sources of corruption and have to be relegated to the realm of hopeless *kufr,* standing in need of not just Islamization but also Arabization:

---

[18] Al-Faruqi 1962:203-4.

[19] Al-Faruqi 1962:204.

[20] El-Mili 1985:49.

[21] Al-Faruqi 1962:199. Faruqi thinks that by virtue of being the original recipients of the Islamic revelation, Arab Muslims are 'at an advantage over those who have to struggle to appropriate this revelation'. Al-Faruqi 1962: 6.

> the Prophet's requirement was that the non-Arab converts ought to be Arabicized and the divine dispensation that the Qur'an — the main fount of Islam — is divine in its Arabic and hence untranslatable, thus establishing once and for all that the ideal values can be reached only through the medium of Arab consciousness.[22]

Translation in Christian and Islamic Missions

The main argument of Sanneh's *Translating the Message* is that scriptural and cultural translations are vintage marks of Christianity and belong to Christian affirmation in ways that it does not with Islam. Sanneh has argued this case very persuasively throughout his works. What needs to be said, however, and Sanneh acknowledges this, is that in the mission experience of the Church, scriptural and cultural translation did not come about on a silver platter. These were fraught with controversies and in many, if not all cases, forced upon the Church by factors other than theological and Biblical concerns.

The early Church itself struggled with translation. Indeed, the Pentecost experience was forced upon the disciples. They did not decide to declare the wonders of God in different languages because they felt it was necessary for the crowd to hear the Gospel in their various mother tongues. The experience was literally forced upon them by the Holy Spirit. Similarly, Peter was the leader of the so-called circumcision party. In Acts 10 and 11, Peter needed a dramatic vision to deal with his deep-seated prejudices about Gentiles and non-Jewish cultures. Paul, who considered himself an apostle to the Gentiles, had to battle with the leadership of the early Church, including Peter, to free Gentiles from having to come to Christianity via the Jewish cultural matrix. Paul talks of his open opposition to Peter in Antioch because Peter used to eat with the Gentiles. But when a group belonging to the circumcision party arrived from Jerusalem, he began to separate himself from the Gentiles because of the fear of being accused of associating with Gentiles.[23]

In Christian mission history, those who regarded themselves as guardians of orthodoxy put up fierce resistance against scriptural translation. The journey of the Christian Bible, from the Septuagint to the Latin Vulgate and to other European languages, was never a smooth one. John Wycliffe's work and ideas of scriptural translation in the 1380s was met with strong opposition from the papacy and when it's full import was uncovered nearly four decades after his death, Wycliffe's bones were dug-up, crushed and scattered into a river. Wycliffe argued that ordinary people should have access to scripture in their mother tongue, while his opponents, the hierarchy of the Church, fought against turning the Bible, which they perceived as "the jewel of the clergy" into "the toy of the laity." One of Wycliffe's followers, John Hus, was burnt at the stake in 1415.

---

[22] Al-Faruqi 1962:204-5.

[23] Galatians 2: 11-13.

Copies of William Tyndale's English New Testament of 1525-1526 were confiscated and burned as soon as the Bishop was able to lay hands on them. The King James version of 1611 was meant to be "the translation to end all translations" while Latin remained the liturgical language of the Catholic Church throughout the world well into the last century!

It is an undisputed fact, that in the 19th and 20th centuries, the Protestant missionary movement initiated vernacular Bible translations across the non-Western world on a very large scale unparalleled in Christian history. Indeed, the Bible has been translated into more languages than any other book in history. Yet, scriptural translation was not always accompanied by cultural translation. Scriptural translation did not always necessarily mean cultural translation, even though 'language is a living expression of culture'.[24] In many instances, the translation of the Bible into the vernacular went hand in hand with strong opposition to the use of indigenous cultural forms, symbols and traditional instruments and dress in worship, i.e. resistance to contextualization. Western missionaries still treated indigenous culture with suspicion and disdain. In the context of this writer's own country, Ghana, Christian villages known as *salems* were established with the view of quarantining new believers from the "corruption" of their indigenous surroundings.

On the Islamic front, Sanneh notes that Islamic mission is properly identified with "cultural diffusion" as compared to Christian mission, which is best identified with translation. As we have pointed out above, it is clear that Islamic orthodoxy is unequivocal on the non-translability of the Qur'an. However, just as the case in Christian mission history, there has been a struggle between the guardians of orthodoxy in Islam and proponents of translations. Early on in the mission history of Islam, Muslims debated vigorously on the need for scriptural translation, and more specifically, the recitation of the *Fatiha*, the first chapter of the Qur'an and the Muslim equivalent of the Christian Lord's Prayer. Three of the four Schools of Law held the orthodox line of non-translation. However, one of the Schools, Hanafi, ruled that recitation of the *Fatiha* in Persian, by persons who could not speak Arabic, was permissible for the purpose of ritual worship, the *salat*.[25]

Long before the perceived threat of non-Muslim translations of their Holy Book in the nineteenth century, Muslims undertook translations of the Qur'an. The earliest is said to be a Persian translation by one Salman al-Farisi, a Companion of the Prophet of Islam, dating back to 744-5 CE. There are said to be over 70 translations into Turkish, made from at least the 11th century onwards.[26] As already mentioned above, Muslim translations of the Qur'an increased dramatically from the 19th century onwards, mainly provoked by Christian missionary translations, and greatly enhanced by the emergence of the

---

[24] Sanneh 1989:200.
[25] See Paret 2001.
[26] Pearson 2001.

printing press. Since then, numerous translations of the Qur'an have appeared in India in various regional languages such as Urdu (first in 1828), Sindhi (1876), Punjabi (1870), Gujarati (1879), and Bengali (1886). The first printed translations also appeared in Turkish (1842), Persian (1855) and Pashtu (1861), as well as African and European languages.[27] The Hanafi scholar of al-Azhar, Muhammad Mustafa al-Maraghi, in an investigation published in 1932, adopted the position that for a Muslim without knowledge of Arabic, the recital of the Qur'an in prayer in an appropriate translation was obligatory. He argued that the thesis, the Qur'an in translation ceases to the Word of God, is valid only with reservations.[28]

Similarly, culturally, in the mission experience of Islam, the orthodox position on the primacy of the Arab factor was challenged right from the beginning. The principal underlying cause for the mainly Persian protest movement culminating in the emergence of Shi'i Islam, as early as 661 CE, was a resistance to, and rejection of, Arab cultural hegemony in the name of Islam. Indeed, right from its inception, Islam was never puritanical as orthodox voices in Islam would have us believe. It is well attested in Muslim sources that the Prophet of Islam was never puritanical or idealistic in his attitude towards indigenous Arab elements. Giving many stories to demonstrate the pragmatic attitude of the Prophet of Islam, Hasan al-Karmi affirms that, 'this spirit of compromise pervaded many of the teachings of Islam. Think of the rules of marriage, the prohibition of wine, slavery, and others: they were all examples of compromise'. This spirit of compromise, the writer goes on to insist, 'was a source of strength rather than weakness'.[29]

Similarly, Mohamed El-Awa, points out that 'Islam was not a legislative revolution directed against all that was known and practised by the Arabs before its emergence', and goes on to state that 'the Prophet, in his capacity as Islam's legislator, made innumerable rulings legalizing Arabian customary law'.[30] Examples, given by El-Awa, include the laws on marriage and divorce, retaliation and the payment of blood-money, and the concept of *shûra*, consultation. Thus, far from being idealistic, puritanical and uncompromising, the Prophet of Islam was a realist and a pragmatist on the issue of appropriating indigenous elements. This attitude of the Prophet of Islam, some Muslims have argued, rather than absolutizing the Arab factor, provides a Prophetic precedent (*Sunna*) for contextualization in Islam just as the Incarnation and the Pentecost event in Christianity.

Throughout Islamic history, Muslims engaged in deep and extensive cultural exchanges with such non-Arab cultures as Jewish, Byzantine, Persian, Hellenistic, Indian, and African. Writing on the cultural transformation during the Abbasid period (from 750CE), I. M. Lapidus notes that 'Persian culture not only became the characteristic style of Iran, but had an important influence upon the

---

[27] See Bobzin 2006:340-354.
[28] Paret 2001.
[29] Al-Karmi 1964:94.
[30] El-Awa 1973:177.

development of Muslim culture in Inner Asia, India, and Indonesia'.[31] In the same vein, it has been demonstrated in North Africa that Berber and Roman pre-Islamic elements have been extensively appropriated into Muslim practices and festivals such as the Muslim New Year, the Prophet of Islam's birthday and the *Muharram* of *Shi'ia* Muslims.[32] The Persian contribution to Islam, in various areas, has been described as 'inestimable' while 'the Moghul Empire of India has also been a major enriching experience in Islamic history, architecture and art'.[33] Sufi Orders have been in the forefront of the Muslim appropriation of indigenous cultural and religious elements.

The story is the same in sub-Saharan Africa. Ahmadou Hampâté Ba, a renowned Malian Muslim mystic, has described the process of inculturation of Islam in Africa in the following words: "*en Afrique, l'Islam n'a pas plus de couleur que l'eau; c'est ce qui explique son succès: elle se colore aux teintes des terroirs et des pierres*'.[34] Literally meaning, in Africa, Islam, like water, has no colour of its own except that of the soil and stones it flows over. In other words, Islam simply absorbs the cultural values and practices of places, wherein it finds itself. Ali Mazrui compares the attitudes of Islam and Christianity to indigenous elements in Africa and comments that, 'On the wider spectrum of comparison, it remains true that Islam has been more accommodating to indigenous African custom and traditions than European Christianity has been'.[35] The battle within Islam as to whether the religion should be freed from its Arab cultural shell continues, and there can be no question as to which side is winning on the ground!

However, it is true that in Africa, as in other parts of the non-Arab Muslim world, there remains a latent and sometimes explicit suggestion that the degree of one's Islam depends on the level of one's connectedness if not rootedness to the Arabic cultural milieu. Writing on the Jakhanke, a pacifist Islamic group in West Africa, Sanneh notes that, even though due to their peaceful dissemination of Islam, Jakhanke Islam, inevitably, has a high degree of tolerance for appropriating local elements:

> Yet both in the traditions concerning the founder of the clerical tradition as well as in the detailed work of the clerical center ... Mecca remains the unwavering point of religious orientation, reinforced by observance of the *salât*, the standing reminder of the *hâjj* obligation, and the use of Arabic in study, teaching, and counselling.[36]

[31] Lapidus 1988:154.
[32] Westermarck 1933:145-75.
[33] Mazrui 1987.
[34] Monteil 1964:41.
[35] Mazrui 1987.
[36] Sanneh 1988 228.

While the above is indisputable, it can be said that the situation is not too dissimilar to a very large proportion of non-Western Christians in their attitude towards the West, in terms of their religious and theological orientation. It is open knowledge that even though Christianity has no geographical centre, no sacred language and no one single dominant culture, and, in fact, is on the decline in the West, many Christians in the Majority World still look up to and draw from the catechetical, liturgical and theological menu cards of the Church in the West. But a more substantive point is that translation took place in the mission histories of both Islam and Christian despite, rather than because of, orthodox instincts in either religion. This raises the question of the agency of translation in both traditions. Is it Islam and Christianity or the indigenous cultures in which they found themselves? In the case of the inculturation of Islam in Africa, for instance, J. S. Trimingham observes that 'when assimilation took place between African and Islamic institutions, the basic institution into which the other was assimilated might be either, but was generally the African'.[37]

However, there is one major contrasting point between the two traditions on the question of translation. While it can be said that Christian orthodoxy, by and large, has come to terms with and embraced translation, Islamic orthodoxy continues to reject translation as a harmful innovation (*bida*) and, therefore, as heretical. In other words, while Christianity has long made up its mind to treat its original cultural, linguistic and geographical contexts and all others as shells, Islamic orthodoxy appears unable or unwilling to make up its mind as to whether to treat the Arab factor as a shell or a shelter. As a result of these contrasting positions, protest, reform or renewal in Christianity have, in the main, been for the cause of translation, whereas in Islam, they have been, in the main, counter to translation. Right from Paul in the early Church, through to the Reformation, to the rise of African Initiated Churches across Africa, protest and reform movements in Christianity have been about turning towards, rather than away from, indigenous elements. In other words, reform and renewal in Christian history has mainly been about hatching the Gospel from one cultural shell into another.

Conversely, in Islamic history protest and reform or revival movements have been mainly about calls for the return to the Qur'an and Sunna, i.e. Islam in its 7th century Arab cultural garb and against the appropriation of non-Islamic elements. In other words, revival moments in Islam have, in the main, been about retaining Islam in its Arabic cultural shell. Within the African context, the main charge against African Muslim clerics was not sufficient knowledge in the Arabic language for the appropriation of indigenous African elements into Islam, according to al-Maghili, a 15th century Tunisian Muslim reformer . He went on to sanction *jihad* against such clerics as legitimate.[38] Hence, the "*jihadists*" of 18th and 19th century West Africa rose up in arms partly, or some would say mainly,

[37] Trimingham 1968:44.

[38] See Azumah 2001chapter 3, for a full discussion on this issue.

because of what they regarded as the corruption of Islam with indigenous elements. They saw their central task as achieving, 'the sacralization of the Arabic cultural milieu,' in black Africa.[39] This is true for other reform movements like the Wahhabiyya of Saudi Arabia and its offshoot, the Taliban in Afghanistan and Pakistan.

However, another significant point worth making is that both Islam and Christianity spread across cultures despite the contrasting attitudes of their respective orthodoxies towards translation. Under the chapter heading, "The Bible versus the Koran: The Battle of the Books and the Future of Two Faiths", Micklethwait and Wooldridge discuss the longer term advantage of the Bible over the Qur'an, on the grounds that 'Christians are much more enthusiastic than Muslims about translating their Holy Book'.[40] To draw conclusions from translation, as necessarily advantageous and non-translation as evidently disadvantageous to mission, is rather simplistic.

Translation can be seen as "good" for mission within the context of a worldview in which religion is understood and considered primarily in epistemological and propositional terms. The alternative is a worldview through which the Supreme Being is viewed as a philosophical concept and religion is treated purely as a social science discipline and subjected to empirical inquiry with the same methods and tools of any other social science discipline. Within the framework of such a worldview, it makes sense to argue for translation for the sake of intellectual enquiry and knowledge. It is this kind of worldview from which translation has taken place in the Christian tradition in the Western context from the modern to the post-modern eras.

At the other end of the continuum are contexts where a contrary worldview holds sway, which sees religion mainly in metaphysical terms, calling for faith and blind adherence with little or no room for intellectual enquiry. This is the worldview in which medieval Christianity found itself. Islam falls into this category with the 9th century, "closure of the gate of independent thinking" (*ijtihad*), and the ushering in of unquestioning adherence (*taqlid*), which only started coming under serious challenge from the last quarter of the last century, but still holds sway in many Islamic communities. Expressing his frustration of blind adherence within the Islamic context, Shaykh al-Amin bin Ali al-Mazrui, a celebrated Muslim thinker of East Africa, writes: 'What kind of [religious] ignorance is this for a Muslim to pray without knowing the meaning of what he reads in his prayer, or to recite the Qur'an like a parrot?'[41]

Non-translation may foster, therefore, unity or rather uniformity and simplicity, but it is also a sure recipe for corruption and abuse. The very reason for which Islamic orthodoxy is opposed to translation, i.e. syncretism, has taken and continues to take place on a massive scale in Islamic history. This is mainly

---

[39] Sanneh 1989:225.
[40] Micklethwait & Wooldridge 2009:273.
[41] Cited in Lacunza-Balda 1933:97.

due to the attitude of Islamic orthodoxy, cultural translation or inculturation in Islam that has mainly been a bottom-up process. The same may be said of the contextualization of Christianity in certain instances. These are the issues with which Islam has to grapple.

To be sure, translation has major advantages for mission. It has been persuasively argued that translating religious phenomena from foreign into familiar idioms is in the interest of mission. If we go by the Christian mission experience of translation in the non-Western world, there can be no question that 'familiarity breeds faith'.[42] On the same token though, it could also be argued that, judging from the same experience in the West, translation may have its drawbacks. While it is true that 'familiarity breeds faith', there is the real risk that familiarity can and does breed contempt. The nature of the spread of Christianity around the world, over the centuries, is now well known and documented as "serial growth", i.e. going through phases of growth followed by decline and not able to hold its ground in the longer term. This is one of the key contrasting points in the mission experiences of Islam and Christianity. Islam has spread across cultures and geographical boundaries without conceding its Semitic cultural and geographical origins, thereby proving that one does not have to sacrifice ones roots in order to branch out to others!

Translation can be compared to the unwrapping of a precious present from its original package. One has the choice of leaving the present unwrapped and exposed, wrapped back into its original packaging or re-packaged into a different package. It seems to me that Christianity in the West, under pressure and influence of post-modernism, pursued the path of completely unwrapping and leaving the present exposed. In such a situation, familiarity can and does breed contempt. Translation in post-modern Western Christianity, in this writer's view, has gone beyond unwrapping into "divulging", "unveiling" and "exposing" the precious present to all kinds of conditions. The element of mystery in religion is now all but "translated" and jettisoned as nonsensical in the West. One wonders, therefore, if translation has played a role in the "serial growth" of the Christian faith.

In the non-Western world, translation, within both the Christian and Islamic traditions, tends to take the second and third paths, i.e. re-wrapped in the original or new package. Writing on the controversies in East Africa surrounding Geofrey Dale's first translation of the Qur'an into Swahili, J. Lacunza-Balda notes that, 'the Arabic language veiled and covered, so to speak, the text of the Qur'an for those without knowledge of Arabic, who were opposed to any uncovering or translation'. Also, 'the Sufi-inspired brotherhoods had underlined the mystical and esoteric dimension of the Qur'an. Translation into Swahili, or into any other language, took away the mystery attached to the Quranic text'.[43] The Muslim fear of scriptural translation is that their precious present is being unwrapped and will

[42] Sanneh 1989:192ff. See also Walls 2002.
[43] J. Lacunza-Balda 1933:100 114.

be left vulnerable. But the other side of the fear is that there is a sense in which unfamiliarity breeds faith.

Translation does not necessarily have to involve divesting a religious tradition of its mystery or strangeness, and, secondly, mystery or strangeness does not necessarily have to mean “foreignness”. Translation, properly understood, does involve re-packaging foreign religious phenomena into indigenous packaging. This includes re-interpreting and re-investing local mysteries with foreign vocabulary, concepts and value preferences. Thus, what takes place, in this form of translation, is a blending or re-casting of local and imported elements resulting in what may be called "home grown mysteries". The ‘indigenisation’ of Islam in Africa, ‘through blind social forces’,[44] has not undermined the mysterious element and, therefore, the appeal of the Islamic tradition. Like the Christian tradition in the African Initiated Churches, local material has been re-interpreted and re-invested with Islamic terminology, concepts and value preferences. Commenting on the ‘syncretizing reality’ of Islam in Africa, C. F. Molla writes:

> Sacrifices are made in the name of Allah, but one is surprised to note that the former gestures have undergone no change whatsoever. Circumcisions are performed but other rites lead up to them and follow them. The new taboos join ranks with old ones.[45]

For instance, in addition to the Arabic Qur'an, the Islamic tradition has been rendered through indigenous religious figures, rites, shrines, etc. In most cases, these religious figures and shrines are a more immediate focus of devotion for ordinary believers than the Prophet of Islam or the *hijaz* respectively. For example, within Mouride Islam in Senegal, followers, according to one writer, ‘have a reputation for revering their *shaykh* as if he were God himself’.[46] Similarly, the *Magal* (the annual pilgrimage to the Mourides' holiest city, Touba), in the minds of ordinary followers is parallel to the annual *hajj* to Mecca. This level of translation is crucial, within cultural contexts, where religion is regarded in metaphysical terms, without necessarily shutting the door to intellectual enquiry.

Conclusion

I have deliberately used the imagery of the “hatching from a shell” to describe the process of translation. No religion is general or culturally neutral. Every religion has a culture into which it was born. The issue about translation is between perceiving and turning the culture into a shell that allows the faith to hatch out of one culture, grow in another culture while taking that culture as its shell and

---

[44] Mazrui 1987:150.
[45] Molla 1967:467.
[46] Lake 1933:217.

continuing with the process, or perceiving and turning a particular culture into an impenetrable shelter for the faith. Christian orthodoxy, after a long struggle, seems to accept culture as a shell; Hinduism and Judaism treat their respective birth cultures as shelters, while Islamic orthodoxy seems to have chosen to watch the show from within the shelter with sporadic outbursts of pious indignation! Our own conclusion, on the issue of translation, is that it could be compared to a chemical fertilizer, causing rapid growth, but prone to abuse and misuse, which, in the long term, can sap the soil of its natural nutrients and render it infertile.

The Word made *Book*: The 1865 Van Dyck Arabic Translation of the Bible and Arab Christian Views of *wahy*

David D. Grafton

Rev. Dr. David D. Grafton is Associate Professor of Islamic Studies and Christian-Muslim Relations at the Lutheran Theological Seminary at Philadelphia

Introduction

The Incarnation is the heart of the message of the New Testament. However, the concept of the transcendent God breaking the great divide between the heavenly realm and the mundane world was considered 'foolish' babble by the Greeks and a 'stumbling block' for Jews, who interpreted their scriptures quite differently from the early Christians. The Christian message of 'God in Christ' was a hard sell, given the predisposed views of the nature of the transcendent, un-nameable God in Jewish piety, and the pluralist cosmologies of widespread Greco-Roman culture. In the 7th century, however, Christians in the East, those on the edge and those outside the jurisdiction of the Roman Empire, were challenged with articulating the Gospel message in a new cultural and religious landscape. With the rise of an Arab Muslim Empire, Greek-speaking and Syriac-speaking Christians needed to articulate their theological convictions in the face of the radical monotheism of Islam and a new *lingua franca*: Arabic. As Arab-Islamic culture became dominant, in what were once parts of the Byzantine and Sassanian Empires, Christians living under the Islamic empires began articulating their convictions in the language and terminology of the new empire. The early Arabic-speaking Christian apologists were not only challenged with the proposition of translating their message from their own languages of Greek, Syriac, and Aramaic into Arabic, but also of fitting those translations and theological propositions into a language that itself had developed as a result of a Qur'anic worldview. While Arabic does begin to appear as a written language in the 4th century, it does not become a widespread written medium until the 7th century, coterminous with the rise of Islam and the Qur'an.[1]

Thus, like Paul in his sermon to the Athenians at the Areopagus, Arab Christians had to articulate their theological convictions to an 'extremely religious' community by using religious terminology from a dominant culture that might help to explain their own distinct religious beliefs (Acts 17:22-31).

---

[1] Hoyland 2001:198-228.

The problem for Arab Christians, however, was that while the Greek and Latin-speaking Christians became part of the dominant culture of the West, the Arabic and Syriac speaking peoples of the East lived in an overwhelmingly Islamic culture. By the 9th century, Islam became the predominant religion of the vast majority of Arabic and Syriac speaking peoples.[2] Over time, as the religious culture of Islam dominated the empires of the Middle East, Central Asia, North Africa and even South Eastern Europe, the indigenous Christians were compelled to undertake catechetical programmes to teach the Christian faith to their own communities who were affected by dominant cultural symbols and concepts.

No issue has been more difficult for the Arabic-speaking Church of the Middle East, since the 7th century, than the nature of 'scripture'.[3] The predominant view of the 'Holy Book' in the Middle East is shaped by the Islamic concept of *wahy*: 'revelation.' The orthodox Islamic view of 'revelation' is that God verbally spoke His message to the prophets and finally to Muhammad; that these messages "came down" from Heaven and were ultimately transcribed into 'The Book.' This has become the predominant understanding of divine revelation.[4] The Qur'an states, 'we have revealed (lit. 'sent down) the Qur'an in the Arabic tongue so that you may grow in understanding' (12:2).

Islamic orthodoxy has taught that Mu□ammad was merely a channel for the literal speech of God that was recited verbatim. The Qur'an is the *ipissma verba* of God, which is unsurpassed in beauty and form. Muslims refer to this as the 'inimitability' of the Qur'an.[5] In the words of the great Islamic exegete al-Tabari (224-?):

> …it is obvious that there is no clear discourse more eloquent, no wisdom more profound, no speech more sublime, no form of expression more noble, than [this] clear discourse and speech with which a single man challenged a people…
>
> each scripture which preceded our Book [however] was sent down to one of God's prophets, may God bless them and grant them peace, in only a single tongue, and when it was changed into a tongue other than that in which it was sent down, this was an interpretation (*tarjama*) and a commentary (*tafsir*) of it, not a recitation according to what God had sent down…[6]

While Jews and Christians have traditionally come to understand the development of their holy texts quite differently than Muslims, it is through the

---

[2] While the roots of conversion among Eastern Christians are still contested, we accept the argument that it was not until the 9th century that the balance of population shifted in the Levant and the 11th century in Egypt. See Bulliet 1979.
[3] While the term 'Middle East' is a 20th century political designation, we will utilize this to speak of the areas of south-west Asia and North Africa, what was in the 18th and 19th centuries called 'the Orient'.
[4] See Surah 12:2.
[5] McAuliffe 2002:526-535.
[6] Al-Tabari 1987:30.

concept of *inspiration* that Arab Christianity has developed within a culture that lives and breathes with the holy otherness of this divine speech. Culturally, the Arabic of the Qur'an has been considered the standard for Arabic. Arabic-speaking Christians, who translated their own scriptures from Aramaic, Greek, Hebrew and Syriac into Arabic, have sought to provide an acceptable translation of their own scripture that respects the quality and dignity of such a 'Holy Book.' The difficulty for Christians has been to find a way in which the Arabic of the Christian (and Jewish) sacred text can be accepted as worthy of revelation. As Kenneth Cragg has stated, Arab Christians have been culturally conditioned by a language that is 'bound over to the Qur'an.'[7]

At the beginning of the 21st century, conversations about a new Arabic translation of the Bible by the Lebanese Bible Society and the Bible Society in Egypt set off renewed theological discussions, centered primarily upon the theological understandings of the revelation of 'the Book, whatever Book that may be. The challenges of developing a new Arabic translation of the Bible have arisen primarily from the problems associated with the predominant Muslim cultural view of *wahy*. For the Arabic *wahy,* translated above as 'revelation' can also be translated as 'inspiration'.[8] Each word, however, has a different theological message. The Christian articulation of the *inspired* Word of God, which serves as the vehicle for the proclamation of the Good News of Jesus the Christ, is quite different from the Islamic concept of the literal Speech of God proclaimed through the conduit of Muhammad's recitation. The role of each Book, within each faith community, functions quite differently. One is a humanly and culturally conditioned narrative, written expressly for the purpose of translating a message into a mundane context, the other is intended to be holy speech that should be memorized *verbatim,* and recited. Both Books provide edification and salvation for their own believers, but role of the Book in that process is quite different.

This chapter will explore the attempt of Arab Christians, focusing on the contemporary Egyptian Church, to struggle with and articulate the Gospel message through their own indigenous scripture. The contested debate over the Arabic translation of the Bible in Egypt, in the early part of the 21st century, demonstrates once again the Arab Christian need for clarity of its own religious terminology within its own culture. In order to interpret this contemporary theological struggle, I will review the origins of the Arab Church's articulation of the Gospel within its own linguistic-cultural context through the development of Arabic translations of the Bible. However, I will focus on the 19th century Van Dyck translation, which has become the official received text of the historic and legally recognized Churches of Egypt. It is this translation that has become the centre of the current controversy surrounding the attempt to produce a new 21st century Arabic translation for the Egyptian Church. My final comments will seek

---

[7] Cragg 1991:65.

[8] See especially 6:19; 29:45; Wensinck 2002:53-56.

to interpret this struggle through the lens of the theological concept of the Incarnation.

Arabic Translations of the Bible

Arabic translations of the Bible appeared quite late among the Eastern Christian languages. In the 2nd century, most of the Christians of the Middle East were introduced to their scriptures either through oral tradition, or through Syriac translations or paraphrases of the Hebrew. Syriac, in its Eastern and Western dialects, as well as Coptic in Egypt, and these quickly became the 'holy languages' of worship and doxology for the early Oriental Churches.[9] Between the 9th and 11th centuries, as a growing number of Middle Eastern Christians began to convert to Islam, and as Islamic culture and Arabic language became the predominant *lingua franca* of the peoples of the Middle East, Syriac and Coptic retreated into the monasteries, so that fewer and fewer Christians were able to read their own holy writ. The earliest Arabic Christian literature, currently available to us, is 'in house' lectionary readings of the Gospels, homilies and prayers from the monasteries in Palestine from the 8th century.[10] Thus, as Islamic culture took root, Middle Eastern Christian bishops and priests were left without any tools to explain their faith to a new generation of young Christians who were growing up speaking Arabic. More specifically, as Islam began to spread and develop a dominant Islamic culture, whose holy writ was found in a 'pure Arabic Qur'an', Arab Christians were faced with a pastoral problem. How were they to continue to teach their Christian faith from a sacred book that was written in a foreign tongue (either Greek or Syriac), while the revelation of the Qur'an was in Arabic – the language of the people? [11] As Stephen of Ramla, a 9th century Byzantine monk wrote: "The language of this community [that is, the Muslims] about God is a clear language, which the common people understand. I mean their saying, 'There is no god but God.'"[12] Once the Arabic of the Qur'an became the standard for articulating the concepts of holy revelation – as opposed to general *inspiration* already recognized among Arab poets of the pre-Islamic period - Arab Christians had to live with a tension between their Christian

---

[9] Although the bibliography on Oriental translations of the Bible is voluminous; two scholars stand out as particularly helpful in terms of assessing the importance of Syriac: William Cureton and Sebastian Brock. See Cureton 1967 [1864]. Sebastian Brock's works are manifold. The most poignant, short essay by Brock that articulates the lack of attention to Syriac texts in Biblical and historical studies is Brock 1973:406-412. See also the extremely well researched works on the development of Syriac translations, through the work of Tatian. These can be found in Moffett 1998:72-74.

[10] See Griffith 1985 pp. 126-167; Griffith 1988:1-28.

[11] The History of Christian-Muslim Relations series published by Brill has put forward a number of very important studies, including Thomas 2008, Thomas 2003, and Thomas 2001.

[12] Griffith 1996:18.

identity and another religious tradition that was determining their cultural identity. Put another way, Arab Christians had the challenge of articulating their own Christian faith in a language in which the terminology has traditionally been defined by Islamic orthodoxy. Sidney H. Griffith has described this theological response in this way:

> In this context, Christians sought to defend the reasonableness of their distinctive doctrines in terms of the same religious idiom as that employed by their Muslim interlocutors and counterparts, who, in accord with the teachings of the Qur'ān, often rejected the central Christian doctrines.[13]

Yet, there was also a need, not only to express doctrines, but also to articulate their Christian revelation. It was necessary to translate the Christian 'Book' into the language of the vernacular, just as it was done over seven hundred years previously (from Greek to Syriac). The earliest tradition of an Arabic Christian translation of the New Testament is that of John, Bishop of Seville, who is said to have made his Arabic translation from the Vulgate in the 8th century. However, we do not possess any copies of this text to date.[14] For that matter, we do not currently possess any full Arabic translations of the Christian New Testament or the TaNaKh until the 9th century. Thus, it is not until the Arabization of culture during the reign of the ᶜAbbassids in Baghdad several hundred years after the coming of Islam, that Arabic translations of the Bible begin to appear.[15]

By the 9th century, we find numerous manuscripts of Arabic translations of the New Testament.[16] Several important manuscripts currently located in the Vatican library, or at the monastery of St. Catherine include *Vatican 15*, the oldest known Arabic manuscript with portions of the Gospels, and *Sinai Arabic No. 151*, the oldest known Arabic text of the Epistles, as well as *Sinai Arabic No. 95*.[17] The first known author of an Arabic text, however, was Sa'adya Gaon, who translated the Pentateuch from Hebrew.[18] Several important later medieval Arabic translations that were made in Egypt included the 'Coptic Vulgate' made by monks from the monastery of St. Anthony in 1205, and two translations of the Gospels, one by Ibn al-Tayyib al-Mishriq in 1045 and the other Hibāt Allah Ibn al-Assal in 1252. These translations were widely used. Lastly, another prominent medieval Arabic translation was of Tatian's Syriac *diatesseron* made by a

---

[13] Griffith 2007:73.

[14] Kilgoue 1916:384; see also Istafanous n.d.:42 and Bailey 1992.

[15] While the first Arabization reforms within the Arab empire occurred under the Umayyad Caliph ᶜAbd al-Malik (646-705 CE) these reforms centered on government bureaucratic systems and did not filter into general culture. Again, a helpful reference is Thomas 2003.

[16] Metzger 1974:160-163.

[17] Bailey 1992:1-7; see also Schaaf 1994:23-28. I am indebted to Nashat Megalaa for his research in this area. See Megalaa 2008.

[18] See Caquot 1989 and Rippen 1986:33-46.

Christian physician at the court of Caliph in Baghdad, ᶜAbd Allah Ibn al-Tayyib in the 11th century. The primary purpose of these translations was to provide opportunities for Arab Christians, primarily priests and bishops, to be able to read and recite their own scriptures in their own language for their own communities.

With the development of the printing press and bookbinding, several partial Arabic translations of the Bible into Arabic began to appear in Europe, commencing in the 16th century. These translations were part of a European interest in Biblical texts. Polyglot Bibles appeared in Genoa (1516) and Constantinople (1546), which included the Psalms, and the Pentateuch in Arabic, respectively. The Paris Polyglot (1546) included the whole Bible in Arabic. This was followed by the London Polyglot (1657). The Dutchman Thomas Erpenius, however, published the first Arabic New Testament by itself, in 1616.

While these bound translations were used for academic study, other Arabic Bible translations originated for purely evangelistic purposes. The first complete Arabic Bible, bound *en toto,* was published in 1671, under the patronage of Pope Urban VIII through the College de Propaganda Fide, whose *reason d'etre* was to bring the Oriental Churches into the fold of Rome. (This translation was authorized by the Bishop of Rome and was intended to help encourage the submission of the Oriental Orthodox Churches to accept the primacy of the Bishop of Rome.) The next complete translation was not published until 1822, when the British and Foreign Bible Society utilized new printing presses, brought by the Bible Societies to Beirut by Western Protestant missionaries, for the sole purpose of winning Jewish and Muslim converts to Christianity. The 1857 Arabic Bible, sponsored by the Society for the Propagation of Christian Knowledge, then followed this translation.[19]

The most important Arabic translation in the modern period, however, was the "Smith-Bustānī-Van Dyck" translation.[20] Begun under the auspices of the American missionary, Eli Smith, in 1848, it was not finally concluded until 1865 through the work of Cornelius Van Dyck, who has received the honour of traditionally having the translation named after him. Seventeen years in the making, this translation has transformed Arabic Christianity in the modern period. A Jesuit Catholic Bible followed the Smith-Bustani-Van Dyck translation in 1880. It was completed under the auspices of Fr. Augsti Rodet in Beirut, along with the help of Ibrahim al-Yazidji, the son of Nasif al-Yazidji, who had assisted Smith.[21] It utilized a Qur'anic calligraphic style of printing, in order to demonstrate the religious value of the text.

---

[19] Kilgoue 1916:387-378; Metzger 1974:162-163.

[20] Usually, and hereafter, referred to as the "Van Dyck," I would like to give credit to the three primary translators of this project; including Butrus al-Bustanī, who is often overlooked.

[21] The "Jesuit Bible" would eventually be followed by a re-translation in 1969. Megalaa 2008:20-21.

The Van Dyck Translation (1848-1865) and its Status

In 1848, the American missionary, Eli Smith, began a major project for the American Board of Commissioners of Foreign Missionaries (ABCFM) in Beirut, by attempting to translate the Bible into modern Arabic. Smith was assisted in the process by at least two Syrian Christians, Mu^{c}allim Butrus al-Bustani and Sheikh Nasif al-Yaziji. Al-Bustani would later go on to found the al-Madrassa al-Wa□aniyya, while al-Yaziji would become a highly celebrated Arab poet.[22] These two figures were quite significant in the development, not only of this redaction of the Arabic Bible, but also the 'renaissance' of Arabic literature throughout the 19th century (*al-nahda*), of which this Bible translation was a part.

The original translation proces undertaken by Smith, Bustānī and Yaziji, was very time consuming, primarily due to Smith's perfectionism. First, Bustānī did an initial rough translation of the Old Testament from Hebrew and Syriac. Smith then reviewed this draft. Sheikh Nasīf evaluated the text for its 'Arabic composition, in reference to grammar, lexicography, and taste.'[23] Smith then once again looked over the text until he was satisfied. He sent these translations out to numerous Arab linguists in Europe, the Middle East, and the United States. After receiving comments and suggestions from these colleagues about the choice of Arabic words, he proceeded to complete each specific portion of the translation. By 1858, ten years after the beginning of the project, Smith had only completed the Pentateuch and a draft of the complete New Testament when he died.[24] Before he died, however, Smith would only authorize the printing of Genesis and part of Exodus. Even at the end of his life, he was not satisfied with the form of his translation.

The ABCFM then asked Cornelius Van Dyck, a Dutch-American doctor, serving in what is now Lebanon, and who was noted as being an eminent linguist, to take up the task. Van Dyck had also worked quite extensively with Bustani and Yaziji, from whom he learned a great deal about Arabic and Arab poetry.[25] However, when Van Dyck took over the translation process he decided to start from scratch. Looking over Smith's work, he noticed that Smith had employed a wide variety of Greek manuscripts of the Bible, including some of the more recent 19th century texts found by Tischendorf, Tregelles and Alford. The use of these new Biblical manuscripts was unacceptable to the American and British Foreign Bible Societies (who were jointly funding the project), as well as to Van

---

22 Barakat 1993:246-247.

23 Smith and Van Dyk 1900:9

24 Smith and Van Dyck 1900:8-10; See also Saliba 1975:257-259. There has been, of late, considerable controversy regarding the role of Bustānī in the translation. It has been argued that the American Mission had a falling out with Bustānī, over their refusal to ordain him. He left the Mission to begin his own school. Thus, it has been argued that Van Dyck, and others minimized his part in the translation process.

25 This information was noted by Edward A. Van Dyck, the son of Cornelius. Caverley 1961:200.

Dyck. They were only willing to accept the Western Text, the *textus receptus*, which was the basis of the 1611 King James Bible. This decision is one that has been second-guessed by later Bible Society members who have argued that this choice has done the translation a disservice in that it did not take advantage of all the available tools of textual criticism.[26] In addition to starting over, Van Dyck also decided not to continue utilizing the services of Bustani and Yaziji. He preferred, rather, Sheikh Yusuf al-Asir, a graduate of the famous Sunni Egyptian institution al-Azhar. Van Dyck stated:

> I preferred a Muslim to a Christian, as coming to the work with no preconceived ideas of what a passage ought to mean, and as being more extensively read in Arabic.[27]

Van Dyck followed a similar translation process to that of Smith, producing a rough draft and then having al-Asir edit it before sending it off to other colleagues, within the region, for comments. Van Dyck, however, worked much quicker than Smith. After only two years, the New Testament was completely translated in 1860 with full vowels added by 1862.[28] The rest of the Old Testament, uncompleted by Smith, was finally translated on August 24, 1864, and the complete Bible printed in 1865. When Cornelius Van Dyck put the finishing touches on this Arabic translation, completing a seventeen-year long process, many felt that a sufficient answer to the linguistic problem of the articulation of Christian Scriptures in Arabic had been solved. The Arab Christians now had a Holy Text worthy of its title!

Even though North American missionaries from the ABCFM initiated this particular translation, it eventually gained a popular following among many different Arab communities, including the Oriental Catholic and Orthodox communities.[29] The 'Van Dyck' Bible has been one of the most popular translations throughout the 20th century, outselling most of the other translations. Despite the fact that Protestants (who are called 'Evangelicals' in Middle Eastern nomenclature) make up only .01% of the Christian population,[30] the Van Dyck translation is by far the most widely read among the nearly 350 million Arab Christians worldwide.[31] This translation has assumed the status of the *textus*

---

[26] Megalaa 2008:58-61.
[27] Hall 1882-1885:280.
[28] Arabic, as a Semitic tri-consonantal language utilizes diacritical marks above and below the text in order to indicate its vowels. Most early Arabic manuscripts, including the early Uthmanic texts of the Qur'an, did not include vowel points; thus leading to the important developments in different schools of thought in pronunciation, or recitation. This was noted very early on by Muslims. Al-Tabari has extensive comments about this in his *Commentary on the Qur'an*.
[29] Megalaa 2008:45.
[30] Courbage and Fargues 1997:209.
[31] Megalaa 2008:48-49.

receptus of the Arabic community in the Middle East, specifically in Egypt where it has been accepted as the official text of the legal and historic churches. The current Patriarch of Alexandria, Shenouda III, the head of the Coptic Orthodox Church, the largest Arabic-speaking church in the world, utilizes the Van Dyck Bible during his weekly Bible study. He has also worked quite closely with the Egyptian Bible Society, providing his blessing to the endeavours of what had been seen as a primarily Protestant institution.[32] While other modern translations have been made and may predominate in certain circles, they have not reached the widespread usage of the Van Dyck. These include the 'Jesuit Bible' (1880/1969), *kitab al-hayat*, or New Arabic Bible (1988), Today's Arabic Version New Testament (1978), the complete Good News Arabic Bible (1993), the Honorable Gospel (1991), and finally *kitab al-sharif*, or the Honourable Scripture (2000).[33]

In 1999, the Egyptian Bible Society and the Bible Society of Lebanon began a project, supported by most of the major Christian denominations of the Middle East, including the Oriental Catholic and Oriental Orthodox churches, to assess the possibility of a new acceptable Arabic Bible Translation for all of the churches. What has resulted from this process did not lead to the development of a new Arabic translation but rather the 'Van Dyck' New Study Bible. In 2006, a New Testament Study edition was published with hopes that the Old Testament will follow by 2013. Rather than a new Arabic translation, the *New Testament Study Bible* has added critical notes and explanations to the existing text of the Van Dyck, adding some 70% more text.

Previously, there had been several other attempts to revise the Van Dyck, which also failed to result in a new translation. In 1906, it was suggested that important changes in the Arabic language and in the field of Biblical studies necessitated some revisions. However, rather than making a complete revision of the translation, references were added along the margins, 'keeping with modern Biblical learning.'[34] In 1916, the American Mission Press in Beirut could not find the support among the church leadership of Syria and Lebanon to re-translate the Bible only sixty years after its publication. The British Foreign Bible Society again faced this same problem in 1928.[35] In 1954, a new translation was proposed in Cairo and worked on for seventeen years, from 1956-1973, but this only resulted in the separate publication of pamphlets of the New Testament books and not a complete translation of the Bible. Thus, the concept of a completely new translation of the Bible received neither ecclesiastical nor popular support.[36] According to John A. Thompson, an American Presbyterian missionary-scholar,

[32] Megalaa 2008:49.

[33] See Schaaf 1994:44-49 for critiques of these translations.

[34] Torrey 1919:106.

[35] Torrey 1919:105; Bishop 1964:170; and The Bible Society of Egypt 2008.

[36] Megalaa 2008:99, cited from Butros Abd al-Malik and Thompson 1958:176. See also Accad 1969:298.

Professor at the Evangelical Theological Seminary at Cairo, and one of the architects of the proposed new translation, the whole concept of the new translation was rejected because, 'no verses can be omitted from the Arabic Revision without arousing misunderstanding and opposition.'[37] There was great suspicion of removing any iota from sacred text, lest the Christians be charged with "corrupting" their texts. These events highlight the particular problem for Arab Christians and the use of the Arabic language as a vehicle for sacred scripture and revelation. The reason lies within the concept of *wahy* in the predominantly Islamic culture of the Middle East.

The Influence of Islamic Views of *wahy* on Arab Christian Views of the Bible

The wide acceptance of the Van Dyck translation, since the 19th century, has been due primarily to the development of an Islamic concept of *wahy* among Arabic-speaking Christians of the Middle East. In classical Islamic thought the Qur'ān is the book from Heaven. The 'revelation' [*wahy*] of this Book, like previous revelations before it, has 'come down' from Heaven and given verbally to the Prophets.[38] The most common word used to describe the act of revelation in the Qur'an is *tanzil* (*nazala*): 'to come down'.[39] Thus, God reveals by sending His words 'down' verbally, whereupon they are written in a temporal book to record the Will of God for a particular people. Throughout history, messengers have received revelations sent down by God from Heaven that were collected in book form (*al-kitab*), most especially to Moses, David and Jesus. However, over time, Jews and Christians have 'distorted' or 'corrupted' (*tahrif*) this revelation, either to suit their own needs, or simply because they did not understand it properly.[40] Muhammad, however, received the final revelation from God in the form of 'The Book' in Heaven. The actual 'Book', or the actual text itself [*mushaf*], is reflective of the literal words spoken from God in Heaven in Arabic, and as it has been traditionally understood, inscribed on a golden tablet (see 12:2): 'Nay, this is a glorious Qur'an (inscribed) in a Tablet Preserved' [*lauh mahfuz*] (85:21-22).

Therefore, the Qur'an is literally the unaltered 'speech of God' in Arabic beyond the bounds of time and space. In the words of the great exegete al-Tabari (224-?):

> …it is obvious that there is no clear discourse more eloquent, no wisdom more profound, no speech more sublime, no form of expression more noble, than [this] clear discourse and speech with which a single man challenged a people…

---

37 Megalaa 2008:99; see Abd al-Malik and Thompson 1958:174-177.
38 See specifically 3:7.
39 Jeffrey 1952:54.
40 For a helpful review of *tahrif* see Saeed 2004:419-436.

> each scripture which preceded our Book [however] was sent down to one of God's prophets, may God bless them and grant them peace, in only a single tongue, and when it was changed into a tongue other than that in which it was sent down, this was an interpretation (*tarjama*) and a commentary (*tafsir*) of it, not a recitation according to what God had sent down…[41]

Medieval Islamic scholars, like al-Tabarī, spent their lives in pursuit of the correct pronunciation of the revelation (*harf),* as God had originally 'sent it down.' These unaltered and perfect utterances of God point to the 'inimitability' (*ᶜijaz*) of the Qur'an for Muslims. Its recitation is unsurpassable in beauty or truth. To put this notion into Christian terms, as Bishop Kenneth Cragg has argued: "In the Islamic faith we have 'the words made scripture', the Book". To put it simply: this is the *Word made Book.*[42]

What adds to this sense of mystery about the divine text is the fact that the Arabic of the Qur'an, especially the pronunciation of the original un-voweled words of the 'pure and clear' Arabic (*'arabi mubin*), is not the common spoken Arabic of the modern Middle East. Qur'anic Arabic continues to be used as the standard for formal speech (*fusha*). And yet, most common communication, both verbal and written, takes place in local dialects. Thus, the language of the Qur'an has become distinctive as the holy language of God and God's will. It is not the language of the people on the street (especially in Egypt, the cultural context of the new Van Dyck Study Bible). Thus, native Arab speakers, who recite the Qur'an, may themselves not be familiar with the words or syntax of the text. This accentuates the mystery and majesty of the Book: God's literal transcendent speech.

This concept of 'revelation', in the Islamic tradition, has become the predominant cultural view in which revealed religion is practiced and lived out among Arabic speaking Christians. Muslims recite and read their Qur'ans, and most importantly, hold, handle and touch the physical text of the 'Book' with a sense of the divine 'otherness' which it represents. The physical book, the *mushaf*, represents the divine in their midst – if we might again use a Christian perspective. Arab Christians, because they live in such a culture and are surrounded by these linguistic usages, have, in many ways, communally internalized this view of *wahy* within popular piety. For many Arabic Christians, especially in the rural areas of the Middle East, the "Book" is that which "came down."

---

[41] Al-Tabari 1987:30.

[42] Cragg 1999:251. I am deeply indebted to Cragg's thinking on this topic. It is his thinking on this issue specifically that is the basis of this work.

Challenges of the Text of the Van Dyck in contemporary Middle Eastern Society

There are several reasons why Arab Christians have come to see their own scripture in the same social-cultural-religious framework as the Qur'an of classical Islam. First and foremost, the Islamic culture that predominates has been absorbed within their own community over some fourteen hundred years. Second, the translation of the Van Dyck, which coincided with the renaissance of the Arabic language in the 19th century (*al-nahda*), has led to a revered status of this translation as 'high' Arabic. This is the Arab Christian answer to the 'inimitability of the Qur'an.' Third, because the 19th century Arabic is difficult and its language and syntax antiquated, its contents are often mysterious. Finally, added to this, is the reality of the rise of illiteracy in the Middle East in the 20th century that creates a stigma of the 'Book' within popular piety.

First, as already stated, Islamic religious culture is predominant and saturates daily interactions in the Middle East. These cultural markers naturally affect the common views of religious minorities. One could argue that a social-religious minority might establish itself as counter-cultural, articulating its own communal ethos as 'other' than that of popular piety. The role of the Amish in the United States, as a separatist Protestant community that has purposefully maintained itself as separate from dominant American culture, would serve as a helpful example here. In this case, however, Arab Christians have had a long history of co-mingling with Arab Muslims socially, economically and politically. Arab Christians are integrated into society. Their identity as a religious minority is not ethnic or linguistic, but rather a communal memory and identity that provides meaning to daily life. If we were to look at the contemporary use of religious language in popular Arab piety, we find very common similarities among Christians and Muslims, such as the use of religious blessings in daily speech. Christian phrases such as *rabbina ma'ak* (Our Lord be with you) are almost as plentiful as *Salam alaykum* (Peace be upon you). Such speech provides a distinctive Christian response as a counterbalance to a Muslim public greeting. In this greeting, 'holy blessings' (*Baraka*) come to be evoked and recognized between members of the faith in public when using particular Christian terminology. While such common language certainly has its roots in pre-Islamic and even pre-Christian Aramaic cultural traditions, the particular usage in popular piety creates distinctive identity markers.

In addition, the portrayal of passages of the Bible in Kufic-style calligraphy, on all manner of ornamentations, adds a visual component to this concept of the 'Words made Book'. Eli Smith, the original translator of the 19th century Protestant translation, insisted on utilizing highly stylized calligraphic Arabic fonts when developing the print form of the Bible. This accentuated the view of the sacred scripture. The intent of Smith, and later the rest of the Protestant translators, was to produce not only a translation, but also a text that 'looked' like sacred scripture, worthy of the public's attention.[43] This visual mechanism has been carried forward into visible sacred art forms that adorn daily public and private space for Arab Christians. An example of this would include the common portrayal of passages from the Bible, as well as the Lord's Prayer, in calligraphic style that adorn Christian shops and homes, just as commonly as the *bismillah*. While, on the one hand, this distinguishes Christians from their Muslim compatriots, on the other hand, such symbols are within the linguistic-cultural framework of Islamic Arabic where the styles clearly denote 'Holy Writ'. Thus, Arab Christians have taken on social customs of Islamic culture as a normal pattern of life.

Second, the development of the Van Dyck translation took place during the beginning of the *al-Nahda* period of the 19th century. It was, during this century, that a literary revival took place in both Beirut and Cairo in which independent Arab societies began founding journals and periodicals. These prominent Arab *literati* or 'men of letters' of this period – both Muslim and Christian – began publishing Arabic literature of a high quality in a wide variety of fields: poetry, history, philosophy, science and politics.[44] Although the origins of this movement are disputed, it ultimately led to the revival of Arabic 'national' and ethnic pride at a time of Turkish occupation, primarily through the wide availability of Arabic periodicals, journals, and books. Native Arab speakers revitalized the Arabic language by promoting the concept of a 'pure and clear' Arabic.

The Van Dyck translation was begun and completed and subsequently published in this atmosphere. Thus, the particular translation – by this I mean the choice of words and phrases, and the presentation of the text itself inside the pages of the book – has become representative of the 19th century standard of Renaissance Arabic. In describing his own system of translation, Eli Smith wrote that:

> clear and impressive intelligibility is labored after, avoiding, as far as may be, all words beyond the circle understood by the more intelligent class of the community. At the same time, it is a rule not to depart from the laws of ancient grammar, nor admit words not sanctioned by classical usage without urgent

---

43 Leavy 1993:7-16.

44 See Chahine 2005:797-824. This is a very helpful review of this movement within Christian circles and argues that it was the Catholic and Protestant missionary schools that gave rise to the movement. The most prominent proponent of this argument was the Greek Orthodox author, George Antonius, who argued that the 'renaissance' of Arabic literature of the 19th was closely tied to the development of printed evangelical texts by missionary communities in Beirut and Cairo and their literary-educational programmes. See Antonius 1945. Another perspective is that of Choueiri 1989:39-67. Choueiri argues that it was the Egyptian invasion of Syria by Muhammad 'Ali and his administrative reforms that gave rise to this development. Both are contributing factors. It must be said, however, that without the Egyptian occupation, the early Catholic and Protestant Mission schools would not have succeeded in their ambitious ideals of educating (and evangelizing) the Syrian population.

> necessity. Rather than do this, we here and there adopt a word, now gone out of use… trusting to the future enlightenment of the nation to bring back the language again nearer to its classical richness and purity.[45]

It has been argued, among Arab Christians, that the use of the Arabic Van Dyck Bible has been unparalleled, and historically has been 'celebrated as one of the best translation of the Scriptures… [and] has been the standard for all Protestant missionary societies working in Arabic-speaking lands throughout the world'.[46] During the 1930's, a Lebanese pastor exclaimed that the Van Dyck translation was so sacred that it was as if 'the pages had virtually fluttered down from heaven.'[47] In such a social-religious environment, where the expectation is that the printed Word becomes holy because it has 'come down', the Arabic of the Van Dyck then has become accepted as central to the understanding of God's Word in the Arabic language.

Even though contemporary Arabic has changed and grown as a used language, the text of the Van Dyck is fixed and has become representative of "holy writ". For example, although many Western Protestant Christians have abandoned the classical style of the "King's English", the traditional King James' version of the *Lord's Prayer* has been maintained by many, for reasons of personal piety or sentimentality (and I do not use that term pejoratively here.) The English Orientalist scholar, Margoliouth, felt that the Van Dyck translation had become as much a part of the Arab Christian 'life and vocabulary as had been the case with the Authorized Version in Britain' of 1611.[48] This respect for the Words and tradition of the text has prohibited scholars from re-translating the Van Dyck Bible.

Third, and building upon this previous concept, the language of the Van Dyck translation has become antiquated, difficult to understand, and even unintelligible to some Arab Christians, especially in the rural areas where the educational opportunities are limited. This has created even more of a sense of mystique about the translation – giving it its own sense of divine majesty of having 'come down'. Just as native Arabic speaking Muslims might ponder over the particular meaning of a Qur'ānic text because of its ambiguity, Arab Christians must also struggle with a vocabulary, grammar and syntax that are unclear. Rev. Dr. ᶜAbd al-Masih Istafanous, former Moderator of the Synod of the Nile in Egypt, in his recent publication *An Introduction to the Bible for the Arabic Reader,* has clearly articulated the problem by outlining several passages, where the development of the Arabic language prohibits readers from truly understanding the original text.[49] The need for clarity within the Arabic of the text is also demonstrated through the publication of the most recent 2006 New Testament Arabic Study Bible of the

---

45 Smith and Van Dyck 1900:9-10.
46 Torrey 1919:105.
47 Bishop 1964:168.
48 Bishop 1964:168.
49 Istafanous 1994.

Van Dyck translation. The text of the New Testament Study Bible includes study notes in the margins, with over seventy percent of the whole text taken up by marginal notes and appendices, the sole purpose of which is to explain unclear idioms and terminology for the native Arab speaker.

Finally, and closely associated with the two issues above, is the fact that a growing illiteracy rate among Arabic speakers within the Arab World contributes to the 'otherness' of the text. Illiterate Christians see the text as a divine mystery that only God can unlock. The 2001 U.N. *Arab Human Development Report* indicates that the Arab World lags far behind every other region of the world in terms of literacy. Even though significant strides were made in educational reforms in the 1990's, throughout the Arab World, the number of illiterate Arabic speakers is increasing, especially among those in poor and rural areas, and especially among women.[50] This social problem enhances the development of an Islamic view of *wahy,* within the popular piety of Christians, especially in the rural areas. In these communities, for example, where fewer and fewer people can read or understand Classical Arabic (*fusha*), the visual images of Arabic Christian calligraphy and the public recitation of a 19th century Arabic, that is often un-intelligible to modern ears, highlight the complete 'otherness' of the sacred text.

In addition, because of the nature of traditional Middle Eastern education is to teach by rote memorization, which is re-enforced with the daily use and recitation of the Qur'an, the Van Dyck translation is the most commonly memorized version. Because the actual pronunciation of Qur'anic passages is vital to the interpretation of certain words, and is an important blessing initself and of itself, the recitation of the Van Dyck has taken on a similar role within the Christian community. To recite or chant the Bible in Arabic has become an important pious act, which brings comfort as the Arab Christian internalizes the very Word of God. Memorization of the Arabic Bible has become an important symbol of faith for Arab Christians. Thus, to change the translation of the Holy Book would be seen as changing God's Words themselves.

Conclusion

In the contemporary Arabic cultural context of the Middle East, I have argued that Arab Christians have come to view their own sacred text as a revelation (*wahy*) which has 'come down.' Given that the Van Dyck translation has become the *textus receptus* of the majority of the Christians of the Arab World, especially within the Egyptian context, the largest Arabic speaking church, and because of its high standard of Arabic that is, in some cases, unintelligible to some native Arab speakers, it has become to be seen as 'otherworldly' and transcendent. More important than this, the *text* itself has assumed theological significance. Whereas traditionally, Christians have utilized three concepts of the term "Word

[50] United Nations Development Progamme 2002:51-52.

of God" (the Book, Jesus, and the power of God in daily life), in this context Christians have given full weight to the concept of the *mushaf* of the Bible as the literal, unalterable 'Speech of God'.

Thus, when a new translation of the Bible has been suggested, such a proposal has been met with great negativity. The proposition of any new translation of the Bible has been rejected because of the predominant culture of the unalterable text as God's speech itself. By even suggesting that the text itself could or should change, Christians fall prey to long-standing Muslim charges of *tahrif*, the corruption of the text. From the orthodox Islamic perspective, because the text itself is unalterable, the wide variety of texts, translations, and styles of Bibles proves that Christians have altered God's Words.[51]

I would argue here that the issue at its root is a theological one, the articulation of a theology of the 'Book'. Arab Christian Churches have been emotionally, mentally, and spiritually uncomfortable with a new Arab translation of their own text because they have been reared in a social-religious environment that has a different theological perspective of the written text. While the Qur'an represents the transcendence of God interjected into human history for the purpose of providing 'guidance', the Christian scriptures, especially the New Testament, represent the "Incarnation" of God in human culture and language. In the case of Arab Christianity, the concepts and status of the Words *within* the Book have been appropriated from Islam. In order for Arabic speaking Christians, then, to recapture their own sense of 'revelation', there must be a reclaiming of the Christian history and tradition of *scripture*.

Recently, Egyptian Christians have begun articulating both the sociological and theological need for a new translation of the Bible by addressing these very issues. It has been argued that the Egyptians have been at the centre of Jewish and Christian translations of their scriptures, beginning with the Septuagint.[52] Thus, by reminding themselves of their own identity as 'People of the Book', in the sense of their writing down and passing on the message of the God's revelation to people in their native tongue, Egyptian Christians might reclaim their historical role as translators of the Bible. ᶜAbd al-Masih Istafanous, in his book *Introducing the Bible to Arabic Readers,* has gone to great lengths to articulate to Arabic readers the reason behind the translation of the Bible from their original languages into other languages all over the world. His point is that it should not be a surprise for Arab Christians to learn that a new Arabic translation is such a novel idea, nor that it undercuts the holiness of the text. Rather, it is inherent in the message of the Gospel that it should be continually translated into

---

[51] A very helpful example of this is the very active website www.AnsweringChristianity.com. This website is very apologetic in nature, pointing out the corruption of the Christian Scriptures. Another website is www.islamic-awareness.org. This website has a very detailed section on the "Textual Integrity of the Bible" 2008.

[52] Megalaa 2008:76.

the languages of all peoples, and that this is how God's Spirit works.[53] It is clear, here, that his intention is to address the contemporary Arab Christian concern regarding how one understands the concept of a revealed scripture. He asserts, 'Christianity does not believe that the Bible descended [*nazala*] from heaven, with its words and letters, but Christianity does believe in inspiration [*wahy*].' Istafanous argues that the Spirit of God was the 'source of their inspiration' and that different texts and translations of the Bible indicate how God's message was intended to be communicated to all peoples of the world. The Word, then, is incarnated into the language of the people.[54]

This historical view of the holy texts has also been put on display by the Bible Society of Egypt, which has recently developed an interactive attraction in Cairo for Sunday Schools called the 'Bible World.' Students walk through this hands-on exhibition, where they learn about the aspects of inscribing texts, printing books, and the translation of scripture from Hebrew and Greek into other languages, including Arabic. This project has the potential to instruct a whole new generation of Egyptian Christians in the history and transmission of their own sacred scripture. The exhibition is also providing a context to explain the concept of *wahy* from a Christian historical perspective. Participants are reminded that the 'Word of God' was transmitted historically rather than 'fluttered down from heaven.'

There is a theological distinction here: complete transcendence versus Incarnation. In order for Arab Christians to reclaim their own text, on their own terms and in their own theological framework within a predominant Islamic culture, will mean the recovery or perhaps the strong articulation of the concept of an incarnational sacred text in history - *in Arabic*. Thus, Arab Christians will need to be clear about their theological understanding of *wahy* as it relates to the Bible as a historically *inspired* text, through which the 'Word of God' speaks as opposed to the literal 'speech of God.' It appears that there is an attempt underway to recover such an incarnational view of the "Book."

[53] Istafanous n.d.:123-124.
[54] Istafanous n.d.:125.

PART III: COMMUNITY

Saints, Incarnation and Christian-Muslim Dialogue: Reflections Inspired by Encountering Bangladeshi Islam

Clinton Bennett

Dr. Clinton Bennett is a Baptist minister and currently teaches at the State University of New York at New Paltz

The Limit of Language

Before becoming a missionary in Bangladesh, I spent a year at the Selly Oak Colleges, Birmingham. In addition to mission studies, I completed the one-year certificate programme at the Centre for the Study of Islam and Christian-Muslim Relations. Later, I earned my M.A. (1985) and Ph.D. (1990) degrees in Christian-Muslim Relations at Birmingham University through the same Centre. During my first period at Selly Oak (1978-79), I discovered the writing of an earlier missionary, Lewis Bevan Jones (1880-1960) and have ever since identified closely with his conciliatory approach to Islam, not least because he and I were both Baptists. He had spent a good part of his career in what is now Bangladesh. As part of my mission studies, I wrote a paper on Jones, which eventually evolved into my master's thesis. One of Jones' suggestions was that, in our Evangelical encounter with Muslims, we should emphasize the "why" rather than the "what" of belief. He contended that beliefs and doctrines are essentially post-experiential attempts to describe, within the poverty and limitations of human language, what people believe to be true about their experience of God. Convinced that Muslim as well as Christian religious experience is genuine, he identified this as common ground.[1] Immediately before this remark, Jones referred to the "very real belief" among Muslims, especially among Sufis, in "God's intimate dealings" with people, adding that some Sufis "carried their doctrine of 'union' with the Beloved to such extravagant lengths that many of them, in days gone by, paid for their temerity with their lives". In this paper, my exploration of the concepts of sainthood and of divine "indwelling" in Christianity and in Islam draws on Jones' suggestion that the language we use to describe the divine-human encounter always fails to express the total truth of what we have experienced. Rather, our language attempts to articulate what can never be comprehensively described. I personally contend that both Christian and Muslim formulations may be true in what they say of God and of the divine-human relationship, but that we cannot claim that they express the whole truth about God. Something similar is found in the writing of Al-Ghazali (1058-1111),

[1] Jones 1938:93.

the great Sufi mystic and Muslim theologian. In asking whether there is any common ground that can reduce the Christian-Muslim divide on Jesus as God-Incarnate, I am interested to see if admitting that our language is limited helps or hinders rapprochement on this issue.

Building on Jones, I suggest that some of the distance between us, when discussing Jesus as God incarnate, may be reduced if we admit the genuineness of each other's *taqwa* (God-consciousness) and that the theological language we use is indicative and provisional, not definitive. On the one hand, differences in the language we use may construct barriers if one side claims that its language is accurate, correct and exhaustive. In this view, the other side is wrong, misguided or heretical. On the other hand, recognition that language has limitations when applied to the divine-human encounter, may build bridges. During over a quarter of a century of involvement in Christian-Muslim encounter, I have tried to combine a scholarly contribution with a pragmatic engagement in bridge-building, assisting Muslim communities in practical ways, such as helping with grant applications, obtaining charitable status and planning permission and even distributing prizes as the chief guest at a Qur'anic school. In what follows, I attempt to ground my reflections on sainthood in Christianity and Islam as a way of helping Muslims to understand what Christians mean by Incarnation in an actual experience of encounter. I begin with an account of how encounter with Bangladeshi Islam alerted me to the possibility that sainthood might be a fruitful area to explore. Next, I shift to a discussion of sainthood in Islam and Christianity as a bridge to understanding Incarnation.

Encountering Bangladeshi Islam

Although I spent a relatively short period in Bangladesh (1979-1982), I have sustained contact with Bangladeshis ever since, living for ten years in a Bangladeshi-majority neighborhood of Birmingham (1982-1992), returning to visit Bangladesh three times (1996, 1998 and 2000) and taking part in many community functions. It was a Bangladeshi Muslim friend and colleague in community work who introduced me to my wife, who is from Bangladesh. For several years, I chaired a neighbourhood Bengali association. In all these years, in conversation with Bangladeshi Muslims, many of whom are Sufis, the issues that have most frequently surfaced surround the person of Jesus, whether as God incarnate, God's son or the second person of the Trinity. In many conversations, my Muslim acquaintance has commented that he cannot comprehend how I can claim belief in One God while insisting on calling God "triune". You call Jesus "God's Son" but God "neither begets nor is begotten".[2] God could not, they insist, stoop to being born as a baby. Yet my Bangladeshi Muslim acquaintances, unlike some other Muslims, whom I know, have never suggested that I am "lost" because I believe that God was present in Jesus of Nazareth. Nor, unlike some

[2] Surah 112: 3.

Muslims, have they ever implied that belief in Jesus' Incarnation means that I think of Mary as God's wife, or that God had sex with her. Often, after identifying the difference between their belief in Unity and my belief in Trinity and expressing puzzlement as to my belief in the latter, they assert that, despite this, we believe in the same God, implying an affirmation of Surah 29: 46, "dispute not with the people of the book … but … say 'we believe in the revelation that came down to you and in the revelation that came down to us, your God and our God is One and it is to Him that we bow." I may be, and probably am, flattering myself, since I am well aware of my faults and failings, yet my gut feeling tells me that my Bangladeshi Muslim friends, many of whom have known me and worked with me for years, without ever casting any aspersions on my spiritual status, think that, despite my flaws, my life is centered on God and my labours on their behalf to improve community welfare are nurtured by my relationship with God. My gut feeling tells me that the genuineness of my religious experience is not at issue, even though my theological formulations may be problematical. This is different from experiences I have had with other Muslims, who make it quite clear that, if I do not embrace Islam, my spiritual state is suspect and my eternal destiny gravely at risk. I recently attended a Muslim Students Association meeting on campus at SUNY, New Paltz. Although advertised as an inter-faith meeting it was really a call to Islam. Speakers declared that only Muslims are certain of pleasing God.

My observations of Bengali Islam suggest to me that religious experience is the centre stage for many Bangladeshis, and is more important than dogma. My instinct is that they do not think that God saves or condemns people for the way they express theological convictions, and that this is secondary to developing genuine God-consciousness, which is not contingent on "orthodox" belief. Prayer, fasting and obligatory external acts of piety are important for Bangladeshi Muslims, but inner renewal is even more important. Hence, the popularity of the Tablighi Jamaat among Bangladeshis: this movement here stresses spiritual growth, peace and tolerance. The annual meeting outside Bangladesh's capital attracts the second largest gathering of Muslims in the world after the *hajj*. With its Deobandi, conservative roots, Tabligh has an anti-Sufi stance but most Bangladeshi Muslims have Sufi tendencies, even if they belong to a movement or organization that officially disapproves of Sufism. Tabligh's founder, Muhammad Ilyas (1885-1944), graduated from Deoband but was also a member of the Chisti order of Sufis, at least before he started the movement.[3] One writer actually confuses the Tablighi gathering with a Sufi convention, "Sufis in Bangladesh organize a huge Muslim gathering annually just outside Dhakka" he writes, adding that, "It is second in size only to the *hajj* in Mecca".[4] Given the popularity of Sufism in Bangladesh, it is easy to see how anyone might assume that such a large gathering would, of necessity, be Sufi. He is correct, though, to

[3] Uddin 2006:146.
[4] Lewis 2005:447.

describe Bangladeshi Islam as tolerant "of other religions" and Bangladeshi Muslims as emphasizing "abstinence and self-denial." Uddin says that it is impossible to estimate the number of Bangladeshis who identify with Sufi orders any more than how many belong to Tabligh or to Jamaat-i-Islam (which won two seats and lost 16 in the 2008 election), "as the level of association with these institutions and with *pirs* varies with each devotee." "Nevertheless", he continues, "Sufi tradition has a long history in Bangladesh, and the *pirs* constituted the main avenue by which Bengalis were introduced to Islam" and "shrines to revered saints" and the rooms where living *pirs* receive pilgrims, "brim with activities and are part of the fabric of Bengali society in Bangladesh". [5] General Ershad, the former military ruler (1982-1990), was a devout disciple of *Pir* Atroshi (or Athrassi) and spared no "expense to spend time" with him.[6] He addressed him as "*amar huzur*" (my Lord),[7] "like any ordinary *murid*" (disciple). *Pirs* are venerated throughout Bangladesh. Esposito, Voll and Bakar refer to sixty-two *Pirs*, "mythical and historical," whose shrines are visited by "hundreds of thousands of pilgrims every year". [8] They also describe the emergence in "recent years" of urban-based Sufi *Pirs*, who enjoy a "large following among military officers, government officials, college and university teachers, and businessmen and politicians".[9] Quite a "large number "of Bangladeshis, they say, "identify … with some *Pir*, living or dead," to whom they look for "spiritual guidance" and even for "intercession for the solution of their worldly problems".[10] One Pakistani *Pir* visits Chittagong annually and collects a large amount of money from that city's "rich business community".[11] *Pirs* channel the divine, having achieved union with God. Before flying to Bangladesh, I did not know much about Sufism, although I knew that Sufi missionaries had evangelized Bengal and that much of Bangladeshi Islam has a Sufi flavour. My experience of Islam in Bangladesh, as well as among Bangladeshis in the diaspora, alerted me to the importance of *pirs* for many Muslims in their personal quest for fellowship with God. This stimulated further study. At some point, I also turned to consider the role of saints in the Christian tradition. Belonging to a denomination, that neither celebrates the feast days of saints, nor possesses any

---

[5] Uddin 2006:146. The popularity of Tablighi in Islam, with its emphasis on inner renewal and ban on political activism has "posed a serious challenge to the Islamic legitimacy of the political alternative offered by Jamaati-I-Islami in Bangladesh" according to Esposito et al. 2008:63.

[6] Uddin 2006:139.

[7] Dey 1996:28.

[8] Dey 1996:60. *Pirs* in Bangladesh include "pioneering settlers," Buddhists and Hindus who have been adopted as Muslim saints and also spirits and natural elements. In an uncertain climate, *Pirs* offer stability and assurance of God's ultimate concern for their welfare (60). Here, Esposito et al. 2008 draw on Roy 1982.

[9] Dey 1996:60.

[10] Dey 1996:60.

[11] Dey 1996:60.

official teaching about saints, this was an informative venture. My encounter with Islam has often led me to learn more about aspects of my own religion. I began by asking what it was about *pirs* or Sufi saints that attract Muslims, helping to nourish their religious experience and assisting them along the spiritual journey. Then I asked whether similarities exist between their role and that of Christian saints. Finally, I asked, if so, can this contribute, in any way whatsoever, to Christian-Muslim discourse on Jesus' as God made flesh? During two visits to Bangladesh, while researching my 2001 book *In Search of Muhammad*, I asked interviewees questions about the role of *pirs*. I refer to this fieldwork below.

Saints in Islam

What follows does not attempt to describe every aspect of saints in Islam, or of their role in Sufi tradition, which is outside the specific scope of this paper. Rather, I focus on how their followers understand their relationship with God, whom some say "dwells in them." If God does dwell within them, this invites a conversation with what Christians mean by "Incarnation". *Hulul* has often been compared with Incarnation; Nicholson cites Abu Nasr al-Sarraj (died 998), "Some mystics … have erred in their doctrine that when they pass away … they enter into the qualities of God" continuing "this leads to incarnation (*hulul*) or to the Christian belief concerning Jesus".[12] Ibn Taymiyya (1263-1328) dismissed "indwelling" with reference to *pirs*, the Shi'a *imams* and Jesus. The term, he said, was unscriptural. Sufis were worse than Christians for claiming union with God, since at least the latter make the claim on behalf of a true prophet.[13] Christians, though, have seized on possible common ground here as a discussion platform, which may explain why an *Encyclopedia of Christianity* has an excellent article on "Sufism".[14] After describing the term used for Muslim saints, I turn to discuss the idea of *hulul*, or divine indwelling, a controversial topic in Islamic discourse. The term for "saint", *wali* (trusted one, or friend) is derived from a Qur'anic passage such as 10: 62, "Behold, verily, on the friends of Allah there is no fear, nor shall they grieve." The plural is *awliya*; women can be *wali* or *Waliyyat* too and include the famous saint, Rabia (died 801CE), a pioneer of "love" mysticism in Islam. *Wali* is usually rendered "saint" in English. Several terms, including *pir*, *sheikh* and *marabout*, depending on geographical location, signify the teacher or guide, the *murshid*, who enjoys the status of a *wali*.

Traditionally, saints trace a spiritual lineage back to Muhammad (*silsilah*). In other words, the living *pir* is appointed by a predecessor, who himself succeeded his own teacher back to Muhammad as the first teacher. One who follows a *pir* is a *murid* or student and, more often than not, offers an oath of loyalty. Many *pirs*, although not all, are heads of an organized order, a Sufi *tariqah*. A *tariqah* is a

---

[12] Nicholson 1914:157.
[13] Ibn Taymiyya 1984:343-4.
[14] See Karamustafa 1999.

path and all Sufis are *salik* (plural *salikun*, pilgrims) as they travel from self-centredness towards God-centredness, from a false self-awareness (*nafs*) towards *fana*, the passing away of "self" into God-consciousness, also described as *baqa*. This is often translated as "union with God". It can be understood as the realization that only God exists, that you "subsist" within God. It is from this that the concept of *hulul*, or "divine indwelling" evolved. What really matters for the *murids* is that the *murshid* has completed the journey, so can channel the divine into their lives, or point the way toward the journey's end. As a friend of God, the *pir* is a conduit of divine grace (*karamat*) and divine blessing (*barakah*). The latter may manifest as miracles granted to the *pir* by God, expressing the former or vice-versa, since *karamat* is also sometimes rendered as a miracle, or an act of grace.

Hulul has always attracted controversy and censure, so much so that Sufis themselves have either avoided using the term or offer various defences of those who felt compelled to express it. Commonly, defences suggest that when Sufis use the language of union or imply that they enjoy this state, they "mis-speak." What Sufis really experience, said al-Sarraj, is the surrender of their will to God so that God's will and their own will coincide in absolute harmony:

> When a man goes forth from his own qualities and enters into the qualities of God, he goes forth from his own will and enters into the will of God, knowing that his will is given to him by God and that by virtue of this gift he is severed from regarding himself, so that he becomes entirely devoted to God; and this is one of the stages of Unitarians.[15]

It was al-Hallaj who expressed *hulul*, crying out "*ana al-Haq.*" Found guilty of heresy, he was crucified in 922.[16] Nicholson commented, "The doctrine of personal deification, in the peculiar form which was impressed upon it by Hallaj, is obviously akin to the central doctrine of Christianity, and therefore from the Moslem standpoint, a heresy".[17] What Hallaj experienced was intimacy with God, and the passing away of the "illusion of subject and object" so that he felt that he had "broken through to the Oneness" and could "either deny that he is anything or affirm that he is all things".[18] Accordingly, he wrote:

> I am He whom I love, and He whom I love is I:
>
> We are two spirits dwelling in one body.
>
> If thou seest me, thou seest Him,

---

[15] Watt 1956:157.

[16] Al-Halaj said "I am Truth", that is, a quality of God, or, put bluntly, he said, "I am God."

[17] Nicholson 1941:151.

[18] Nicholson 1941:161.

And if thou seest Him, thou seest us both."[19]

According to Knysh sainthood was "particularly suspicious in the eyes of the guardians of Islam's purity" because if Sufis claim that saints, like Muhammad, "have direct access to the source of divine revelation"[20] they usurp Muhammad's role. Ibn 'Arabi refers to the fact that *wali* "is applied to both God and man, whereas the word 'prophet' is attributed exclusively to man".[21]

Explaining why Hallaj was not really a heretic, but still wrong for expressing his inner experience of intimacy with God as he did, Al-Ghazali said that he mis-spoke. In the ecstasy and intoxication (*wajad*) of *baqa*, "drowned in the absolute of Oneness" he and others become "lost in" the "Abyss ... they become persons struck dumb, and they [have] no power within them except to recall God" not "even the power to recall themselves." Thus, "there remains with them nothing but God". "Drunk with a drunkenness wherein the sense of their own intelligence" disappears, they cry out words that should remain hidden "and not spoken".[22] Rumi (1207-1273) explained "mystical *hulul*" by saying that his sense of self receded, leaving only an awareness of God: 'There's nothing left of me. I'm like a ruby held up to the sunrise. Is it still a stone? Or a world made of redness? It has no resistance to the sunlight.'[23] The saint's will, desire and self aligns so completely with God that they "flow into God". Notice how here the movement reverses the flow that Christians traditionally associate with Jesus, who was God made man, not a man who flowed "into God." Karamustafa writes:

> The Sufi ... could flow into God, but movement in the other direction was off limits, or at least extremely limited, since such as flow from the divine into the human could pave the way for divinization of the human and thus led to the suspect, even heretical, doctrine of incarnation and inherence.[24]

Does this undermine the possibility of identifying common ground between *hulul*, saints and Jesus as God-Incarnate? Not necessarily, if we pause for a moment to consider "why" Islam is reluctant to speak of movement from the divine to the human. Jones lists several Muslim objections to Incarnation, including "to attribute a son to the Divine Being in a literal sense is to attribute an imperfection to him which is met with in human beings", "has Allah a wife that he should have a son" and "communion is not attained by bringing down God to man in the sense of incarnation, but by man rising gradually".[25] The last objection informs the idea that flow is from the human to the divine not vice

[19] Nicholson 1941:151.
[20] Knysh 1999:53.
[21] Knysh 1999:321 n.97.
[22] Peters 1994;342-3.
[23] Berjak 2006:277.
[24] Karamustafa 1999:222.
[25] Jones 1938:57.

versa. Jones suggests that the rather crude ideas of sexual relations between God and a consort refer to stories associated with pre-Islamic Arabian deities.[26] Yet is there any plausible reason why we should place limits on what God can and cannot do? Jones says that in "seeking to safeguard the High and Lofty One from what he deems derogatory" the Muslim "is persuading himself that he knows the Mind of the Eternal." We do indeed possess knowledge of God but we cannot "speak as though the view-point of the Deity were our own".[27] The Qur'an affirms God's absolute, not limited, power. A God who can say "Be" and "it is,"[28] so that Mary conceives Jesus without sexual congress, is also able to pass into the human realm, which, as God's own creation can, in some respects, be understood as an extension of God's-self. I argue that God created us to enjoy direct communion with Him but that sin and forgetfulness on our part prevents this. God moves toward us in love and mercy to save us from ourselves and to unite us with God's-self. What lies at the root of the concept of sainthood in Islam is the belief that the saint's will and God's will correspond exactly. Whether they pass into God, or God passes into them, may be playing with words, a matter of semantics. What people intend to explain is their experience of intimacy with God, an experience that no human vocabulary can adequately describe. Perhaps talk of movement of one to the other is itself metaphorical, since what really happens is the dissolution of any barrier between us and God and vice-versa.

Before turning to Christian saints, a word about the other Muslim criticism of the *wali*, that they usurp Muhammad's role. There is a story about Muhammad appearing in a dream to Rabia to challenge her if she truly loved him, presumably because she did not constantly refer to him in her discourse. She replied, "O Prophet of God, who is there who does not love thee? But my love to God has so possessed me that no place remains for loving or hating any save Him".[29] Rabia rightfully pointed out that, once the *salik* has travelled to the end of the journey, there is room for none but God, yet it seems to me that without Muhammad's example, there would be no *wali*. Rabia had to follow Muhammad to reach the goal. Once there, Muhammad recedes, since his task is complete. The path that Sufis walk, the religious ideas they employ, all stand on Muslim ground. They imitate Muhammad, not anyone else. When they proclaim the *shahadah*, they declare that Muhammad is the messenger of God. In interviewing Bangladeshi villagers, I asked them whether the role of *pirs* relegates "Muhammad to a less significant role." In reply, they suggested genuine *pirs*, not moneymaking charlatans, do not usurp Muhammad's place because they "point to the *pir*, who is Muhammad".[30] The existence of saints in Islam can be taken as proof that the

[26] Although a verse such as Surah 4: 171 was almost certainly addressed to Christians.
[27] Jones 1938:69.
[28] Surah 3: 47; 59.
[29] Smith: 2009:123-4.
[30] Bennett 2001:255, 199.

path Muhammad taught and walked leads people into a loving, intimate relationship with God.

Christian saints are these whose lives exhibit high levels of holiness, whose words and acts mirror Jesus. In Colossians, all Christians are referred to as "saints" (Col 1: 2). Later, the designation was restricted to a smaller number of Christians whose lives stood out, even among other Christians, as especially holy. In early Christianity, there was no formal procedure to determine sainthood. Later, a complex canonization mechanism was created. Whereas one criterion was a sound doctrine, another was a proof that miracles were associated with the saint. Saints are also those in whose lives the Holy Spirit operates, which all Christians believe to be true of their experience. Just as Muslim saints follow the path of Muhammad, so Christians follow Christ. The Muslim saints' experience of intimacy with God, of *taqwa* rests on Muhammad's prior experience, while the experience of intimacy with God of Christian saints rests on that of Jesus. For Christians, says Jones, "the voice of conscience itself is proof to us that the Divine Spirit can and does indwell man, while the lives of prophets and saints bear witness to the way in which God's spirit endues man with power and insight". People, he says, were created by God in a way that makes it possible for them to "receive such Divine self-impartation", the "quality and intensity" of which "depends ... upon the receptiveness of the individual"[31] In Jesus, the movement of the divine toward the human met with "a perfect human response." Thus, God could reveal through Jesus God's redemptive purpose. Christians, of course, regard Jesus as unique among men but nonetheless as a man. Jones says that it was Jesus' consciousness of his intimacy with God as the Father that led to his followers recognizing that, as well as being a man, Jesus was also God's Son. He points out, though, that when Christians began to speak of Jesus as God's Son and as the second person of the Trinity, most of them were Jews for whom the conviction that there is only One God was unshakeable. They chose the language they used "due to the poverty of human language" as an attempt to describe their "apprehension of the redemptive operation of God's Holy Spirit within us" but they did not for a moment intend to compromise their monotheistic faith.[32] Jesus was so intimately linked to their experience of God and of God's Spirit that they felt compelled to express this through language that spoke of a triune God. They "concluded that Christ belonged, in some mysterious way, to the category of God".[33] However, "no Christian claims that even the most widely accepted definition of the Trinity is adequate to the ultimate truth about God.[34]

Muslims have never called Muhammad "God," or applied to him the language of divine son-ship, although it can be argued that some Muslims approach the former, as Kenneth Cragg comments: 'Islam, in spite of itself, finds place for

---

[31] Jones 1938:71.
[32] Jones 1938:93-4.
[33] Jones 1938:91.
[34] Jones 1938:94.

categories of relationship between divine ends and human means, between the eternal and the historical, unlike and yet akin to those that are at the heart of Christian experiences in Jesus as the Christ.'[35]

Yet just as Christians believe that Jesus leads them to communion with God, so Muslims believe that Muhammad's role of pointing the way toward God is essential. In Islam, it is Muhammad's experience of intimacy with God that paves the way for those who replicate this in their own lives, becoming *wali*. For Christians, Jesus is the "pioneer and finisher of our faith" (Hebrews 12: 12), who shows us the way. Arguably, Muslims and Christians use different language to describe the same experience, the same mystery. Given that the experience behind the language is a mystery, all language used in description is allegory and metaphor, and not scientific. Both descriptions may be true yet neither may represent the whole of the truth. Jesus, for Christians, was "God" as well as a man yet exactly how Jesus was God and at the same time "man" has proved extremely difficult to define. Traditionally, Christians affirm that God's eternal Word entered a human embryo, that of Jesus. Jesus was then born as a man, with a human mother, Mary but without a human father.[36] Muslims, for their part, argue that God's eternal Word was revealed through Muhammad as a Book. Both the man Jesus, and the Book revealed through Muhammad, represent finite physical objects. Yet God's eternal Word dwelt or dwells within these physical objects. This does not imply that the whole of God resided or resides therein but that a quality or aspect (or in traditional Christian language a "person") did. This quality or person, though, is wholly divine. What Christians see in Jesus is the movement of God toward humanity, to save and to redeem, so that Jesus' life, death and resurrection represent definitive moments in the history of the divine-human encounter. What we affirm when we say that God or God's Word dwelt in Jesus is that God was present in him in a unique and special way. I can affirm that Jesus was God or God made flesh without knowing how. As I have written: 'I do not know whether Jesus was ontologically God, or whether he was so intimate with God that the distinction between who he was and who God is became blurred, which Muslims describe as a harmony of Jesus' will with God's will.'[37]

Similarly, I can affirm that somehow "God made God's Word enter Muhammad, and pass through him into what became a physical, material object, a Book" while remaining unable to explain the mechanics involved. "The actual process of *Incarnation* and of *Bookification*" I continue "can be regarded as mysteries while their reality and truthfulness can be affirmed." There is, of course, a difference here, in that, for Christians Jesus is God's Word, while Muhammad, for Muslims, was the vehicle through which the Word was revealed,

---

[35] Cragg 1984:65.

[36] Most Muslims also accept the Virgin Birth of Jesus, based on such passages as Surah 3: 47 and 3: 59.

[37] Bennett 2008:215.

rather than the embodiment of the Word. Muslims ascribe the divine quality to the Book, not to the Prophet and only ever speak of Muhammad as a man. Yet they speak of him as a very special man, as unique, as the perfect man. Christians go further, applying God language to Jesus. While problematical for Muslims, this language may actually express the same conviction. In practice, the relationship between Muhammad and the Qur'an is so intimate that, while theologically the correct parallel is Jesus with the Qur'an not Jesus with Muhammad, functionally, Jesus and Muhammad occupy "a commensurate place … in believers' hearts".[38] Muhammad lived the message contained in the Book. He is the Book's best interpreter. Knowledge of his life sheds essential light on the Book's meaning. If we can speak of Book-Prophet as a single unit, there is a sense in which the "divine" also dwelt in Muhammad. Muslims will certainly object to this on the same grounds that they reject the idea that God dwelt in Jesus *if a literal meaning is intended*. My suggestion is that what we are describing is spiritual experience, so that all the language we use is metaphorical not literal.

If, as a Christian, I am able to accept that God spoke through Muhammad and through Muhammad's Book, does this mean that God speaks to me through the Prophet-Book revelation? Some Christians accept Muhammad as a genuine prophet but argue that Muhammad's message was intended for the non-Christian world.[39] I do not have a problem accepting that God spoke through Muhammad after speaking through Jesus. The Gospel says that the Holy Spirit will lead us into all truth (John 16: 13). The creeds that some Christians recite were written after the time of Jesus, as were the books of the New Testament. God continues to speak to us through saints, too. Following Jones, I can affirm that the self-revelation of God in Jesus "is in every way adequate to human need." I agree with Jones that it is "distinctive," that "there can be no uncertainty about the quality of the life revealed" yet I also agree with him that we "cannot claim that God" in "Jesus in exhaustively revealed". We cannot limit God, claiming that His "Word" exhausted itself in Jesus. God still speaks. I believe that God spoke through Muhammad and through Muhammad's Book. Jesus, for me, represents the defining paradigm of divine love in action. Muhammad, for me, adds some detail to the demand to order the whole of society so that human action harmonizes with God's will, upholding justice, treating all people with equity, alleviating poverty and suffering, ending exploitation and the elevation of profit and power over the quality of life. Some Sufi orders have distinguished histories of humanitarian and philanthropic service and of ordering their communities so that economic justice is achieved. Sufi saints usually live as married men and women, so they show those of us with families and jobs in the world that we can achieve harmony with God in the midst of human society. Rabia, though,

[38] Bennett 2001:227.

[39] This was the position adopted by Paul of Antioch (1140-80) in his Letter to a Muslim; see Bennett 2008:107-8

remained celibate. Many Christian saints were celibate.[40] They lived lives isolated from the world and so teach us little about what we might call the external aspects of living in harmony with God's will. Like Jesus, they teach us more about the inner life of faith. The "officially recognized" saint that has most attracted my interest is Francis of Assisi, yet he wrote such a strict rule for his community that it was modified before the Church would sanction it. As inspirational as his life is, which, of course, is also instructive for Christian-Muslim dialogue, his example does not help us to put food on the table, to pursue a career in the workaday world of family and marriage or to fulfil our responsibilities within the wider society towards the body politic, encouraging good governance and global responsibility.

I argue that, "If neither Muslims nor Christians insist on the absolute nature of their doctrinal articulations, movement towards God and away from either of our formulations takes place".[41] By insisting that the language we use to describe the most intimate, transforming aspects of the divine-human relationship exhausts everything that can be said or is completely comprehensive and adequate, we elevate doctrine above spiritual experience. Doctrines are essentially human efforts to describe what transcends our finite natures. This experience cannot be fully comprehended or rendered into language. By elevating our doctrines above experience, we lift the human above the divine. This might be *shirk* or the false attribution of a partner to God. The lives of saints who, following Jesus' path, shone with God's presence and goodness, indicate that we also can experience what they experienced. The lives of those, who achieved sainthood in Islam by imitating Muhammad's example, show us that intimacy with God and selfless service are real, achievable goals. Of course, this depends on accepting that Sufi saints can attain communion with God; some Christians argue that even as great a Sufi as al-Ghazali could only seek God, and that, without faith in Jesus, he did not find God.[42] Does an examination of sainthood in Islam and Christianity, then, establish any common ground that can reduce the Christian-Muslim divide on Jesus as God-Incarnate? I suggest an affirmative answer, provided that, when we speak of a divine indwelling with reference to Jesus or to the Sufi saints, we are affirming that what people experienced was a profound intimacy with God, which even the language of "indwelling" and "Incarnation" only provisionally

---

[40] This refers to the official Roman Catholic and Orthodox list of saints. Given the expense involved in promoting the cause of a candidate for canonization and the resources of religious orders to do so, a disproportionate number of "saints" have been monks and nuns.
[41] Bennett 2008:216.
[42] For example, Zwemer (1920) described al-Ghazali as a Muslim "seeker after God" adding that "No one can read the story of Al-Ghazali s life, so near and yet so far from the Kingdom of God, so eager to enter and yet always groping for the doorway, without fervently wishing that Al-Ghazali could have met a true ambassador of Christ" (12). Jones argued that what matters is not the Name but "but the experience of His redemptive work in our hearts and lives (80) so a Muslim can be saved without having named the name of Jesus.

describes. The hymn, "None of Self and All of Thee" expresses, for me, the aim of Christians and of Muslims, who set out to imitate the pioneer of their respective faiths and of those who have replicated this experience:

Higher than the highest heaven,
Deeper than the deepest sea,
Lord, Thy love at last has conquered:
"*None* of self, and *all* of Thee."
None of self, and *all* of Thee,
None of self, and *all* of Thee,
Lord, Thy love at last has conquered:
"*None* of self, and *all* of Thee." [43]

If these sentiments are blasphemous, so be it. The hymn is based on John 3: 30. Jones suggested that if, when we use the God-language of Jesus in dialogue with Muslims, we explain that this is an "attempt" to describe "our apprehension of the redemptive operation of God's Spirit in our lives within us," while this "might still seem unacceptable" to them, they may also "see that it is no longer unreasonable and certainly not blasphemous".[44]

---

[43] Arranged by Theodore Monod. Public domain available at: http://library.timelesstruths.org/music/None_of_Self_and_All_of_Thee/ accessed on 08/01/10

[44] Jones 1938:93.

Matam and emerging Vitality: Community, Ritual, and Commemoration in a South Asian Muslim Sect

Mary Kay McVicker

Mary Kay McVicker is Director of the Asian Institute of Intercultural Studies, India

Introduction

Matam calls the faithful to recount passionate narratives in the battle at Karbala. This vibrant chest-beating rhythm where the faithful remember the life of Hussain and companions, his family, and important Islamic figures who fought for the family of Islam illustrates one of the many multisensory communication[1] elements that express the Muharram rituals of the Dawoodi Bohra community. While diverse historical traditions and unique cultures created a rich veneer for Islam throughout South Asia,[2] Islam, observed in the Dawoodi Bohra community, reflects its Fatimid history,[3] its remnants of Yemeni culture, and its Nargees Brahmin beginnings in the Indian states of Gujarat and Rajasthan.

The premise of this paper is the community life, ritual, and commemorations of Islamic figures through the multisensory communication elements not only shape the women of the Dawoodi Bohra community but its impact offers fresh perspective for reflection on Jesus and the Incarnation. Rather than examining the theological concept from a primarily abstract view, the unfolding discoveries describe the immense importance of the experiential dimensions in the participants' understanding and engagement. The contextual observations in this community underline the physical, psychological, social, emotional as well as soteriological factors present and emerging in the lives of the women, similarly for the men also, through the Muharram ritual. As a methodological means to

---

[1] Anthropologist Ruth Finnegan's exhaustive exploratory volume on communicating inspires the adoption of the term multisensory communication that will be discussed further in the paper and describes communicating as humans calling on gestures, sounds, writing, images, material objects, bodily contacts with its interaction and mutual influence and activating our voices, touches, movements, and emotions shared with others and using pictorial displays, graphics, and artefacts to inter-connect over space and time. See Finnegan 2002:6.

[2] For diverse expressions of observed Islam, see Asani 1996 and Ahmad and Reifeld 2004.

[3] The current *da'i* has prioritized the strengthening of its Fatimid heritage which can be seen through his support of Fatimid architecture throughout the globe. See Abdulhussein 2001.

unpack this topic, I rely on a qualitative research approach where I engage in "active listening."[4]

To understand my own experience of Jesus the Messiah and the Incarnation, as a follower of Christ,[5] I begin by listening to the community who opened the door to my research where I sought to discover the impact of multisensory communication in the lives of the women and families.[6] In this anthropological reflection, I become a participant observer at community rituals and converse with the Dawoodi Bohra women to learn their perspective.[7] At the same time I reflectively inquire, how observing, participating with, and listening to the Dawoodi Bohra community inform my own experience of Jesus the Word who became flesh and of Jesus who, in fulfilment of the prophet Isaiah, was called Immanuel, meaning God with us. I respond by noting the emerging discoveries I observe particularly among the Dawoodi Bohra women, and then I query how the discoveries provoke my experience, perspective, and communication of the revelation of Jesus, Immanuel.

The Community Life

The Dawoodi Bohra community belongs to India's minority Shi`i sects in Sunni majority India. Of the two larger sects, Ithna Ashari (known as Imami or

---

[4] Holstein and Gubrium 1995 articulate an approach based on relationship and constant mutual sharing that seeks to balance the what (content) and the how (process that concentrates on the respondent).

[5] I do not presume that my view is unbiased, yet to conduct this anthropological exploration seeking to be an objective researcher, the main requirement was absolute vulnerability and transparency. In the process I found that people, who either welcomed me to participate with them (even sharing food together at the family *thal*, not expected of non-community or even non-family members) or in conversation, may not be satisfied with answering my questions but are intent to learn my views (including the leader of the local community when I sought his permission to conduct research he required to know my perspective of the sect so I explained why I chose the community as well as the assurance of the demonstration of being a peace-loving people). Not uncommon was meeting women who insisted on first interviewing me. When fully satisfied with who I was and my purpose and intention, they opened the door wide and some even became advocates of the research.

[6] For further exploration of the dynamic communication spheres and multisensory communication, see McVicker 2007. This paper focuses primarily on reflections among the Dawoodi Bohra women as my gender gives me privilege to enter the women's world. Yet as Islamic historian Kamran Aghaie reveals, in his impressive collection of Karbala ethnographic essays, these gender dynamics are relevant to both the women and the men (2005:45-63), which can also be observed today.

[7] The methodology I employed for this paper draws from that research and relied on participant observation in community rituals, life stories, informal conversations based on structured questionnaires, and library research. I conducted the field community research in 2005-2006 which was my primary concentration with this particular sect, and have lived and been among various South Asian Muslim communities for more than twenty years.

Twelver) and Isma`ili, the Dawoodi Bohra follow the latter as Tayyibi Musta`li Isma`ili Shi`i. As followers of Musta`li, they await the return of the 21st hidden *imam* who is represented by the *da`i al-mutlaq*, the present day leader; known as the Syedna or his title, His Holiness; and affectionately referred to by the community as *aqa moala*, meaning the respected, benevolent master. The *da`i al-mutlaq* presides over all spiritual matters[8] in a well-organized religious system and guides the community in temporal matters.

More than one million people, the community extends around the globe with the largest population in Mumbai and concentrated in western India as well as key cities across India, Pakistan, Sri Lanka, East Africa and beyond. The Dawoodi Bohras speak Gujarati influenced by regional dialects, yet the formal language of the community is Lisan al-dawat, an Arabised Gujarati. Bohras are multi-lingual, essential for their occupation as traders, the meaning of Bohra.

Like all of their imams and religious hierarchy, the Dawoodi Bohra descend from Fatima the daughter of prophet Muhammad, and follow the Fatimid school of jurisprudence. "*Walayah* (love and devotion) for Allah, the Prophets, the *imam*, and *da`i* is the first and most important of the seven pillars."[9] A distinctive feature of the community, that expresses the priority of this first pillar, is their ritual calendar.[10] The calendar is based on the Fatimid lunar calendar that sets the number of days for each month that is normally two to three days ahead of the other Muslim communities. Every home and business keeps a copy of this wall calendar. It informs the dates and prayer timings, and each day states the name and details of the Islamic figure(s), who is remembered.[11]

The Fatimid lunar calendar begins with the month of Muharram, devoted to the commemoration of the battle of Karbala. The 10th day called Ashura is the most solemn, important observance of the ritual calendar for Shi`ites. Hussain and the martyrs are remembered for their courage. He led his followers into battle to fight Yazid. Though far outnumbered, Hussain and his 72 companions fell by the sword that day.[12]

---

[8] The *da`i al-mutlaq* developed a policy in order to make uniform community ritual practices and in particular to prioritise adherence to Islamic orthopraxy.

[9] Abdulhussein 2005; and an additional pillar, '*taharah* (purity and cleanliness),' both pillars are not found in the Sunni tradition.

[10] For a further discussion and its significance in the women's ritual life in the community, see Ghadially 2003b.

[11] The Dawoodi Bohra leads the way in virtual community where the calendar has a prominent role. Sites provide the ritual calendric information in detail. Mumineen.org boasts the "official" website of the community that includes reports of His Holiness' itinerary often accompanied by colourful photography describing recent ritual events. In the community's trend toward modernisation, advanced technology not only provides pertinent information for community members but also offers official services required for rituals, available online.

[12] See Yusuf, 2009 for a Dawoodi Bohra narrative on the day of Ashura.

The Dawoodi Bohra women actively engage in *walayah* to remember the saints through their devotion. They honour the *panjatan pak*, translated the holy five, referring to the prophet Muhammad, Fatima, Ali, and their two sons Hassan and Hussain. They lament Hussain and his companions and grieve with the women who suffered the loss of their kin at Karbala as though it was yesterday. They express loyalty to and affection for the *da`is* and others who have struggled for the survival and honour of the Dawoodi Bohra community.

The Ritual

The ritual in the Dawoodi Bohra community is fundamental and a primary part of the women's lives. Ritual practices guide her through the lifecycle, both for her and her family.[13] And her religious activities revolve around the ritual. In particular, the Muharram ritual energizes and invigorates the community as at no other time.[14] The first ten days of the month of Muharram culminates at the Ashura event. It is this energy that infuses the calendrical rituals throughout the year and relives this event on a regular basis through the multisensory communication elements reflective of the Karbala narrative. In the Ashura ritual, the *matam*[15]- using the right hand and forearm to beat the left side of the chest with one's flattened hand in a rhythmic manner, in unison with the other participants - for both women, and men, form the foundational element to participate in the sacred event, yet it does not stand alone for numerous multi-sensory communication elements create primary experiential dimensions in their lives.

Finnegan's multiple modes of human connectedness[16] provide a theoretical framework to observe the multisensory communication in the rituals of the Dawoodi Bohra women. These interconnecting multiple modes of

---

[13] For an overview of the rituals of Dawoodi Bohra life, see Blank 2001:53-81.

[14] Ghadially 2005:187.

[15] Generally the term *matam* can mean a funeral lamentation. While many Shi`ites refer to it for observances performed during Muharram to honour Hussain and the martyrs at Karbala, a Shi`ite from Hyderabad, India captured the devotion of the event, 'the Qur'an tells us to love *Ahl-e Bayt*, and *matam* shows our love for them.' See Pinault 1992: 99, 101. *Ahl al-bayat* refers to the 'people of the household,' considered the Prophet's family, to whom the Dawoodi Bohra share a sense of loyalty with the pan-Islamic community.

[16] Various disciplines offer descriptions, analysis, and considerations of the multiple factors that influence the human communication process including Don Smith's twelve signal systems which examines each signal as a function in culture that may be used and understood differently in each culture and Allan Canfield's symbolic inter-actionist perspective that identifies key factors effecting non-verbal communication; see Smith 1992 p. 144 ff. and Canfield 2002 respectively. While Finnegan's theory employs similar categories and processes, she shifts, or balances, the focus from the modes, systems, and factors to call attention to - using Birdwhitsell's approach to communication - the "active dimension of human interconnectedness" in Finnegan 2002:6ff.; also see Birdwhistell 1968:25-26.

communication describe the vast, elaborate multisensory activity in the ritual[17] that, through affect resonance in an active dimension, can trigger understanding. The elements of multi-sensory communication to observe[18] are the bodily senses, body movements and gestures, the affect or emotion, artifacts, and space. Time and social factors also contribute to the multisensory communication. The multisensory communication elements become the identifiable markers that are both intricate to the ritual and the community as well as pertinent to understand the identity and communication of the women and their community.

Schore's attachment theory[19] then provides a framework for multisensory communication to analyse the affect resonance that the women experience in the midst of the Muharram ritual through the active dimension of the multisensory communication. As humans connect with one another - or objects or their environment - an affect resonance results through positive socio-emotional or bodily sensations; when the negative sensation is communicated a disconnection occurs. If the other person(s) responds with a positive sensation and resonance occurs, the two regulate each other through the connection; with repeated affect regulations including when 'dysregulations' are repaired, multiple connections form between the persons which creates a secure attachment. As attachment takes place - or when absent, the opposite occurs - a safe haven evolves, mutuality is created, and the participants are reciprocally active or 'tuned into one another.' This is the process of interconnectedness where a place forms through multiple connections with the other(s), objects, or environment and gives rise to understanding. And ongoing attachments between people create a secure attachment where a sense of belonging emerges and identity is reinforced. Affect resonance, its multiple connections, and the process, reveal the importance of the multisensory activity in the women's lives and its physical, psychological, social, emotional, and soteriological impact emerges through this ritual experience.[20]

The Dawoodi Bohra women participate in Muharram rituals, both in public and private spaces. During the first ten days of Muharram, which climax at Ashura, the women join the men at the mosque in a passive role for the daily *wa'az*, sermon and *majlis*, dirge; while the men occupy the main floor and lead the event, the women are present on the upper floor(s) that looks onto the main

---

[17] Schubel asserts how ritual 'provides an expression of religious piety that is apprehensible to all of the senses,' 1993:1.

[18] A research instrument was designed to identify the multisensory elements and its affect resonance can be found in McVicker 2007:108-117.

[19] Affective neuro-scientist Allan N. Schore provides an extensive study of attachment that demonstrates how the formation of the human brain and its structure is responsible for human attachment, and in another ground-breaking work, Muslim-Christian relations scholar Evelyne A. Reisacher reveals its significance for inter-cultural relations; see Schore, 1994 and its sequel and Reisacher 2001 respectively.

[20] Analysis of the affect resonance and attachment is beyond the scope of this paper. Rather it acknowledges the methodology used for the observations and factors discussed. See McVicker 2007 for further analysis.

floor behind a short decorative lattice. Like every Bohra, the women long to join the Syedna - and many do - wherever he holds his annual *majalis*, plural for dirge - in order to be close to him.[21] While the men's experience of Muharram is in the mosque as well as at the stalls that they set up in the market to give water and refreshment for the faithful called *sabils*, the women are in semi-public places including the mosque and community halls or in the private space of homes. This includes an initial feast - with potentially 52 dishes in honour of the current 52nd *da`I* - in the home with family members around the *thal* where the food is shared on the eve of Muharram called *phele rath*, and immediately following Ashura the women conduct *majalis*.

Commemorating the Heroes of the Faith

In post-Ashura, the Muharram theme continues as the Dawoodi Bohra women commemorate the heroes of the faith. The women's *majalis* commences after Ashura for 40 days of lamentation and encouraged by the *dawat* - the modern day Bohra clergy - to hold this important daily event in the mosque though historically women met in homes.[22] Important Islamic figures are remembered including the *panjatan pak* in their struggle for Islam to be established and founded by Muhammad, the last of the *panjatan pak* Hussain in the battle at Karbala, and the *da`is* who have struggle for the Dawoodi Bohra community culminating with the *da`i al-mutlaq* today.

On the 36th day of the *majalis*, I followed my hostess for a short walk to the mosque. Women, clad in *rida*, women's traditional attire, that includes a long skirt, cape, and bonnet to cover the hair, neck, and chest in colourful fabrics with embroidery and lace designs, bustled from both directions of the small lane and made their way up the clean marble steps to the area's Dawoodi Bohra mosque for the evening women-only *majlis* to commemorate the heroes of the faith. At the top of the steps, my friend - whose husband visited the clergy for that locality called the *amil* earlier in the day to secure my invitation to join the event - and I quickly removed our sandals along with the others and entered the majestic main floor that was already half-packed with women. The white marble mosque with its gleaming interior as well as the refreshing breeze and gleaming sun that began to set added to the buzz of whispering voices and excitement that filled the room

---

[21] Even if they are not able to travel to the international city of the Syedna, the community relays his annual *majalis* live to Bohra centres all over the world so that all members can participate with him.

[22] Numerous channels provide expression for commemoration including aroma. 'We always burn the incense, the *bukhur*, during the 40 days of Muharram.... In cleaning and preparing the home for the ritual, the *bukhur* will be burned. When it is burned, it is like a perfume. It gives a very good smell. From that smell we connect. The *bukhur* connects to a holy thing. For example, I burn incense every Friday in my home. It is a good scent, and I feel it in my home. This scent is used only by our community, from our Yemeni heritage. Our own people make it and sell it.' Amina 2006b.

as women quickly found a place to sit on the floor. The mosque's sparse ornaments reflected the community's devotion with the *bismillah* praising God and names of the *panjatan pak* revering the prophet and his family etched in beautiful Arabic on the wall, a life-sized photo of the Syedna on the opposite wall, and a diamond-like chandelier in the shape of his *topi*, or ornamental hat. Dressed in nearly every pastel shade, the women each in *rida* looked like a moving rainbow.

Just after 5 pm the cantors began as women, some even with small children in tow, continued to arrive, the *majlis'* daily timing made it accessible for all women to participate as their household responsibilities were completed. While part of the expansive hall remained unused, we sat close to each other with legs tucked under the body. While others might have felt the fatigue of the taxing posture, at least for my untrained body, accustomed to a crossed legged position, no complaint was heard as the disciplined community etiquette expressed devotion for Hussain and the heroes of the faith. The shared, unspoken physical pain with fellow worshippers during the Muharram rituals relived the tragedy and created a sense of connection with one another that I too felt, even as a guest.

As the cluster of ten or so women cantors recited the first narrative, the participants joined in with slow *matam* beating our chest in unison. Despite the difficulty of the formal language even for the most learned women (though Dawoodi Bohra are women nearly 100 percent literate), the momentum kept growing as the women embodied each narrative. Regardless of full comprehension, we consistently repeated the chorus or phrases expressing grief with Sakina for the loss of her father Hussain. Passionately beating one's chest in varying degrees, tears began to spill as weeping broke out across the room as though we were reliving Sakina's tragedy-her father, the family, his companions, and the dreams for victory destroyed. The anguish wailing of the recitation as we echoed the cantors, the thumping chests in crescendo, and sniffling that moved into grievous unquenchable weeping as though mourning side-by-side with Sakina filled the hall. The recitation resounded with the women's voices at Karbala as the cantors led the next one in honour of Fatima. While the wailing dissipated, a strong, unified *matam* accompanied the sense of loyalty and devotion focused toward Fatima, a part of the *panjatan pak*. The *matam* kept growing stronger, sounding like a herd of elephants passing on the lane, accompanied by an assertive chanting in tandem with the cantors, "*Ma Fatima*!" as though exclaiming that we are the daughters of Fatima.

The mood shifted slightly as the third *da`i* was remembered. We continued to beat our chest and honour the third Musta`li *da`i* in Yemen, named Hatim Shamsuddin ibn Ibrahim al-Hamidi, who played a fundamental part in supporting the 21st hidden *imam*. In the meantime, open coconuts circled around the room, so each one of us shared a small piece. The coconut, brought by one or two women who had held a special occasion, symbolised a token of blessing for the one giving and for the one receiving.

The event climaxed when the cantors led to the finale. A eulogy for the *da`i al-mutlaq* affirmed the centrality of his leadership to the life of the community. As all of us rose to our feet, many of the women joined the cantors in the chorus, and it began to feel like the room was moving as the volume swelled. Nearly all of the women chimed into the closing section, 'may you have a 1000 more years, for the *da`i al-mutlaq*.' We returned to the sitting position and the *majlis* was over, greeting one another informally. We joined the surge to the front to greet the *amil's* mother who presided over the event and seated next to the cantors. I pushed my way forward with the rest as my hostess gave me a final nudge to reach the respected leader. As I greeted her in the traditional Bohra *salaam*, the community hand kissing gesture, she responded by inquiring about me, invited me to come tomorrow, and insisted that I wear the *rida* next time.

Shoulder to shoulder with the other women, we moved toward the exit, and when we reached the door a small group of women handed each participant a brightly coloured box of Mala's strawberry jam. In an affectionate expression of devotion toward the 3rd *da`i*, the women prepared the jam on his designated remembrance day. We found our shoes and while descending the steps we discovered that the women travelled from all parts of the city, even where they had their own mosque, in order to take part in and join the larger group of the faithful for the event.

Emergence from the Ritual

The participation in the Muharram ritual moves this story of Karbala from the abstract to the narrative and to experiencing it today. From the ritual expressions and multi-ensory interconnections of the experience emerges a concrete understanding that impacts on daily life. The ritual enables people to gain a new perspective. Realising through the acting out of the stories, immersing oneself in the suffering of the *ahl al-bayat*, grieving with the women of Karbala, honouring important Islamic figures, in particular the *da`i al-mutlaq*, Dawoodi Bohra women find strength for their own lives. In addition to participant observation including the above, listening to the Dawoodi Bohra women's reflections informs what physical, psychological, social, emotional, and soteriological factors emerge through the *matam* and its Muharram rituals. The women describe their experience thus:

> First of all, it is the mind concentrating and the physical activity. The physical activity is *matam*. In unison, we beat our chest. We weep. You do not need to pretend, tears just come automatically. That is the physical activity, and mentally you are involved in listening to whatever suffering that he [Hussain] has gone through and listening to all of the things.[23]

---

[23] Amina 2005.

PHYSICAL

In the lives of today's Dawoodi Bohra women, the physical factors in the rituals provide a crucial foundation to their experience. Whereas Shi`i sects in South Asia[24] and the globe[25] use artefacts or instruments to relive the narrative, the Dawoodi Bohra woman uses her body. In contrast to the other sects, including the majority Ithna Ashari where physical artefacts, parades or processions, and self-immolation play crucial roles in performing Muharram rituals, these traditions are mostly absent from the Dawoodi Bohra experience. Rather, the Dawoodi Bohra women, like the men, rely on their bodies and emotions in acts of devotion to the *panjatan pak* and the important Islamic figures who have fought or died for Islam.[26]

Their Muharram experience is not restricted to an annual procession nor reserved for access to particular instruments in contrast to the other Shi`i communities, but takes place in the familiar space of homes, the community, and the mosque and repeated with their bodies throughout the year. They use daily items to express their devotion so that it is integrated into ther lives. *Matam,* for the Dawoodi Bohra, is repeated in nearly every ritual practice and religious activity of the women. *Matam* becomes a primary vehicle to demonstrate their devotion especially at celebratory events. Capturing the excitement from the physical participation of the narrative, one woman reflects:

> When everyone is there together, the excitement is real. I don't know much, but we remember what Imam Hussain went through and the sacrifice that he gave. We remember the events of his life. This is the passion for doing *matam* when you are at the mosque. The men and the ladies do it with vigour. It is not merely sitting and doing the action. No, it is the actual beating our hearts and doing it with a loud noise. We beat our hearts and call out his name, "*Ya Hussain.*" We honour his name. We call out the names of his whole family, all those who have been martyred. We call out all the names of the martyrs.27

Commenting on if Muharram helps to fulfil one's identity as a Dawoodi Bohra,' she exclaimed, 'As a human being!'[28] *Matam,* reciting in unison the names of the honoured, with calligraphic reminders of the *ahl al-bayat*, the aroma of *bukhur,* and meals around the *thal,* provides channels for her to embody

---

[24] See Pinault 1992 and D'Souza 1998.

[25] See Flaskerud 2005.

[26] Ethnographer Jonah Blank observed the impact of *matam* at Ashura particularly among men from the upcoming generation and secularists who thought the 'arcane language' of the sermon difficult to understand, showed preference for the 'gut-level pull of a physical display' rather than 'long-winded oratory,' felt 'bored by the speechifying,' and enjoyed 'the opportunity to demonstrate their faith with actions rather than words' so *matam* was 'a welcome break from the liturgy.' See Blank, 2001:91.

[27] Fatima 2005.

[28] Amina 2006a.

Islam as a way of life. Her bodily senses and emotions are triggered and affirmed through repeated daily connections that began at a very early age.

PSYCHOLOGICAL

The emerging physical factors in the Muharram ritual create an environment to consider their psychological impact. The Dawoodi Bohra woman comes with burdens that she is facing in life. She listens to or recites the women's experiences at Karbala. As she participates in the physical narrative, she is able to see her own burdens in light of what the revered women on the *panjatan pak* faced. It is an invitation for her to engage in the suffering of another, beyond herself. Her experiential re-enactment of the Karbala event enables her to live-it so intensely. Entering the lives of the Karbala women, she experiences their sacrifice. In this process she releases her burden. And she finds relief from the mental anguish of her burdens:

> For me personally I am involved totally [in Muharram]. I always pray for the well-being of my family, my children, my husband, and my friends for all the areas of their life including health and finances. I always think that my prayer will be heard at this time because it is the most auspicious day of the year. If my prayer is not heard this day, then when will my prayers be heard? That is how I feel. Most of the time I am praying prayers rather than the *namaaz*-ritual prayer. The *namaaz* is a part of it but not the whole time. When we remember the martyrdom of Imam Hussain at that time I am remembering so many things that happened to me and also my family.... So I am automatically crying and praying to Allah for all of these things. We remember you Imam Hussain. Then afterwards we can forget all of these difficult times. We feel better and that everything turns out to be good for good. We feel like crying all of the time, yet we should be happy [she laughs intensely at the paradox].... It so happens that you get involved in such a way that you don't even know whether you cried or thought whether it is the mass congregation being together or the Imam Hussain's martyrdom or that it was because you remembered your own children and your own problems. So sometimes it is so difficult.... At that point then you think, I must put all of those things aside and let the bad things turn away. And then I can once again focus properly.[29]

SOCIAL

Three important social aspects emerging from the experiences of the Muharram rituals are social cohesion, the place of community impacting identity or belonging, and a support structure. Whether the women's *majlis* above, a mixed gender event like Ashura, or a celebratory ritual during the year, vigorously beating one's chest in unison with women and other community members in *matam* to remember the *panjatan pak* brings a sense of social cohesion among its participants. Also it affirms their belonging to the community as *matam* and

29 Amina 2006a.

numerous multisensory communication elements grant a distinctive identity. Recollecting the Ashura event, a young woman leader described her devotion to identify with Hussain at Karbala:

> That's why we forget everything. We go as a family and we only concentrate on that one thing, on Imam Hussain. Right from the time we get up in the morning. We forget our sleep. We forget our eating. We forget to drink. We give our total concentration.... It's the participation together that is most important.[30]

Participating in the Muharram rituals, the women chant in unison, beat their chest together in rhythm, weep together, let the tears pour down their faces, sway back in forth as they mourn with Fatima, and grieve for Sakina in the pain of losing her father. It is a process of being heard and being felt. This emerging sense of belonging and social cohesion also enables new learning.[31]

The Dawoodi Bohra women organise themselves to be actively involved in the ritual activities, adjusting the time to the women's schedule for the optimum number of women to be able to join. With three women groups for the community according to age, each one has officers, pays dues, and plans and hosts rituals. Participation with the other women at the rituals and the women's groups provides an acceptable channel for women to depart from her children and home, and join the group of women where she has support.

EMOTIONAL

Two primary factors describe the profound place of emotion that emerges from the women's participation in the ritual. First, the bodily re-enactment of the Karbala narrative creates a fundamental channel to express her devotion to important Islamic figures. In this process, she identifies with the family of Islam in an intimate way that as the stories are retold she enters the scene of the battle and its outcome. Through her emotions she experiences the Karbala tragedy and its martyrs and the grief of the women who have gone before her and identifies with the depth of their suffering. Secondly, taking it a step further, this channel provides a way to vent her own emotions in life: her pain, her grief, her sorrow and her anger. Through her emotions, the burdens in life find an outlet to freely vent everything. She cries with them. As the body participates, the emotion is vented. A feeling of hope arises.

---

[30] Khadijah 2005.

[31] Here is one reflection: Up to the 10th of Muharram, the story is told how it started. And why do we have to know? Otherwise we will not know many of the things which we have to follow in our daily life. It is apart of *gathering* that we can be informed about many things. The Dawoodi Bohra practices the prayer, the meditation, and telling about the ways to do things, not in an explicit way, but one that people can understand. See Amina 2006a.

While her own re-enactment of the narrative creates a channel to express her devotion and to share in the suffering that enables her to vent her own emotions, the evoking of these powerful emotions leads to spiritual impact.[32]

SOTERIOLOGICAL

The culmination of these factors embodies the faith of the Dawoodi Bohra women, her love and devotion for Allah, the prophets, the *imams*, and *da`is*. The centrality of the *da`i al-mutlaq* to Dawoodi Bohra faith, as the representative of the hidden *imam* who will return, forms the women's soteriological perspective.

First, her *walayah* and her piety demonstrated through participating in the ritual, giving food, and hosting ritual activities, describe her soteriological motivation. Second, her devotion also reflects her search for help and guidance from important Islamic figures. 'These religious figures are not only of historical significance but are living, spiritual entities whose presence and assistance can be evoked by various ritual activities.'[33] This is affirmed by the *da`i al-mutlaq* who encourages the faithful to express their sorrow and reveals how intercessory help is available. 'It is a time of sorrow of course. Syedna says at that time, you ask whatever you want-you wish. So you can fulfil your wishes *by* showing your sorrow.'[34] Finally, there is a deep longing to be close to the *da`i al-mutlaq*. His living presence is a reciprocal relationship for their *walayah*, a channel for help and guidance, and the model who guides them in mourning. When he is not present, his photo is always present as a reminder of the relationship. "For all Bohras-you can ask anyone, they will say 'he is our father'-Syedna is our father. He might not be my biological father, but he is my father. I want to be with my father."[35]

The integration of these factors reflects the multiple interconnections of the women's multisensory communication elements in their active dimension of the ritual. The resulting affect resonance produces fresh vitality in the women's lives. The performance of *matam* gives her hope for the future and grants strength for her daily life. This concrete perspective experienced in her body and lived out through her emotions triggers understanding of her faith. Repetition of the rituals through distinct multisensory communication elements during each event of the calendrical year affirms her identity and creates a sense of belonging.

Revelation

By listening to the Dawoodi Bohra women, I discovered the primary place of their revelation takes place in *walayah* where the body's participation,

[32] See D'Souza 1997 for the intense impact that the Muharram songs of lament have on the Shi`is of Hyderabad, India.
[33] Ghadially 2003a:312.
[34] Farzana 2006.
[35] Amina 2006a.

psychological concerns, social environment, affective intersection of one's life and the narratives at Karbala, and the soteriological devotion to Allah, the *panjatan pak* and the *da`is* meet. Since *walayah* provides the pathway toward paradise, its practical and regular expression explains the power of the ritual and the significance of *matam* that gives invitation and opportunity to show devotion to the *da`i al-mutlaq* by honouring Allah, the *panjatan pak* and the *da`is* in every aspect of their lives.

As I observed the Dawoodi Bohra's *walayah* and its ritual infused with multi-sensory communication as an integral part of embodying their faith by attainment and through expression I query, how do I experience and communicate my own faith?

As *walayah* is important to the Dawoodi Bohra, devotion to Jesus Christ is foremost in my faith and life in God. The expression of my love follows the pattern of David the prophet and passionate psalmist as I turn my worship to the Almighty God alone. My devotion does not focus on merit or demonstrating piety, but rather as a follower of Jesus, I seek to grow in relationship with God and submit everything to Him. In worship I thank Him for His remarkable gift in Jesus, for the message of eternal life, and for those who follow Him, for the gift of the Holy Spirit, who guides in all truth, fills with peace, and gives power to all who believe in Him. Though I am absolutely unworthy, the all-knowing God offered these, the greatest gifts of eternal life and the power of His Spirit, so I gladly accepted His gifts.

As illustrated in the description of my devotion, the perspective of my faith can easily remain, or at least be communicated, in the abstract. Yet the Dawoodi Bohra women and her community demonstrate that faith is experiential and must find tangible expressions.

My response to that challenge leads me back to our theme, Jesus and the Incarnation. Jesus the Messiah entered the life of the 1st century Palestinians as a craftsman, followed the rituals, and obeyed the requirements of the law including circumcision. His cultural experiences, social expectations, and religious activities including circumcision were significantly closer to the Dawoodi Bohra than my own. Yet He introduced a new way. Rather than being bound by the law, Jesus fulfilled it and gave a new commandment, love one another. He made a new covenant, the Lord's Supper. And he gave a new concept to live by, to wash one another's feet. Jesus lived and modeled the new way for his disciples to follow.

As Jesus invited people to follow and experience the new way, He demonstrated the importance of multisensory communication relating to people in their context. Living the new commandment to love one another, Jesus called others to do likewise.[36] In one example,[37] Jesus went to Simon the Pharisee's home to share a meal, and a woman knelt at his feet, kissed them repeatedly,

---

[36] John 13:34-35, Matthew 22:36-40; Mark 12:28-31.
[37] Luke 7:36-50.

bathed them with her own hair, and anointed them with oil. Seeing that Simon was appalled, Jesus told him a story about one small debtor and one large debtor whom the creditor forgave both. Jesus asked which one loved him more, and Simon said the one who had the greater debt cancelled. And Jesus affirmed his answer and then noted how his host had not brought water for his feet, nor greeted him with a kiss, nor anointed his head with oil. He said, yet this woman's sins are many but she will be forgiven because she expressed great love. In the midst of his socio-cultural surroundings, Jesus accepted the expression of devotion-with tangible expressions through her physical body, emotions and perhaps psychological cries not hindered by the social stigma. Rather respected through the acceptance by the other, forgave her sins, and honoured her initiative while using it and the story to rebuke and instruct the Pharisee and his guests.

Jesus' commandment to love one another as I have loved you, the new covenant expressed through 'the Lord's supper' with bread and wine to remember Jesus' body given and his blood shed, and the new concept to wash one another's feet as Jesus did engage the multisensory communication, call for participation, and trigger understanding. The experiential act of each one relives Jesus' message that calls for a fresh examination of one's own life-to love one another, to die to self and live in Christ, and to serve one another.

Conclusion

Her chest-beating hand in *matam,* throughout the calendrical year, affirms the cry of pain, summons help, and seeks hope. The Dawoodi Bohra women focus their *walayah* through bodily expressions, affective resonance, and social connections that leads to being close to the *da`i al-mutlaq*. This living representation of the hidden *imam* who is expected to return provides guidance, help, and soteriological hope for their lives. His living presence addresses the longing of humans to be close to the divine.

While anthropology and neuro-science provide the foundation for this study, the relevance and usage of multisensory communication and affective resonance cannot be overlooked in Islamic contexts. For the presence of Jesus to be comprehended, his followers must embody a 'theology of love'[38] with concrete expressions that can be experienced in the body, felt in a significant way, and embraced through meaningful relationships. There new vitality can emerge.

[38] Glasser 2008:138ff.

The Roles of Humanity and Jesus in the Sainthood of Ibn 'Arabi

David Emmanuel Singh

Introduction

Christians have experimented with different approaches to Islam. Muslims approaches to Christianity too have been more diverse than we think. The story of Christian-Muslim relations is not exhausted by the verbal/written discourses and physical conflicts/violence. Undoubtedly, polemical engagements and physical conflicts did happen but largely from contacts between 'exoteric' rather than 'esoteric' traditions. The latter being simply dismissed as 'heterodox' often did not get a real hearing and a chance to be an alternative. If one gave these traditions a hearing, one might find there a promise of an alternative means for thinking on Christian-Muslim relations.

According to S.J. Samartha, 'Through His incarnation in Jesus Christ, God has relativised Himself in history. Christian theologians should therefore ask themselves whether they are justified in absolutising in doctrine whom God had relativised in history.'[1] There is a serious philosophical problem here which needs to be addressed. In attempting to do a theology of Islam, one is compelled to ask: how can the Jesus of Nazareth continue to act beyond his time; and if the reality of this Jesus is indeed universal how can ordinary human beings rise above their creaturely limitations to respond to this Jesus? Rather than attempting to address these questions as part of the 'Christian' theology of religions, I propose an unconventional approach from within an esoteric Islamic tradition represented by one of the greatest Sufi (Muslim mystic) Islam has ever known, Ibn 'Arabi (1165-1240).[2]

I will first discuss Ibn 'Arabi's theory of humanity to show its prominent place in his philosophical system. It also explains, like Plato's idea of the Soul, why humanity, despite creaturely existence, possesses the capacity to relate to God, and to receive and grasp His knowledge. I will then examine the question of the person of Jesus and his role in the scheme of God as conceived within this system of thought. The underlying question is: how is Jesus different from the rest of humanity and particularly the Prophet Muhammad?

---

[1] Samartha 1987:16.

[2] Ibn 'Arabi was a Spanish-Arab mystic-philosopher (known to the Spanish philosopher Averroes; 1126-1198) and widely known throughout the Muslim world, for good reasons, as the *shaykh al-akbar* (the greatest Sufi master).

Ibn 'Arabi is a difficult writer to understand. Some of the difficulties in reading him arise from not only the language he wrote in (Arabic), his idiosyncratic use of it, and the esoteric nature of his discourse, but also to the fact that his ideas were revolutionary in the context of mainstream exoteric Islam. However, throughout, a spirit of ecumenicity characterizes his writings. Another difficulty arises from the fact that almost an impossible number of books/treatises have been attributed to him. He certainly did not write all of these and not all of them are extant or accessible to interested readers anyway. For the purpose of this paper, therefore, I have focused on a limited number of well-known primary and secondary sources.[3]

The Idea of 'Perfect Humanity'

In the works I have scanned, I see a mystic-philosopher for whom world humanity has a special place – not merely as 'slaves' (*'abd*) and creatures bound by culture, religion, language, time and space but all of these with the potential for spiritual perfection. Ibn 'Arabi's view of humanity stands in sharp contrast to the 'mainstream' Islamic view of man being fundamentally different in being and distant from the transcendent God. Ibn 'Arabi is a reconciler. He likes intractable contradictions in religious thinking but rather than seeing them as antitheses, he ingeniously attempts their reconciliation. Thus, for instance, humanity for him is not simply an entity of the 'sensible world' (to use the Platonic image) because each human is part of a spiritual 'reality of humanity' which embraces both God and His creation. Whereas humanity, as a physically localized entity, serves God as the *'abd*, the 'reality of humanity' transcends the exoteric sense of 'servanthood'. The saints (Muslim mystics) down through the centuries serve for him as the examples of the meeting of the opposites. Muhammad and Jesus were to him the greatest examples of perfect slavehood where both physical humanity and substantial unity with God (*jawhar*) were amply manifest.

This is revolutionary stuff. Ibn 'Arabi presents his arguments therefore in carefully selected Islamic imageries and a language that is deliberately complicated and layered. He piles these imageries one on top of the others but even obvious repetitions do not seem bothersome but instead serve the positive purpose of reinforcing his arguments. His world is dualistic in the Platonic sense; but rather than setting up an antithetical scheme, his conception of the supposed 'whole affair' embraces the spiritual and the physical. In his idealistic conception of the 'whole affair', thus, the divine becomes manifest in the differentiated world of humanity through 'the Perfect Manhood' (PM) of his supreme veneration, Muhammad and Jesus.

---

[3] Corbin 1998; Ibn 'Arabi 1911a, 1959 & 1960, 1980, 1987a, 1987b; Morris 1986a & 1986b; Nyberg 1919.

The term used for 'man' is *insan,* a Qur'anic term, referring normally to ordinary human beings.[4] A deliberate connection is therefore intended between the PM and 'man' arguably to explain two complementary processes: creation of beings bound in time and space and their return to the spiritual reality (as for instance denoted by the idea of *logos* or the Neoplatonic Soul or Intellect). This happens 'imaginally' (*khayal*) first and, then, in 'actuality' (after death). *Insan* thus becomes the locus in whom the process of the return to God occurs. In this conception of the whole affair, the PM is said to be the image of the invisible and transcendent God. God in Himself, in His essence, remains forever beyond the reach of the creation and ordinary humanity.

Hakim Tirmidhi's (c. 820-908) was a Muslim mystic from what is now northern Afghanistan. He was a major source of influence upon the Sufi thinkers after the 9th century. One of his works, *Sirat al-awliya',* is particularly well-known. Already, B. Radtke has argued for Tirmidhi's influence particularly on Ibn 'Arabi.[5] We know this also from Ibn 'Arabi's own engagements with Tirmidhi. In his writings, Ibn 'Arabi's discourses are often presented as answers to Tirmidhi's questions. One such question is, 'What is the crown of the King (*taj al-malik*)?' An interesting, though, rather abstract description of humanity emerges from the answer to this question. A number of metaphors are employed to illustrate a conceptual view of the creation and the appearance of humanity in it and the creative Divine Thought/Word before its actualization in the concrete universe. If one peels off the Islamic images, one observes, in this description, fundamental similarities with Neo-Platonist thinking which were absorbed in Islam through the Ishma'ili and Arab philosophies.

The first compound metaphor used is the 'crown of the king'. The 'crown' is a sign or symbol of kings. A king without the crown is no king. Likewise, Ibn 'Arabi argues, the entire creation is the sign of God. The creation as a whole (macrocosm) remains however 'non-conscious' without humanity. It finds its own fulfilment with the appearance of humanity. The creation needs a conscious being to comprehend itself and the Creator who has given it being.

The second metaphor is used then to confirm the first point about the role of humanity in the created realm but more importantly to illustrate the Creator-creation-humanity relations. These are the 'writing' or the 'edict'. A piece of writing or an edict of the king is worthless without the king's signature. Likewise, the creation without humanity is meaningless. It is not by accident however that humanity is the real 'crown' of the 'king' or the 'signature' or 'seal' on the divine 'edict'. Through the capacity for the Creator and its knowledge, humanity in the world of material creation is potentially the image of God. The creation is derived from the Creator but humanity fulfils its potential by returning the knowledge and praise of the creation back to the Creator. In possessing this capacity, humanity is unique.

---

[4] See Surah 76.

[5] Radtke 1989.

This idea of the special connection between the Creator and humanity therefore lends itself to the notion of the Creator/God being the Perfect Man (PM). These metaphors also work to illustrate the nature of the PM. Before the creation comes into being ('edict' or 'writing'), it exists as Thought or Word. However, just as the piece of writing or edict remains nothing until it is personally owned through the signature of the owner or crowned by his personal authentication, the Thought or the Word remains nothing until sealed by the personal name of the owner. The edict is effective only when the signature is put on it, the signature 'includes' the content of the edict. The PM is conceived to be the signature of God on the writing of the Existence. Since the PM authenticates and actualizes the 'edict', he is said to encompass it all. Thus, the PM is himself the 'crown' of the king. In the same way, the writing of an edict by the King himself presupposes its preconception in the King's Thought, who in intending to actualize the edict, thus conceived, actually puts his signature on the thought of an edict. The signature is therefore the main thing. The edict in differentiation or existential actuality follows the intention of the author who gives the finality to it by 'objectifying' the intention through the final signature.

Ibn 'Arabi couches his revolutionary concept of God as the PM by using Qur'anic images. The images of the crown, writing and edict are Qur'anic but impersonal. Since, 'thought' and 'knowledge' are thought to be central to his view as much as being or 'ontology', he also uses some other 'personal images' from the Qur'an to speak of the relationship between humanity and God. Muhammad and Jesus are right at the heart of this. *Insha' al-dawa'ir* is one of Ibn 'Arabi's shorter treatises. The central focus of the treatise is the doctrine of what he called, 'the Third Entity' (*al-shay' al-thalith*). Here, he appears to be suggesting that divine and human affairs belong to two different orders – one is the Thing or Entity itself (as the reality or the cause) and the other is the effect. But, a closer look reveals that for lbn 'Arabi the traditional distinction between the human and God in this sense cannot be maintained in an absolute and strictly dualistic sense. The divine and the human are closer than traditional dogmatics would permit. There is an ontological connection which explains the human capacity for grasping the revelation and the human desire or longing for God. This accords a very special position to humanity among all of God's creatures on earth. The evidence for this is offered through an extremely subtle and idealistic means i.e. by arguing in favour of the idea of a correspondence between humanity and the Creator. The idea is explained in terms of our 'Third Entity' assumed to be the interface between two poles of the 'Entire Affair'. On the one end of the pole is Being or God-in-Himself and on the other end is the physical universe. God who brings this universe into being is the Third Entity (identical to the notion of the PM). He is outwardly undifferentiated but contains the universe in a potential state of will, intention, and thought. On the side of the universe, the being that corresponds with the Third Entity as its 'image' is humanity. The correspondence with the Third Entity is fundamentally (when viewed from within the perspective of time and space) epistemic, i.e. exhibited in the capacity for grasping the divine knowledge personified in the notions of the Third Entity or the PM.

This revolutionary view is however again expressed differently and repeatedly in traditional terms. Thus, an example of the PM is sometimes is said to be Adam, the first man. Another example is the Prophet Muhammad and yet another example is Jesus. When speaking of Adam, Muhammad or Jesus, Ibn 'Arabi is not thinking of mortal embodied beings but of the incorporeal being of the Third Entity, the Creator God, the PM as discussed above. These are mere conditioned names of the very form of God which incorporates all of existence like a hidden treasure.

The Doctrine of Jesus

The idea of the Third Entity unlike that of the PM is not apparently anthropocentric. It does not clarify how Muhammad or Jesus relates to this Entity. A useful line of thought is provided by another of Ibn 'Arabi's works, *Shajarat al-kawn* where he speaks of Muhammad having two sides to him: the human prophet and the 'reality' behind it. He calls the latter 'the Muhammadan Reality' or 'the Reality of Muhammad'. A. Jeffrey who translated this treatise suggests that this work may be Ibn 'Arabi's contribution to raising Muhammad's status above the other prophets in a manner similar to the Christian doctrine of the *logos*. Muslim exegetes, traditionalists, popular preachers, story tellers and Sufis have in their own way contributed to the growth of the Prophet's veneration. Jeffrey attributes the motive for this to the desire 'to interpret the significance of their prophet as unique not only in his own community but also in cosmic history,' and of course to raise the status of Muhammad higher than the Qur'anic Jesus.

There is no question that Ibn 'Arabi thinks of the Reality of Muhammad to be ontologically prior to Adam: 'Muhammad was a prophet when Adam was between water and clay.' 'Adam was created in the form of his name for his name is Muhammad.' There is therefore no competition from Adam. It is not the Adam whom the angels worship but the Reality of Muhammad which is the principal source of Adam's origin. It is this Reality and not Adam that is greeted by the angels as they fall down 'doing obeisance' and saying, '…the possessor of the Throne forever.' Muhammad's pre-existence is implied. In expounding Muhammadan pre-existence, Ibn 'Arabi also speaks of what he calls the 'light of Muhammad'. This light is another image of his notion of the Third Entity. It is to him the very source of every light of knowledge. This Light or Reality of Muhammad is first in 'thought' [as the Word] but last in 'actuality' [as the seal of the prophets]'.

The same could be said of Jesus; but the description of Jesus is significantly different. Jesus is presented by Ibn 'Arabi, especially in his *Fusus al-Hikam,* as an exceptional instance of the work of God:

> From the water of Mary or from the breath of Gabriel, in the form of a mortal fashioned of clay, the Spirit came into existence in an essence purged of nature's taint, which is called *sijjin*. Because of this, his sojourn was prolonged, enduring, by degree, more than a thousand years. A Spirit from none other than God, so that he might raise the dead and bring forth birds from the clay. And became worthy to be associated with his Lord, by which he exerted great influence, both high and low. God purified him in body and made him transcendent in the Spirit, making him like Himself in creating.[6]

Here, Ibn 'Arabi appears to be suggesting that existence is a product of interaction between the Spirit (God) and the Nature (matter). The language of engendering duality is clearly typically concrete and biological. If the Spirit is the father of the universe and the human (macrocosm and microcosm) then one must suppose the existence of a mother. Something called 'Nature' is supposed by him to be the mother. In the 'creation' of Jesus for example, Mary denotes the Nature and the Angel Gabriel signifies the Spirit. Jesus' coming into being thus becomes the supreme example of the highest order of Spirit-Nature interaction. D'Souza, in his study of this section, equates Gabriel with God. He speaks of the three stages of Mary's perception of Gabriel:[7] i) when She saw Him as a man (*nasut*) 'who desires to lie with her,' thus 'she sought refuge in God; ii) when she saw the pure divine in Him, she experienced a state of ecstasy. This state of Mary before receiving the Spirit was important: 'Thus, she attained to perfect presence with God, which is the [perversion of] the unseen spirit. Had He blown [His Spirit] into her at that moment, Jesus would have turned out too surly for anybody to bear, because of his mother's state;' iii) this stage is a combination of the divine and human. This is the state when she accepted the Spirit and brought forth Jesus.

Clearly, there is a problem here. How could the human Jesus be brought forth through a combination of the Spirit and the Nature? Ibn 'Arabi overcame the problem through his notion of imagination (*khayal*):

> (Thus) the body of Jesus was created from the real water of Mary and from the imaginary [water] of Gabriel which flowed into the moisture of that breath (nafs) since the breath of an animal body is moist because it has an element of water. Thus Jesus' body was formed from the imaginary water and real water and Jesus was born in a human form ...8

One might suggest that being Muslim, Ibn 'Arabi's primary concern would be to guard the unquestionable Qur'anic notion of Mary's virginity. This is indeed true, but searching for a basis for Jesus' uniqueness is as much his concern as preserving the traditional notion of virgin birth - inspired not by Mary but by Jesus. Interestingly, the first quote above says that Jesus came into being 'From

---

[6] Ibn 'Arabi 1980:ch.15.
[7] D'Souza 1982.
[8] Ibn 'Arabi 1980:217.

the water of Mary or from the breath of Gabriel....' The second quote above says that the body of Jesus was created from 'the real water of Mary' and 'the imaginary water of Gabriel.' Though, the second quote has the conjunction 'and,' signifying that Jesus came into being in 'the form of a mortal fashioned of clay' through a union of the real water (genetic material) and the imaginary water (spiritual engendering material), the first quote has the word 'or,' signifying that in actuality only one of the two 'materials' actually engendered Jesus. The Jesus of Ibn 'Arabi was thus created only in 'the form of a mortal fashioned of clay'. His true nature entailed the exclusive agency of the Creator but not in the sense of *ex nihilo* because that would mean he was created out of nothing. Ibn 'Arabi's argument is that Jesus was unique in that he was 'created' with/by the very substance (*jawhar*) of the Creator. Thus, to him, Jesus was the Spirit come into existence, the Spirit of God. The material which brought Jesus into being was 'imaginary' not in the sense of being unreal but 'spiritual' (as opposed to material). The Spirit produced all the effects of being. The Spirit alone actually formed the whole person of Jesus. This form of creation was a unique instance of creation. No other being has ever been conceived in the manner in which God brought Jesus into being.

This is the basis on which Ibn 'Arabi explains Jesus' access to and grasp of God and His knowledge. His knowledge of God is complete and eternal by virtue of his substantial oneness with Him (as the embodiment of the Word). This is therefore, also the basis for his claim for Jesus being 'the Seal of Universal Sainthood'.

Out of the terms used to describe the actual mode of the Spirit's operation are the words 'inform' and 'word-enunciation.' The idea of the word 'inform' is related to the phenomenon of prophecy since the word *nubuwwah* (prophecy) comes from the root *nab'a* (to inform). A *nabi* (prophet) thus is one who has had the Word of God informed into him: '...God purified his body and elevated his spirit and made him a model in His act of creation' [there is a sense here in which Jesus' pre-existence is presupposed in the sense one reads about Jesus in the Book of Philippians]. Each *nabi* is a microcosm. There is, thus, a double meaning in the account of Jesus' coming into being: the Spirit brings Jesus into being in a unique way and also word informs or incarnates the divine Word. We are told that when Gabriel blows into Mary the breath, her 'breasts expanded' (*insharah sadru-ha*) just as the Prophet Muhammad's breast expanded in order to receive the revelation of the Qur'an. But, there is a fundamental difference between Jesus and Muhammad, forMuhammad is comparable to Mary in that, just like her, he received the Spirit in order to have it form the revelation in his heart. Both Mary and Muhammad are mere instruments. Jesus is, in contrast, the very Incarnation of the Divine Word. 'He is not an instrument but, rather, the end of the activity of the Spirit. The point is that, in this sense, lbn 'Arabi considered Jesus to be unique even in relation to the Prophet.

It is not surprising that Ibn 'Arabi, as a Sufi (Islamic mystic), was attempting to address the question: who is the 'heir' of prophecy/prophets? Does the manifestation of God and his Word end with 'the Seal of Prophecy', Muhammad? If not, then how how is prophecy related to sainthood and prophets with saints, Muhammad with Jesus?

According to Ibn 'Arabi in the *Tarjuman*: 'When she kills with her glances, her speech restores to life, as though she, in giving life thereby, were Jesus.' Chittick commenting on this verse has noted that "the reason 'Her speech' is compared to Jesus and not to the life-giving breath mentioned in the verse is 'courtesy'."[9] The Spirit or the Word spoken of here is spoken of in the feminine form. Ibn 'Arabi notes its essential function in relation to the creation of humans: 'molding of man when the Spirit is breathed into him.' This creative medium of God is linked essentially to Jesus. Jesus is, therefore, not just the end of the activity of the Spirit as the Word, but 'a Spirit from God and none other.' It was because of this status of Jesus that he was able to resuscitate the dead and make the birds of clay come to life. In his calling, Jesus was the seal of the saints (*khatam al-awliya'*). As a saint (*wali*) of this high order, he is one who embodies the Word and is indeed the Word himself. He knows God and his mind more intimately than anyone/anything else in the entire affair. Whereas the other saints may be sent/called for and to their own generations, Jesus as the seal of all saints transcends historical appointment. He is the saint of saints for eternity. The phenomenon of sainthood (*al-walaya*) is eternal in this sense and does not necessarily start after the prophecy. It incorporates both prophethood (*nubuwwa*) and apostleship (*risala*). Sainthood is a higher spiritual state than prophethood.

This is a problematical conclusion in the context of traditional Islam and this is where Chittick's idea of 'courtesy' is helpful. Prophecy occupies the highest level of authority in traditional Islam. Sufis like Ibn 'Arabi were Muslims and they wished to remain within the notional boundaries of Islam. They achieved this by means of the principle of courtesy for Muhammad and the traditional notion of prophecy. The Prophet Muhammad is for them a saint too, in the sense that he had gained (upon his heart) the knowledge of the divine Word, but with his passing away the category of 'the Seal of the Prophets (last prophet incorporating the knowledge of all previous prophets) came to an end. However, the phenomenon of sainthood continued through the saints. The Prophet Muhammad is accorded also the position of being the 'Seal of Sainthood' (i.e. within the realm of Islam), whereas Jesus is accorded the distinctive wider status of being 'the Seal of Universal Sainthood.' Huge claims these may be but they were based on Ibn 'Arabi's own experiences as a saint in terms of his religious affiliation within the order of the Prophet Muhammad (in the 'Muhammadan' sense) and secondarily in the order of Jesus (in the ecumenical and 'universal' senses). His esoteric teachings were thus based on his own experiences of the divine at these two planes of sainthood. A form his experiences took followed the famous Qur'anic ideas of the Prophet's *Isra'* and *Mi'raj* (the 'nocturnal journey'

---

[9] Chittick 1994:79.

and the 'ascension.').[10] These journeys with 'the Realities of Muhammad and Jesus' serve as the basis of his claims:

> Hence God does not move a servant from place to place in order that (servant) might see Him, but rather 'so that He might cause him to see of His signs ...' He said: 'Glory to Him who made His servant journey one night from the sacred place of worship to the farthest place of worship ...'[11]

Mi'raj and *Isra'* were the reward for the prophetic faithfulness as the *'abd* of God. It was in this symbolic framework of 'servitude' into which Ibn 'Arabi filled new content and opened up a potential experience for the saints. The Muslim saints, in his view thus, participated in the heritage of Muhammad by being given the opportunity to meet with and interact with the different levels of spiritual realities in a hierarchical vision of the heavens. These levels of entities formed the substance of the realm between the transcendent Being of God and the physical universe. These represented the diversity within the 'Third Entity'; the intermediate world (*isra' al-ruhaniya barzakhiya*) of the Creator.

The Prophet's journey and ascension were not unique to him. The saints too share these experiences. Ibn 'Arabi's claimed himself to have experienced these. In one such journey, he recounts his encounter with Jesus in heaven:[12]

> He was looking for us when we entered upon this Path we are following today; I returned [to God: *tubtu*] at the hands of Jesus; Our return to this path was through good tidings (*mubashshira*) at the hand of Jesus ...; We found that station [of immediate spiritual 'feeding'] within ourselves and had the immediate experience (*dhawq*) of it at the beginning of our journeying with the spiritual Reality (*ruhaniya*) of Jesus.

Ibn 'Arabi thus recognized Jesus' special influence on him in leading him to God. Since the universal spiritual element was, in his view, the essential characteristic of Jesus, his role as the Seal of Sainthood was not limited to a particular people (Arabs or Muslims) or time in history (history of Muslim saints). The knowledge he imparted was 'immediate' because the Jesus he met was not bound by time, space and history of any particular religion but was the very Spirit that gives being to the world.

Concluding Remarks

I began by surveying Ibn 'Arabi's anthropology. His notion of humanity transcends physical delimitation. The affinity with God gives humanity the power to 'imagine' the true nature of reality. If this is what all humans could potentially achieve, how much more can the one brought into being by the Universal Spirit!

---

[10] Surah 17.1 & 60.

[11] Ibn 'Arabi 1987b:358.

[12] Morris 1986a/b: I, 15.26; IV, 77.30;IV, 172.13; Ill, 43 20, 21.

Ibn 'Arabi and his Isawi connections (Jesus centeredness) experienced what all humans have the potential for finding. He had no direct knowledge of the Jesus of Nazareth or of the Jesus of the Christian faith (although, he was aware of and possibly met with Christian monks). His knowledge and experience of Jesus was rooted in his direct experience of the very 'Reality of Jesus'. His story concerns his meeting with this Jesus and not the historical Jesus. What he saw in this Jesus led him to believe that not only was the historical Jesus unique in the way he was brought into being in history, but also this was the evidence of what his direct experience of him denoted. Firstly, this Jesus was 'the Seal of Universal Sainthood' by which is meant that he was the very fount of the knowledge of God and his revelation. Secondly, his knowledge of God and his universal sainthood rested in his ontological or substantial unity with God described variously as the PM, Word, Spirit etc. The reality of Jesus was indeed 'relativised' in history, but was never disconnected from its universality as the Spirit.

His unique coming into being in history and his 'special substance' gives him the exalted position of being 'the 'Universal Spirit'. This would indicate not only his exalted ontological status but also his grasp of the full knowledge of God for humanity. Here is possibly a parallel idea with the Word or *logos* of the Christian faith which can potentially provide one with the substance for dialogue with Muslims.

The discourse about Jesus in Christianity is plural but we are not concerned with that in this paper. We are concerned with a lesser known perspective within Islam which in itself throws up interesting challenges for an intra-Islamic debate on Islamic Christology and 'Prophetology'. This Christology draws its inspiration from the scriptures but was not restricted by either its plain textual sense or its meanings subscribed to by theologians for whatever reasons. This Christology relies on 'the imaginal faculty' or on direct experience. This is interesting because what it assumes is that the scriptures are the Word of God but like all words are not precise enough to capture the richness and inexhaustible nature of God. The scriptures are, as St. Ignatius of Antioch believed, historical 'archives' with Jesus himself as 'the Door' to the particular stories of the prophets and the inexhaustible mysteries of the Father. The scriptures bear witness to the truth. In arising from particular historical locations, these archives reflect the appreciation of the truth and its understanding then but these also bear witness to the inexhaustible nature of the truth. As archives these are reliable witnesses to the truth but not the truth itself. The truth is personal and not literal. It assumes shapes to connect with humanity but is like the scriptures that bear witness to the all comprehensive person of God who creates, communicates, wills, loves, shows mercy and judges.

Ibn 'Arabi took enormous risk in drawing the attention of his readers to an all-comprehensive reality behind the particular incarnate Jesus. This was not a matter of a mere mental exercise in philosophy but an outcome of his irresistible and direct experience. The reality of Jesus to him was neither exhausted by the scriptures nor by the crude caricaturing of him in the witnesses to his Incarnation, his coming into being in history (to which the scriptures bear witness). What can be said in words is that the Incarnation was a mystery as the coming into being of the universe was a mystery. God has the power to create things that eludes the human capacity to comprehend. His coming into being as Jesus was an instance of His power and mystery. This expressed mystery however is *for* humanity. Its purpose is to point to the reality of Jesus that is at the root of all creation and revelation.

Christian Contextualisation in Central Asian Islamic Society

Peter F. Penner

Dr. Peter F. Penner has throughout the last 18 years been involved in theological education for and in the region of the former Soviet Union

Introduction

As Luong remarks,[1] "until now, Central Asia has been treated as peripheral, both in the study of the Soviet Union and in the development of social science theory." Only during the recent decade this has started to change. The region of Central Asia by definition includes India, touches Russia and partly China and comes in the south-west down to present Pakistan, Iran and for some even up to Turkey. This article will primarily focus on those Central Asian countries that previously were part of the Soviet Union. We will include present Turkmenistan, Uzbekistan, Kazakhstan, Tajikistan and Kyrgyzstan, a territory that with its 4,000,000 sq. km. is larger than all of Western Europe. From East to West it measures up to 3,000 km and from North to South some 2,500 km. Presently about 54 million people live in this vast region; they represent at least 130 different nationalities and are predominantly Turkic ethnic groups.[2] Half of the present population is under 30 years old. The region stand at the same time for very young political entities created after the collapse of the Soviet Union and for centuries-old traditions and customs with their histories of wars, abundance and poverty.

Only a quick and careless glimpse at the region could suggest the prevalence of a monolithic Islamic tradition. Quite to the contrary, the region comprises an unusual diversity of Islam and of major religions beyond it.[3] Central Asia displays a variety of different Islamic as well as other religious communities located in countries which try to separate religion and state while attempting to continue the model of a secularized state introduced throughout the time of the Soviet Union. After their unexpected independence due to the fall of the Soviet

---

[1] Luong 2004:1.

[2] Menges 1994:60. The region can therefore be identified as Turkestan because primarily Turkic languages are spoken here. But we find also Iranian influence in the region and the use of non-Turkish languages. Still, the region was known in the past as Turkestan. See Fuller 1992:4ff.

[3] Van Gorder 2008:134,135.

Union, all countries are involved in and struggle with the growth of different religious movements in the region.[4]

This article will primarily look at the region's Evangelicals, a group that represents about 15 % of the entire population of Central Asia, and their ability to incarnate and contextualise. I will need to look at the history of the region as it explains much of the present. I also will look at the present and try to envision a possible future and the issues that may surface with it.

Central Asian History of Christianity till the Collapse of the Soviet Union: *Early religious developments in the region*

The Silk Road brought wealth to the region of Central Asia in ancient times. It was also the road used by mighty warriors who introduced different cultures to the region, for example Alexander the Great and his Hellenisation. The same road was used by various religious messengers to transmit their religious views to the people of the land.[5] According to reports from the Persian Synod, "along the Amur Darja river … already in the 5th century witness of Christian churches" is found.[6] But as the Silk Road was a point of intersection of various cultures, it allowed a number of different religious communities, such as Buddhists, Zoroastrians, and Manicheans[7] to live side by side and influence each other. In the seventh century, Islam entered the region to become the dominant missionary religious movement in Central Asia.[8] All of the mentioned five religious communities found their entry from the economical centres of the Silk Road and moved from there into the countryside, where a still tribal animistic tradition was rooted. This tradition was assimilated by the different incoming religions, as we can still find it presently in folk Islam settings in Central Asia.[9]

Prior to the dominance of Islam, the mission activities of the Nestorian Christians had reached Central Asia. The missional monastic groups, well-trained in theology, art, medicine and many other academic sciences and in trade, were sent from the Persian Empire to build up Christian communities in different parts of Central Asia.[10] Their appealing outreach and their independence from

[4] Roy 2007 points out the problem of nationalism, which we will only partly touch on in this article.

[5] Irvin & Sunquist 2001:311-314.

[6] Irvin & Sunquist 2001:311.

[7] A Persian prophet Mani is the founder of this religion which incorporated major elements from Buddhism, Zoroastrianism and Christianity. "So close did Manicheans and Christians become in Central Asia that it is often hard to tell whether a particular text belongs to one faith tradition or the other. " Irvin and Sunquist 311,312.

[8] Christian 1998 is a very helpful book on the origins of Central Asian civilisation and Islamisation, especially looking at the early Turkish Islamic influence.

[9] Irvin & Sunquist 2001:312.

[10] Dickens 2001:1,2.

missionary support – they had their own businesses and practiced a tent making approach in their witnesses to Christ – were the reasons for the quick growth of Christianity in the region.[11] By the 5th and 6th century local bishops were in place to look after the flock.[12] Dickens remarks that "Huns and Turks were … evangelized during this period prior to the Arab invasion, resulting in a Christian presence amongst the Central Asian Turks that would last until the 13th or 14th centuries."[13] Cemeteries of Nestorian Christians from that time can be visited today in the region and remain a witness to an early and vital Christian life in Central Asia, even during the time when Islam spread in the region. After a time of almost complete extinction of Christian witness, European settlers brought back Christianity which had earlier flourished in the region for 1000 years.[14]

European Christianity in Central Asia

During the last 140 years the region has experienced a strong Russification process due to the influx of Europeans and especially of Russian speaking individuals and groups and through the process of becoming part of Tsarist Russia and later the Soviet Union with all its influences. But already earlier Europeans came here, sometimes as business people, travellers or conquerors, but also as slaves. Russian Orthodoxy, the primary Christian face to the region, and Islam met at different levels with little problems, with a few incidents of Russians becoming Muslims and Central Asian individuals becoming Orthodox. As apostasy was detestable to both religious groups, the religious encounter was kept at a minimum.[15] The Tsars showed very little interest in Christianisation and enculturation of the region until the mid-19th century, even so this was happening, for instance, in Siberia; the interest was primarily vested in trade relations. Catherine the Great was not interested in Christian mission to Central Asia, as she hoped that Islam would, in fact, advance Tsarist power. With Alexander II (1865-1881), Islam was perceived as a threat which needed to be confronted by Russian Orthodox missionaries who were directly financed by the Russian government. While "Russian Orthodox missionaries struggled and often died proclaiming the true and ancient faith",[16] some of the outreach happened

---

[11] Owens 2005:4.
[12] Müller 1981:306.
[13] Dickens 2001:4. As Islam "gained the upper hand in Central Asia" Christianity experienced harsh persecution. By 1380 the large Nestorian communities of the past were erased in the region (Van Gorder 2008: 51).
[14] The persecuted church in Persia has also learned to continue its mission in times of anti-Christian governments and severe persecution. This probably is one of the reasons why the church in Central Asia was prepared to survive under difficult circumstances (see Walls 2000:108).
[15] Edward 1994:5, 32.
[16] Van Gorder 2008:55.

with use of political power as well as for "economic and social advantage".[17] With the Soviet Revolution and latest during Stalin's antireligious campaigns "Russian Orthodox missions among Muslims ended".[18]

Some more interest in evangelising native Central Asians was demonstrated by the Catholic Church, primarily through the Jesuit mission.[19] The early phase of Pietism included a grand vision to reach the different ethnic groups of Central Asia. A dissertation on the Herrnhut mission to Russia and Central Asia points to that grand vision by two Pietist leaders, Gottfried Wilhelm Leibniz and August Hermann Francke, already in the 18th century. It seems that indeed some attempts have been made by Pietistic groups to organise local mission centres in the region, as for example by Zinzendorf.[20] A caravan from Petersburg to China, going the route every three years, seemed to be a vehicle used by the Herrnhut missionaries to witness to Christ.[21] Later, some Pietists expected the return of Christ in the region and settled there as end-time communities.

British and North American missionaries entered the region already before the 1917 revolution. They generally remained without much effect and were primarily adventurers with no notable churches being established.[22] A Scottish mission group has also been involved, with little results.[23] As an important milestone in reaching ethnic communities in Central Asia "two Swedish missionaries named Hermanson and Ahlbert were active in translating the New Testament into the Uzbek language shortly before the Russian Revolution".[24] This marked the beginning of the Swedish Bible translation work that was picked up again and fostered from Stockholm during the time of the Soviet Union.[25] The turn to Christianity was costly for all ethnic Central Asians and often led to their martyrdom inflicted by the hands of relatives and neighbours. With the Soviet rule any foreign mission stopped. But soon after the revolution Russian and German speaking settlers from inside the Soviet territory moved to the region and established their communities often isolated from the local ethnic communities. They came from different Christian backgrounds, such as Russian Orthodox, Roman Catholic, Lutheran, Baptist, Pentecostal and Mennonite.[26]

The beginning of the Second World War saw the Soviet government engage in major resettlement activities and large groups of German Catholics, Lutherans

[17] Van Gorder 2008:56.
[18] Van Gorder 2008:57.
[19] Zugl 2005:83. See also Wessels 1999.
[20] Zugl 2005:21, 22.
[21] Zugl 2005:148.
[22] Van Gorder 2008:57.
[23] Zugl 2005:52.
[24] Van Gorder 2008:57.
[25] Bible translation has been conducted already during Soviet times by the Slaviska Mission from Bromma, Sweden. Others have also been involved, and since the collapse of the Soviet Union also Wycliffe Bible Translators. Van Gorder 2008: 181.
[26] Van Gorder 2008:33.

and Mennonites were forced to move to Central Asia in September 1941. Approximately 1.25 million people were resettled and lived under "a special command that functioned like forced labour camps".[27] In the process of liberalisation of those very strict rules, German speaking churches arose under the careful watch of the secret police. Some of the German Pietists and Mennonites joined hands with the Russian speaking population and established various Evangelical churches (Baptist, Pentecostal, etc.) that became part of the Union of the Evangelical-Christians and Baptist churches. Throughout the many persecution waves initiated by the Soviet government, the churches developed in numbers, were able to build church buildings and had some limited freedom in using it for Evangelistic outreach, which was primarily focused on the European population of Central Asia with a few exceptions. At the end of the Soviet reign, only a few hundred ethnic Central Asians belonged to one of the Christian communities. Most were not even on the radar for local mission efforts. A story is told from that time of an Imam who on his death bed told his children that he has not found answers in Islam. "Go, therefore, - he commented to his children, - to the Christians and find the true religious way." But when they arrived in a local Evangelical church, church members sent them away because they could not understand why these people would be interested in Christianity. Similar encounters with ethnic Central Asians widened the horizons and initiated Evangelistic activities toward non-Europeans in the region. In the late 1980s, Western Evangelicals added to this development the '10-40 window' perspective, viewing the region of Soviet and post-Soviet Central Asia as a doorway to the 10-40 countries.

Post-Soviet Developments and Issues: *Emigration of Europeans to Europe and North America*

With the family reunion agreement signed 1972 between West Germany and the Soviet Union (Brezhnev and Brandt) an exodus of ethnic Germans began from Central Asia which reached its climax in the 1990s. "More than 35.000 of their number had left by the end of 1990. Many of the strongest independent churches in Central Asia were reduced to a remnant".[28] A Mennonite Brethren church in Karaganda had more than 1000 members, yet after the exodus the church was almost empty.[29] This also affected Lutheran and Baptist churches. Baptist communities had mixed ethnic origins, Slavs and Germans who met as a Russian speaking church; even they were sometimes overnight reduced to a small flock, like the Baptist church in Kant, with about 1000 members counted by 1990 only a few hundred members. Emigration had also affected other ethnically 'white' people who moved to Russia, Ukraine and, in the early nineties, on refugee

[27] Sawatsky 1994:252.
[28] Sawatsky 1994:266.
[29] Sawatsky 1994:266.

status, to the United States. Books, such as *'Welcome to the United States: a guide for new immigrants'* by the United States Department of Education, offer to the Christian immigrants, advice in Russian language on how to integrate into this multi-ethnic country. They have built their own churches and denominations there and keep the traditions of their homeland alive.[30]

European Settlers: Mission Involvement

But a constantly shrinking remnant continues to minister in the region. Religious freedom that was introduced under Gorbachev allowed for tremendous missionary and Evangelistic activities, often initiated and supported financially by missionaries from the West. In the meantime, local evangelical communities went through some change in how they perceived ethnic Central Asians and whether they deserved their witness or otherwise. While earlier, their primary targets were Russian speaking inhabitants of the region, now they increasingly focused on the ethnic peoples of Central Asia.[31] Mission agencies mushroomed, probably more than 70 % being of Evangelical origins.[32] Different traditional mission agencies, such as Light to the East, had started to translate Christian literature already before the 1990s but intensified efforts after the collapse of the Soviet Union. Bible translation, that had started already in the underground in the Soviet time, was now able to openly demonstrate its first fruits, offering parts of or the whole Bible in the Kyrgyz language, for example, to different ethnic groups in Central Asia. This active evangelisation of all inhabitants of the Central Asian states, independently of ethnic origins, helped at least partly to fill the empty spaces in church buildings, built before the 1990s and before the exodus. At the same time, new churches developed with predominantly native ethnic communities and so new church meeting places were established.

Some of the emigrants, who had left already in the 1970s or later as well as the recent emigrants to the West, felt a calling to help their former neighbours back in Central Asia. They registered mission agencies in different Western countries, often with a focus on humanitarian aid, in order to help and support church and mission leaders in continuing the mission both to the Europeans and the Asians in Central Asia.[33] Also, vital communities in Moldova and especially

[30] Various Baptist and Pentecostal Unions can be found on the east as well as west coast of the USA. Cities like Sacramento have absorbed thousands of Russian and Ukrainian-speaking immigrants (they comprise about 10 % of the population) and host their churches.

[31] Snyder 2002:43,44.

[32] Tabyshalieva 2006:1.

[33] Friedensstimme was one of the first agencies to be registered in Germany to help the underground churches in the former Soviet Union, followed by a number of other mission agencies founded by emigrants from Central Asia.

Ukraine saw the need to help and enhance the mission work in the region by sending co-workers to the region.[34]

Foreign Mission Involvement

Foreign mission involvement in Central Asia was a reality already before the fall of the Soviet Union. Bible translation, radio programmes focused on Central Asia, smuggling activities, underground discipleship groups go back to the late seventies. With Gorbachev's dawn of religious freedom financial and material help came more regularly, and so Bibles and Christian literature were distributed, technology like VCR's with Evangelistic materials found their way into the country and more western visiting ministers/missionaries were seen in churches. In the early nineties missionaries arrived from North America and Europe[35] as well as from Asia (Indonesian and Korean missionaries). Through the foreign missionaries, the local communities were enriched and helped but also new Evangelical churches as well as Christian and other cults entered the region and were quite successful among the European and Asian population of Central Asia.

Some foreign missionaries from the West and from Asia tried to work with the local denominations and churches but felt that the locals were not enthusiastic enough in their views of mission. Others could not cope with the conservative focus of the local churches which were strongly culturally oriented toward Eastern European Evangelicals, with their expectations about clothing, hair style, church praxis and worship. They soon identified for themselves these churches as legalistic and quickly separated from them in order to start their own churches and mission work. Some completely ignored any Christian local church from the time before *perestroika* and claimed to finally bring Christianity to this region of the world. These problems, but especially the different personal agendas and sometimes issues of power and control, were mainly reasons for church splits and a waste of energy. Competition was part of the motivation to reach out especially to the ethnic Central Asians.[36] On the positive side, a variety of different methods and approaches of ministry were used and different ministries were generated to witness on different social and ethnic levels in Central Asia.

Surprisingly, thousands of ethnic Central Asians became Christians. While visiting traditional Baptist churches in Kyrgyzstan, I have not seen a church without at least a handful of Kyrgyz or Uygurs attending. But at the same time I have also met a number of Kirgiz pastors from churches with pure Kyrgyz membership. Churches and Unions that have not been in existence in the region before *perestroika* usually have a higher degree of ethnic Central Asians. This is

---

[34] Today there are dozens of Ukrainian missionaries in the region. The college in Kishinev uses a different strategy and trains a number of MBB's in their theological programmes but also has an extension campus in Central Asia.

[35] Snyder 2002:43-44.

[36] Van Gorder 2008:94.

especially true for the variety of charismatic groups. While some major language and ethnic groups have a Bible or at least parts of it in their language, there still is a need for basic Bible translation into some ethnic language groups in Central Asia. Without such solid groundwork, there is little hope that local ethnic churches will remain vital in the long-term or permanently.[37] As the emigration of Europeans, but also of some Asians from Central Asia continues, mission activities are more and more focused on those people groups which will most probably stay. Serious leadership training is therefore needed as well as contextual studies to strengthen this group and enable long-term Christian witness in the region.[38]

Theological training seems to be one of the key activities that is able to respond to the present developments of Evangelical changes in Central Asia. Already during the Soviet time church-based education took place through extension education materials and programmes were allowed to be offered under the umbrella of the Union of Evangelical Christians and Baptist churches in the Soviet Union. The majority of pastors, preachers, presbyters, and other active members and leaders of the church were educated through the church's preaching activities, Bible study groups and personal studies.

Biblical Education by Extension through Logos International, already in the late 1980s, offered church-based education. However, only in the early 1990s, Bible schools, colleges and seminaries developed.[39] In the first phase, they primarily trained ethnic Europeans in Central Asia, but slowly also Asians from and for the region. The language in the nineties was almost exclusively Russian, as this was still the *lingua franca* for the whole former Soviet Union. However, in the late 1990s slowly local languages gained sufficient strength as languages for theological studies. Presently each of the Central Asian countries has at least one theological institution, usually there are more and they are established by different denominations. There is also a variety of educational models that can be observed in different Central Asian settings. While in the past, many theological institutions were focused on full-time residential studies, today there is a plenitude of models, probably dominated by part-time on-off campus studies. But there are also pure extension programmes, TEE programmes, etc.[40]

Only in the last few years have native students increasingly appeared in local institutions, and, among them, a growing proportion of academically prepared students and gifted future leaders. Some classes are offered in the native languages, even though most subjects are still delivered in Russian. Theological literature is almost non-existent in the local languages, so that again the Russian

[37] Smith 2009.
[38] Shamgunov 2009:270.
[39] Shamgunov 2009:19.
[40] Shamgunov 2009:19-33.

language literature is used.[41] However, the younger generation is not always able to use Russian anymore, so translation and publishing in native languages will be of increasing importance. Co-operation between theological institutions is just in its beginning and their place in the wider Evangelical theological world is still to be determined. Should they orient themselves toward the Eastern European groups, such as the Euro-Asian Accrediting Association, to the Asian Accrediting Association to which they belong geographically but not historically, culturally or theologically, or possibly to the Middle East Evangelical Accrediting Association which is closer contextually?[42]

Central Asia is divided at different levels. The present borders of Central Asian countries go back to Soviet rule which divided some of the territories that historically and ethnically belonged together, similar to what Great Britain has done in the Middle East. But the division across theological and denominational lines is also clearly visible among Evangelical communities. There are some attempts to co-operate and have regional conversations and projects that would overcome barriers. Co-operation is indeed needed to strengthen an Evangelical presence and witness in the region. Very often co-operation is fostered by the ethnic European representatives from the region. But the divisions are also mostly a result of old or recent splits among ethnic Europeans. The ethnic Central Asians usually try to connect with partners at least in their own country and are usually not too well connected to the wider region. Links beyond the region depend on the context from where the people come.

In response to an intensive involvement of evangelical groups on different levels, governments of different Central Asian countries have introduced laws on religious freedom, some following recent models of the Russian government and some those of the former Soviet Union. As a result, some restrictions on church and mission ministries are starting to be felt in Kazakhstan, Tajikistan and Kyrgyzstan, and massive restrictions as well as partial persecution, including imprisonment of Evangelicals, are observed in Turkmenistan and partly in Uzbekistan.[43] Various websites and other publications inform of such persecution and provide examples.[44] However, these problems seem not to stop mission and Evangelistic work even in countries with persecution. It seems that persecution results in the opposite reaction in this context and invites missionaries and Evangelists to adopt very creative approaches.[45]

---

[41] Shamgunov in his Ph.D. dissertation points to "cross-cultural issues" which create problems and that, beside literature, many other aspects of theological education are lacking solid ground. Shamgunov 2009: 245-247.

[42] All of these accrediting associations are united under the International Association of Evangelical Theological Education, as part of the Theological Commission of the World Evangelical Alliance.

[43] See Shariphzan 2009.

[44] See Tabyshalieva 2008.

[45] Uzbekistan may be an interesting case, where we see the Christian faith grow. Officially the numbers of Christians, with a huge proportion of ethnic Central Asians, are given as

At the same time, especially during the last decade, there is a strong Islamisation in the region, fostered both from inside, partly as a response to Evangelical mission work, and from outside, through Arabic and Turkish influence. The latter are involved, similar to Evangelicals, with foreign missionaries as well as with training institutions. They also offer young people an education outside of the country in their often fundamentalist theological training institutions.[46] Publications, such as Naumkin's,[47] may overstate the danger but they also point to real difficulties that are created in the region through fundamentalist militant Muslim groups.

Historic churches, such as the Russian Orthodox community, usually have not been missionally active toward the native population of Central Asia. They were often also offered a privileged role among Christian groups, because they primarily reach out to the Slavic population of Central Asia. Lutheran communities were mainly focused on German ethnic groups in Central Asia, with only a few exceptions of some Pietistic church leaders who have attempted to reach out to Central Asians. The Catholic community does not limited itself to historically Catholic ethnic groups in Central Asia but is quite missionary minded and faces persecution and restrictions, as do Evangelicals.

Toward a Future of Christianity in Central Asia

The future of Evangelical presence and witness will depend on many factors, which need to be decided now. (a) There are issues of ethnic leadership development going along with the whole issue of contextualisation. (b) Much will depend on the new waves of Islamisation. (c) One important factor will also be the political links the region will have and how empire(s) will relate to Central Asia. Those three components seem to exert major influences on the process. At the same time there is the expectation that God will be in control and the promise of Mt 16:18 – "I [Christ] will build my church, and the gates of Hades will not prevail against it" – will hold true. The promise was addressed to Peter, the disciple, and underlines the human context. While God will intervene, Christians also need to be involved in the process, with reasoning, wisdom, sensitivity and respect in and toward the social, cultural and religious context.

10,000. Unofficial numbers that include believers in Christ who are not joining local Christian churches may be up to 40,000. The hesitancy concerning joining a Christian church sometimes has cultural elements. Some Uzbek men have accepted the Christian faith, but have difficulties in joining Christian churches where women are the majority in attendance. To participate in such communities, Uzbek men have to overcome their traditional understanding of honour.

[46] Snyder 2002:43, 44.

[47] Naumkin 2005.

Issues of Contextualisation

It seems important to maintain both the European and the Asian Christian presence in the region. Such a balance seems only beneficial for times when most missionaries will have gone or will be restricted in regions where already now some persecution is obvious, or in situations when governments attempt to balance the growth of religious groups with new laws on religious freedom trying to limit all religious movements from dominating politics and society in an attempt to maintain a secular state.[48] To retain ethnic European churches in the region, in spite of all limitations by laws and under the pressure of Islamic groups, will keep this ethnic Christian community's witness. Historically this has always been a possibility, even under a strict Islamic rule. Those cells of Christian presence and witness were able to hold up the light, help ethnic Asians to keep their Christian faith, continue a formal dialogue with the Muslim leaders and spread Christianity, as in the past, when society opened up for possibilities of such witness. But these ethnic European churches and leaders, together with missionaries from North America, Europe and Asia, must train leaders from out of the Central Asian ethnic communities and pass on the power and their contacts with international Christians to those native leaders,[49] (under the title "Implications for Theological Institutions").

During this time of relative freedom it is important to test options in contextualisation, experimenting with the C1 to C6 issues that have some roots in the region. One needs to learn from other evangelical communities how they contextualise in the different regions where Islam is the majority religion and to find an authentic Central Asian Christian witness, which retains the message of the Gospel and at the same time attracts onlookers, as it is grounded in the social and cultural life of the different contexts of Central Asia.[50] There is a need to develop versatile and holistic approaches to this, allowing and respecting creative differences in Evangelical Christian witness.[51] Much is already happening, for instance, a contextualised translation of the Bible into Russian that uses names of people and places in the same way as they are used in the Qur'an. Community celebrations need to pick up local customs and traditions and transform them for

---

[48] Van Gorder 2008:91ff.

[49] Schamgunov2009: 277-288.

[50] An issue of male honour has been discussed before in this article (fn. 17). Is there an appropriate way to deal with honour and shame in the different cultures in Central Asia? Many studies need to be conducted on social and anthropological levels. The role of women in society needs to be carefully evaluated. On the one hand, there is a Biblical mandate to strengthen the place of women in society through Christian faith. The cultural praxis in some parts of Central Asia of selling women as brides to the bridegroom's family for them to serve as servants/slaves is an issue. Christian faith here needs to carefully but clearly maintain a countercultural position and transform the local culture. There are no simple solutions in contextualisation and transformation of the culture and they should not lead to imitating western praxis. See Luong 2004:29-89.

[51] Van Gorder 2008: 110-111.

use in Christian communities. A contextual approach to issues of how to experience church, celebrate worship services, Bible reading, prayer, baptism and the Lord's Table is presently being discussed inside different Evangelical communities. This clearly includes also adapting to the way people are dressed and behave in particular situations and cultures.[52] Should a young Christian ethnic community be encouraged to participate at burial ceremonies which have some animistic elements and are perceived by some ethnic European Evangelicals as worshipping other gods? How can a person who comes from an Islamic context be helped to grow in Gospel faith and at the same time remain in a meaningful relationship to relatives and friends who do not appreciate this move? Many more issues are in the air and under discussion, which gives hope that relevant and much needed contextualisation is on the way.

The Result of a new Wave of Islamisation

While in countries such as Turkmenistan, Uzbekistan and Tajikistan the Islamic community was well established already before the fall of the Soviet Union and could quickly regain its role in society and on the political scene, often even developing militant Islamic groups in particular geographic areas, Kyrgyzstan and Kazakhstan, on the contrary, were historically and culturally leaning toward folk Islam. It seems that this context is changing and a more sophisticated Islam takes over regions even where folk Islam was rooted for centuries.[53] When travelling through Kazakhstan and Kyrgyzstan, the Muslim presence is quite obvious. Many small and large mosques have been built in the last ten years and the number of new mosques is constantly growing.[54] A new generation of Muslim religious leaders is aggressively involved in mission to lead people with ethnic Asian but also European backgrounds to Islam.[55] Visits from house to house and personal invitations are regular events and after a few negative responses people reconsider and decide to visit a local mosque.

The new Muslim religious leaders often are well trained, either in local theological institutions or abroad in Turkey, in different Arabic countries or in Egypt. Some adopt a more moderate position, but many are very active in their mission work in the region. Mainly they are not aggressive toward other religious groups, but some are. They are also in conflict with the older established Islamic communities and leaders who have kept the traditions and survived the Soviet persecution.[56] Looking closer at some of the tensions, similarities in mission work between Evangelicals and the new waves of Islamisation can easily be recognised. The government clearly prefers traditional Islam which has survived

---

[52] Sookhdeo 1996:137-138.
[53] Van Gorder 2008:73ff.
[54] There were at least 10,000 mosques built during the time of 1991 to 1995. This process continued also after 1995, often sponsored by Arab or Turkish money.
[55] Sookhdeo 1996:130.
[56] More than 56,000 *imams* were deported under Soviet persecution.

and adjusted throughout Soviet times and accepts the Central Asian style of secularisation.[57] But exactly these groups, connected to the governments and clans, are special targets for the more militant Islamic groups. Sometimes those Wahhabite militant groups also demonstrate their power to other religious groups as they seem to them as part of the society to which they respond aggressively. But there is hope that in the end Central Asian Muslims may be able to not only curtail these militant and extremist foreign influences but offer "hope to other Islamic communities encountering similar transitional challenges" to overcome such extremist tendencies in their societies.[58]

Central Asia between the Empires

When I visited Kyrgyzstan a few years ago during an anti-government uprising it was interesting to recognise in what ways other countries were involved in this power struggle. While I was given a tour through Bishkek to see the demonstration in front of governmental buildings, I was also shown large department stores that were looted by demonstrators. These were Chinese, Russian and Turkish shops and the interpretation given was that the looting was a response of the locals to the three major regional players and the threat they were perceived to be for the country. The Russian store represented Russian dominance that is still felt even after the collapse of the Soviet Union. The Chinese five-storey building was burned in response to the constant threat from the 'big neighbour' who quietly sneaks into the country and strategically takes over all areas of economics. Surprisingly, also a large Turkish store was looted because Turks, seemingly, treat ethnic Kyrgyz as second class people while they nostalgically maintain their dream of a large Turkestan. Not far from Bishkek, the capital of Kyrgyzstan, large military bases of the Russian Federation as well as of US troops demonstrate their presence and interest in the region. The Arab states and Iran are the other main players in the region and all of them compete for who, in future, will dominate the territory.[59]

Those who will win the power play will also influence the ways in how politically, economically and religiously things will develop in the vast land of Central Asia. Beside oil and gas, many other natural resources have been discovered and identified in the region.[60] The behaviour of the victors will also partly influence how Christians will be treated in the region. Western European

---

[57] After 2005, most Muslim missionaries from abroad have been expelled by Central Asian governments as a response to unrest and new movements in Islamic communities in the region. But today, there are many locally trained Muslim missionaries who continue the task of expatriate missionaries.

[58] Van Gorder 2008:89-90.

[59] A report from the BBC by Shenker 2009, one year later, finds that no significant change has been achieved. See on issues of influence of other countries in the region also Loung 2004:11 and van Gorder 2008:112ff.

[60] Luong 2004:13.

or North American influence may not guarantee more freedom, as the imperial influence from those countries could trigger a negative local response toward Evangelical Christians viewing them as spies of the powerful West, with results similar to the looted shops representing empires already present in Bishkek. At the moment it looks somewhat as if the West has lost the battle, at least in some regions of Central Asia and may lose it altogether.[61] The economic crisis has, for instance, caused Kyrgyzstan to sign a long-term agreement on military and economic cooperation with Russia, which limits the Western presence on all levels. The Kirgiz government had to go this direction because the country is bankrupt and Russia was the only partner who offered real economic help, honing its own interests to strengthen its own positions. At the dawn of the post-Soviet time governments and inhabitants of Central Asia opened up their countries to the West, expecting a change after one hundred years of Russian dominance. Western institutions were started as well as many other initiatives to enhance Western influence. Now the process has been reversed and, instead, we find more and more closing doors.[62]

The recently accepted law on religious freedom in Kyrgyzstan is far more restrictive and difficult for Evangelicals as compared to other Central Asian countries.[63] But the praxis and how it will be applied in the country will probably be more important than the actual fact of an existing law. Uzbekistan may be a good example for the opposite where the laws are less restrictive but the praxis is more demanding, and it is difficult for Evangelicals to continue witnessing to Christ and his Gospel. As the time of total religious freedom has passed and was only partly used wisely for the witness of the Gospel of Jesus Christ, the countries still find themselves at crossroads on different levels and the future is still undecided. Continuing contextualisation and dialogue will be needed, in order to secure a future of Christianity in Central Asia, where the population will continue its rapid growth.

[61] Van Gorder 2008:130-133.

[62] Patrick Sookhdeo refers to these tendencies as "anti-Western resentment". It seems Central Asia has moved beyond the crossroad point.

[63] See Bayram 2009 on the effects of the recently introduced law.

PART IV: DIALOGUE AND WITNESS

Defending the Incarnation in the early Christian Dialogue with Muslims

Mark Ivor Beaumont

Dr. Mark Beaumont is Vice-Principal of Birmingham Christian College, UK

Introduction

The advent of Muslim rule in the largely Christian Middle East during the seventh century brought a direct challenge to Christian belief in the Incarnation. The Islamic scriptures taught that Christ was a messenger of God who had been sent to God's people Israel to confirm the *Torah* that had previously been given through Moses and to lead them back to devotion to God.[1] He had an unusual conception without a human father,[2] he had a special measure of God's Spirit,[3] he performed prodigious miracles,[4] and he did not seek faith in himself but rather pointed others to God.[5] That there was no room for the Incarnation was particularly obvious in the repeated denial of the Christian title for Christ as Son of God. The loud volume of denial created by the sheer number of instances of this repudiation of sonship drowns out the rest of the message about Christ in the Qur'an.[6] It is hardly surprising that Christians who attempted to defend the Incarnation had to deal with this repeated rejection of a title for Christ that was embedded in their own scriptures as an entirely appropriate name. They also had to respond to two arguments that Muslims developed from the Qur'anic attack on divine sonship; firstly, Christ was human and not divine so Christians have misunderstood him, and secondly, any supposed union between divinity and humanity in Christ would have seriously damaging consequences for the divinity.

Denial of Divine Sonship

One of the earliest examples of a debate between Muslims and Christians shows how central the denial of divine Sonship was for Muslims. The Caliph al-Mahdi, who had summoned Timothy I, the Patriarch of the East Syrian Diophysites

---

[1] Surah 3:49-51; 5:46; and 61:6.
[2] Surah 19:19-21.
[3] Surah 2:87, 253; and 5:110.
[4] Surah 3:49; and 5:110.
[5] Surah 5:116-7; and 43:57-64.
[6] Surah 2:116; 4:171; 6:101; 9:30; 10:68; 17:111; 18:4; 19:35, 88-92; 21:26; 23:91; 25:2; 37:152; 39:4; 43:81-2; 72:3; and 112:3.

(Nestorians) in Baghdad, to answer questions about Christian beliefs around 781-2, opened his questioning about Christ with the following, "How can someone like you, knowledgeable and wise, say that the Most High God took a wife and had a son?"[7] The Caliph evidently thought that Christians held to a biological connection between God and Jesus through a physical union with Mary. The fact that Christians would never have said such a thing demonstrates that this idea arose from the interpretation of the texts denying that God had a son. The Qur'an never actually accuses Christians of believing that God took Mary as a wife, but al-Mahdī probably thought of Surah 4:171, "People of the book…Do not go beyond what is right in your religion. Confess God's truth; the Messiah, Mary's son, is only a messenger…Do not speak about a trinity…since God is one. Far be it for Him to have a son", implied that Jesus, the son of Mary, had been transformed by Christians into Jesus, the son of God, via Mary, in strictly physical terms. Timothy reacted by exclaiming, "who has uttered such blasphemy?" and avoiding Sonship terminology altogether, spoke of his belief in "the Word of God appearing in the flesh for the salvation of the world." [8] Al-Mahdī pressed his case about Christian use of the title Son of God and Timothy responded by separating Christ's eternal sonship from his temporal one; "The Messiah was born of the Father as His Word and he was born of the Virgin Mary as a man. His birth from the Father is eternal before time and his birth from Mary took place in time without a human father."[9] The discussion later returned to the concept of two kinds of sonship. Al-Mahdī accused Timothy of believing in two Messiahs, one eternal and the other temporal, but Timothy argued that there was perfect unity between the eternal and temporal origins of Christ after the Incarnation. "There are not two Messiahs or two sons but one Messiah and one Son who has two natures, divine and human, because he is the Word of God who took a human body and became a man."[10] In other words, the Muslim allegation that God took a wife and had a son was met by the Christian claim that the eternal Son of God took a human body and became human.

Another defence of the sonship of Christ from the 8th century is found in an *Anonymous Apology for the Trinity and the Incarnation* that was produced in the Palestinian Christian monastic community.[11] In dealing with the repudiation of

---

[7] Arabic text (c. 795) edited by L. Cheikho in *Al-Machriq* 19 (1921) 359-374 and 408-418 is reproduced as *A Dialogue between the Caliph al-Mahdī and the Nestorian Patriarch Timothy I* in the appendix of Putman 1975. Here, appendix, 7.
[8] Putman 1975.
[9] Putman 1975.
[10] Putman 1975:10.
[11] Arabic text (Sinai 154) is edited with an English translation by Gibson 1899. S. K. Samir discovered that Sinai 154 contained the following statement not noticed by Gibson, "If this religion was not truly from God, it would not have stood firm nor stood erect for seven hundred and forty six years". He calculated that this reflects a date of just before 750. See S. K. Samir, 'The Earliest Arab Apology for Christianity (c. 750)' in Samir and Neilsen 1994:57-116, 61. M. Swanson calculated 746 years, not from the birth of Christ

Christ's sonship in the Qur'an, the author rejects the accusation that Christians believe that God gave birth to a son. "We do not say that God brought forth (*walada*) his Word, as humans give birth to offspring."[12] Christians do say that God the Father brought forth his Word as the sun produces rays, or the human mind words, or fire heat. As there cannot be heat without fire, rays without the sun or words without a human mind, so there cannot be the Word of God without God.[13] This emphasis on Christ as the Word of God is an attempt to deflect attention from the biological reading of sonship in order to persuade Muslims that sonship may have a non-biological sense. The author quotes from the Qur'an to support this view. "Believe in God and His word; and also in His spirit, who is sent down from your Lord as mercy and guidance."[14] In other words, Christians could refer to the Muslim scripture to uphold their understanding of Christ's relationship to God, and in so doing hoped to shift the debate onto more harmonious ground on which Muslims might see the reality of the Christian conviction that Christ was the Son of the Father.

The Father-Son relationship so central to the Christian scriptural witness was defended early in the 9th century by Abu Qurra (c. 755-c 830), at one time Chalcedonian Bishop of Harran in northern Mesopotamia, who had a reputation for debating with Muslims. One of his short treatises addressed to Muslim concerns deals with the Sonship of Christ and is entitled, 'God has a Son who is His equal in nature and exists forever with Him'.[15] He summarises the Muslim challenge in the following way: "How can God give birth in the light of the fact that a man only has offspring after intercourse with a woman? Surely it is not right to speak this way about God?"[16] Abu Qurra says that this is a futile question and that a Muslim might just as well ask how God sees or hears when only humans have eyes and ears. Does the Qur'an really mean that He has eyes and ears like ours?[17] He poses his own question to the Muslim. "If you accept that God can be called the one who hears and the wise, and these titles do not demean Him, why can't you accept that He can be called the Father in the same way?"[18] He answers the question by declaring that the Son is not part of the created order, nor has he a beginning in time, therefore God cannot be accused of taking a Son

---

but from the beginning of the church and arrived at a date in the 780's. See Swanson 1993:118-141, 140.

[12] Gibson 1899:75.

[13] Gibson 1899:75.

[14] Gibson 1899:75. The quotation is an amalgam of *sūras* 4:171 and 16:102.

[15] See Bacha 1904:91-104.

[16] Abū Qurra, 'God has a Son who is His Equal in Nature and who Exists Forever with Him' (*Maymar yahqiqu an li-llah ibnan huwa `adilu-hu fī-l-jawhar wa lam yazilu ma`a-hu)* in Bacha 1904:94.

[17] Bacha 1904: 95.

[18] Bacha 1904: 96-7.

to himself as the Qur'an states, since the Son lives forever with the Father and is equal in nature to him.[19]

Abū Qurra shows his awareness of a debate amongst Muslims about the attributes of God, between the Mu`tazila who denied that He had attributes and the Traditionists who held that He did. Al-Ash`ari (d. 935-6) reported that, "all the Mu`tazila agree that God is one with nothing resembling Him. He is the hearing and seeing one without being matter, spirit, body, shape, flesh, and blood, person, substance or accident…He is not limited by space or time."[20] While the Mu`tazila rejected God's hearing and seeing as literally true, the Traditionists believed that God did see and hear although humans do not know how He did so. Abu Qurra sidesteps this debate by emphasising that both sides accept the language of hearing and seeing being applicable to God without damaging His character. Thus the attribute of Fatherhood can be applied to God without compromising His nature, if such Fatherhood is beyond space and time just as His hearing and seeing. Nevertheless, the basic problem with this comparison of anthropomorphisms is that hearing and seeing are predicated of God in the Qur'an but Fatherhood is not. The notion of the Sonship of Christ has no adequate anchor in Islamic language, and the Incarnation of the Son is so much more difficult to discuss as a result.

Acceptance of Jesus' Humanity but Denial of Jesus' Divinity

Since the Qur'an portrays Jesus as God's messenger to the Jews to confirm the *Torah* brought by Moses, Muslims argued that Christians ought to be content to affirm this and not believe that Jesus was more than a messenger somehow sharing the divine nature.[21] One of the first surviving responses to this Muslim treatment of Jesus is found in the *Anonymous Apology for the Trinity and the Incarnation.* Despite the apparent Qur'anic denial of divinity in Jesus, the author finds support for his divine nature in the way his miracles are reported in the Qur'an. "Christ created whereas only God creates. You will find in the Qur'an that Christ spoke and created from clay what looked like a bird, then blew on it and it became a [real] bird by God's permission." [22] The author appears to have noticed that the verb *khalaqa* (created) is normally reserved for the work of God in the Qur'an and yet Jesus is said to have shared in that exclusively divine action, an attribute not ascribed to Moses who also performed miracles according to the Qur'an.[23] On this Islamic foundation, the author builds an edifice of data

[19] Bacha 1904:97-8.
[20] al-Ash`ari 1963:155.
[21] For example the Caliph al-Mahdi did not accept that God could unite with a human being and maintain His distinctiveness, so Jesus had to be human and not divine. See Putman, appendix 1.0
[22] Gibson, 84; referring to Surah 3:49 and 5:110.
[23] For Moses' miracles see Surah 2:60; 7:109-26, 160; 10:79-82; 20:56-73; and 26:38-51.

from the Gospels, including Christ forgiving sins, multiplying food for the hungry, casting out evil spirits, giving the Holy Spirit to his disciples, judging humanity and granting eternal life to the righteous. His conclusion is that only God who "veiled Himself in a sinless human being" could do all these things. [24]

Muslims developed a tradition of appealing to the Christian scriptures to prove the humanity of Jesus and disprove his supposed divinity. The Caliph al-Mahdī quoted John 20:17, "I am going to my God and your God"[25] and Matthew 26:39, where Jesus prostrated himself and pleaded to God to remove the cup of suffering from him, although he would abide by God's will. He held that these texts demonstrate both Jesus' humanity and his awareness of his being different from God. "If Christ prayed, prostrating himself, he is not divine, and if he were divine he would not have prayed, prostrating himself." [26] The earliest extant writing by a Muslim to use the Gospels in the same way is al-Qasim ibn Ibrahim al-Hasan al-Rassi's *Refutation of the Christians* (c. 820 CE).[27] He knows that Christians claim that the title, 'Son of God' implies the divinity of Jesus and seeks to refer to Gospel passages that must mean that this Sonship is shared with others. There are many references to Jesus encouraging his disciples to call God their 'Father'. Since there was no natural kinship between Jesus and his followers, it follows that, "if they were all sons of God their father, then this interpretation of fatherhood and sonship is not what you Christians teach…You claim that Jesus is the (only) Son of the Father." [28] Therefore, when Jesus is called "my beloved Son" by the heavenly voice [Mt 3:17], and when Peter says, "you are truly the Son of God" [Mt 16:16], this is best understood through the analogy of adoption. At the time the Gospels were written, Jesus' Sonship was thought of as the kind of Sonship granted by "those who adopt out of love and the children obtain favour with them, not through physical generation." [29] It follows that when Jesus claims to be God's Son he does not see himself exclusively so, but wants others to be the Sons of God just like him. He can say in John 8:31-58, that he is God's Son and God is his Father, that he has come from his Father, and that if his hearers obey God then they will be God's Sons, so, "Christ made God Father of those who obey and please Him…So Christians must interpret everything in their gospels about fatherhood and sonship according to the way they are presented in the gospels." [30]

---

[24] Gibson 1899:85.

[25] John 20:17 was the most quoted Gospel text by Muslims who debated with Christians in succeeding centuries since it succinctly stated that Jesus saw himself as subordinate to rather than equal with God. See M. Accad, 'The ultimate proof-text: the interpretation of John 20:17 in Muslim-Christian dialogue (second/eighth-eighth/fourteenth centuries)', in Thomas 2003:199-214.

[26] Putman 1975:appendix 21

[27] Al-Qasim ibn Ibrahim year:301-331.

[28] Al-Qasim ibn Ibrahim year:321.

[29] Al-Qasim ibn Ibrahim year: 322-3.

[30] Al-Qasim ibn Ibrahim year: 324.

This kind of interpretation of the Gospel accounts by Muslims had to be dealt with by Christians who defended the divinity of Christ. An example of Christian response comes from the apologetic writing of Jacobite, (Syrian Miaphysite) Habib ibn Khidma Abu Ra'ita, associated with Takrit, who was active in the early decades of the 9th century, and was a contemporary of al-Qasim.[31] His *Letter on the Incarnation* contains forty four answers to questions about the Incarnation which might typically be asked by Muslims. Question 41 asks how Christians can claim that Christ is God when he said that his Father was his God [John 20:17], that his Father was greater than he was [John 14:28], that he did not know the hour [Mark 13:32], that he could not give places to people in his kingdom [Matthew 20:21-3], and when he appealed to his Father in the face of death [Matthew 27:47]? Abu Ra'ita accepts that these texts show the humanity of Christ, but he indicates other texts that show Christ's divinity:

> He whom you describe as saying: 'I am going up to my Father and your Father, to my God and your God'...is he who said: 'The one who sees me sees my Father' [John 14:9], 'I am in my Father, and my Father is in me' [John 10:38], and 'I and my Father are one' [John 10:30]...and that he always was, before Abraham existed [John 8:58], and other sublime statements that point to his divinity.[32]

In order to affirm the truth of Christy's humanity and divinity, Abu Ra'ita argues that the subordination of Christ in the texts included in the question is an indication of his Incarnate state in which he shares the limitations of all other humans.

If the defence of Christian readings of the gospels was one possibility for Christian apologists, another approach was to put forward explanations for the Incarnation that might appeal to Muslims. After all, it was one thing to assert that the Gospels provided clear evidence for the humanity and divinity of Christ, it was much more challenging to give cogent reasons for this union of divine and human natures in Christ, since the Qur'ān appeared to forbid it altogether. A ninth century Nestorian (East Syrian Diophysite) theologian, `Ammar al-Basri, put forward four reasons for the Incarnation in his *Book of the Proof.*[33] The first is that the Incarnation is a more complete manner of revelation than the sending of messengers. While God had sent men with His message it was His intention ultimately to reveal Himself in person to remove any doubt that humans might have about Him. "He appeared to human beings in human flesh and spoke to

---

[31] He was named as a participant in a synod held in 828 in The Chronicle of Michael the Syrian. See Chabot, *Chronique* 1899-1910:50.

[32] Abu Ra'ita, 'Letter on the Incarnation' (*al-Risala fi-l-tajassud*) in Keating 2006:268-71.

[33] `Ammar al-Basri, 'The Book of the Proof' (*Kitab al-Burhan*) in Hayek 1977:19-90. This work must have been written after 838 since it alludes to the conquest of Amorium by the Caliph al-Mu'tasim, 'a king in our time who left his kingdom with all of his armies for Rome to look for a woman in a fortress' (Hayek 1977:38).

them about Himself, revealing His authority and power to them."[34] While this argument reflects John 1:14-18 and Hebrews 1:1-4 which favourably compare seeing God in Christ with hearing God through previous messengers, it directly challenges the Islamic confinement of revelation to God's speech that safeguards Him from contamination by what He created, or limitation in some aspect of His creation. `Ammār evidently thought that Muslims could be persuaded that the revelation of God in person was more valuable than the revelation by speech through messengers.

Secondly, God understands that human beings long to see Him since they make images of the divine in their quest for Him. Rather than leave people searching for Him, God chose to come Himself to demonstrate His true likeness in Christ. This is a bold claim given the insistence of the Qur'ān that humans had gone astray by attempting to make images of divine beings, but `Ammār presents God as One who condescends to human weakness out of compassion for those who had gone astray, and who chooses the union of divinity and humanity to make visible His true nature. Thirdly, if it is the case that all humanity will meet God as Judge, then is it not an act of kindness for the Judge to make Himself known to the accused? However, it was not possible for the Judge to appear directly, so He decided to "veil Himself with human nature."[35] Perhaps `Ammār believed that the Muslim denial that God can be seen by humans may be met by conceding that indeed the Judge wears a veil over His face, but this would be to play down the very point of the Incarnation made in John 1 and Hebrews 1 that in Christ God is seen in all His glory. Fourthly, by taking a human body, God has elevated humanity to rule creation both in time and eternity, showing just how highly He thinks of us humans. This fourth reason is illustrated in another apologetic work by `Ammar, *The Book of Questions and Answers.*[36] Question twenty-seven in section four on the Incarnation asks how the merit of Christ relates humans to God. Imagine a king, replies `Ammār, who wants to identify with his people to the fullest extent so decides to have a son born among them. The son inherits his father's kingdom and possesses all his authority yet he is one of the people. Because he stems from both the king and the people, the latter are included in the kingdom he inherits. "In the same way the Incarnate one by taking a human body relates humanity to his divine inheritance by taking humanity into that which belongs to God."[37] In the final analysis, `Ammār boldly contested Muslim convictions about the absolute otherness of God, in the confidence that the Incarnation would commend a better view of God's dealings with humanity. Yet the reality probably was that Muslims would not have

[34]Hayek 1977: 62.
[35] Hayek 1977:69.
[36] `Ammar al-Basri, 'The Book of Questions and Answers' (*Kitab al-masa'il wa-l-ajwiba*) in Hayek 1977: 178-265.
[37] Hayek 1977: 222.

accepted the terms of these arguments that so fundamentally breached the transcendence of God.

This reality can be illustrated from the *Refutation of the Incarnation* by Abū `Īsā al-Warrāq [d. 861].[38] In the most thorough criticism of the Incarnation by any Muslim writer in the early Islamic period, al-Warrāq argues that the supposed union of divinity and humanity in Christ is logically impossible and therefore not a true account of the way God relates to the world He created. When Christians speak of the divine 'Word' in Christ they might mean that "the Word showed itself to the creation through this body…and they saw it and touched it", or they might mean that the Word "appeared in him as control, which indicated the wisdom and power of the controller". [39] The first meaning is incredible because God cannot be restricted to a body, and the second does not guarantee that Jesus uniquely reveals God since God controls all bodies, animal and human.

Al-Warrāq was treated to a point by point reply by the renowned 10th century Jacobite philosopher and theologian, Yahya ibn `Adi [893/4-974]. [40] His response to the above discussion is to say that Christians do not want to affirm either of the interpretations given by al-Warraq. They mean to say that "the Word was revealed united with the human being by means of what was revealed from the actions of the one substance (*jawhar*) of Christ formed from the substance (*jawhar*) of the Word and the substance (*jawhar*) of the human being." [41] In practice this means that the Word is revealed in the miracles performed by Christ that cannot be ascribed to human capability but must arise from a "divine substance" (*jawhar ilahi*), as well as from the divine power that allows no room for him to lie in his proclamation that "he was God, and Son of God, and that he and his Father, who is God, were one, and that whoever had seen him had seen his Father." [42] By quoting John 10:30 and 39, along with John 14:9, ibn `Adī demonstrates that the language used by Christian theologians ultimately reflects the language found in the gospels, and that theology is a form of faithful interpretation of scriptural sources. In other words, his reply to misinterpretation by al-Warraq is based on reference back to the original statements of Christ in order to show how the developed theology of the churches is true to the master's teaching. The fact that al-Warraq refers only once to the teaching of Christ in the Gospels in his long refutation of the Incarnation makes this appeal to the Gospels

---

[38] Abu `Isa al-Warraq, 'Refutation of the Incarnation' (*al-radd `ala al-ittitad*) in Thomas 2002.

[39] Thomas 2002:172-3.

[40] Yahya ibn `Adi, 'Reply to the Refutation of the Incarnation by Abu `Isa al-Warraq' (*Jawab Yahya ibn `Adi`an radd abi `Isa al-Warraq `ala al-Nasara fi-l-Ittihad*) in Platti 1987.

[41] Platti 1987.490:88.

[42] Platti 1987.490:88.

by ibn `Adī all the more poignant and demonstrates the gulf between Muslim and Christian apologists. [43]

Allegation that the Union of Divinity and Humanity adversely affects the Divinity

The most serious challenge to the Christian belief in the Incarnation came from the Muslim claim that the otherness of God would be damaged by the union of the divine and human. Al-Qasim argued that associating the created with the Creator weakens His power, and believing that God should take a body is to limit Him. "He is God the Creator…who has no partner in his power or timelessness...who is not, composed of various parts, weak, embodied, or limited." [44] Therefore, Christians were under pressure to defend God from apparent threats to His sublime character when they claimed that the Word of God had become human in Jesus Christ.

Abu Qurra addressed such Muslim difficulties in a treatise entitled "*A Reply to the One who refuses to attribute the Incarnation to God*." [45] He attempts to answer the following question posed by an anonymous Muslim, "How can the divine Son take a body and experience suffering?" Abu Qurra replies that "God is not effaced or cancelled out by appearing to His creation." [46] He appeals to texts from the Bible where God is sitting on His throne and argues that God is both seated on His throne and in control of the whole universe. While he does not refer to any of the eighteen passages in the Qur'ān that refer to God sitting on His throne, it is probable that Abu Qurra is aware of discussion among Muslims about the interpretation of these texts. [47] He seems to be asking Muslims to agree that God can sit in one location yet control everything since the Qur'an affirms this. On this basis, he argues that God can both be in Jesus and in control of everything. "The eternal Son is in every place…He is not at all limited or restricted, apart from being in the body in which he experienced pain and suffering." [48]

Nevertheless, the anonymous Muslim is allowed to come back with the observation that the analogy of the throne with the human body is unacceptable. "It is undeniable that God sits on the throne but He does not take up residence in the body…The throne is pure but the human body is not suitable for God." [49] In

---

[43] Thomas 2002:198-9; al-Warrq quotes John 10:30, "I and my Father are one."

[44] Al-Qaasim ibn Ibrahim 309.

[45] Abū Qurra, 'A Reply to the One who refuses to attribute the Incarnation to God' (*Maymar fī-i-radd `ala man yankaru li-llah al-tajassud*) in Bacha 1904:180-186.

[46] Bacha 1904: 180.

[47] Surah 7:52, 9:130, 10:3, 13:2, 17:44, 20:4, 21:22, 23:88 and 117, 25:60, 27:26, 32:3, 39:75, 40:15, 43:82, 57:4, 81:20, 85:15. See further, Rissanen 1993:120-123, and Beaumont 2005:33-36.

[48] Beaumont 2005:182.

[49] Beaumont 2005:183.

response Abu Qurra suggests that the human body is the finest aspect of God's creation and although human beings are sinful, the body taken from Mary was not touched by sin. In fact the Holy Spirit cleansed that which was taken from Mary so that the Eternal Son was able to unite with "a body which was pure, clean, immaculate and beautiful" fit for the residence of the divine. [50] As a result how can anyone deny "the residence of God (*hulul Allah*) in the human body? [51] Here Abu Qurra may be alluding to *sūra* 19:19 where Mary is informed of the gift of a pure child, in the hope that Muslims may come to see that the Incarnation does not impugn the character of God, and that God may associate with His creation in a manner that does not undermine His transcendent majesty. In the final analysis, Muslims would probably have insisted that transcendence precluded the embodiment of divinity, but Abu Qurra's apology is a notable effort to engage appropriately with Islamic presuppositions.

Other arguments in support of the suitability of the human body taken by the Word are put forward by `Ammar al-Basri in *The Book of Questions and Answers.* Several of the fifty one questions on the Incarnation relate to the supposed negative impact of the human body on the divine Word. Question five asks, whether or not human nature affects the divine. The answer is that the divine affects the human but not the other way around, for just as coal is made hot by fire but does not pass on blackness to it, so the human nature in Christ does not affect the divine. [52] Question eight wonders whether only one or both the divine and human natures of Christ ate and drank and suffered. `Ammar replies that it was "from his human nature (*nasuti-hi*) he grew up, ate, drank, changed, and developed, not from his divine nature (*lahuti-hi*)." [53]

`Ammār attempts to defend the divine from contamination by union with the human by insisting that the actions of the human nature of Christ have no adverse impact on his divine nature. Development and change do not touch the divine so the Muslim questioner should not be anxious that the Christian notion of Incarnation undermines the integrity of the transcendent One. However, this separation of the human activity from the divine nature of Christ results in a Jesus that is divided into two personal centres, one divine and the other human. In other words, there is a union of two natures in Christ but they do not function in a united way, but seem to alternate depending on circumstances.

Question eleven is, how is it possible for the divine nature to clothe itself with human nature without becoming limited by it? The answer refers to the analogy of the sun giving light to a part of the earth without being limited to that place. "The eternal substance (*al-jawhar al-āzalī*) took a body for himself by uniting with it, a temple which he indwelt...yet the body that he put on did not enclose

[50] Beaumont 2005:184.
[51] Beaumont 2005.
[52] `Ammar, 'The Book of Questions and Answers' (*Kitab al-masa'il wa-l-ajwiba*) in Hayek 1977:183.
[53] Hayek 1977:191.

him, or his habitation limit him, or hold him back, or his temple restrict him." [54] God interacts with his creation without being confined to a particular connection, a concept a Muslim could affirm, but the next question is concerned with the embodiment of God, a step too far for the anonymous Muslim. `Ammar replies that he does not want to speak about God's body. "God the Word became human" (*Allah al-kalima ta'annasa*). [55] This is analogous to a man becoming dressed, or taking up arms, or putting on a turban. "He did not become a turban or weapons or armour. Likewise we say that God the Word became embodied (*tajassada*), became human (*ta'annasa*). In other words, he brought into being (*ahdatha*) a body (*jasadan*) and clothed himself with it. He created a human being and put it on (*tadarra`a-hu*)." [56]

This portrait of Christ as providing complete freedom for the divine Word from limitations apparently imposed by indwelling a human body would probably imply for a Muslim reader that the body in this Christian presentation is merely a set of clothes that can be put on and off at will. However, real human beings are more than an outer shell but involve integration between mind and body as a functioning unit. Was Christ, for Christians, a real human being, or was he, according to them, the divine Word appearing in a human body as al-Warrāq suggested above? To make matters worse, al-Warraq complained that a union of the divine and human substances in Christ would result in the transformation of the one into the other. "If the substance of one of them was transformed into the substantiality of the other, the temporal would become eternal or the eternal temporal." [57] Safeguarding the integrity of the divine was central to Muslim thinking and the objections of al-Warraq show just how insistent Muslims were in the face of Christian talk of Incarnation of the divine in Christ.

An answer to this query was offered by Yahya ibn `Adi in his comparison of the union of the Word and the human body with the union of the human mind and body:

> We find the soul (*al-nafs*) and the body become one substance (*jawhar*) by their being joined together, and this is the animal (*al-hayawan*), without the substance (*jawhar*) of the body being transformed from its substantiality (*jawhariyya*) or the substance (*jawhar*) of the soul being transformed from its substantiality (*jawhariyya*), but their substantialities remain as they are and another, third substance (*jawhar*) comes into being in which are found the two substances…It does not follow that the contingent becomes eternal or the eternal contingent. [58]

In other words, just as a living human being is the union of spirit and body which do not become transformed into the other but remain distinct, even though

[54]Hayek 1977:194.
[55] Hayek 1977:196.
[56] Hayek 1977:196.
[57] Al-Warraq in Thomas 2002: 138-9.
[58] Platti 1987.490:56.

they are joined together in a being that acts as a union of soul and flesh, so Christ is a union of divinity and humanity which do not become transformed into the other but keep their separateness, even though they are joined together in a being that acts as a union of divine and human. Al-Warrāq returned later to the same issue charging Christians with absurdity in their attempt to keep the divine intact when united with the human. They could not "reject the claim of anyone who said that black is white, or the physical body is an accident, the impossible is possible, right is wrong, and other kinds of contradiction."[59] Ibn `Adī responded by pointing out that a human can be both black and white in colour without this causing any difficulty. "An African has white eyes and teeth, but he is not described as a white person."[60] Thus we say that he is black because for the most part his body is black in colour even though he has some white aspects. In the same way, we say of Christ "that he is eternal and contingent from two different aspects, eternal from the aspect of his divinity (*ilahiyya*) and contingent from the aspect of his humanity (*insaniyya*)."[61] What is clear from this argument is that the Christian defence of the Incarnation had to deal with the charge of contradictory claims and that suitable analogies from life needed to be found to demonstrate the appropriateness of seemingly paradoxical language.

Conclusion

Christian apologists first of all had to defend the nature of the Incarnation from Muslim misunderstanding of the kind of relationship Jesus had with his Father. If he was the Word of God who took a human body then there was no biological link between the Father and the Son. Therefore, it is possible for Fatherhood to be an acceptable attribute of God. Secondly, they needed to develop appropriate justifications for Jesus' divinity in the light of Muslim refusal to countenance any union of divine and human. One apologist noticed that the Qur'ān gave Jesus creative powers belonging to God alone. Muslims found lots of evidence in the Gospels for a human Christ so Christians were forced to appeal to Gospel passages showing his divinity. One theologian came up with imaginative reasons for God to want to reveal Himself in human form out of compassion for humanity, but that was probably a step too far for Muslim conceptions of God's mercy. Thirdly, they took pains to so portray the union of divinity with humanity in Christ that there would be no adverse effects on the divinity from uniting with the humanity. One appealed to God sitting on his throne yet being everywhere at the same time, to uphold the ubiquity of the divinity while united with the localised humanity in Jesus. Another separated the human actions from the divine nature of Christ so that the latter remained untouched by the former, by picturing the body as clothing or a temple for the divine Word. Muslim challenges to the

[59] Al-Warraq, in Thomas 2002:242-3.
[60] Platti 1987:178.
[61] Platti 1987:178.

rationality of this idea were met by the analogy of the human soul indwelling the body without being tainted by that union. If the soul can remain untouched by the influence of the body then the divine can be unaffected by the human in the Incarnation. Christians in the early centuries of encounter with Muslims defended the Incarnation with the aid of careful Scriptural interpretation, more or less appropriate analogies, and dialectical argument in support of the truth of paradoxical language.

Newbigin's Reformulation of Christology and its Implications for a Christian-Muslim Dialogue

Jose Abraham

Rev. Dr. Jose Abraham is Lecturer in Religion and Culture at the United Theological College, Bangalore, India

Introduction

Lesslie Newbigin (1909-1998), a missionary of the Church of Scotland, served as Bishop of the Madras Diocese of the Church of South India. He spent nearly forty years shepherding and nurturing the church in different parts of India. During this time he also actively participated in the world wide ecumenical movement and held key positions in the International Missionary Council and the World Council of Churches. After his retirement as bishop in India, he taught Missiology at the Selly Oak Colleges and continued his pastoral ministry in Birmingham. He has written a number of books and articles and delivered numerous sermons through which he articulated his theology of mission and challenged the Western churches to rethink their commitment to the Gospel of Christ. His writings, which were born out of his rich cross-cultural experience as well as his sharp critical insights as a missionary, rejuvenated fresh thinking among Christians about their responsibility towards people of other faiths and ideologies. No wonder he continues to be regarded as a highly respected and relevant theologian of religion.

Exclusivism, inclusivism and pluralism have been three dominant theological positions that explain Christian attitudes towards non-Christian religions. The main preoccupation of these positions has been with the issue of the salvation of non-Christians. Though exclusivists and inclusivists believe that salvation is only through Christ, the former hold that there is no salvation outside the church and Christianity; the latter believe in God's salvific plan for humanity through Christ, irrespective of their religious persuasions. Pluralists argue that Christ is just one of the ways for salvation and God may have other plans to save non-Christians. Newbgin was an active participant in these discourses. Since these theological positions were dominated by a discourse on salvation rather than rethinking traditional Christology, he believed them to be insufficient to deal with the issue of Christian responsibility towards people of other faiths and ideologies. Therefore, he attempted to reformulate a Christology based on the Trinitarian doctrine of God, which is especially important for a Christian-Muslim dialogue. This is because it is Jesus Christ who is shared between Islam and Christianity but he is also a source of theological conflict between them. Whilst Jesus is understood as divine in Christianity he remains only as a prophet of God in traditional Islam. Traditional Christologies have historically failed to negotiate the tension resulting from this. This paper is an attempt to explore the extent to which Newbigin's Christology is relevant for bridging this impasse.[1]

Context of Newbigin's Reformulation of Christology

Indeed, there was an immediate European context for Newbigin's thinking about Christian responsibility towards people of other faiths and ideologies.[2] In the second half of the 20th century, the churches in Great Britain and Ireland realized they lived in the presence of Muslims, Hindus, Sikhs and others as their neighbours and fellow citizens. Newbigin wrote the following to explain the gravity of this situation:

> The accelerating explosion of world population is on such a stupendous scale that it is difficult for us to grasp its significance and to recognize that it creates a radically new situation for the human race. It is only a short time ago that we were like small tribes inhabiting a vast forest, so large that we only occasionally met for mutual trading or for inter-tribal skirmishing. Today we are more like the inhabitants of an overcrowded slum where several families have to share a single flat. We are already fighting among ourselves – even the wealthy nations of the West – for the diminishing stocks of food.[3]

According to Newbigin, during the colonial period, Christian missionaries, who engaged in Evangelism with the support of British colonial rulers, understood Christian mission as 'crusade' and promoted a kind of 'aggressive Evangelism.'[4] However, the contemporary European Christians of his time hesitated to involve in this kind of evangelism because they wished to become agents of reconciliation. Moreover, their association with Muslims, Hindus and Sikhs as their fellow-citizens reinforced their ambivalence towards crusading spirit of Evangelism:

> They discover that these are not enemies of the truth to be subdued, nor backward people to be civilized. They can very easily see that they are … more devout, God-fearing and law-abiding than many of the natives of these islands. If they have the opportunity of more intimate friendship they will find much more:

[1] See Newbigin 1977, 1989, 1991 and 1969.

[2] Newbigin firmly believed that Christian mission is not limited to people of other faiths alone but also included those outside the religious fold, such as atheists and people who follow political ideologies, such as Marxism.

[3] Newbigin 1977:2.

[4] In Newbigin's understanding, this is a model that the medieval Christians learned from Muslims. He explains European colonialism as an extension of the Crusades against Muslims. Newbigin 1977:2.

> evidences of a level of devotion of commitment and of spiritual experience which make the average Christian aware of the shallowness of his own. Traditional concepts of evangelism do not fit this situation.[5]

In this situation, the contemporary European Chrsitians thought that it would be improper to share the Gospel with their fellow Muslims, Hindus and Sikhs. However, Newbigin warned, "our shame and penitence as we remember the sins of arrogance and pride which have so often marked our witness in the past" should not keep us away from fulfilling our responsibility towards non-Christians.[6] To him human history is replete with God's covenantal action with human beings. The church is entrusted with the responsibility of witnessing to this covenant.[7] Evangelism is for this reason an essential part of the churches' ministry. Christians are mandated to be the bearers of the Gospel for all mankind and this is 'the central Christian tradition.'[8]

Islamic Understanding of God (*Tawhid*)

The Qur'an used the Arabic word *Allah* for God, which appears more than 2500 times in it.[9] The root of the word *Allah* is constituted with the letters A, L and H. It was the same root letters that all Semitic languages, such as Hebrew, Syriac, Aramaic, Chaldean, Himyarite and Arabic, combine to denote the Supreme Being.[10] For instance, in pre-Islamic Arabia, poets used the term *Ilah* to refer to the Highest Being or the Creator of the universe. According to Abul Kalam Azad, the term *ilah* had probably been derived from the root *'lah*, which was an exclamatory expression of "wonder or helplessness."[11] Therefore, "the term *Allah* came to be used as the proper name for the Creator of the universe in respect of whom man can express nothing except his sense of wonder which increases in intensity, the more he thinks of Him, only to admit eventually that the road to the knowledge of God begins and ends in wonder and humility."[12] This explains the reason why various aspects of the beliefs and practices of Islam encompassed the Reality of God and are designed to make and keep Muslims aware of that Reality.[13]

Tawhid is the technical term that is used in Islamic theology to describe the Qur'anic understanding of God. The words *tawhid* and *wahid* have been derived from the same root which means "one." Therefore, the doctrine of *tawhid* is

---

[5] Newbigin 1977:2.
[6] Newbigin 1977:8.
[7] Newbigin 1977:13.
[8] Newbigin 1977:3.
[9] Rahman 1994:1.
[10] Azad 996:14-15.
[11] Azad 996:15.
[12] Azad 996:15.
[13] Miller 2000:35-36.

defined as the belief in the oneness or unity of God. In the Quranic understanding, God is the Absolute Reality (112:2). He is the self-subsisting (20: 111; 2: 255), all embracing, all knowing (2:115), eternal (112:2), most high, most great (31:30) and sovereign God (59: 22-24; 62:1). He is the first and the last, the seen and the unseen (57:3). He alone is infinite while everything else is finite (13:16). God, who is pure and holy, is free from all defects and imperfections and there is no other being in the category of God. God has no partners, associates or co-equals and there is nothing to which He can be properly compared. He is unique in His being and in His characteristics. Therefore, "God cannot be regarded as an existent among other existents … [and] there can be no democratic and equal sharing of being between the Original, the Creator, the Self-Necessary and the borrowed, the created, the contingent."[14] According to Miller, this doctrine of God explains the Muslim hesitation about representational art in relation to God. "God who is incomparably divine in quality cannot be compared to what is creaturely in origin or form. And human language suffers the same deficiency as art. It also is inadequate to describe the Being and Character of the Almighty, and all human statements about God therefore be regarded as having a provisional quality."[15] In Islamic theology, the term *tanzih*, which means "to declare something pure and free from something else,"[16] is used to describe the doctrine of God in this perspective.

Muslims hold that it is impossible for human beings to understand God unless God reveals himself to us. Therefore, the first step to fathom out God is to understand the Qur'an, the word of God.[17] The Qur'an employs several names in an attempt to shed light on the essence and attributes of God. It is commonly believed that there are 99 beautiful names for God, which are sometimes categorized as 'glorious' and 'terrible' names. While the majority of these names are found in the Qur'an, some of them are drawn from traditions. According to Murata and Chittick, the names of God's essence, such as One, Holy, Glorified, Independent, and Transcendent, as well as 'the majestic and wrathful names' could only reveal how God is different from the rest of creation and infinitely beyond the petty affairs of the creatures.[18] Since these names cannot describe God's essence in positive terms, they could only talk to us about human limitations and thereby affirm that God is beyond all imperfection and limitation. Since God, who alone is Real, is so great and so majestic, everything else is unreal and not worthy of consideration. Therefore, there is little room left, from the *tanzih* perspective, to argue for some sort of similarity between God and the creation.[19]

---

[14] Rahman 1994:4.
[15] Miller 2000:43.
[16] Murata & Chittick. 1994:71.
[17] Murata & Chittick. 1994:47.
[18] Murata & Chittick. 1994:70-71.
[19] Miller 2000:59.

From the above discussion, one can make out that affirming the divine-human divide is fundamental to the Islamic doctrine of God. God and humanity are thought of in polar terms and any suggestion for intimacy between divine and human beings was simply thought impossible.[20] Therefore, confessing the unity or oneness of God is a cardinal principle in Islamic tradition. Due to the same reason, associating partners to God, denoted by the term *shirk*, which means "to share, to be a partner, to make someone share in, to give someone a partner, to associate someone with someone else,"[21] is considered as the greatest sin in Islam. While God is being the "absolute creator, master, king, deity and majesty," humanity stands antithetical to Him as "creature, servant, worshipper, lowly-humbled creature full of awe of the other."[22] God being so transcendent, prophecy is the authoritative mode of divine revelation in Islamic tradition. Angels and prophets are the mediums through which God revealed himself to human beings throughout history. It is significant to note here that the prophets never shared intimacy with God in Islamic understanding. This explains the reason why the notion of the divinity of Jesus, who is one of the prophets of Islam, is completely rejected in the Qur'an.

However, in Islamic theology, God is also understood from another perspective known as *tashbih*. *Tashbih* is 'to declare something similar to something else,' which affirms that God must have some sort of similarity with the creatures.[23] The names of God's attributes, such as life, knowledge, desire, power, mercy, generosity, and provision, designate God's qualities and characteristic. Even though these attributes belong truly to God, they are also shared in a certain degree by human beings.[24] In other words, these attributes declare that even though God is the only Reality truly worthy of the name, He is not totally separated from His creation. Therefore, in *tashbih* perspective, God embraces the entire creation and discloses His nearness to the creation and His deep concern for the creatures.[25]

In this context, it may be relevant to note the meaning of two names of God in the Qur'an, *ilah* and *rabb*. Singh notes, "[O]ne of the meanings of *ilah* in the Lexicon speaks of *ilah* as the object of intense feeling of the worshipper. *Ilah* in turn also reciprocates this feeling."[26] The intensely intimate relationship of *ilah* with the devotee is captured by the picture of the joining together of a lost baby camel and its mother. In such a union both the parties have intense longing for finding the other or being found by the other. Similarly, Singh suggests the word *rabb* (another name of God) can be imagined like a foster mother "bringing up a

[20] Singh 2002:240.
[21] Murata & Chittick 1994:49.
[22] Singh 2001:178.
[23] Murata & Chittick 1994:71.
[24] Murata & Chittick 1994:60.
[25] Murata & Chittick 1994:71.
[26] Singh 1999:119.

child under her care, supervising improvement, nourishing and caring for the child with an ultimate aim of bringing the child to 'a state of completion by degrees.'[27] In this picture also there is a sense of mutual benefit. While the child's physical needs are met by the mother, 'the child also meets some needs of the mother, which acts as her motivation to care.'[28] In the same way, human beings trust in God to receive God's mercy and love, but, in return, God also receives human response of worship: 'God's intense love for humanity is realized when He accepts human knowledge of him (as *ilah/rabb*) as a true representative of His deity.'[29]

In Islam, Muslim mystics and philosophers especially held the possibility of the relationship between God and His creation. As we have already noted, Muslims traditionally believe that it is through prophecy that divine knowledge has been conveyed to human beings. However, under the influence of Greek wisdom, Muslim philosophers maintained that the human intellect is capable of gaining divine knowledge directly, without any intermediaries.[30] They integrated Greek philosophy with Islamic theology and popularized the Islamized Greek worldview, which made it possible 'in Islam what was impossible within the purview of the traditional transcendental view of God. It made it conceivable to think of the possibility of Divine-human intimacy.'[31] In Ibn Sina's understanding 'creation itself is intellection by God of His own Essence. It is this intellection (*ta'aqqul*) and knowledge (*'ilm*) of His one Essence that brings all things into being.'[32] Thus, creation is part and parcel of the essence of God and it manifests Him. Ibn 'Arabi believed that the starting point of the activity of creation was God's self awareness that He is 'the hidden treasure'. From being a hidden treasure God longed to be known and it was this longing that burst forth into a sigh, which caused the creation to come in to existence.[33] If God is the One and Only Reality, then creation cannot be placed as another reality, completely divorced from God.[34] This understanding, which will reduce God and creation as two separate entities, will eventually negate the very principle of *tawhid*. Therefore, according to Nasr, creation is 'a manifestation of a vastly greater world which transcends it and from which it issues.'[35]

Muslim mystics, naturally, attempted the possibility of emphasizing their experience of human intimacy with God without compromising the cardinal

[27] Singh 1999:119.
[28] Singh 1999:119.
[29] Singh 1999:122.
[30] Singh 2002:243.
[31] Singh 2002:241.
[32] Nasr 964:213.
[33] D'Souza 1988:147.
[34] Nasr 1964:5. If God is One and the only Reality, according to Seyyed Hossein Nasr, then *tawhid* is the belief in the Oneness of Reality. Therefore, in its most profound sense, *la ilaha ill Allah* means that there is no reality outside of the Absolute Reality.
[35] Nasr 1992:94.

Islamic principal of *tawhid*. But to them their intimacy was with God was the secret of their direct access to the divine knowledge.[36] Sufis went to the extreme (and still do) of portraying God as their bridegroom, and of themselves as the lovers or friends of God. It is highly significant to note here that Sufis are venerated by a large number of Muslims in many parts of the world and their tomb complexes (also called the *dargah*) are often the focal point of popular Islam. Thus, even though the notion of divine-human divide is fundamental to traditional Islam, it is not uniformly accepted in practice by all Muslims.

Christian Understanding of God

There is no doubt that the Christian understanding of God can be categorized as monotheism. However, the Christian understanding of monotheism is interpreted rather differently than that of the Jews' and Muslims'. The disciples of Jesus and early Christians were rooted in Judaism and they believed in the dogmas of monotheism. However, "the first disciples lived with Jesus, saw how he prayed, how he spoke of God, how he preached, how he treated people, particularly the poor, how he faced up to conflict, how he suffered and died and rose again; they also saw what happened in the community that believed in him, especially after Pentecost."[37] It is through the life and work of Jesus that they understood various dimensions of the essence and attributes of God. They also experienced the work of the Holy Spirit in the church. Therefore, early Christians were struggling to express a doctrine of God without compromising their monotheistic belief as well as their experience of the work of Jesus and the Holy Spirit. It is this struggle that gave rise to the Christian doctrine of the Trinity, which Leonardo Boff defined as 'one God in three persons, or one nature and three hypostases, or three Lovers and a single love, or three Subjects and a single substance, or three Uniques and one communion.'[38] Therefore, even though the early Christians held the belief that God is one, their monotheism was rooted in the belief that God is a triune.

Christology is part and parcel of the Christian doctrine of God. Christians cannot formulate the doctrine of God without Jesus Christ and the Holy Spirit. Therefore, in Christianity there is no way of doing theology without reference to Christology and Pneumatology. In fact, the early Church devoted its time and energy not to formulating a doctrine of the oneness of God, which was never disputed in Christianity, but to explain the relationship between the Father, Son and Holy Spirit - the three persons of the Godhead. If God's transcendence dominated the Islamic doctrine of God, it is God's imminence that became central to Christian theology. God is divine and human at the same time and He identified himself with the creation in its joy and suffering. God reconciled the divine-human divide in Christianity through the self-giving love of Jesus Christ

---

[36] Singh 2002:242.
[37] Boff 1988:1.
[38] Boff 1988:2.

and offered His continued guidance to human beings through the work of the Holy Spirit. Since the essential nature of God is love, who expressed it in the self-sacrifice of Jesus Christ, the divine-human, creator-creature, master-servant, deity-devotee disjunction is reconciled in Christianity, though it is a blasphemous notion from an Islamic understanding. Therefore, it is not a heresy in Christianity to address God as Father and Jesus as brother and bridegroom of the church or lover.

If we compare our discussion on Muslim understanding of God as above with that of the Christian understanding, it should be possible to find parallels between them. In both the Christian and Muslim perspectives there lie profound mysteries and complexities in understanding the essence and attributes of God. Any label that we attach to God would be inadequate to describe His Reality in human language.[39] Therefore, according to Clinton Bennett, 'in the orthodox Muslim doctrine of Attributes (*sifah*) we have an understanding of God that is not very far removed, if removed at all, from the Christian understanding of Trinity.'[40] This means that the Trinitarian doctrine of God is not entirely a foreign idea to Islam, which should open the possibility of dialogue between Muslims and Christians. Such a dialogue will be possible because the subject of the dialogue would not simply rehash the traditional understanding of Jesus, as a prophet or the son of God (in biological terms). The starting point of dialogue would be the mystery of God rather than the divinity or humanity of Jesus.

Newbigin's Reformulation of Christology

Newbigin's Christology gives one a clue to analyzing his understanding of the Christian responsibility towards the people of other faiths and ideologies. According to him, even though Christians are monotheists they understand God in the Trinitarian (three-in-one, as Father, Son and Holy Spirit) rather than in Unitarian (one) model.[41] Therefore, though the understanding of God as the ultimate reality is central to non-Christian religions, the Christian doctrine of God is distinctive. Christians believe that God revealed Himself through the person of Jesus Christ and, therefore, Jesus Christ is 'God as he really is.' Early Christian communities very well understood Jesus as God in this sense. Therefore, even when they were a tiny minority religious community, they did not think of Jesus as one among the many ways for salvation. Rather they believed that Jesus, who is the 'head of the church,' is also the head of the entire cosmos. He is the Lord of all, and, in the end, all things will be united in Christ.[42]

In Newbigin's understanding there is one more thing that makes the Biblical doctrine of Jesus unique and thus different from the conceptions of God in other

---

[39] Bennett 2001:268-269.
[40] Bennett 2001:265.
[41] Newbigin 1977:7.
[42] Newbigin 1977:8.

religious traditions. In Christianity, even though God is understood as all-knowing, all-powerful and all-present, he is also conceived as 'a crucified man.'[43] Jesus, who himself is God and came to proclaim the reign of God, was crucified "as a defeated, condemned and excommunicated man, that among his last words was the terrible cry: 'My God, why have you forsaken me?' It is this Jesus whom the church proclaims as the risen and victorious Lord and King."[44] According to Newbigin, 'it is the total reversal of everything that men normally accept as the truth about God and about history.'[45]

Against this conception of Jesus, Newbigin noted, contemporary Christians think of God in a Unitarian, rather than Trinitarian model, in an attempt to make Christology relevant for people of other faiths. John Hick's Copernican revolution was one such attempt.[46] He rejected John Hick's repositioning of Christianity.[47] Likewise, he believed that while some religions may recognize Jesus as one among many saviours, they fail to understand the complexity of the Christian doctrine of Christ. The 'search for historical Jesus,' a Christian movement based on rational thinking in the West, makes a distinction between the 'Jesus of history' and the 'Christ of faith', and it too cannot hold Christology in its entirety.

Significance of Newbigin's Christology

Newbigin's Christology is in the affirmation that Jesus is the 'God as He really is.' This is significantly relevant to explain how the non-Christian world is related to God. Since Jesus is God, every part of the whole created world and every human being are related to him. In Newbigin's opinion this was the reason why St. John wrote that 'Jesus is the Word through whom all things came to be, that he is the life of all that is and that he is the light that gives light to every men.'[48] This implied that the person and work of Jesus should not be confined to Christians or Christianity. It means that Christians should not 'deny the reality of work of God in the lives and thoughts and prayers of men and women outside the Christian church.' In fact, they should be looking for and rejoicing in the evidence of such works.[49]

---

[43] Newbigin 1977:6.
[44] Newbigin 1977:14
[45] Newbigin 1977:14.
[46] Traditionally Christians imagined that Christianity was the centre of the universe of faiths, and that the other religions circled at varying distance around it. According to John Hick, God is the centre and all the religions, including Christianity, are planets that circle around him.
[47] Newbigin 1977:5-7.
[48] Newbigin 1977:10.
[49] Newbigin 1977:10.

> Therefore there is something deeply wrong when Christians imagine that loyalty to Jesus requires them to belittle the manifest presence of the light in the lives of men and women who do not acknowledge him, to seek out points of weakness, to ferret out hidden sins and deception as means of commending the Gospel. If we love the light and walk in the light we will also rejoice in the light wherever we find it – even the smallest gleams of it in the surrounding darkness….Here I am thinking, let it be clearly understood, not only of the evidence of light in the religious life of non-Christians, the steadfastness and costliness of the devotion which so often puts Christians to shame; I am thinking also of the no less manifest evidences of the shining of the light in the lives of atheists, humanists, Marxists and others who have explicitly rejected the message and fellowship of the church.[50]

This implies that Christians should have the 'readiness for frank and searching discussion' with those outside the church in their day-to-day conversations. They should also meet with the people of other faiths and share with them in a common life, 'as neighbours, as citizens, as workers, as people who care about music or sport or politics.'[51] They should not encounter them 'as strangers but as those who live by the same life-giving Word, and in whom the same life-giving light shines.'[52] In this common human enterprise of living and building up a common life, Christians need 'to learn as well as to teach, to receive as well as to give.'[53] Even though Newbigin did not deny the importance of meeting scholars of different faiths in a formal 'dialogue,' he opined that it was in the day-to-day human living and relationships that we share each others' experience and hopes and fears and fundamental beliefs.[54]

Rationale for the Church in Dialogue with Non-Christians

In God's sight there is no distinction between Jew and Greek and Christian and non-Christians. It is the same God who is the Father of all and who purposes the salvation of all. For this reason, we have been chosen, called and sent into the world as members of the Church to continue the mission of Jesus in dialogue with the people of other faiths and ideologies. But Newbigin often reminded the Christians of the fact that they were entrusted with this commission even though they were 'a sinful company, sometimes more sinful than the world around them,' and, therefore, they should not think that their calling and commissioning was due to their merit.[55] In fact, they were no better, competent, enlightened, wiser, stronger, or more able than others. 'We have been chosen for this task, that

---

[50] Newbigin 1977:10.
[51] Newbigin 1977:18.
[52] Newbigin 1977:11.
[53] Newbigin 1977:11.
[54] Newbigin 1977:18.
[55] Newbigin 1977:17.

is all.'[56] Consequently, '[w]henever the church has imagined that it had a claim upon God which others did not have, it had already fallen away from Grace. The church is servant and not master. It is appointed to a stewardship on behalf of all, not to a privilege from which other are excluded.'[57]

Even though we are called to bear witness to God's mission, our understanding of 'Jesus as he really is' is conditioned by the whole of our culture – like any other knowledge. This is not to deny the fact that the fullness of God is not to find in Jesus, but to reiterate that the church does not yet possess all his fullness. We know in part, but not in full. Being an empty vessel, the Church is the place where the filling of the fullness of God is taking place (Eph 1:23). We are continually pressing on towards the fullness of knowledge of God in Jesus Christ, but have not reached the goal. Therefore, even the whole testimony of the Christian community as it is now is not enough to say who Jesus is.[58] It means that:

> [t]he church … faces the world not as the exclusive possessor of salvation, not as the fullness of what others have in part, not as the answer to the questions they ask, and not as the open revelation of what they are anonymously. The church faces the world rather as *arrabon* of that salvation, as sign, first-fruit, token, witness of that salvation which God purposes for the whole.[59]

Therefore, the church does not go into the world as the body 'with nothing to receive and everything to give.'[60] On the contrary, the whole church is learning by living continually in open and humble dialogue with the world. In this process, a Christian not only learns from his fellow Christians of another culture, but also from his fellow men or women of another faith or ideology. It can only be at the end, when every tongue confesses him as Lord and 'when all things have been summed up in him' (Eph 1: 10), that we shall know the fullness of all that he is.[61] In this journey, it is the Holy Spirit, who is Lord over the church, who guides her from the limited, partial and distorted understanding of and embodiment of the truth into the fullness of truth in Jesus.[62] Therefore, Newbigin understands Christianity as a growing and developing movement:

> It grows and develops not merely by extending the circle of its membership, but because in the encounter of the Gospel with new cultures, new aspect of the fullness of God in Christ are brought to light. We have seen this illustrated in the encounter of Peter with Cornelius. The result of that encounter, and of the full meeting of the Gospel with the world of classical culture, was that Christianity

[56] Newbigin 1977:25.
[57] Newbigin 1977:17.
[58] Newbigin 1977:9.
[59] Newbigin 1977:20.
[60] Newbigin 1977:19.
[61] Newbigin 1977:9.
[62] Newbigin 1977:23.

> could no longer be a sect of Judaism but began to be a world religion.... It is through the meeting with all these cultures that the church learns more of Jesus and is thereby more fitted to be the house of all mankind.[63]

God's Universal Salvific Plan vis-à-vis Salvation through Christ

Newbigin acknowledged that the enduring tension between the Biblical doctrine of God's salvific plan for all and the salvation of a few through Christ. On the one hand the New Testament holds that God purposes the salvation of the whole world. In this perspective, Jesus, who is the unique saviour, is also the universal saviour. And, yet, on the other hand the same New Testament maintains that those who reject Jesus, the light of the world, will go into darkness. He is the Lord of all but only a few will find themselves as the object of His saving grace and all others will be judged by Him for eternity.[64]

In Newbigin's understanding, Christian theologians always try to relieve the perpetual tension between these two accounts of God's salvific plans. In this process, a group of theologians, who hold on the universal salvific doctrine of the Bible, argue that all roads must in the end lead to the same goal, as all rivers flow into the sea. These scholars exclude the possibility of eternal loss. Newbigin maintained that this stance needed to be rejected because it 'robs human life of its seriousness by denying the reality of human responsibility.'65 In an attempt to escape the tension, another group of theologians, who insist the salvation of the few through Christ, derived a doctrinal formula that explicated who were to be finally saved and who were to be lost. Newbigin rejected this solution as well on the grounds that it 'contradicts the central emphasis of the New Testament teaching about final judgment, which is that judgment will always be surprising and that it will be those who are sure they belong inside who find themselves outside.'66

Newbigin maintained that '[t]he real issue here is between the quest for a kind of assurance which has the future securely programmed in advance, and the summons to a kind of faith which trusts everything to the living Lord.'[67] It is true that we are called to be bearers of the Gospel to all humanity but we are not promised that we will be successful in converting all peoples to faith in Christ. God purposes the salvation of all but 'we are not to be anxious about our 'success' or otherwise in winning men and women to the faith. This is not in our hands. We are rather to be believing and hopeful because we trust the promise given to us.'[68]

---

[63] Newbigin 1977:18-19.
[64] Newbigin 1977:24.
[65] Newbigin 1977:24-25.
[66] Newbigin 1977:25.
[67] Newbigin 1977:25
[68] Newbigin 1977:17.

Conclusion

Newbigin's proposal for Christian responsibility towards people of other faiths and ideologies is relevant for our contemporary explorations in the area of the Theology of Religions because it clearly maintains the aspect of mystery of Christian doctrine of God. He maintains that 'Jesus as who really is,' who is God, and 'Jesus as we know him' is not the same. Therefore, he calls upon the Christians to live with people of other faiths and ideologies a life in dialogue seeking the mystery of 'Jesus as who really is'. He attempted to reformulate a Christology based on the Trinitarian doctrine of God, which is especially important for a Christian-Muslim dialogue because it is the doctrine of Christ that is commonly shared between Islam and Christianity but the same doctrine also became a point of contention among these two religious traditions. Thus, he affirmed that it is not possible develop a Christian doctrine of God without paying serious attention to Christology. He also maintained an aspect of mystery in the concept of salvation. We are called to proclaim the Gospel but at the same time we are also summoned to live a life of faith and obedience striving to enter the narrow door of salvation because salvation is not guaranteed to anyone in advance.

Christological Reflection in the Apologetic of Hamran Ambrie (1921-1988) of Indonesia

Jonathan E. Culver

Dr. Jonathan E. Culver did his cross cultural research at Fuller Theological Seminary and has been serving in Indonesia with OC International since 1982

Introduction

"God cannot have a son, for He has no need of a wife".[1] For more than thirteen hundred years Muslims have persistently rejected the Christian affirmation that Jesus is divine and that he is the Son of God. Thus, Christology remains one of the classic stumbling blocks in Christian-Muslim dialogue. Part of the problem lies in the way that Christians—mostly from the West—have explained the person of Christ. Many years ago, James W. Sweetman lamented the inadequacy of statements on Christian doctrines in languages spoken by Muslims. Furthermore, Sweetman noted that "mistakes are to be found which must be a stumbling block and which could have been avoided with a deeper knowledge of Islamic theological usage…."[2]

If what Sweetman says is true would not Christian converts from Islam who deeply understand that religion be more effective in explaining the person of Christ to Muslims, especially if they could adequately contextualize their statements? An answer to this question surfaces in an interesting way in the case of Hamran Ambrie of Indonesia. Ambrie was a former imam, a promoter of independence from Dutch rule and a regional leader of the South Kalimantan branch of Muhammadiyah, a prominent Islamic reformist party in Indonesia. He became a Christian apart from missionary or national Christian proselytism. He never went to Bible school or seminary, nor was he ever systematically discipled in a local church setting. Consequently, the Christology that later emerged in his apologetic writings took on something of a Qur'anic and local flavor. But how effective was he as a Muslim convert-apologist? And did his contextualization of Christology stay within Biblical boundaries?

Conversion and Calling, 'God Whispered to My Soul'

Ambrie's journey towards Christ began in 1962 while he was preparing a sermon for the Friday worship in a Jakarta mosque. During his preparation Ambrie read

[1] See also Surah 6:101.

[2] Sweetman 1945-1955:Part 1.vii.

sura 5:68 in the Qur'an: "Say: 'O people of the book (Jews and Christians)! You have no ground to stand upon unless you stand fast by the Torah (*taurat*) and the Gospel (*injīl*) and all the revelation that has come to you from your Lord.'" Ambrie had read this passage hundreds of times before, but at that moment, he says, "God whispered to my soul that the Torah and the Gospel mentioned in the Qur'an are the Torah and the Gospel found in the Bible now."[3]

At this point Ambrie became totally confused. Since childhood, Islamic religious teachers had taught him to believe that God had sent down the Gospel to Jesus. However, the original had been lost and the Gospel the Christians used today had been hopelessly corrupted. As a result, when the voice in Ambrie's soul kept saying that the Torah and the Gospel found in the existing Christian scriptures were true, his mind shouted back, "No! The Torah and the Gospel in the Christian scriptures have been falsified!"

To resolve this raging conflict, Ambrie asked God for a sign by praying a special *tahajud* midnight prayer. In his prayer Ambrie pleaded:

> Oh God, Creator of heaven and earth, God of the Muslims, Christians and Buddhists … Please show me the truth about what is mentioned in the Qur'an concerning the Torah and the Gospel … if the truth in the Torah and the Gospel mentioned in the Qur'an means the truth found in the Bible now, I beg you to open my heart so that I will be more eager to study the Bible honestly.

The following day Ambrie experienced a profound change in his attitude toward the Bible. From that time he regarded the Bible 'as a friend and not as an enemy.'

This experience, in which a verse in the Qur'an pointed him to the Bible, made a deep impact on Ambrie and very likely influenced his apologetic approach in later years. If God could speak to him through the Qur'an and Islamic thought forms, would not this also be true for other Muslims? This does not mean that Ambrie felt that the Qur'an was inspired. On the contrary, he emphatically asserted: "I am absolutely certain that the Qur'an is not the revelation of God. Rather, it contains the private opinions of Muhammad."[4] While this statement reveals a commendable clarity on Ambrie's part, it also reflects a polemical style of engagement that later brought him into sharp conflict with his former co-religionists.

From that time (1962) until his baptism in 1969, Ambrie lived as a secret believer. On Friday he continued to worship in the mosque, at least for the next two years, but on Saturday he surreptitiously attended the Seventh Day Adventist Church, and on Sunday various Protestant churches in Jakarta. He listened to the sermons and looked for evidence of idolatrous practices but he

---

[3] Ambrie 1978:6. All further biographical information is taken from this source unless otherwise noted. For further details of Ambrie's life see my Th.M thesis written under the pseudonym, Mansur 1990.

[4] Ambrie n.d.i:8.

found none. As a result he decided to leave Islam, but he did so quietly, and waited five more years before he told his wife and family, who then followed him into Christian baptism. During this period of transition, Ambrie also questioned different pastors and Evangelists by asking why Jesus was called the Son of God and what the meaning was of the term "Trinity". Ambrie noted later that they gave explanations with fluency, but he could not comprehend their answers. This was due, Ambrie said, to the fact that these Christian leaders had never made a comparative study of the teachings of Islam and Christianity "to discover where the actual points of difference lay, and then to find a meeting point to bridge these differences." As a result, their answers "went into the left ear and came out the right ear; they did not enter my heart at all."

So once again Ambrie turned to God for guidance, this time to find out the truth concerning the meaning of the Trinity and the Son of God. "God helped me," Ambrie exulted, "through His true Spirit, that is the Holy Spirit who worked in my heart." But the seeds planted by the Holy Spirit were placed in the soil of a heart that still beat with an Islamic rhythm.

By 1970, Islamic leaders heard about Ambrie's baptism and began sending letters to demand that Ambrie give an account of his apostasy, indeed to "repent" and return to Islam. Ambrie found that he could not keep up with the correspondence, so he began to privately publish the questions raised in these letters along with his answers. "God used them," Ambrie observed, "to raise me up, so that I became an active Christian and gave testimony about the truth concerning the divinity of Christ."

'Christian *Tawhid*'

We will now focus on Ambrie's Christological views, but before we do so we first need to briefly review some of his Trinitarian thought. This is necessary because as Bernhard Lohse correctly notes, 'Every Christological affirmation always contains a certain understanding of the Trinity and, conversely, every Trinitarian affirmation contains at the same time a Christological one.'[5]

The major hurdle that Ambrie faced in his dialogue with Muslims on the subject of the Trinity was the Muslim confession that God is one, or *tawhid.* The Islamic doctrine of *tawhid* emphasizes the simple, undifferentiated unity of God and gives to Islam its distinctive Unitarian theology. Therefore, when Christians assert that God is one in trinity, Islam equates this with *shirk*, the mortal sin of ascribing partners to God Almighty to share in His essence and glory. Clearly then, Ambrie's first task was to convince Muslims that the Trinity does not violate *Tawhid.* Accordingly, Ambrie proposed that Muslims consider 'Christian *Tawhid*', a term that 'is very strange to our ears.'[6] What Ambrie means here is that both Christians and Muslims understand *tawhid* as the Muslim, but not the

[5] Lohse 1985:71.
[6] Ambrie n.d.a:1.

Christian concept of God. For Ambrie this was most unfortunate as it lead to a breakdown in Christian communication with Muslims.

If Islam's concept of God is Unitarian and Christianity's concept is Trinitarian how is it that Ambrie finds the Trinity and *tawhid* to be compatible? Ambrie answers by first of all explaining that Christianity 'unequivocally confesses that God is One' and that he alone is worthy to be served and worshipped (Deut. 6:13; Jos. 24:14-15; Matt. 4:10; Lk. 4:8). But the key iblical verse that harmonizes with *tawhid* is Deuteronomy 6:4, 'Here O Israel, The LORD our God, the LORD, is one.'

Clearly the Jews were monotheists, but what about Christians? In his book, *Tauhid dan Syirik*, Ambrie points to Mark 12:29-30 where Jesus gives the foremost commandment that must be obeyed by both Jews and Christians: '… Hear, O Israel: The Lord our God, the Lord is one ….' Next, Ambrie turns to Paul's teaching on the unity of God to show that it is in harmony with Jesus' teaching, namely: Ephesians 4:6, 'one God and Father of all …' and 1 Tim. 2:5, 'For there is one God, and one mediator between God and man, the man Christ Jesus.'[7]

Secondly, Ambrie points out that Christianity does not acknowledge the existence of other gods in any shape or form whatsoever (Ex. 20:3-5), whether they be idols, stones, magical objects, 'even if the object of worship is called the *ka'bahbaitulah*' (a sarcastic allusion to Islam's veneration of the black corner stone in the Ka'bah shrine in Mecca). Thus with 'total honesty' Ambrie affirms that 'this is Christian *tawhid,* a *tawhid* that is most superior and most pure.'[8]

God in Three Powers

While Ambrie successfully demonstrated that Islamic *tawhid* does not conflict with clear Biblical statements on the oneness of God, how does he harmonize *tawhid* with other clear statements in the Bible relating to the three-ness of God as Father, Son and Holy Spirit? This is a much more complex issue and it stretches Ambrie theologically to provide an answer.

In explaining this three-fold aspect of God's unity, Ambrie does not shy away from using the traditional language of 'three Persons'. Yet, in Trinitarian discussions with Muslims he seems most comfortable with the term 'Powers'. Indeed his "Trinity of Powers" represents his own original concept. We can see how he develops this idea in an exchange with Ali Yakub Matondang, who accused Ambrie of teaching that God is uni-plural (*satu majemuk*) and not absolutely one (*satu mutlak*). Ambrie responds by noting that uni-plural does not mean more than one in unity. Rather it means 'One essence of God in three authorities of the Power of God' (*satu zat Allah dengan tiga kewibawaan*

[7] Ambrie, n.d.i: 6.
[8] Ambrie n.d.a:37-39.

Qudrat-Kuasa Allah).[9] In another context Ambrie elaborates further by referring to Genesis 1:1-3, where God creates, the Spirit of God hovers over the face of the water, and God speaks. 'Thus we conclude" says Ambrie, "that there are three Powers of God, namely to create, to give life and to speak something into being.'[10]

At first glance Ambrie gives the impression that his 'Powers' imply impersonal forces. But his actual motivation is to avoid tritheism. He also labours to avoid the impression of depersonalizing the Trinity and lapsing into some form of modalism, though we must realize here that up to this point Ambrie had never heard of the concept of 'modalism', let alone the name Sabellius.[11]

Accordingly, Ambrie explains that each Power 'represents a Person'. The one who creates is called the Father, because in Matthew 11:25 Jesus prays, 'I praise thee, O Father, Lord of heaven and earth.' Whereas the Spirit of God hovering over the face of the waters means 'that He blessed or gave life to everything that He did or would create.' The one who gives life 'is known in the New Testament as the Holy Spirit.' Then God spoke and created, and this work of speaking 'clearly points to the work of a Person.' This Person was incarnated in Jesus as stated in John 1:14. From this it is clear, Ambrie concludes, that the Christian doctrine of the Trinity, 'in no way means three Gods who become one, but rather, God, the One, the only creator, in his three essential Powers.'[12]

It is interesting to note here that Ambrie's 'Powers' terminology has some point of contact with ancient Jewish thought and early Patristic terminology. Thus, when Jesus responded to the high priest to confess that he was Messiah, Jesus said: 'From now on you will see the Son of Man seated at the right hand of Power and coming on the clouds of heaven' (Mat. 26:64). In a comment on this verse the online New English Translation (www.Bible.org) notes that 'Power' was one of the indirect references to God that were common in 1st century Judaism out of reverence for the divine name. Among the early Eastern Church Fathers we find Origen referring to God as a 'beneficent and creative power', while Athenagoras spoke of the Father, Son and Holy Spirit as 'united in power'. Hippolytus adds, 'For there is one Power which proceeds from the sum of things; the sum is the Father, out of which the Power is the Logos.'[13] These Patristic formulations reflect an instrumental concept of the Trinity which is not all that far from what Ambrie tried to express.

---

[9] Ambrie n.d.h:79, 97.

[10] Ambrie n.d.e:11-12.

[11] Later, a Christian pastor wrote to Ambrie and accused him of teaching a modalism akin to that of Sabellius in Church History. Ambrie angrily replied that he had never heard of this concept nor had he ever heard of Sabellius, he was simply trying to follow the teachings of the Bible. Ambrie 1982

[12] Ambrie 1982.

[13] Prestige 1964:68-69, 131.

The Son of God

By saying that the Word of God is one of the three essential 'Powers' of God, Ambrie implies that Jesus is of the same essence as the Father. But this issue of Christ having one essence with the Father became an explosive one for Ambrie when he addressed the problem of Jesus' divine Sonship. From Islam's perspective, the deity of Christ and the related Sonship doctrine is sheer blasphemy. This is true because it seems to deify a mere man to form a second god and suggests to the Muslim that God physically generated a son, reminiscent of the myths found in paganism. The Qur'an builds a strong case against this idea when it expressly declares: "they say: 'God has begotten a son': Glory be to Him—Nay....";[14] and 'How can He have a son when He has no consort?'[15]

In order to combat this deep-seated Muslim loathing for the term 'Son of God', Ambrie emphatically insists that the sonship of Christ in no way whatsoever refers to physical sonship. Rather, it is an analogous term. To prove his point Ambrie turns to Surah 18:4 which says: "warn those who say, 'God has begotten a son' (*takhadzal-hu walad*)." Here Ambrie points out that the word *walad*, the Arabic term for 'son', means 'son' in a physical and biological sense. Christians also reject this gross, physical concept of sonship when speaking of the 'Son of God'. Instead of *walad* we should use *ibn*, which according to Ambrie, 'does not contain a biological meaning.' In fact this very word is used in the Arabic Bible, notes Ambrie, for Jesus, Son of God, or *yasu'a ibn 'Allah*, which is quite different than saying *yasu'a walada' llah*. Therefore, Ambrie concludes that Surah 18:4 is not aimed at Christians but rather at the polytheists of Muhammad's time.[16]

Is Ambrie correct in saying that *ibn* is free from biological association and thus connotes a spiritual or metaphorical idea? In looking at the Qur'an itself we do find some support for Ambrie's assertion. For example in Surah 2:215 we see a metaphorical usage for *ibn* in the term *ibnus sabil*, literally 'son of the road' which means a traveller. On the other hand Ambrie neglects to mention that the Qur'an also refers to Jesus as *ibnu Maryam* or "son of Mary". Thus *ibn* can also imply physical generation and raise troublesome questions about Jesus as 'Son of God'. *Ibn* also frequently appears as 'son of' in Arab genealogies,[17] but with one important qualification; a male figure is always the progenitor. Thus it appears that *ibnu Maryam* forms an exceptional case in Arab custom. This brings the focus back to Jesus' miraculous and divine origins. Ambrie does not seem to be aware of these subtle distinctions. Thus he misses the opportunity to harmonize divine sonship with the Qur'anic teaching that Jesus came into being by God's command, 'Be! And he was'.[18]

---

14 Surah 2:116.
15 Surah 6:101.
16 Ambrie n.d.b:23.
17 See Lewis and Donzel 1978. 3:670.
18 Surah 3:47.

Ambrie concludes by arguing that the 'Son of God' is a title given to Jesus as an analogous term or metaphor to describe his role as the 'Word of God' (*kalimat'ullah*) as revealed in John 1:1-4.[19] As the Son of God he has his origins from the Word and the Spirit of God, and from this standpoint (as Word and Spirit of God) he is in fact of the very essence of God.[20] But the 'Son of God', is not a physical descendant of God, nor is he equal with God, indeed he is not God.[21] Here Ambrie makes a tentative statement on the two natures of Christ but he does so without precision.

Some modern Sufi-inclined Muslims might allow the term 'Son of God' in a spiritual or metaphorical sense. A. Yusuf Ali, for example, is willing to admit that 'in a spiritual sense we are all children of God.'[22] On the other hand, the vast majority of orthodox Muslims would probably agree with Efiz Fahmi who emphatically informed Ambrie that "Islam does not recognize the term 'Son of God', whether an adopted son, a proclaimed son, an imaginary son, an incarnated son, a son of a lock [*anak kunci*, the Indonesian word for 'key'], an honorific son, or whatever else."[23]

What Efiz Fahmi seems to be saying here is that the term 'Son of God' is off limits for discussion, a blasphemy that cannot be entertained. Indeed, a number of Muslims will not even open a Bible for fear that their eyes will chance upon this blasphemous term and bring judgment upon themselves! This being the case, we would have to conclude that Ambrie may have convinced some Muslims that the 'Son of God' lies within the acceptable range of analogy and metaphorical language. But for most Muslims even a metaphor is an unacceptable intrusion into the majesty and oneness of God, a problem which modern Muslim-oriented translations of the New Testament have struggled with arduously.

One Hundred Percent Man and God

On the subject of the two natures of Christ, Ambrie adheres, without the slightest hesitation, to the Christian orthodox and seemingly paradoxical statement that Jesus is fully God and fully man. When asked whether Jesus is Creator (*khalik*) or creature (*makhluk*), Ambrie answers that Jesus has to be viewed from both standpoints: 'He is most assuredly hundred percent man but He is also hundred percent God.'[24] During a dialogue with Muslim leaders in Jakarta, a prominent Muslim scholar, Hasbullah Bakry, tested Ambrie on his two natures theology by asking, 'when did Jesus utter the first person pronoun 'I' as a man and when did he utter it as God?' Ambrie replied that Jesus spoke as God when he said, 'The

---

[19] Ambrie n.d.c: 6.
[20] Ambrie n.d.d:36-37.
[21] Ambrie n.d.d:36-37.
[22] Ali *1977:*49.n119.
[23] Ambrie n.d.f: 47.
[24] Ambrie *n.d.a:*8.

Father and I are one' (John 10:30), and 'Before Abraham was I am' (John 8:58). On the other hand, Jesus spoke as a man, says Ambrie, when he said, 'The Father is greater than I' (John 14:28).[25] Ambrie's answer was fearless, bold and Biblical, and an eye-witness present at that dialogue, John Haurissa, told me that Bakry and the other participants were momentarily stunned.[26] But as we shall see later, Bakry remained unpersuaded, his Qur'anic worldview untouched by these quotes from the Bible.

Thus, Ambrie acknowledges both the divine and human natures in Christ, but in the end he gives far more attention to the divinity of Christ than he does to humanity. The reason for this, as Peter D. Latuihamallo correctly notes, is that the deity of Christ 'remains the crucial point in his encounter with Muslim scholars who have condemned him according to the law of apostasy.'[27] As Ambrie himself complains, 'The problem with the Muslims is that they only view Jesus from the standpoint of his humanity, whereas Christians view Jesus 90% of the time from the standpoint of his divinity, and only about 10%—perhaps less than that—from the standpoint of his humanity.'[28]

The Humanity of Christ

Ambrie's heavy emphasis upon the deity of Christ does not mean that he maintains a defective view of his humanity. Ambrie affirms that Jesus was born as a man (Rom. 1:3; 1 Tim. 2:5). In his status as a man he was a servant and a creature of God (Matt. 12:18; 1 Cor 3:23; Acts 4:27-30). He was finite; he had a beginning and an end. His beginning took place when he was born in Bethlehem; his end occurred on the cross at Golgotha. His human attributes were the same as any other human being. He felt hunger and thirst because he needed to eat and drink. He also experienced joys, sorrows and anguish. He arose at dawn and prayed to God, the Creator of the universe. 'All these experiences prove' Ambrie concludes 'that the Lord Jesus (*Tuhan Yesus*) was a man.'[29]

The Incarnation

To speak to the Muslim about the humanity of Christ presents no difficulty, even if he was born of a virgin. According to the Qur'an Jesus and Adam had one important thing in common: they came into being by God's command: 'Be! And he was'.[30] The problem comes when the Christian says that God became incarnate in Jesus Christ. To Muslim ears, this sounds as if God abandoned His

[25] Ambrie *n.d.f:*37-38.
[26] Haurissa 1988.
[27] Latuihamallo 1984:87.
[28] Ambrie *n.d.f:*2-33.
[29] Ambrie *n.d.g:*11.
[30] Surah 3:47.

glory or shared His majesty with a creature, resulting in a pagan mixture of God and man. And if He, the infinite, the One God, should incarnate Himself in a finite form, then it follows that He Himself becomes finite.[31]

In addressing this apparent impasse, Ambrie first establishes certain principles about God's nature upon which, he says, Muslims and Christians agree: He is One; God is Spirit; there is nothing like God; God does not change. Yet, even though Muslims strictly adhere to these attributes of divinity, which differentiate God from His creatures, Ambrie points out that certain suras in the Qur'an lend support to the idea of God incarnate: 'Verily those who plight their fealty to thee (Muhammad) do no less than plight their fealty to God: The Hand of God is over their hands:'[32] and, 'He is the First and the Last, The Evident (*zahir*, i.e., manifest, visible) and the Immanent (*batin*, i.e., interior, invisible)'.[33]

Among Muslims there is a debate about the meaning of the 'hand of God' in Surah 48:10. For many orthodox Sunni Muslims it is simply a symbolic statement of the power of God. Others hold to a literal interpretation but at the same time they claim that it is impossible to say in what sense or manner God has a hand.[34] Either interpretation would severely restrict an argument for the Incarnation. Ambrie is on firmer ground with Surah 57:3. The term *zahir* is frequently used in Islamic theology to express that which is 'manifest' about God as distinguished from *batin* or that which is "interior" or 'immanent' or possibly 'hidden'.[35] But Muslims would carefully guard what it is that God manifests about Himself. A. Yusuf Ali, for example speaks of God manifesting His signs in creation which are evident in the entire universe.[36] Nevertheless, this verse clearly declares that some degree of self revelation is part of the very nature of God. As such it provides a fruitful opening for a discussion on the degree that God could be made manifest through the person of Jesus Christ, the Word of God. It is unfortunate that Ambrie provides no discussion and application for this verse. Apparently he felt that the implications for the Incarnation were self-evident in the Qur'anic statement.

Nestorian Tendencies?

Ambrie expresses himself adequately and Biblically on the subjects of the humanity and the divinity of Christ, insofar as these are treated separately. Yet he does affirm that the two natures are joined together as one, and he calls the resultant union *manusia ilahiyat*, or the Divine Man.[37] However, when he

---

[31] Ambrie *n.d.f:* 31-32.
[32] Surah 48:10.
[33] Surah 57:3.
[34] See Hughes 1994:21.
[35] Hughes 1994: 698.
[32] Ali, 1997: 1393 n.4877 and 1497 n.5276.
[37] Ambrie 1983:116.

attempts to solve the problem as to how Jesus can be God and man at one and the same time, he inadvertently uses problematic terminology. In answering the question, 'which part of Jesus is divine and which part is human,' he explains: 'The part which is God is the invisible or the Spirit which is in control in the person of Jesus. He [the Spirit] is the one who is in control and accomplishes things according to His will.' On the other hand, the human part is the visible Jesus, whose humanity, says Ambrie, 'only forms a mediatory instrument between God and other men.'[38]

At first glance Ambrie's 'instrument' terminology appears to be similar to the statement of Nestorius when he expressed his opposition to calling Mary *theotokos* or bearer of God: 'A creature [Mary] did not produce the Creator, rather she gave birth to the human being, the instrument of the Godhead ... he formed out of the Virgin a temple for God the Logos, a temple in which he dwelt.'[39] An Indonesian pastor, Rudy Herman, noticed this apparent similarity between Ambrie and Nestorius, so he sent a letter to Ambrie accusing him of reviving the Nestorian heresy. Ambrie, in his reply to Pastor Herman says: 'If I use the term 'instrument' in reference to His humanity, it is because of my understanding of the Biblical passage found in 1 Tim. 2:5... one mediator also between God and man, the <u>man Christ Jesus</u>.' For Ambrie, therefore, 'instrument' refers to the humanity of Christ, the 'visible flesh, truly man, which God used as an instrument of proclamation of God to man.' [40] Thus for Ambrie Christ's humanity is an instrument for proclamation, which is quite different than saying that it was a temple for the divine *logos*.

It seems then that Ambrie's affinity with Nestorianism here is more apparent than real. Nestorius distinguished the two natures in order to uphold Christ's true humanity against those who tended to minimize it. For Ambrie, on the other hand, the main concern is to maintain Christ's divinity in order to achieve his apologetic aim: to refute Islam's insistence that Jesus is merely a man—precisely the opposite concern of Nestorius. His sharp demarcation between the two natures helps him to achieve this objective, a demarcation which sounds Nestorian but is not really.

Perhaps Ambrie is more 'Nestorian' in his understanding of the hypostatic union, the union of the two natures in the one Christ. Ambrie adequately defended the divine and human natures of Christ and he confessed that they were united in what he called the *manusia ilahiyat* or the Divine Man. But like Nestorius, he did not give a clear theological statement describing the *nature* of this union. The closest that Ambrie came to making such a statement is when he said: 'It is extremely improper to maintain that he (Jesus), the visible human

---

[38] Ambrie n.d.c:15.
[39] "Nestorius First Sermon Against the Theotokos," cited in Norris 1980:125.
[40] Ambrie 1982; the underlined words are Ambrie's.

being, is God. The truth is that the invisible power behind that physical body, the Spirit, is the Person of Divine Power'.[41]

So for Ambrie, the union is one of an invisible presence, the Spirit, whom Ambrie describes as "behind" Christ's human body. Could it be that this statement reflects a pattern of thinking, ingrained since childhood, that the divine Majesty is not begotten, does not beget and is therefore *with* or 'behind' the human Jesus unable to actually *assume* human flesh? Or is this a retention, however faint, of a Gnostic type of spirit-flesh dualism evident in the theosophical mysticism that pervades Javanese *kejawen* philosophy? According to Clifford Geertz, a noticeable theosophical tinge persists even in Ambrie's native South Kalimantan.[42] This is a hard question to answer. In his apologetic encounters with Muslims, Ambrie was never called upon to describe the union of the two natures. And since he had never studied Church history, Ambrie remained uninformed about this subject. Thus he could easily have spoken in terms that arose from his own cultural frame of reference. Yet it is important to note is that he intentionally and willingly confessed the unity even if he did not understand it. And really, who does actually understand it? At best, human minds can only suggest a theoretical framework against unscriptural statements.

Conclusion

Ambrie lived as a Christian for twenty-four years. Nevertheless, his Christological views bear the marks of Islamic influence. His Trinity of 'Powers' is probably rooted in Islam's own emphasis on the power and wisdom of God, while his 'Nestorian' sounding Christology reflect his overriding concern to preserve the majesty and unity of God for the sake of dialogue with Muslims. Yet, we do see that Ambrie's reflections were based on clear Biblical statements.

Without doubt Ambrie was a helpful guide and encouragement for Muslims who were on a spiritual journey, converting from Islam to Christianity. He also equipped Christians to be better witnesses for Christ in the Islamic context. It is also true that some Muslims gained a more accurate understanding of Christology even if they did not desire to convert to Christianity. For instance, in a much publicized debate with H. M. Rasjidi and other Muslim dignitaries in 1979, Ambrie reports that he received several letters from Muslims who were present at the debate expressing their sympathy for his viewpoint.[43]

However, for the majority of Indonesian Muslims, Ambrie proved to be a huge embarrassment and thus he was reviled as an apostate. For them no amazing contextual breakthrough or convincing explanation on his part would avail. For example, Hasbullah Bakry, a well known Muslim figure in the 1970s and 1980s, dismissed Ambrie's apologetic as the efforts of a man whose knowledge of both

[41] Ambrie n.d.i:26-27.
[42] Geertz 1971:12.
[43] Ambrie 1983:137, 153.

Christianity and Islam was 'extremely shallow,' whose only strong point 'is to audaciously proclaim … without any trace of shame, his move from Islam to Christianity, as if this was the result of deep, intellectual investigation.'[44]

Even some Indonesian Christians were not altogether happy with Ambrie. A few who possessed a more intellectual bent felt that Ambrie moved toward Nestorianism. Many more from across the theological spectrum thought that Ambrie was too confrontational in his approach. Peter D. Latuihamallo, former head of the Indonesian Council of Churches, felt that Ambrie had contributed much to Christian-Muslim dialogue, nonetheless, 'it is to be regretted that the more Ambrie spends his time on written dialogue, the more tense the situation becomes.'[45] Similarly, Dr. Chris Marantika, a well known Evangelical leader in Indonesia, while affirming that Ambrie was an 'honest bearer of the Cross", also asked, "Is confrontation the only way to Calvary?"[46] As it turned out, in 1982 the Indonesian Attorney General's office (*jaksa agung*) ordered that Ambrie cease from writing his apologetic booklets and forbade any further sale of his works.

In the last analysis, Ambrie shows us that there are ways to present Christology in the Muslim context without resorting to credal statements or wooden literal translations of the Bible. At the same time Ambrie's case reveals that we need to approach Muslims in the right way, and not only with the right message.

---

[44] Bakry 1982:29-31.
[45] Lautihamallo 1984:89.
[46] Marantika 1984:370-371.

The Incarnation Expressed Through a Conversion Testimony from Indonesia: The Role of the Qur'an

Peter Riddell, Ailish F. Eves, Bernie Power

Dr. Peter Riddell is Professorial Dean of the BCV Centre for the Study of Islam and Other Faiths, Melbourne

Dr. Ailish F. Eves was formerly Lecturer in Missiology at London Bible College

Dr. Bernie Power is Lecturer in Islam and Christian Muslim Relations at the BCV Centre for the Study of Islam and Other Faiths, Melbourne

Strangers On a Train[1]

In January 1981 I paid my third visit to Java, Indonesia. After a few days in the congested, polluted coastal capital of Jakarta, I moved inland to visit Indonesian friends in the more laid-back city of Bandung in West Java. From there I took the *Mutiara* overnight train to Yogyakarta, the cultural capital of the island.

I installed myself in one of the train carriages, and found myself sitting opposite an Indonesian man and his wife. Initially there was silence between the Indonesian couple and myself, but after a time I made a few comments about the scenery to the Indonesian man facing me. When he realised that I spoke Indonesian, he quickly showed a great interest in talking.

He told me about his family, his children and his village. He also told me about his work, pastoring a small church in Central Java. He had assumed that I was Christian; in his mind a Westerner was necessarily a Christian. It wasn't long before his conversation moved onto the matter of his conversion from Islam to Christianity.

During the journey I became friends with that Indonesian man, whom I will identify by the initials A.B.D. When he left the train at his destination, some way before Yogyakarta, he gave me a small *kenang-kenangan*, something to remember him by. This was in the form of a testimony of his spiritual journey, written by hand in a dog-eared grimy notebook. I recently stumbled upon this gift while clearing out some old files, and want to share its contents with others, as it

[1] The translation and analysis of the following conversion testimony was prepared by Peter Riddell, who served as foundation Director of the Centre for Islamic Studies at London School of Theology from 1996-2007, and is presently foundation Dean of the Centre for the Study of Islam and Other Faiths at the Bible College of Victoria, Australia.

contains a fascinating account of how one man came to make a decision about his faith.

The testimony is concisely written, with each sentence laden with multiple layers of meaning and significance. He begins as follows:[2]

> *Autobiographical details:* I was born on 10 December 1952 in Palembang. I was born a Muslim but am now a Protestant Christian. I formerly lived in Palembang, but have now settled in Central Java.[3] My father worked as a *penghulu*, or mosque official, and had received Islamic religious instruction from childhood. By the age of four I had been taught to recite verses from the Qur'an. I went on to study recitation, translation and Arabic. After I undertook these in-depth studies, what happened?

Why Did I Embrace Christianity?

> After I closely studied the translation of the Qur'an verse by verse, and also studied Arabic,[4] it was clear to me that there was a difference between the [Indonesian] translation and the Arabic original... The meaning of the Qur'anic verses had been altered by the translator. Moreover, the translator's explanation was that which my teacher had taught me. Beloved brothers and sisters in the Lord,[5] after scanning through the true contents of the Qur'an, it was obvious that the path to salvation identified by the Qur'an was Jesus son of Mary (Jesus Christ).

Some comments at this point of the testimony would be useful. The region of South Sumatra where Palembang is located has long been regarded as one of the more devoutly orthodox Muslim regions in the Indonesian archipelago. This would have been a key motive in the author's move to Central Java, as neither family nor community would have responded well to his decision to leave Islam. A complete relocation to a distant place and different ethnic area would have provided a much more secure future.

Even more significant in terms of a negative family response to his conversion must have been the fact that his father was a mosque official. He probably had dreams of his son following in his footsteps, and trained him from an early age in the key Islamic subjects, to ensure that he was well equipped to become an expert in the Islamic sciences.

Clearly here was a young man with an inquiring, critical mind. He was obviously gifted; it is no easy task to acquire a sufficient mastery of Arabic to be

---

[2] The original testimony is written in Bahasa Indonesia.

[3] These first few sentences actually appear in list form in the original document. I have converted the list to prose to match the rest of the testimony. No details have been altered.

[4] The original text has "Arabic dictionary" (*kamus* Arab) here.

[5] This phrase is interspersed throughout the testimony. Only this first occurrence will be rendered in the translated text.

able to decipher the text of the Qur'an and to scrutinize translations for accuracy or error. He elaborates on the questions which were being raised in his mind through studying the Qur'an, and goes to considerable lengths to identify the Qur'an as the instrument of his conversion, rather than any influence from Christian individuals or books. He stresses this in the following statement:

> The reason I became a Christian was not because of the efforts of an evangelist or a priest or the influence of Christians. I was fanatical, and refused to associate with Christians. As for reading the Christian Gospels, this I had never done. I became a Christian because I came to understand the [true] contents of the Qur'an.

He then proceeds with his account, seeking to lead his audience on the same journey which he took. We will let the remaining testimony speak for itself:

An Analysis of the Key Verses of the Qur'an

Let us examine each of those verses in the Qur'an which declare Jesus Christ to be Saviour.

Surah19:19: [The angel] said, "I am but a Messenger from thy Lord, to give a boy most pure."[6]

In this verse of *Sura Maryam* (the Chapter of Mary), God declares His promise to Mary through an angel, that Mary will be given a holy son.

If we take note of this phrase… a holy son… it is clear that Jesus is that holy son, born of the Virgin Mary according to God's will.

Surah 21:91: And she who guarded her virginity, so We breathed into her of Our spirit and appointed her and her son to be a sign unto all beings.

In verse 91 of *Sura al-anbiya'* above, God orders mankind to remember that Mary will be given a child through a/the Spirit. What is that Spirit (the Holy Spirit)? God is Spirit. John 4:23-4 specifies that God is Spirit. So if it is the Spirit which is breathed into Mary, is it not then God who will be born into the world, in the form of a man?

Why would God take the form of a man? Because God will save mankind... He is also called Son [of God] because He was born via his mother Mary. He is called God because his mother Mary gives birth according to the will of God. He is called the Holy Spirit because the Spirit was breathed into Mary. Such is the basis of the Trinity.

In order to clarify that He is the Son (of God), let us note the following verse:

Surah 3:47: "Lord," said Mary, "how shall I have a son seeing no mortal has touched me?" "Even so," God said, "God creates what He will. When He decrees a thing, He does but say to it 'Be,' and it is."

---

[6] English renderings of Qur'anic verses are taken from Arberry 1964.

From verse 47 of *Sura Ali Imran* it becomes increasingly clear that God brought about His birth through Mary.

Surah 3:45: When the angels said, "Mary, God gives you good tidings of a Word from Him whose name is Messiah, Jesus, son of Mary; high honoured shall he be in this world and the next, near stationed to God."

After reading verse 45 of *Sura Ali Imran*[7] we are able to affirm that with the words "high honoured shall he be in this world and the next", if He is not God in human form, then he could not be held in honour. This verse clearly demonstrates that:

He is God who has been born in the world in the form of a man (cf. Psalm 24:7-10);

[He is] the most noble of rulers (cf. Matthew 1:21-23);

He atones for the sins of all who believe. Any who believe and are baptised will be saved (Mark 16:16)

From the above, why would I not therefore believe? In fact, I didn't even believe that it was Jesus who was crucified. Because my teacher said that Jesus was not dead, but that Judas had been crucified in His place, was this story true? After I read verse 55 of *Sura Ali Imran*:

Surah 3: 55: When God said, "Jesus, I will take thee to Me and will raise thee to Me, and I will purify thee of those who believe not. I will set thy followers above the unbelievers till the Resurrection Day. Then unto Me shall you return, and I will decide between you, as to what you were at variance on."

If it is claimed that Jesus had not yet died, and that the one who was crucified was not Jesus, when will the above verse take place? This verse, referring to death and being raised up, shows that after his death he was raised up. Why then is it still maintained that it was not Jesus [who was crucified]?

This becomes more convincing, plausible and impressive if we note the following verses:

Surah19:15: Peace be on him, the day he was born, and the day he dies, and the day he is raised up alive![8]

Surah19:33: Peace be on me, the day I was born, and the day I die, and the day I am raised up alive!

Surah19:34: That is Jesus, son of Mary, in word of truth, concerning which they are doubting.

Once we have read the above three verses, we are increasingly convinced that it was He who died and rose again. If we continue to say that it was not Jesus

---

[7] Verse numberings in the Qur'an differ slightly according to the edition. I have reproduced exactly the verse numbering given by the author of this testimony, though the numbering of most English translations varies from that presented here to a minor degree. This is not significant for interpretation of the Qur'anic text.

[8] The author includes this verse, which actually refers to the life and death of John the Baptist, to provide a context proving that the following two verses testify to the death of Jesus.

who died on the cross, is it not that the translator is in conflict with the above-mentioned verses from the Qur'an?

Thus I repeat that if the translation alone is followed, [then we are depending] only on the translator, not the original meaning. It is therefore important to study the Arabic original text [of the Qur'an], not merely the text in translation.

Let us note in the following verse the function of Muhammad [to determine] whether he was a Messenger or Prophet. This verse is taken from *Sura al-Ahzab*:

Surah 33:63: The people will question thee concerning the Hour. Say: "The knowledge of it is only with God; what shall make thee know? Haply the Hour is nigh."

It is clear from this verse that Muhammad was not empowered. When people asked about the resurrection he had to say that knowledge of it was by the side of God (*'ind Allah*). As for knowledge about the resurrection, we recognise that among the 25 prophets specified by Islam, Jesus was the only one who returned to the side of God, while even Muhammad admitted that [the believers should look] to the side of God.

From the above let us return again to examine the verses of the Qur'an so that we can find the true path to salvation. The true path to salvation is Jesus alone. Read *Sura al-Zukhruf* verse 61:

Surah 43:61: It is knowledge of the Hour; doubt not concerning it, and follow me. This is a straight path.'

At this point the testimony ends. In many ways this remarkable piece of writing raises more questions than it answers, and it embodies a number of factors that deserve our attention. Firstly, implicit in this testimony is the author's belief in the Qur'an as a valid instrument to lead people like himself to faith in Christ. The author clearly affirms the Qur'an as a source of truth, a view which contrasts with that of many former Muslims who turn against the scripture of their former faith. This represents a significant reinterpretation of Qur'anic content as traditionally understood by both Muslims and Christians.

Secondly, the author also reinterprets the role of Muhammad vis-à-vis Jesus, especially in terms of traditional Muslim interpretations. The author portrays Muhammad as not especially empowered himself, yet he nevertheless seems to serve as a signpost, pointing Muslims in the direction of the message of Jesus.

Conversion testimonies (in both directions) provide a rich field of investigation for those interested in the dynamics of the Christian-Muslim relationship. Although Christians would have diverse opinions about the method of this particular man's faith decision, this short testimony clearly shows that motives for a change of faith can be very individual, often triggered by factors other than direct missionary endeavour.

Ailish Eves[9] Responds: Some Missiological Thoughts on "Strangers on a Train"

Can a person come to Christ and truly know him without any witness from a Christian believer or reading the gospels? Mr. A.B.D. says, 'Yes!' His testimony encourages us to believe that the Holy Spirit is at work beyond the boundaries of organised church and mission activity.

Yet there are human factors at work as well. Indonesia is an easy place for even the most inward-focussed Muslim community to know Christians and what they believe. Mr. A.B.D. grew up in Palembang, a provincial capital, where there are a number of thriving churches. People from all over the archipelago meet and mix daily there, united by their constitutional commitment to the *Pancasila*, to 'belief in one God' and to 'unity in diversity'.

In this social context his teachers, interpreting the Qur'anic texts to the young Mr A.B.D., can hardly have done so without saying, "Christians say 'X', but the Qur'an says 'Y'. Islamic apologetics planted seeds in his mind with contrary opinions for which he then found textual and grammatical justification in the Qur'an. Apologetics can be a dangerous business!

May the Qur'an be used in Witness to Muslims?

The extraordinary thing is that this young man reads within, or into, the Qu'ranic texts beliefs which set him at odds with his family and community. He addresses Christians in his testimony, buttressing his Qur'anic quotations with references from both Old and New Testaments. Is he therefore proposing that the Qur'an, rightly reinterpreted, can be a vehicle to bring someone to acknowledge Jesus Christ as the incarnate Son of God, the crucified Saviour? If there has been more than an intellectual paradigm shift and he has had an existential encounter with Christ how can our witness continue to treat the Qur'an in such a way?

Admittedly, in any new believer, the firmly held beliefs of years take time to change and adjust. It seems that Mr A.B.D. has yet to process the full implications of the Christian teaching on the self-revelation of God, finally and completely, in the Old and New Testament scriptures. Yet by the time Peter met him he was already a pastor. Presumably, then, he had been a Christian for quite a while and had received some theological training. So it is somewhat surprising that he still uses the Qur'an as though the Arabic original is an inspired and infallible text.

It may be argued that the seeds of the Word *logoi spermatikoi* are present in the Qur'an as a result of Muhammed's interaction with Jews and heterodox Christians in the Arabian peninsula of his day. These would be the truths implanted in the Muslim holy text and might still be used to lead people to an

[9] Ailish Eves spent 20 years in Indonesia and lectured in Missiology for many years at London Bible College.

acceptance of Christ as Saviour and Son of God. Though John Mbiti[10] suggested that the pre-Christian beliefs of any person may be stepping stones to lead to fulfilment in Christ, even for Muslims it is not very advisable to treat the Qur'an as a text of evangelism. Such a faith, a castle erected on the wafting mists of reinterpreted Qur'anic texts, is not sufficient to sustain the convert from Islam in true, lifelong Christian commitment.

We may doubt the reliability and veracity of the witness's experience, but it would be very unwise to use it as a pattern for witness within the Muslim community so as to lead others along the same journey. God, through his Holy Spirit, 'blows where he wills' and so can spark off a search for Himself, through a Star Trek video, a Harry Potter novel, or a pop-song. As human ambassadors for Christ, however, we would be ill-advised to base our Evangelistic apologetic on any of the above creations of human imagination and skill.

Another Witness Needed?

Mr A.B.D. was speaking to Peter in 1981, at a time when the case of another convert and Palembang man was fresh in everyone's mind. In 1979 A.M. Yusuf Roni came to trial at last, after 5 years imprisonment, to face charges of 'subversion'. He told the court how, as a propagandist for Islam, and studying the New Testament, he had become convinced that 'the Lord Jesus' was the one who could give him assurance of forgiveness and salvation which he did not have in Islam[11]. Though he had produced, written and recorded materials in which he interpreted the Qur'an in the light of the Bible, he had done so for the Christian community and not with the intention of offending Muslims. By 1980 he had been released from these charges and began to work in Methodist churches.

Mr. A.B.D. must have known that his own testimony could also be regarded as a dangerous attempt to destabilise this 85% Muslim country by sowing distrust in the sacred Qur'an. May it have been that in his meeting with Peter, consciously or unconsciously, he was getting rid of this potentially incriminating written testimony, to distance himself from this approach?

Yusuf Roni has become a fiery evangelist and controversial church leader, the founder of a Bible College and active in Christian service to this day. As far as public ministry goes he no longer uses the approach of reinterpreting that Qur'an in his teaching. One wonders if Peter's friend was in the process of taking the same journey when he surrendered this document into his hands. He would certainly have been wise to do so for political reasons, but also I would suggest, for reasons of securing firm theological foundations for his future.

---

[10] Bediako 1992:320.

[11] Yusuf Roni 1979.

Bernie Power[12] Responds: More Missiological Thoughts on "Strangers on a Train"

'Kevin' was the first local believer that I met on the Arabian peninsula in an officially one hundred percent Muslim country. He came to a faith in Christ in the same way as A.B.D. As a young man, he had never met a Christian or seen the Bible. He recounted to me that one day he was sitting in a mosque reading the Qur'an. 'As I read, I realized that Jesus was more powerful than Muhammad. Jesus could heal the sick and raise the dead, but Muhammad could not. Jesus was sinless, but Muhammad was not. Jesus was alive in heaven, but Muhammad was dead in his grave in Medina. From that day forward, I decided to follow Jesus.' The African theologian Moussa Bongoyok asserts: 'There is enough evidence in the Qur'an to help a genuine Muslim seeker of the Truth to understand that Jesus is not only a simple human prophet among others.'[13]

No Christian would doubt that God can and does use different methods to draw people to Himself. The percentages of converts from Islam reporting dreams and visions are considerable. One commentator calls it 'a large percentage'.[14] Otis refers to 'at least 35 percent of all recent Turkish converts'.[15] In a ten year survey of some 600 Muslim background believers from over 35 countries, Woodberry and Shubin reported that 'over one-fourth of those surveyed state quite emphatically that dreams and visions were key in drawing them to Christ and sustaining them through difficult times.'[16] One third of attendees at a Central Asian Women's conference in 1996 claimed to have come to faith in Christ through dreams.[17]

Remarkably one study found that about the same proportion of former Muslims cited the significance of the Qur'an in bring them to Christ, even though those engaged in Evangelism amongst them did not recognize its value. Mogenson discovered that 'the vast majority of those involved in mission projects [among Nigerian Fulbe] attached no importance to the use of the *Qur'an* [in witness], but thirty percent of the converts stated that it had a great influence on their conversion.'[18]

God's sovereign use of means such as dreams and the Qur'an in situations where a human witness was lacking is, however, a different matter to missionaries choosing to use the Qur'an themselves in their witness to Muslims. It is to this thorny question that I will now turn.

---

[12] Bernie Power has lived and worked among Muslims in Asia and the Middle East for over 20 years, and currently lectures on Islam and Arabic at the Bible College of Victoria.

[13] Bongoyok 2008:299.

[14] Cate 1992:233.

[15] Otis 1991:159.

[16] Woodberry &.Shubin 2001.

[17] Robinson 2003:254.

[18] Mogenson 2000:223.

The Bible's Attitude to other Writings

I begin by examining the Bible itself. In Lebanon, some Christian scholars and missionary practitioners formed "The Beirut Muslim Study Group." They wrote a report on 'The Use of the Quran in Reaching Muslims.'[19] They began with the caveat 'there is no exact parallel in the Bible to our situation regarding the use of the Qur'an. Nevertheless, a study of the use of non-Biblical literature by Biblical writers gives us guidelines that aid us in our thinking.' They outlined six principles: i. Biblical writers were clearly familiar with the religious and secular literature of their neighbours. ii. Biblical writers borrowed words and expressions freely from non-Biblical sources. iii. Biblical writers borrowed ideas and concepts freely e.g. Paul's use of *musterion* (mystery), an idea taken from Greek mystery religion. iv. Biblical writers sometimes used material without adaptation. v. Biblical writers sometimes adapted material that they borrowed. vi. Borrowing did not imply approval of everything in the original."

The Bible was not revealed in a vacuum. Many nations existed nearby as Holy Scripture was being revealed to the Jewish nation, and we find evidence of the ideas and cultural forms of these communities in the Bible.

Biblical examples of borrowing and adaptation of ideas from other religions and traditions are evident. In Gen.14:18-22, the name of the Canaanite high god, *El*, is applied to *Yahweh*, the God of the Hebrews. The Babylonian high god *'elahh* is similarly adopted. This Chaldean word for 'God' occurs as an appellation for Yahweh ninety-five times between Ezra 4:24 and 7:26, and Dan.2:11 and 6:26. [20] Abraham followed Nuzi inheritance laws in working out his family bequests.[21] Hittite Suzerainty treaties may have provided a template for the Mosaic Law,[22] the Elamite Code of Hammurabi had some similar content,[23] and close parallels existed between Jewish and Hittite sacrifice laws.[24] Solomon's temple appears to be based on Phoenician architecture of the same era.[25]

An Old Testament scholar sees the divine hand in all this. LaSor speaks of "the condescension of God in utilising literary forms and legal customs as the most suitable vehicles for revealing his purposes to his children in the most easily understandable and clearly comprehensible manner."[26]

---

[19] This was never published, but copies were circulated amongst those working among Muslims.

[20] Strong's concordance ref. H.426; it also occurs once in Jer.10:11 in Aramaic, where it refers to the pagan gods who will perish.

[21] Pritchard 1969:219 H (2) = Gen.15:2,3; p. 543 (4) = Gen.16:1-4; p.220 (3) = Gen.17:19-22.

[22] Thompson 1979.1:791.

[23] Youngblood 1998:71.

[24] Rogerson & Davies 1989:96

[25] La Sor *et al* 1996:194 and Meyers 1992:5:330-369. This is not surprising, since the builders were Phoenician (1.Kg.5:1).

[26] Youngblood 1998:71.

Although warned against mimicking the pagan idolatry of the nations around them (Dt.18:9), the Israelites adopted and adapted some of their cultural forms. In some cases this led to apostasy or syncretism, but in other cases it led to God's people living in a way that 'made sense' to their neighbours. The new form became a perfectly adequate way of operating faithfully under the rule of Yahweh. The anthropological distinction between 'form' and 'meaning' is a helpful one here, where a particular 'form' or cultural object or activity (denotation) may have a different 'meaning' or association (connotation) in another context.[27]

The Old Testament writers were clear that they were operating in a literary context of other documents. There are references to other books, as shown in this table:

<table>
<tr><td>The Book of the Wars of the Lord</td><td>Num.21:14, 15</td></tr>
<tr><td>The Book of Jasher</td><td>Josh.10:13; 2.Sam.1:18</td></tr>
<tr><td>The Records of Nathan the Prophet</td><td rowspan="3">2.Chr.9:29</td></tr>
<tr><td>The Prophecy of Ahijah the Shilonite</td></tr>
<tr><td>The Visions of Iddo the Seer</td></tr>
<tr><td>The Book of the Annals of King David</td><td>1.Chr.27:24</td></tr>
<tr><td>The Book of the Annals of Solomon</td><td>1.Kg.11:41</td></tr>
<tr><td>The Book of the Annals of the Kings of Judah</td><td>1.Kg.14:29; 15:7,23; 22:45; 2.Kg.8:23; 12:19; 14:18; 15:6, 36; 16:19; 20:20; 21:17,25; 23:28; 24:5</td></tr>
<tr><td>The Book of the Annals of the Kings of Israel</td><td>1.Kg.11:41; 14:19; 15:31; 16:5,14,20,27; 22:39; 2.Kg.1:18; 10:34; 13:8,12; 14:15,28; 15:11,15,21,26,31; 2.Chr.20:34; 33:18</td></tr>
<tr><td>The Book of the Annals</td><td>Neh.12:23; Esther 2:23</td></tr>
<tr><td>The Book of the Annals of the Kings of Medea and Persia</td><td>Esther 10:2</td></tr>
</table>

Although some of these may refer to material already included in the Biblical canon (e.g. the books of 1 and 2 Chronicles), others do not. Unnamed poets are also quoted (Num.21:27-30).

In a number of situations, there seems to be a direct literary succession. The Wisdom literature of Israel shows remarkable similarities to the teaching of nearby nations. These include the Egyptian *Teaching of Amenemope*,[28] Babylonian *Counsels of Wisdom* from the Kassite period (1500-1100 B.C.),[29]

---

[27] Kraft 1996:132 ff.
[28] Eliade 1967:553, 554.
[29] La Sor et al. 1996:449.

Egyptian *Instructions of Vizier Ptah-hotep,*[30] Mesopotamian literature in Sumerian and Akkadian[31], and some quotes comparable to the Book of Job in a Babylonian theodicy from the period c.1000 B.C.[32] Akhenaten's hymn to Aten[33] 'is quite similar to Psalm 104, and some direct borrowing is possible.' [34]

The New Testament

This approach continues in the New Testament. Jesus quoted well-known proverbs (Lk.12.54) and even nursery rhymes (Lk.7.32), although He clearly did not accept all popular wisdom (c.f. Jn.9.2). Every item in the Lord's prayer has parallels in the Old Testament or Jewish literature (e.g. Ben Sirach, Pirke Aboth).

The following is a list of books quoted from or alluded to in the New Testament: Jewish non-Biblical books: Judith (8:4-6) - Lk.2:37; 8:24,25 – 1.Cor.10:9,10. Book of Wisdom (3:5,6) – 1.Pe.1:6,7; 3:7 -Mt.13:43; 7:26,27 – Heb.1:3. Tobit (12:12,15) - 1.Cor.15:29; Rev.5:8; 8:3,4. Ben Sirach (5:11) - Jam.1:19. Baruch (3:29) – Jn.3:13; 3:38 – Jn.1:14; 4:7 – 1.Cor.10:20; 4:9 – Lk.13:29. 2 Maccabeus (7:1-29) - Heb.11.35b; 12:44 - 1.Cor.15:29. Psalms of Solomon (2:6) - Rom.16:7. Ascension of Isaiah (1:9; 5:2; 5:14) – Heb.11:37. Assumption of Moses - Jude 9,14. Apocalypse of Isaiah : Martyrdom of Isaiah - Heb.11:37. Apocalypse of Elijah - 1.Cor.2:9; Eph.5:14. Enoch (1:9) - Jude 4,6,13, 14-16. Book of Jannes and Jambres - 2.Tim.3:8. Ecclesiasticus (36:20) - 1.Cor.6:13. Greek books: Aratus' *Phaenomena* - Acts 17:28b. Epimenidas' *Cretica* - Titus 1:12; Acts 17:28a. Menander's *Thais* – 1.Cor.15:33. Euripides' *Bacchus* - Acts 26:14. An Unknown book: Book of the Wisdom of God – Lk.11:49

Paul even called a pagan poet 'a prophet' (Epimenedes in Titus 1.12). There are at least 133 references or quotes from other books in the New Testament.[35] A Lausanne Paper concludes: 'Biblical writers were familiar with the religious and secular writings of their neighbours. Biblical writers borrowed certain expressions and concepts from other sources. So did Jesus. Borrowing did not imply total agreement with the original, which was sometimes adapted even to the extent of teaching a totally different point from the original. Paul contextualised his message to suit Greek or Jewish audiences. This would suggest a similar freedom in the use of the Qur'an.'[36]

If we allow that the Qur'an has some place in witness to Muslims, how might it be used? The Beirut Muslim Study Group enumerated five possibilities

---

30 La Sor et al. 1996:48.
31 La Sor et al. 1996:450.
32 La Sor et al. 1996:52-453.
33 Pritchard 1969:369, 370; this was the work of Pharaoh Amenhotep IV who ruled c.1370-1360 B.C.
34 Rogerson & Davies 1989:94.
35 Accad 1997:26.
36 Lausanne Occasional Paper 1995:32.

for its use (or non-use): View 1: 'The Qur'an should never be used". View 2: "Use the Qur'an if and when necessary'. View 3: 'Use the Quran but against itself'. View 4: 'Use the Qur'an only as a starting point'. View 5: 'Use the Qur'an as a source of Truth'.

I will outline these approaches in some detail.

VIEW 1: NEVER USE THE QUR'AN

Some reasons have been suggested why those ministering among Muslims should never use or refer to the Qur'an: the Qur'an is only the Qur'an in Arabic. Arguments based on the English version will not generally be accepted. To use part of it may place you in the position of having to accept its authority on other matters. Otherwise you may have to say you accept some parts but not others. Some people feel that using the Qur'an or anything else of a different spiritual origin is dangerous, and may place you under its authority. You may be called upon to state whether you believe it is from God, and this could place you in a difficult legal position in some countries. 'Ignorance is bliss'. If you do not know anything about it, you can neither confirm nor deny its truth. This then leaves you free to take about the things that you do know about, i.e. Jesus and the Bible. Why use the Qur'an when you can use the Bible? As one person put it, 'Why use the devil's blunt instrument when you can use the Spirit's sharp sword?'[37] It may be counter-productive. Muslims, seeing a *'kaafir'* (infidel) having a greater knowledge of the Qur'an than they have, may feel ashamed and feel that they should study their own scriptures more before studying some-one else's scriptures.

VIEW 2: USE IT WHEN NECESSARY

There are some situations where it is helpful to use the Qur'an or at least to have read it: it is an accepted teaching principle to work from the known to the unknown. Muslims will find the Qur'an is familiar, and be happy to accept what it says. 'In treating the great truths which are common to the two religions, the Christian can speak freely and heartily, and in so doing he can awaken a glow of sympathy in the hearer which will at least dispose him to listen to what one has to say in regard to distinctive Christian doctrines.'[38] To use the Qur'an shows that you accept them and take them seriously, and have thought about their beliefs. This is a good spiritual principle, at least as a starting point. To have read the Qur'an can put you in a strong position in a discussion. 'I have read all four of the holy books – the *Taurat* (Torah), *zabuur* (Psalms), *injiil* (Gospel) and the Qur'an. How many have you read?' When asked what you thought of the Qur'an, you can reply: 'I read it but there were a lot of words I did not understand. The Qur'an itself admits that some of its verses are not clear and only God understands them (Q.3:7). Do you understand every word when you read the

[37] Personal communication.
[38] Jadeed 1904/1980:19.

Qur'an?' (Usually they will say: 'No'). Then ask: 'Would you like to read a book from God that you can understand?' (I usually carry a New Testament to give away in such situations)

VIEW 3: USE THE QUR'AN AGAINST ITSELF

The Qur'an and Islamic teaching can be used against themselves, to point out their inconsistencies. Jesus applied the teachings, traditions and practices of the Pharisees as a polemic against them (Mt.23.13-36). The Old Testament prophets did the same with pagan idolatry (Isa.44:9-20; 45.20; 46.5-7; Jer.10.1-5). Richardson comments: 'We must learn to use quotes from his (Mohammed's) Koran to undermine Muslim confidence in him and his writings.'[39] Websites such as 'Answering Islam' outline lists of contradictions in the Qur'an,[40] and the Qur'an's grammatical errors have been made public.[41]

VIEW 4: USE THE QUR'AN ONLY AS A STARTING POINT

This approach is taken by the "Camel Method' developed by Kevin Greeson. He states: "The primary method of reaching Muslims in Bangladesh is using the Koran as a bridge. Evangelists use passages in the Koran to begin speaking with Muslims about Jesus. Then, when they find those who are interested in hearing more about Jesus, they take them from the Koran to the Bible."[42] He bases his approach on one passage of the Qur'an.[43] Having established the uniqueness of Christ from this passage, he quickly moves to the Bible for a fuller picture.

VIEW 5: USE THE QUR'AN AS A SOURCE OF TRUTH

A Lausanne paper notes that "[t]here are 'stepping stones' in the Qur'an that can lead Muslims to Christ, notably the references to Jesus himself. It is like a palimpsest written over an imperfectly erased Biblical text. Our calling is to help Muslims 'see the Biblical text underneath'."[44] William Temple Gairdner of Cairo referred to Islam as a *preparatio evangelica.*[45] The Lebanese Christian scholar Fuad Accad stated that: 'After studying the Qur'an for over 30 years, I have found it to be overwhelming pro-Christ, pro-Christian and pro-Bible.'[46]

Although everyone may not share such a glowing analysis of the Qur'an, it certainly can be used as a means of countering typical objections raised by Muslims as well as in presenting the Gospel to Muslims. Topics would include the veracity of the Bible, the death of Christ and the divine Sonship of Christ.

---

[39] Richardson 2003:219.
[40] 'Contradictions in the Qur'an' 2009.
[41] al-Fadi 1995:173.
[42] Greeson 2007:6.
[43] Surah 3:42-55.
[44] Lausanne Occasional Paper 1995:32.
[45] Kerr 2002:13.
[46] Accad 1997:10.

Most Muslims claim that the Bible has been corrupted. Yet the Qur'an itself can be used to dispute this claim. The following verses outline an approach for this. God's Word does not change.[47] There is no difference between the Bible and the Qur'an.[48] God protects His scriptures.[49] Muslims should ask Christians when they are in doubt.[50] Do not dispute with Christians.[51] Muslims must believe the Bible ('the Book sent down before').[52] Christians must believe the Bible.[53] The Qur'an confirms the previous scriptures.[54]

Many Muslims claim that Jesus did not die on the cross. Again this can be challenged using the Qur'an. Its proof text on this issue[55] asserts that the Jews did not execute or crucify him. Historians would agree, for crucifixion was a Roman technique, never used by the Jews. The Jewish method of capital punishment was stoning. The Qur'an asserts that many prophets were killed,[56] so for Jesus to die a violent death would not be unusual. God's angels protect a messenger until he had delivered his message to humankind.[57] Jesus was aware of this, for several times he said: "My time has not yet come.' (Jn.2:4; 7:6 also Jn.16:32). Later he said: 'The hour has come for the Son of Man to be glorified." (Jn.12:23). In the Qur'an, Jesus spoke of his coming death. 'So Peace is on me the day I was born the day that I die and the Day that I shall be raised up to life (again)!'[58] Likewise God said: "Behold! Allah said: 'O Jesus! I will cause thee to die (*mutawaffika)* and raise thee to Myself and clear thee (of the falsehoods) of those who blaspheme'".[59] Similarly Jesus spoke of his death afterwards, presumably to His Father in heaven: 'And when Thou didst take me up cause me to die (*twaffaytani*), thou wast the Watcher over them and Thou art a Witness to all things'.[60] The word *twaffa* means 'die' in almost every one of its twenty-three occurrences in the Qur'an.[61] The onus of proof is on those who deny that Christ

---

47 See Surah 3:2,78; 4:135; 6:34; 10:64; 18:26; 35:42; 50:28,29.
48 See Surah 2:136; 3:2,3; 9:111.
49 See Surah 15:9.
50 See Surah 10:94; 21:7.
51 Surah 29:46.
52 Surah 4:136.
53 Surah 5:46,47; 5:68.
54 Surah 2:41,89, 91,97,101; 3:3,81; 4:47; 5:46,48; 6:92; 10:37; 12:111; 35:31;46:30; 61:6.
55 Surah 4:157.
56 Surah 2:61,87,91; 3:21, 112, 181, 183; 4:155; 5:70.
57 Surah 73:27,28.
58 Surah 19:33.
59 Surah 3:55.
60 Surah 5:117. The Bible also speaks of the Father's protective guard over Jesus' disciples after Christ's death: "I will remain in the world no longer, but they are still in the world, and I am coming to you. Holy Father, protect them by the power of your name- the name you gave me- so that they may be one as we are one. (Jn.17:11).
61 Surah 2:234, 240; 3:193; 4:15,97; 6:60, 61; 7:37, 126; 8:50; 10:46, 104; 12:101; 13:40; 16:28, 32, 70; 22:5; 32:11; 39:42; 40:67, 77; 47:27 and also 6:60 & 39:42 which refer to 'sleep'.

died, for evidence from Qur'anic, biblical and historical sources suggest that He did.

There is much in the Qur'an that Christians can use in sharing Christ with Muslims. The information in the following table illustrates how topics such as the divine Sonship of Christ and the fallibiility of Muhammad could be raised:

	God (Allah)	**Jesus also**	**But Muhammad**
is holy & sinless	Q.59:23; 62:1	Q.19:19; 3:45,46	asked for forgiveness: 4:106; 40:55; 47:19; 48:2
had clear signs	2:159;	2:87; 43:63	could perform no miracles: 6.8,9,109; 17.90-93; 29:50 His only sign was the Qur'an: 21:3,5,10
creates	6:102; 13:16	3:49; 5:110	
heals	26:80; 41:44	3:49; 5:110	
raises dead	22:6; 42:9	3:49; 5:110	
fed the hungry	6:14; 26:79	5:112-115	
is kind	3:30; 9:117	19:32	disregarded blind man 80:1-12
changed the law	73:20	3:50	could not change the law: 10:15; 66:1
knows hidden things	5:109; 20:7; 72:26	3:49	did not know the hidden things 6:50; 7:188; 10:20
knows last hour	7:187; 31:34; 33.63; 41:47	43:61	did not know the last hour 72:25
has universal impact	1:2; 2:29	19:21; 21:19; 3:45	was only a warner : 7:184; 13:7
is in heaven	2:255; 5:112	3:55; 4:158	was uncertain what would happen to him 46:9

However, it must be admitted that the Qur'an does not give a full presentation of the nature of God, the person and work of Christ, or the Gospel. If it did, the Bible would be superfluous. The Qur'an contains statements which are used by Muslims to deny basic Christian doctrine, such as the Trinity,[62] the Sonship of Christ,[63] the death of Christ,[64] substitutionary atonement[65] and salvation by faith.[66]

---

[62] Surah 4.171; 5.76.

[63] Surah 4.171; 5.75, 9.30.

[64] Surah 4.157, 158.

[65] Surah 4:112; 17:15 ; 6:164; 35:18; 39:7; 53:38.

[66] Surah 6:70. The Italian scholar Basetti-Sani proposes that "Mohammed never knew the doctrine of the Catholic Church, of orthodox Christianity; hence he was unable to reject it. He rejected *distortions* of Christianity." Basetti-Sani 977:31.

Do these glaring faults mean that it cannot be a vehicle for truth? Not necessarily. I would suggest that the Qur'an contains a mixture of truth and error. There is a difference between using the Qur'an as a source of truth, and using it as the source of truth. The Qur'an needs to be used with discernment. Truth can be found in many places. The goal of this methodology is to find the common ground shared by Muslims and Christians. There will be shared truth which can be openly declared. "We will want to see how far we can walk along the same road with the Muslim before we come to the fork where our paths diverge."[67] This can occur without denying or betraying one's own faith-commitment. There can be forward movement side-by-side, like a pair of railway tracks, without stepping in the other's footprints. Yaqoob ibn Ishaq al-Kindy, 'the Arab Philosopher' (801-873 A.D.) states: "We should not shy away from welcoming and acquiring the truth regardless of where it came from, even if it came from distant races and nations that are different from us. Nothing is more important than seeking the truth, except the truth itself. We should not belittle the truth, or those who utter it or bring it."[68] Christian apologists have long suggested that all truth comes from God, for Jesus is the *logos* of the universe, through whom the world was created. Justin Martyr may have been the earliest advocate of this view.[69] The scriptures proclaim about Christ: "In Him are hidden all the treasures of wisdom and knowledge." (Col.2:3). St Augustine of Hippo is reputed to have said: "Truth, wherever it is to be found, it is the Lord's. Even the gold of Egypt is still gold."[70] Echoing this, Parshall notes that "truth is truth wherever it is to be found."[71]

Steve Bell tells the story of an Egyptian man. "[E]ven the prophet Muhammad and the Qur'an became stepping stones facilitating Ahmed's journey to Christ. It had become clear to him that Jesus' moral and spiritual authority was total and that what he demanded from Ahmed was not some new external observance alongside his Islam but the redirecting of it."[72]

---

[67] Chapman 1995:324.
[68] *AHDR* 2003:32
[69] Macquarrie 1966:19.
[70] Bell 2006:68.
[71] Parshall 1983:19.
[72] Bell 2006:37.

Incarnating Christian Witness within Popular Islam

Phil Parshall

Dr. Phil Parshall is a missionary-at-large with Serving in Mission (SIM)

Introduction

Incarnation as a lifestyle concept has an attractive, even compelling quality about it. When we place God into an Incarnation mode, we find his Son Jesus modelling such exemplary traits as humility, identification, and intimacy. How essential it is for the messenger of Christ to adopt these spiritual realities into his/her life. Muslims particularly are eager to evaluate the behaviour of Christians. Often they have become convinced that followers of Christ are profligate persons given over to swine eating, alcohol consumption, and engaging in various modes of sexual immorality. A godly Incarnation of a pure life will do much to offset such a generalization. Who then, specifically, would be those who would profit from such a contextualized witness?

Definitions

Popular Islam, Folk Islam and Sufism are all found within the broad embrace of Islam. In contrast to a rigid orthodoxy these manifestations of the faith are more emotional and intense. The devotees seek a personal relationship with Allah that is centered in love rather than cold, repetitive ritual.

Some years back I had the privilege of observing a group of seventy-fine Muslims engage in just such a heart-quest for God. The setting was in the courtyard of a home in Khartoum, Sudan. Few Western Christians have ever attended the Thursday evening worship sessions of this group. Men sat on chairs facing the modestly dressed Sudanese women. Well behaved children sat off to the side. Under the gorgeous star-studded, pollution-free sky, all began to sing in melodious harmony praises to Allah. At one point a thirteen year old girl sang a few lines of a song immediately followed by an antiphonal response from the group. It was powerful in beauty and intensity. After an hour of such expressions of joy and praise, a man led the group in what appeared to be extemporaneous prayer. He stood with hands lifted toward Heaven as he petitioned the One Whom he worshipped as the creator and sustainer of the Universe. Next come men to men and women to women embraces. Gaiety filled the air as Arabic words of fellowship flowed between the devotees. Tea and cookies were then served to all present. We, as Christians, were treated as royal guests. Such was my memorable experience with a gathering of Sudanese Muslims, which touched both my mind and my heart. Would such a group best be identified as Folk Muslim, Followers of Popular Islam, or as Sufis or as all three? The following is a brief overview of religious belief and practices that are more tolerated then embraced within the strict parameters of Islamic orthodoxy.

The term 'Popular Islam' is an overarching designation for all religious beliefs and practices outside of mainstream Islam. So then, in what sense can it be called 'popular'? It is my considered opinion that well over fifty percent of Muslims worldwide are either in this category or are significantly influenced by it. They may or may not be organized into entities or orders. Rather, their more mystical belief system is likely to be kept personal and even border on the esoteric. When speaking of 'Folk Islam', I am referring to Muslims who have incorporated certain animistic features into their religious observances. They would particularly focus on the spirit world. These devotees would offer gifts and sacrifices to unseen forces that have a bearing on their well being. There is a huge component of fear in the lives of these Muslims. Having ministered to Filipino Muslims for over two decades, I can testify to the vast influence former animistic practices have had on these converts to Islam. One can easily discern the ongoing power of such belief. These Filipinos continue their visits to the shamans and offer rice cakes to the spirits in the shape of the all-powerful alligator. They somehow have syncretized this un-Islamic worldview with an Islamic profession of faith. I have observed similar 'non-contradictory contradictions' particularly in sub-Saharan Africa and in other parts of Asia.

The origin of the word 'Sufism' is unknown, but it is speculated to have derived from the Arabic word, *suf*, which means wool. This word then would refer to early Muslim mystics who were ascetics caring nothing for this materialistic world. While carrying on their ministry as itinerant preachers, they dressed in simple wool garments. Sufism took deep root in the Indian subcontinent, though it can be found worldwide. Hinduism, with its mystical practices, has provided an interesting opportunity for syncretism with Islam. What should be antithetical has in some instances become a selective amalgam. Sufis have developed a counterpart to Hinduism's seven stages toward merging with the ultimate being. The guru of Hinduism has become the *pir* (holy man) of the Sufis. Temples attract Hindus for annual pilgrimage. And the 'empowered' tombs of departed saints beckon Muslims to visit. Sufis are the most structured of all Folk Muslims. The Sufis divide into Orders led by a *pir* to whom the adherents pledge absolute devotion.

The four main Orders are as follows: 1. <u>Chishti</u> that embraces an emphasis on music, which is said to kindle a fire for loving God. Orthodox Muslims denounce the use of music in worship. Chishtis also are known for the importance they place on sharing food, a practice that is said to picture a spiritual fellowship and camraderie. When I would first meet a Muslim in Islampur*[1] who insisted on taking me to a stall for tea and biscuits, I would always ask, "*bhai, Apne kon*

· Pseudonym (also on following pages).

tarikay achen?" (Brother to what order of Sufis do you belong?) The surprised answer would invariably be 'Chishti..., but how did you know I am a Sufi?'

2. Suhrawardi the leading saints of which are known for performing miracles. Hafiz Muhammad Ismail was born in 1586 in what is now Pakistan. He had an extraordinary ability to assist his disciples in memorizing the entire Qur'an. Even today, Madrassa students commute to Ismail's tomb and munch on the herbs and leaves found near the elevated gravesite. Their conviction is that by partaking of these empowered plants they can more easily commit the Qur'an to memory.

3. Qadiri was not established until three hundred years after the death of its founder, Abdul-Qadir Julani. The drawing power of this sect that has flowed down through the centuries was the oral tradition concerning the *pir's* miracles. One story illustrates the conflict often found between Orthodox Islam and Sufism. Muhammad Fudayl was a native of Afghanistan who travelled to India where he acquired perfection in the Qadiri mystical path. Upon his return to Kabul he once neglected to say his obligatory prayers. An imam heard of this oversight and threatened to punish him. Fudayl argued that such rituals like ablution were quite unnecessary. Angrily, the imam poured water on the "heretic's" body. All were amazed to see the arms and hands of the saint's body did not even become wet.

4. Naqshbandi established by Ahmad Faruqi in India, though it later spread to the Middle East, Europe and Africa. At the time of Faruqi's birth, the spirit of Prophet Muhammad is reported to have come near the infant and repeated the name of Allah in his ears. The father was then instructed by Muhammad to not allow any musician to play an instrument in celebration of the birth. Thus Naqshbandi devotees to this day are forbidden to use music in their worship. Other prohibitions flowed from the convictions of Faruqi. No Sufi-style dancing was allowed. Prostration before a *pir's* tomb was forbidden, as were all forms of religious ecstasy. Though Faruqi was a mystic, he was careful to harmonize Qur'anic teaching with his belief system. His 644 writings are now published in three large volumes. He was said to have performed seven hundred miracles.

Seven Stages

Sufis of all types are well acquainted with the seven stages through which a devotee passes in order to become intimately acquainted with Allah. This is a lifelong quest in which the true worshipper slowly progresses spiritually upward: *Ubudiyah* (Service) focuses on providing assistance to others and is the entry level requirement for anyone in his or her journey to obtain oneness with God. The aspiring Sufi seeks opportunities to offer help to the needy. Good works prepare the soul for an ascent heavenward. Emphasis on *ishq* (love of God) shows the more emotional side of Sufism coming to the fore. This is distinct from a cold, bookish theology or philosophy. Many Sufis will write poems or become musicians as they seek to express their love for Allah in a heartfelt manner. Like-minded worshippers will seek out each other and form small groups in which their hunger for Allah can be nurtured. *Zuhd* (seclusion) is a sort of meditation to be practiced apart from worldly distractions. The performance can be solitary or with others who are on a similar pilgrimage. Beads are commonly utilized to guide the believer in repeating the 99 names of God. Extended seclusion is seldom practiced as Sufis are generally quite relational in personality. *Marifah* (knowledge) is the means of exploring the metaphysical. Informal groups meet together to discuss issues like Allah's role in creating the universe and why an all-powerful God doesn't intervene and stop the suffering of mankind. Sufis recognize they, as mere mortals, will never be able to comprehend all of the deep mysteries of God, but there is fulfilment in the journey. The unknown is not to be ignored. Satisfaction is gained from any new insight gleaned through their pursuit of the supernatural. *Wajd* (ecstasy) is the way by which the devotee deepens his/her relationship with ultimate knowledge, a desire arises to somehow express the joy and excitement that such insights bring. To many, a ritual of high octane emotion provides just such an outlet. *Dhikr* is a ceremony which centers on the repetition of the word 'Allah.' The earnest seeker may continue speaking this word in a forceful manner up to the point where joyful ecstasy, even intoxication with God is reached. Feeling, not cognition, is the goal. *Haqiqah* (truth) takes the aspirant beyond knowledge and into the Holy of Holies. Allah is said to become as real as the intake of one's breath. Al-Hallaj, in the tenth century went so far as to proclaim, "I am Truth." He was said to have regarded Jesus as his example, not Muhammad. Such heresy was not to be tolerated by the Islamic scholars of Al-Hallaj's day. He was threatened with hell-fire if he did not repent. This was not an option for this 'saint' who regarded himself as intimate with God. Al-Hallaj was sentenced to be crucified. As he went to the cross, he was heard forgiving his executioners and asking Allah to have mercy upon them. Few, if any, Muslims have made such a profession as this, and for good reason. *Wasl* (union with God) is the last stage of enlightenment. The Muslim Sufi is said to no longer be mere man, but is transubstantiated into Allah. He can then declare *"Ana-L-haqq"* (I am the real). This profession is not to be regarded as blasphemous for it is not the utterance of mere man, but is the Word of Allah through flesh and blood. It is the communication of the Infinite through the finite. At the end of the eighth century Abu Yazid stated, "Verily I am God, there is no god beside me, so worship me!" I could find no record of how he was treated by Islamic Fundamentalists, but one can speculate![2]

In what follows, I will not attempt to draw rigid lines between allegiances to beliefs or orders or rituals. The common theme will be the incarnation of Christian witness among Muslims who care more about loving God than observing the five pillars of Islam. To them, feeling God is more essential than fearing the fires of Hell. Worship is free-form rather than being strictly prescribed. Allah's mercy is elevated over a long list of dos and don'ts that stifle rather than liberate the soul. The mystical Muslim regards the cage as one's body.

---

[2] Parshall 2007.

Inside this prison is a bird (soul) longing to be released to fly free and soar into the heavenlies. This, to them, more than creed or dogma, is authentic, unstructured spirituality.

Incarnation of Lifestyle

Three Cups of Tea3 is an outstanding example of an American who, moved by compassion, decided to assist illiterate girls to learn how to read and write in the wild, lawless region of Pakistan's Northwest Frontier. There are no indications of Mortenson being an Evangelical, though he is the son of Lutheran missionaries. His early years growing up in East Africa prepared him well for the rigours of living among the needy and deprived. Mortenson, early on, discovered he would be required to incarnate his words and behaviour into a Muslim mode of thinking and being. Otherwise his desire to build schools for young girls would go unfulfilled. Mortenson took the theoretical concept of contextualization and applied it to the people he served to a degree I have seldom seen among other Christian missionaries.

Joseph was for fifteen years a missionary among extremely devout Muslims in Western Africa. His compelling (even obsessive) desire was to assist Muslims both physically and materially. Joseph and his team of multinationals laboured tirelessly to accomplish this goal. Some years ago I lead a retreat with this group of stalwarts living on the edge of the Sahara. Joseph, dressed in his multi-layered, colourful African dress, greeted me at the city's small, rather dilapidated airport. Driving across town, seeking to avoid ubiquitous potholes, was a challenge. As we proceeded along dust-saturated lanes, it became obvious we were moving toward the poorer section of the city. Arriving at Joseph's rented home, we walked through a wooden gate and into a 50 foot long open verandah. Off to the right was a small room with a hole in the middle, a brick on either side. This primitive squat toilet promotes excellent leg muscles, as Julie (my wife) and I can testify. We used a similar facility in Islampur for 8 years. A nearby pail of water is utilized for body washing as well as toilet cleaning. On the left was the first of four twelve foot by twelve foot rooms. It was occupied by a Muslim family of six. Joseph, his wife and two children lived in the next two interconnected rooms. One was the living/dining and kitchen area. Cooking was on a one burner kerosene stove. The second room served as the family bedroom. Mattresses where spread on the floor. Nails protruded from the walls serving as clothes hangers. There were no tables or chairs in either room. The scarcity of material goods was blatant.

At the end of the verandah was the fourth room, the guest room. There I slept on the floor on a thin mattress over which hung a mosquito net. My only problem

---

[3] Mortenson 2006.

was that the blood-sucking critters preferred to domicile inside rather than outside of the net. Memorable was the screaming of two women just outside my window. These wives were literally fighting over who would get to spend the night with a more than harassed husband.

No lights, no fans, no running water. How could this Ivy League-educated American couple with two small children live in these deprived circumstances for fifteen years? In the summer temperatures soared above 120 degrees Fahrenheit. Dust storms from the desert blanketed the city and penetrated into the interiors of even closed rooms in the home.

On the day of the retreat thirty alert team members gathered together to consider spiritual and methodological initiatives within such a harsh and religiously adversarial context. The Muslim director of social services of that country was invited to bring greetings to this group, which was under his direction.

Following his brief remarks opportunity was given for interaction. One of the young ladies asked the government official, 'Sir, what can we do to be of greater help to the poor of your country?' I will never forget the answer. With a sweeping gesture of his hand, he pointed toward Joseph and said, 'If you want to be of the greatest assistance to us, then just be like him.' I felt overwhelmed. Here is a Muslim official commending a Christian missionary as an exemplary person of dedication, accomplishment and integrity. This testimony for Christ was outworked in one of the most hostile religious environments in Africa and within a harsh lifestyle context. All of the above makes my family's 'deprived' incarnation into Muslim situations look fairly insipid. True, we spent half of our twenty years in Islampur without reliable electricity and with no running water. Our first five years in a village were pretty basic. Then in the Philippines we lived in a simple apartment adjacent to a busy street. We were surrounded by three huge slum areas. For 22 years in Manila we witnessed the pain of the deprived. Our small effort at living a contextualized lifestyle was appreciated by those among whom we dwelt. We consider it a wonderful privilege to have invested our lives with our Muslim friends.

Incarnation of Ministry

In 1974, our team in Islampur decided to make a radical departure from the norms of Muslim outreach as practiced there. Our target community was the nominally religious folk Muslim. Methodology that was then considered 'radical' is now much more of a norm. In the early 1800's, William Carey entered the area which is now Islampur. His focus of ministry was to reach Hindus. This was particularly reflected in his choice of language which would be appreciated by his target group. *Ishwar* is a Hindi word for God. Carey felt Christians could use it and, therefore, even today Islampur Christians who are of Hindu background worship *Ishwar*. Some of their songs use *puja*, a Hindu temple-worship word, as an expression of devotion to God. Such vocabulary is totally repugnant to

Muslims. Therefore it soon became apparent that relations with Muslims would require a new direction, not only in Biblical vocabulary, but even in everyday conversation. Islamic greetings, such as *asalam-alaikum* (Peace be upon you), are actually more of a New Testament concept than is the Hindi salutation, *namaskhar*.

Bible Translation

Viggo Olsen, a missionary surgeon of the Association of Baptist for World Evangelism in Islampur put aside some of his medical responsibilities and, for years, worked on producing a linguistically appropriate New Testament for Muslims. Olsen's choice of vocabulary was brilliant and it's packaging in sympathy with locally preferred colours and design Operation Mobilization rose to the challenge of distributing these New Testaments throughout the length and breadth of Islampur. Thousands of Muslims, for the first time in their lives, had access to the Bible. It became the bestselling book in the country in the late 1970's. Accompanying the book sale was an invitation to enrol in the Islampur Bible Correspondence School. During those years my wife and I were directors of this BCS. Without a doubt, this all laid the foundation for a movement that was to follow. The Gospel had become incarnated. Jesus' words were now understandable.

Worship Forms

The traditional church in Islampur had historically incorporated Western worship forms into its worship. It became perfectly natural for Hindu-background believers to fit into the rhythm of the same liturgy as a church found in London or in Dhaka. After all, if William Carey instituted it, one must accept it as bearing the imprimatur of God! Fine for the adaptive Hindu, but what about the Muslim?

Contrasts

Mosque	**Islampur Traditional Church**
Obligatory washing prior to prayer	No washing
Men wear prayer hats	Not worn
No wearing of shoes	Shoes were worn
Worshippers always sit on rugs or mats	Optional
No musical instruments for worship	Important for worship
Singing totally disallowed	Always practised
Prostration during prayer	Sitting or standing for prayer
Embracing after service	Optional

The Incarnated witness will seek to be sensitive and adaptive to Muslim preferences. Actually, the rhythm of prayer postures practiced in the mosque come out looking more Biblical then those found in the average church.

Standing, hands raised, kneeling, and prostration are found throughout the scripture, but are often absent in the average Evangelical church.

Pirs (Holy Men)

In southern Islampur there is a large plot of land that is believed by folk Muslims to be spiritually energized through the medium of a holy man who has been deceased for centuries. My wife, daughter and I walked down a dusty lane flanked by small stalls which were stocked with an unusual product. Scores of long thin sticks were neatly lined up on the counter. At the tip of each was a generous portion of raw meat. Sales were brisk.

We continued on and came to a large, polluted pond. Swimming around in the greenish water were scores of turtles of all sizes. Standing at the pond's edge were large numbers of boys, girls, men and women. Each held their stick of meat close to a turtle which immediately snapped the titbit into its mouth.

I walked among the crowd and took an informal survey as to why these well dressed, obviously intelligent Muslims were concerned enough for the welfare of turtles to make pilgrimages from distant towns in order to feed them. Some answers I received included: 'I know that these turtles' ancestors were alive in the *pir's* days, so there is power passed on from him to us through them.' 'If I feed the turtles, then the pir will be pleased with me and intercede to Allah in my behalf.' 'I am sick, so I will pour some of this energized pond water into this bottle and drink it when I get home. Then I believe I will be healed.' And finally, a handsome young student stated with obvious satisfaction, 'I was very concerned about passing my college entrance exam. So I prayed to the *pir* to petition God for me. I told him I would come and feed his turtles if I passed. I did and so I'm here to fulfil my vow.'

Immediately behind the pond was a high hill upon which was built an attractive small cement room. No women were allowed inside, so my female family went to a side window where they could watch but not be watched! As I was of the privileged gender, I took my shoes off, went inside, and joined the solemn procession circumambulating the above-ground tomb. The men had written out prayer requests which were deposited near the crypt. Expectation was that the pir would read these petitions and then intercede to Allah on behalf of his devoted followers. All exited the room walking backwards as it would dishonor the *pir* if he (or his spirit) had to gaze upon our backsides. Outside, all were expected to place money in a large box which would pay for upkeep of the premises… and presumably make the *pir* happy in his ongoing task of intercession. Lastly, the men prayed toward the tomb, not toward Mecca.

What do orthodox Islampur Muslims think of such quasi-pagan practices? By and large the country's Muslims are more folk than fundamentalist. Some religious leaders object, but not too loudly. When Saudi *ulema* visit Islampur, they are extremely displeased. But they come and go, and folk Islam practices continue unabated. I have found many opportunities to talk to Sufis concerning our risen intercessor, Jesus Christ. Definitely these Muslims are more open to spiritual discussions.

Evil Influences

Folk Muslims are sensitive to the power of Satan and his demons. They are fearful of his attacks upon life and property. This evil force is identified by most Muslims as *jinn,* a spirit-being that seemingly is omnipresent and just waiting for an opportunity to cause hurt and destruction. *Jinn* are known to live in garbage dumps, cemeteries, wells, certain trees, and toilets. They move about freely at night seeking to accomplish their evil deeds. Diagnosis of a *jinn* attack is done by divination. A power practitioner is called, who may sleep with an afflicted person's clothes and then devise a cure. The remedy may require donating money to a mosque or in some instances to wear special tiny brass containers tied to their neck and arm. Inside are small pieces of paper upon which are written Quranic verses that are applicable to the problem of the afflicted.

In Khartoum, Sudan, I watched a bearded old man sit beside a dirty road with a blackboard and chalk in hand. I was curious to see him write verses from the Qur'an on the board, then wipe off the chalk into a glass of water which would be drunk by a Muslim. He explained that this empowered word of Allah would, after being ingested, protect one from all evil and sickness. In Islampur, I was invited by our Muslim neighbor to watch an exorcism ceremony. A house helper was said to be demon possessed. An exorcist had been called to come and cast out Satan's representative from this 14 year-old girl. Upon entering the living room, I was stricken by the sight of the young girl writhing on the floor in obvious agony. Her hands and legs were being thrown about uncontrollably. Gurgling sounds mixed with saliva exited her mouth. Clearly this girl was in dire distress and needed immediate attention. Within a few minutes the exorcist entered, who was also a carpenter who had done some interior work for me. He first drew a chalk line around the girl's body. While chanting the Qur'an he blew cigarette smoke into the girl's ears. He took red chilies and passed them around her head. Lighted incense sticks filled the room with a sickening, strong odour. Slowly, the girl stopped shaking and making unintelligible sounds. The exorcist declared she was healed, collected his fee, and departed.

The Muslims were all pleased at this divine intervention. Faith was vindicated, Satan's work defeated. As for me, rational being that I am, I concluded the girl was afflicted with epilepsy. My conviction is that Pentecostals and Charismatics are the best equipped people to engage in power encounter experiences with Muslims. Calvin Olson was my close Assemblies of God missionary friend while we were in Islampur. He was able to identify the real from the false. Calvin was at home in dealing with the spirit world. In any event, we find that Sufis are indeed appreciative of Christians who take their fears seriously and engage in some kind of ritual that affords them relief.

Dreams

Over the years, I have encountered Muslims who have had vivid dreams of Muhammad. The Prophet has exhorted them to forsake the sins of their flesh and return to the ways of Allah. In at least some instances this dream has prompted repentance. Conversely, many are the instances of Muslims having a nocturnal vision of Christ which has brought them to a radical conversion experience. Bilquis Sheikh was a wealthy divorcee who lived in a huge home in the northwest area of Pakistan. One night she had a vivid dream of John the Baptist. This caused her to make an unannounced visit to the home of nearby team missionaries, Dave and Sinova Mitchell. Bilquis wanted to know who this John the Baptist was. She was open to the Gospel and soon became a true believer. I had the privilege of meeting her twice and was immensely impressed with her life and verbal testimony. Her autobiography is published under the title, *I Dared to Call Him Father.*[4] It all started with a dream. So many Muslims are open and even responsive to some supernatural visitation that they are convinced is a message from God. Therefore, it seems proper to me to pray for the Lord to use dreams and visions to bring Muslims to Himself.

Conclusion

Spiritual encounters, for Muslims, are diverse and, at times, enigmatic. But if we are honest, this also is true of those who profess to follow Christ. We should be open to evaluate experiences of a divine nature wherever they may be found. For Evangelicals it is important to use the Bible as a guidebook for this critique process. The Incarnation of life and witness will mean different things in each context. The Christian should be alert to all legitimate methods by which to share his or her faith.

---

[4] Sheik 1978.

Bibliography

Abazov, R. 2007

Culture and Customs of the Central Asian Republics (Westport, Conn.: Greenwood Press)

Abdulhussein, M. 2001

Al-Dai Al-Fatimi Syedna Mohammed Burhanuddin: An illustrated biography (London: Al-Jame'ah al-Saifiya Trust)

Abdullah, A. 1997

Morals and Manners: An Islamic Perspective (Plainfield, Ind.: Islamic Society of North America)

Abdulhussein, M. 2009

'Bohras: An article on Bohras taken from the OUP Encyclopedia of the Modern Islamic World,' cited at http://archive.mumineen.org/publications/oup/bohras.html accessed on 25th April 2009.

Accad, F.E. 1969

'A new Arabic common Bible' *Christian Century* 86, no.9 (February)

Accad, F. 1997

Building Bridges (Colorado Springs, Col.: NavPress)

Accad, M. 2003

'The ultimate proof-text: the interpretation of John 20:17 in Muslim-Christian dialogue (second/eighth-eighth/fourteenth centuries)', in D. Thomas (ed.) *Christians at the Heart of Islamic Rule* (Leiden: Brill)

Aghaie, K.S. 2005

'The Gender Dynamics of Moharram Symbols and Rituals in the Latter Years of Qajar Rule' in Kamran Scot Aghaie (ed.) *The Women of Karbala: Ritual Performance and Symbolic Discourses in Modern Shi'i Islam* (Austin, Tex.: University of Texas Press)

AHDR 2003

The Arab Human Development Report 2003 (New York: United Nations Development Program), cited at http://www.arab-hdr.org/publications/other/ahdr/ahdr2003e.pdf accessed on 20th Januray 2010.

Ahmad, I. & H. Reifeld (eds.) 2004

Lived Islam in South Asia: Adaptation, Accommodation and Conflict (Delhi: Social Science Press)

Ahmad, S. 2004

'Satanic Verses' in J. D. McAuliffe (ed.) *Encyclopedia of the Qur'an* 6v. (Leiden: Brill)

Ali, A.Y. 1977

The Holy Qur'an, Translation and Commentary 2nd ed. (Indianapolis, Ind.: American Trust Publications)

Allworth, E. 1994

Central Asia, 130 Years of Russian Dominance: A Historical Overview 3rd ed. (Durham, N.C.: Duke University Press)

Ambrie, H. n.d.a,
Allah Tritunggal yang Maha-Esa [The One Triune God] (Jakarta: P.B.K. Sinar Kasih)

Ambrie, H. n.d.b
Allahu Akbar [God is Great] (Jakarta: P.B.K. Sinar Kasih)

Ambrie, H. 1982
'Correspondence with Rudy Herman, July 1', 17, Copy in personal files of Puranwan Tenibemas, Institut Alkitab Tiranus, Bandung, Indonesia.

Ambrie, H,n.d.c.
Dengan Kasih Kita Jawab [We Reply with Love] (Jakarta: P.B.K. Sinar Kasih)

Ambrie, H. 1983
Dialog [Dialogue] (Jakarta: P. B. K. Sinar Kasih)

Ambrie, H. 1978
God Has Chosen for Me a New Life in Christ (Jakarta: P.B.K. Sinar Kasih)

Ambrie, H, n.d.d
Kenapa Yesus Disebut Anak Allah? [Why Is Jesus Called the Son of God?] (Jakarta: P.B. K. Sinar Kasih)

Ambrie, H. n.d.e
Kritik Muhamad Zulkarnain Mengenai Kristologi yang Keliru [Criticism by Muhammad Zulkarnain Concerning an Erroneous Christology] (Jakarta: P.B.K. Sinar Kasih)

Ambrie, H. n.d.f
Membahas Buku: Ke-Ilahi-An Yesus Kristus [Examining the Book: The Divinity of Jesus Christ] (Jakarta: P.B.K. Sinar Kasih)

Ambrie, H. n.d.g
Menjawab Tantangan [Responding to the Challenge] (Jakarta: P. B. K. Sinar Kasih)

Ambrie, H. n.d.h
Surat dari Mesir [A Letter from Egypt] (Jakarta: P.B. K. Sinar Kasih)

Ambrie, H. n.d.i,
Tauhid dan Syirik (The Unity of God and Polytheism) (Jakarta: P.B.K. Sinar Kasih)

Amina, Mrs. 2005
Personal conversation with author in Pune, India on December 22

Amina, Mrs 2006, a
Personal conversation with author in Pune, India on February 28

Amina, Mrs 2006 b
Personal conversation with author in Pune, India on March 14

Antonius, G. 1945
The Arab Awakening (New York: Capricorn Press)

Arberry, A.J. 1964
The Koran Interpreted (Oxford: Oxford University Press)

Asad, M. 2009
The Qur'an at http://www.islamicity.com/quransearch/default_thebookfoundation.asp, accessed 5th July 2009.

Asani, A.S. 1996
'Propagating the Message: Folk Songs and the Spread of Islam in South Asia,' Abstracts of the 1996 AAS Annual Meeting, Association for Asian Studies, Inc., Honolulu, HI, posted at http://www.aasianst.org/absts/1996abst/southasi/sa201.htm, Accessed 25th April 2009.

Al-Ash'ari, 1963
Kitāb Maqālāt al-Islāmīyīn wa Ikhtilāf al-Musallīn (ed.) H. Ritter (Wiesbaden: Franz Steiner)

Aslan, R. 2006
No God but God: The Origins, Evolution, and Future of Islam (New York: Random House)

Athanasius 1957
The Incarnation of the Word of God: Being the Treatise of St. Athanasius De Incarnatione Verbi (tr.) C. S. Lewis (New York: Macmillan)

Athanasius 1996
On the Incarnation: the treatise de incarnatione verbi dei (Crestwood, N.Y.: St Vladimir's Seminary Press)

Attridge, H.W. & W.C. Meeks (eds.) 2006
Harper Collins Study Bible rev.ed. (San Francisco, Calif.: Harper San Francisco)

Ayoub, M. 1978
Redemptive Suffering in Islam: A Study of devotional Aspects of 'Ashura in Twelver Shi'ism (New York: Mouton)

el-Awa, M.1973
'The Place of Custom ('Urf) in Islamic Legal Theory' in *The Islamic Quarterly,* Vol. 17, Nos. 3 & 4 (July-December).

Azad, Abul K. 1996
The Tarjuman al-Qur'an (ed. and tr.) Syed Abdul Latif v.1 (New Delhi: Kitab Bhavan)

Azumah, J. 2001
The Legacy of Arab-Islam: A Quest for Inter-Religious Dialogue (Oxford: Oneworld)

Bacha, C. 1904
Les Oeuvres Arabes de Théodore Aboucora Évêque d'Harran (Beirut: al-Matba'ah al-adabiyah)

Bailey, K.E. 1992
Arabic Versions of the Bible: Reflections on their History and Significance (Cairo: n.p.)

Bakry, H. 1982
'Membantah Terhadap Hamran Ambrie' [Refuting Hamran Ambrie] *Panji Masyarakat,* 21 March, 29-31

Barakat, H. 1993
The Arab World: Society, Culture, and State (Berkeley, Calif.: University of California Press)

Basetti-Sani, G. 1977
The Koran in the Light of Christ W.Russell Carroll & Bede Dauphinee (tr.) (Chicago: Franciscan Herald Press)

Bauckham, R. 1998
God Crucified: Monotheism and Christology in the New Testament (Grand Rapids, Mich. and Cambridge: Eerdmans)

Bauckham, R. 2006
Jesus and the Eyewitnesses: The Gospels as Eyewitness Testimony (Grand Rapids, Mich.: Eerdmans)

Bauckham, R. 2007
The Testimony of the Beloved Disciple: Narrative, History and Theology in the Gospel of John (Grand Rapids, Mich.: Baker Academic)

Bauckham, R. 2008
Jesus and the God of Israel: God Crucified and Other Studies on the New Testament's Christology of Divine Identity (Grand Rapids, Mich. and Cambridge: Eerdmans)
Bayram, M. 2009
'Kyrgyzstan: Crackdown follows new Religion Law', Forum 18 News cited at http://www.forum18.org on 28th May 2009.
Beaumont, M. 2005
Christology in Dialogue with Muslims (Carlisle: Paternoster)
Bediako, K. 1992
Theology and Identity (Oxford: Oxford Regnum)
Bell, S. 2006
Grace for Muslims? (Milton Keynes: Authentic)
Bennett, C. 2001
'Christian Trinity and Muslim Attributes: An Invitation to Spiritual Exploration' in David Emmanuel Singh and Robert Edwin Schick (eds.) *Approaches, Foundations, Issues and Models of Interfaith Relations* (New Delhi: ISPCK/HMI)
Bible Society of Egypt, 2008
'The First Ever Arabic (Van Dyke) Study New Testament: Understanding the 140-year-old Arabic Bible' *Bible Society of Egypt,* cited at www.bsoe.org.eg, accessed 4th June 2009.
Birdwhitsell, R.L. 1968
'Communication' in D.L Sills (ed.) *International Encyclopedia of the Social Sciences* v.3 (New York: Macmillan and Free Press)
Bishop, E.F.F. 1964
'The Arabic Bible after a Century' *The Bible Translator* v. 15, no. 4 (October)
Blank, J. 2001
Mullahs on the Mainframe: Islam and Modernity among the Daudi Bohras (Chicago: University of Chicago Press).
Blomberg, C. 2001
The Historical Reliability of John's Gospel (Downers Grove, Ill.: Apollos)
Bobzin H. 2006
'Translations of the Qur'an' in McAuliffe, J.D. (ed.) *The Encyclopaedia of the Qur'an* v. 5 (Leiden: Brill)
Boers, H. 1970
'Jesus and the Christian Faith: NT Christology since Bousset' *Kurios Christos, JBL* 89.4 (December)
Boff, L. 1988
Trinity and Society Paul Burns (tr.) (London: Burns & Oates)
Bongoyok, M. 2008
'Islamism and Receptivity to Jesus' in J.D Woodberry (ed.) *From Seed to Fruit: Global Trends, Fruitful Practices, and Emerging Issues among Muslims* (Pasadena, Calif.: William Carey Library)
Bouwsam, W.J. 1988
John Calvin: A Sixteenth-Century Portrait (New York: Oxford University Press)
Brock, S.P. 1973
'An Occidental View of the Bible: A Review Essay' in *Journal of the American Academy of Religion* XLI, 3

Brown, P. 1971
'The Rise and Function of the Holy Man in Late Antiquity' *The Journal of Roman Studies* 61
Brown, R. 2007
'Biblical Muslims' *International Journal of Frontier Missiology* (24) 2, Summer, 65-74
Brueggemann, W. 1991
'Introduction to the Apocrypha/Deuterocanonical Books' in B. M. Metzger and R. E. Murphy (eds.) *New Oxford Annotated Bible* (New York: Oxford University Press)
Bulliet, R.W. 1979
Conversion to Islam in the Medieval Period: An Essay in Quantitative History (Cambridge, Mass.: Harvard University Press)
Bennett, C. 2001
In Search of Muhammad (London: Cassell)
Bennett, C. 2008
Understanding Christian-Muslim Relations Past and Present (London: Continuum)
Berjak, R. 2006
'Sufism' in Leaman, Olive (ed.) *The Qur'an: An Encyclopedia* (London: Routledge) 276-7
Cate, P. 1992
'What Will It Take to Win Muslims?' in *EMQ* (July)
Catholics New Service. 2009
http://www.catholicnews.com/data/stories/cns/0805000.htm accessed on 27th February 2010.
Catholic Online International News. 2009
http://www.catholic.org/international/international_story.php?id=29812 accessed on 27th February 2010.
Caquot, A. 1989
La version arabe de la Bible de Sa'adya Gaon, L'Ecclésiaste et son commentaire Le livre de l'Ascèse (Paris: Maisonneuve & Larose)
Caverley, E.E. 1961
'Cornelius Van Allen Van Dyck' *Bible Translator* 12, no.4
Chabot, J.-B. 1899-1910
Chronique de Michel le Syrien: Patriarche Jacobite d'Antioche v. 3 (Paris: Ernest Leroux)
Chahīne, J. 2005
'Christians and the Arab Renaissance' in Habib Badr (ed.) *Christianity: A History in the Middle East* (Beirut: Middle East Council of Churches)
Chandler, P.-G. 2008
'Can a Muslim Be a Follower of Christ? The Arresting Story of a Devout Believer' in *Mission Frontiers* (30), 4 July-August
Chapman, C. 1995
The Cross and the Crescent: Responding to the Challenge of Islam (London: InterVarsity Press)
Chittick, W. 1994
Imaginal Worlds: Ibn al-'Arabi and the Problem of Religious Diversity (Albany, N.Y.: State University of New York Press)

Christian, D. 1998
A History of Russia, Central Asia and Mongolia v.1: Inner Eurasia from Prehistory to the Mongol Empire (Oxford: Blackwell Publishing)

Choueiri, Y.M. 1989
Modern Arab Historiography (London: Curzon Press)

Clifford, G. 1971
Islam Observed (Chicago, Ill.: University of Chicago Press)

Cohn-Sherbok, D. (ed.) 1991
Islam in a World of Diverse Faiths (New York: St. Martin's Press)

'Contradictions in the Qur'an' 2009
Cited at http://www.answering-islam.org/Quran/Contra/ accessed on 4th November 2009.

Corbin, H. 1998
Alone with the Alone: Creative Imagination in the Sufism of Ibn 'Arabi (tr.) R. Manheim (Princeton. N.J.: Princeton University Press)

Courbage, Y. & P. Fargues 1997
Christians and Jews under Islam (Oxford: I.B. Tauris)

Cragg, K. 1988
Readings in the Qur'an (London: Collins Liturgical)

Cragg, K. 1991
*The Arab Christian (*Louisville, Ky.: Westminster/John Knox)

Cragg, K. 1994
The Event of the Qur'an: Islam in its Scripture (Oxford: Oneworld)

Cragg, K. 1984
Muhammad and the Christian: A Question of Respons (London: Darton, Longman and Todd)

Cragg, K. 1999
Jesus and the Muslim: An Exploration (Oxford: OneWorld)

Cragg, K. 2004
A Certain Sympathy of Scriptures: Biblical and Qur'anic (Eastbourne: Sussex Academic)

Cragg, K. 2005
The Qur'an and the West (Washington, D.C.: Georgetown University Press)

Cragg, K. 2009
'70 Years' Study of Islam'; a lecture at Song School, St Stephen's Hall, Oxford; 6 May, 2-4 PM

Cumming, 2009
'Muslim Followers of Jesus?' in *Christianity Today*, December, 32-35

Cureton, W. 1864/1967
Ancient Syriac Documents Relative to the Earliest Establishment of Christianity in Edessa and the Neighboring Countries (London: Reprint: Amsterdam: Oriental Press)

Cuypers, M. 2009
The Banquet: A Reading of the Fifth Sura of the Qur'an (Miami, Fla.: Convivium Press)

Davis, S.J. 2008
Coptic Christology in Practice: Incarnation and the Divine Participation in Late Antique and Medieval Egypt (New York: Oxford University Press)

DeSilva, D.A. 2006
'Apocrypha, Deuterocanonicals' in *New Interpreters' Dictionary of the Bible* 5 v. (Nashville, Tenn.: Abingdon Press) 1.195-200
Dey, A. 1996
Sufism in India (Calcutta: Ratna Prakashan)
D'Souza, A.F. 1988
'The Concept of Revelation in the Writings of Modern Indian Muslims: A Study of Ahmad Khan, Azad and Mawdudi' (Ph.D. Dissertation, Institute of Islamic Studies, McGill University)
Dickens, M. 2009
'Nestorian Christianity in Central Asia' cited at http://www.oxuscom.com/Nestorian_Christianity_in_CA.pdf accessed on 20th April 2009.
Donaldson, J.W. 2009
Christian orthodoxy reconciled with the conclusions of modern Biblical learning (BibliolLife, LLC. Originally published in London by Williams and Norgate, 1957)
Doughty, C.M. 1921
Travels in Arabia Deserta 2v. (London: Jonathan Cape and the Medici Society)
D'Souza, A. 1982
'Jesus in Ibn 'Arabi's Fusus al-Hikam' in *Islamochristiana,* 8,185-200
D'Souza, A. 1998
'In the Presence of the Martyrs: The `Alam in Popular Shi`i Piety' in *The Muslim World* (88) 1, 67-80
Dunn, J.D.G. 1989
Christology in the Making. A New Testament Inquiry into the Origins of the Doctrine of the Incarnation 2nd ed. (Philadelphia: Westminster Press)
Eliade, M. 1967
From Primitives to Zen (London: Collins)
Esposito, J.L., J.O. Voll, & O. Bakar 2008
Asian Islam in the 21st Century (Oxford: Oxford University Press)
Eusebius, 1890
Church History in Philip Schaff (ed.) *Nicene and Post Nicene Fathers* v.1 (Edinburgh: T&T Clark)
al-Fadi, A.A. 1995
Is the Qur'an infallible? (Villach: Light of Life)
Al-Faruqi, I. 1962
On Arabism; 'Urubah and Religion: A Study of the Fundamental Ideas of Arabism and Islam as its Highest Moment of Consciousness (Amsterdam: Djambatan N.V.)
Farzana 2006
Personal conversation with author in Pune, India on 23rd February
Fatima 2005
Personal conversation with author in Pune, India on 29th September
Fee, G.D. 2007
Pauline Christology: An Exegetical-Theological Study (Peabody, Mass.: Hendrickson)
Finnegan, R. 2002
Communicating: The Multiple Modes of Human Interconnection (London: Routledge)

Flaskerud, I. 2005
'Oh, My Heart Is Sad. It Is Moharram, the Month of Zaynab: The Role of Aesthetics and Women's Mourning Ceremonies in Shiraz' in Kamran Scot Aghaie (ed.) *The Women of Karbala: Ritual Performance and Symbolic Discourses in Modern Shi`i Islam* (Austin, Tex.: University of Texas Press)

Fowden, E.Key. 1999
The Barbarian Plain: Saint Sergius between Rome and Iran (Berkeley, Calif.: University of California Press)

Fuller, G.E. 1992
Central Asia: The New Geopolitics RAND Report (Santa Monica, Calif.: RAND)

Gaudeul, J.M., 2000
Encounters and Clashes: Islam and Christianity in History v.2 (Rome: P.I.S.A.I)

Ghadially, R. 1998
'Women's Vows, Roles and Household Ritual in a South Asian Muslim Sect' in *Asian Journal of Women's Studies* (4) 2, 27-52

Ghadially, R. 2003a
'A Hajari (Meal Tray) for `Abbas Alam Dar: Women's Household Ritual in a South Asian Muslim Sect' in *The Muslim World* (93) 2, 309-321

Ghadially, R. 2003b
'Women's Observances in the Calendrical Rites of the Daudi Bohra Ismaili Sect of South Asian Muslims' in Islamic Culture (77) 3, 1-20

Ghadially, R. 2005
'Gender and Moharram Rituals in an Isma`ili Sect of South Asian Muslims' in Kamran Scot Aghaie (ed.) *The Women of Karbala: Ritual Performance and Symbolic Discourses in Modern Shi`i Islam* (Austin, Tex.: University of Texas Press) 183-198

Gibson, M.D. 1899,
A Treatise on the Triune Nature of God (London: C.J. Clay)

Glasse, C. 2002
The New Encyclopedia of Islam (Walnut Creek, Calif.: AltaMira Press)

Glasser, I. 2008
'Cross-Referencing Theology: Speaking, thinking and living the cross in the context of Islam' in D. E. Singh (ed.) *Jesus and the Cross: Reflections of Christians from Islamic Contexts* (Oxford: Regnum Books International)

Grafton, D.D. 2008
'The Arabs' in the Ecclesiastical Historians of the 4th/5th Centuries: The Effects on Contemporary Christian-Muslim Relations' *HTS Teologiese Studie/Theological Studies* 64/1, 177-192. Cited online: www.hts.org.za/index.php/HTS/article/viewFile/14/11 accessed on 28th February 2010.

Grams, R. 2008
'God, the Beneficent-the Merciful, and Jesus's Cross: From Abstract to Concrete Theologising.' in D. Singh (ed.) *Jesus and the Cross: Reflections of Christians from Islamic Contexts* Ed. D. Singh (Oxford: Regnum/Paternoster)

Grams, R. 2008
'Some Geographical and Intertextual Dimensions of Matthew's Mission Theology' in R. Grams, I. Howard Marshall, P.Penner, R.Routledge (eds.) *Bible and Mission: A Conversation between Biblical Studies and Mission* (Schwarzenfeld: Neufeld Verlag)

Greeson, K. 2007
The Camel Method Training Manual (Richmond, Va.: WIGTake Resources)

Griffith, S.H. 1985
'The Gospel in Arabic: An Inquiry into Its Appearance in the First Abbasid Century' *Oriens Christiannus* 69

Griffith, S.H. 1988
'The Monks of Palestine and the Growth of Christian Literature in Arabic' *The Muslim World* LXXVIII, no. 1 (Jan.)

Griffith, S.H. 1996
'The view of Islam from the Monasteries of Palestine in the Early 'Abbāsid Period: Theodore Abu Qurrah and the Summa Theologiae Arabica' *Islam and Christian-Muslim Relations* 7, no. 1 (March)

Griffith, S.H. 2002
The Beginnings of Christian Theology in Arabic: Muslim-Christian Encounters in the Early Islamic Period (Aldershot: Ashgate)

Griffith, S.H. 2007
The Church in the Shadow of the Mosque: Christians and Muslims in the World of Islam (Princeton, N.J.: Princeton University Press)

Haleem, M.A. 1999
Understanding the Qur'an: Themes and Style (London, and New York: I. B. Tauris)

Hall, I.C. 1882-1885
'The Arabic Bible of Drs. Eli Smith and Cornelius V.A. van Dyck' *Journal of the American Oriental Society* 11

Harnack, A.von. 1897
History of Dogma v.1 (London: Williams and Norgate)

Harrington, D. J. 2006
'1 Maccabees' in H. W. Attridge and W. C. Meeks (eds.) *Harper Collins Study Bible* rev. ed. (San Francisco, Calif.: HarperSanFrancisco)

Hasan, Y.F. 1985
'Comments' in K. El-Din Haseeb (ed.) *The Arabs and Africa* (London: Croom Helm)

Haurissa, J. 1988
Interview by Jonathan Culver, 6 August, Jakarta, Indonesia

Hayek, M. (ed.) 1977
'Ammār al-Ba'rī': Apologie et Controverses (Beirut: Dar al-Machreq)

Hengel, M. 2008
'The Prologue of the Gospel of John as the Gateway to Christological Truth', in R. Bauckham and C. Mosser (eds.) *The Gospel of John and Christian Theology* (Grand Rapids, Mich.: Eerdmans)

Hick, J. (ed.), 1977
The Myth of God Incarnate (London: SCM Press)

Hick, J. and Meltzer, E.S. (eds.) 1989
The Three Faiths-One God: A Jewish, Christian, Muslim Encounter (London: Macmillan)

Hick, J. 2005
The Metaphor of God Incarnate: Christology in a Pluralistic Age (Louisville, Ky.: Westminster/John Knox Press, 1993)

Hick, J. 2005
'Religious Pluralism and Islam,' Lecture delivered to the Institute for Islamic Culture and Thought. Tehran, cited at http://www.johnhick.org.uk/article11.html.accessed, accessed 1st Januray 2010.

Hick, J. 2009
'Islam and Christianity,' in a lecture to the Iranian Institute of Philosophy, under the auspices of the Iranian Institute for Interreligious Dialogue in Tehran, March 2005, cited online http://www.johnhick.org.uk/article12.html accessed on 3rd April 2009.
Holstein, J.A. & J.F.Gubrium 1995
The Active Interview (Thousand Oaks, Calif.: Sage)
Hoyland, R.G. 2001
Arabia and the Arabs (London: Routledge)
Hughes, T.P. 1994
'Hand' in *Dictionary of Islam* (Chicago: Ill.: Kazi)
Hurtado, L. 2003
Lord Jesus Christ: Devotion to Jesus in Earliest Christianity (Grand Rapids, Mich.: Eerdmans)
Ibn al-'Arabi 1911
Tarjuman al-Ashwaq: A Collection of Mystical Odes (tr.) R. A. Nicholson (London: Royal Asiatic Society)
Ibn al-'Arabi 1980
(Fusus al-hikam) The Seal of Wisdom – Muhyid-din Ibn 'Arabi (Norwich: Diwan Press)
Ibn al-'Arabi 1981
Bezels of Wisdom (tr.) R.J.W. Austin (Ramsy N.J.: Paulist Press)
Ibn al-'Arabi 1987a
Theory of the perfect Man and its Place in the History of Islamic Thought (Tokyo: Insitute for the Study of language and cultures of Asia and Africa)
Ibn al-'Arabi 1987b
Les lluminations da la Mecque: The Meccan Illuminations (*Futuhat al-Makkiyya*) M. Chodkeiwicz, W.C. Chittick, Ch. Chodkiewicz (tr.) (Paris: Sindbad)
Ibn al-'Arabi 1959 & 1960
Shajarart al-kawn in *Studia Islamic* XI, 43-77 and X, 113-160
Ibn Taymiyya [T. Michel (ed.)] 1984
A Muslim Theologian's Response to Christianity: Ibn Taymiyya's Al-Jawab Al-Sahih. (Delmar, N.Y.: Caravan Books)
Irenaeus, 1885
'Against Heresies' 5.14. in A. Roberts and J. Donaldson (eds.) *The Ante-Nicene Fathers v.1 The Apostolic Fathers—Justin Martyr—Irenaeus* (Buffalo, N.Y.: The Christian Literature Publishing Company)
Irvin, D.T. and S. Sunquist 2001
History of the World Christian Movement (Maryknoll, N.Y.: Orbis Books)
Istafanous, [c]Abd al-Masih
Asihiyya wa'l l-masihiyun loghat al-[c]arabiyya [Christianity, Christians and the Arabic Language] (Cairo: Istafanous)
Irvin, D.T. and S. Sunquist 2008
Taqadim al-kitab al-muqudas ila al-qara' al-[c]arab [An Introduction to the Holy Bible for the Arabic Reader] (Beirut: Bible Society of Lebanon)
Jadeed, I. 1980
Christian Reply to Muslim Objections (Light of Life, Austria, 1904, [Fotoreprint])

Jamous, R. 2003
Kinship and Rituals among the Meo of Northern India: Locating Sibling Relationships (New Delhi: OUP)

Jeffrey, A. 1952
The Qur'an as Scripture (New York: R. F. Moore)

Jones, E.S. 1928
Christ at the Round Table (New York: Abingdon Press)

Jones, L.B. 1938
Christianity Explained to Muslims (Calcutta: YMCA Press)

Jukko, R. 2007
Trinity in Unity in Christian-Muslim Relations: The work of the Pontifical Council for Inter-religious Dialogue (Leiden: Brill)

Luong, P.J. 2004
'Politics in the Periphery: Competing views of Central Asian States and Societies', in ed. P.J. Luong (ed.) *The Transformation of Central Asia –States and Societies from Soviet Rule to Independence* (London: Cornell University Press)

Karamustafa, A.T. 1999
'Sufism' in E. Fahlbusch and G.W. Bromiley (eds.) *The Encyclopedia of Christianity* (Grand Rapids, Mich.: Eerdmans) 221-224

Al-Karmi, H. 1964
'The Prophet Muhammad and the Spirit of Compromise' in *The Islamic Quarterly*, Vol. 8, Nos. 3 & 4

Käsemann, E. 1968
The Testament of Jesus: A Study of the Gospel of John in the Light of Chapter 17 (Philadelphia: Fortress Press)

Kaplan, B. 2007
Divided by Faith: Religious conflict and the practice of toleration in early modern Europe (Harvard, Mass.: Harvard University Press)

Kateregga, B.D. & D.W. Shenk 1980
Islam and Christianity: A Muslim and a Christian in dialogue (Nairobi: Uzima Press)

Keating, S.T. (ed.) 2006
Defending the 'People of Truth' in the Early Islamic Period: The Christian Apologies of Abū Rā'i'ah (Leiden: Brill)

Keener, C.S. 2003
The Gospel of John: A Commentary 2v. (Peabody, Mass.: Hendrickson)

Kerr, D. 2002
'Christian Mission and Islamic Studies: Beyond Antithesis' *IBMR* 26/1 (January).

Keston News Service. 2009
'Central Asia: New Laws Restrict Religious Freedom', cited online at http://www.barnabasfund.org/Index.php?m=7%238&a=566 accessed on 27th March 2010.

Khadijah 2005
Personal conversation with author in Pune, India on December 22.

Khatami. M. 2000
Islam Dialogue and Civil Society (Karachi: Foundation for the Revival of Islamic Heritage and the Cultural Centre of the Islamic Republic of Iran)

Khodr, G. 1981
The Economy of the Spirit in G. H. Anderson and T. F. Stransky (eds.) *Faith Meets Faith* (New York: Paulist Press and Grand Rapids, Mich.: Eerdmans) 36-49
Khurshid A. and D. Kerr (eds.) 1982
Christian Mission and Islamic Da'wah: Proceedings of the Chambesy Dialogue Consultation (Leicester: Islamic Foundation)
Kilgoue, R.H. 1916
'Arabic Versions of the Bible' *The Moslem World* 6, no. 4 (October).
Kleist, J.A. 1946
The Epistle of St. Clement of Rome and St. Ignatius of Antioch (Mahwah, N.J.: Paulist Press)
Knapp, Arthur Bernard. 1988
The History and Culture of Ancient Western Asia and Egypt (Chicago, Ill.: Dorsey Press)
Knysh, A.D. 1999
Ibn 'Arabi in the Later Islamic Tradition: The Making of a Polemical Image in Medieval Islam (Albany, N.Y.: State University of New York Press)
Kors, A.C. and Peters, E. (Eds) 2001
Witchcraft in Europe, 400-1700: A documentary history (Philadelphia: University of Pennsylvania Press)
Kraft, C. 1996
Anthropology for Christian Witness (New York: Orbis Books)
Lacunza-Balda, J. 1933/1977
'Translations of the Quran into Swahili and Contemporary Islamic Revival in East Africa' in D. Westerlund & E. E. Rosander (eds.) *African Islam and Islam in Africa: Encounters between Sufis and Islamists* (London: Hurst)
Lake, R. 1977
'The Making of a Mouride Mahdi: Serigne Abdoulaye Yakhine Diop of Thies,' in D. Westerlund & E. E. Rosander (eds.) *African Islam and Islam in Africa: Encounters between Sufis and Islamists* (London: Hurst)
La Sor, W.S., D.A. Hubbard, F.W.Bush & L.C. Allen 1996
Old Testament Survey (Grand Rapids, Mich.: Eerdmans)
Latuihamallo, P.D. 1984
'Who is Jesus in an Islamic Society? The Case of Indonesia' *Reformed World* 38 (June)
Lapidus, I.M. 1988
A History of Islamic Societies (Cambridge: Cambridge Univiversity Press)
Lausanne Occasional Paper 1995
Ministry in Islamic contexts (Nicosia: Lausanne Committee for World Evangelisation)
Leavy, M.R. 1993
'Eli Smith and the Arabic Bible' *Yale Divinity School Library Occasional Publication, No. 4,* (New Haven, Conn.: Yale University Press)
Lewis, B.E., & E. van Donzel (eds.) 1978
'Ibn 'Arabi' in *The Encyclopedia of Islam* 2nd ed. v.3 (Leiden: Brill)
Lewis, R.D. 2005
When Cultures Collide: Leading Across Cultures: A Major New Edition of the Global Guide (Boston: Nicholas Brealey International)

Lohse, B. 1985
A Short History of Christian Doctrine (tr.) Ernest Stoeffler (Philadelphia: Fortress Press)

Macquarrie, J. 1966
Principles of Christian Theology (London: SCM Press)

Mandelbaum, M. 1994
Central Asia and the World: Kazakhstan, Uzbekistan, Tajikistan, Kyrgyzstan, and Turkmenistan (Council of Foreign Relations)

Mann, T. 1933/1978
Joseph und seine bruder (tr.) H.T. Lowe-Porter *Joseph and his Brothers* (Harmondsworth: Penguin)

Mansur, Y.D. (pseudonym) 1990
'To Give an Anwer to Every Man: Trinitarian and Christological Views in the Apologetic of Hamran Ambrie of Indonesia', Th.M. thesis, (Talbot Theological Seminary, La Mirada, Calif.)

Marshall, D. 1999
God, Muhammad and the Unbelievers (Richmond: Curzon)

Mazrui A., 1987
'The Africans: A Triple Heritage', at Ann Arbor: Ann Arbour Public Library, London: BBC (audio-visual)

Marantika, C. 1984
'Toward an Evangelical Theology in an Islamic Context', in Bong Rin Ro and Ruth Eshenaur (eds.) *The Bible and Theology in Asian Contexts* (Taichung, Taiwan: Asia Theological Association)

Martin. R.C. 2002
'Inimitability' in J.D. McAuliffe (ed.) *Encyclopedia of the Qur'an* v. 2 (Leiden: Brill)

McAuliffe, J.D. (ed.) 2001-2006
Encyclopedia of the Qur'an 6 v. (Leiden: Brill)

McVicker, M.K. 2007
'Multisensory Communication among *Dawoodi Bohra* Muslim Women: Invitation at the *Thal*,' PhD thesis submitted to Fuller Theological Seminary.

"Meet persecuted Christians in Central Asia." 2009
Open Doors, accessed on the 5th Aprilhttp://oduk.infogateway.org/meet_c_asia.php. accessed on 05.04.2009

Megalaa, N.H. 2008
'The Van Dyck Arabic Bible Translation After One Hundred Fifty Years', Unpublished MATS Thesis (Cairo, Egypt: Evangelical Theological Seminary in Cairo)

Menges, K.H. 1994
'People, Languages, and Migrations' in Edward Allworth (ed.) *Central Asia, 130 Years of Russian Dominance: A Historical Overview* (Durham, N.C.: Duke University Press)

Menken, M.J.J. 1985
'Numerical Literary Techniques in John: The Fourth Evangelist's Use of Numbers, of Words and Syllables' *Nov.Test.Supp.* 55 (Leiden: Brill)

Metzger, B.M. 1974
'Early Arabic Versions of the New Testament' in M. Black(ed.) *On Language, Culture, and Religion: In Honor of Eugene A. Nida* (Paris: Mouton)

Metzger, B.M. & R.E. Murphy (eds.) 1991
New Oxford Annotated Bible (New York: Oxford University Press)

Meyers, C. 1992
'Temple, Jerusalem' in Freedman, D.N. (ed.) *Anchor Bible Dictionary,* v.6.
Micklethwait, J. & A. Wooldridge 2009
God is back: How the Global Rise of Faith is changing the World (London: Penguin)
El-Mili, 1985
'Comments' in Khair El-Din Haseeb (ed.) *The Arabs and Africa* (London: Croom Helm)
Miller, R. 2000
Muslim Friends: Their Faith and Feeling (Chennai: Orient Longman)
Moffett, S.H. 1998
A History of Christianity in Asia v. 1 (Maryknoll, N.Y.: Orbis Books)
Mogenson, M.S. 2000
'Contextual Communication of the Gospel to Pastoral *Fulbe* in Northern Nigeria, Ph.D. diss., Pasadena: Fuller Theological Seminary), cited online at www.intercultural.dk/index.php?mainid=51&subid=571 accessed on 8th January 2010.
Molla, C.F. 1967
'Some aspects of Islam in Africa south of the Sahara' in *International Review of Missions*, October, Vol. 56, no. 224
Monteil, V. 1964
L'Islam Noir (Paris: Éditions de Seuil)
Morris, J.W. 1986a
'Ibn al-'Arabi and his interpreters part I: Recent French translations' in *Journal of Oriental Society* 106.3
Morris, J.W. 1986b
'Ibn ;Arabi's Esoterism: the problem of spiritual Authority' in *Studia Islamic* LXXI, 37-64
Mortenson, G. 2006
Three Cups of Tea (New York: Penguin)
Moule, C.F.D. 1977
The Origin of Christology (Cambridge: Cambridge University Press)
Müller, C. D., D.G. Caspar & H-G.B. Müller 1981
Geschichte der orientalischen Nationalkirchen (Gottingen: Vandenhoeck & Ruprecht)
Muir, W. 1897
The Mohammedan Controversy (Edinburgh: T. & T. Clark)
Murata, S. and Chittick, W.C. 1994
The Vision of Islam (St. Paul: Paragon House)
Muslim dialogue 2010
Cited online at http://www.muslimdialogue.com/, accessed 6th March 2010.
Nasr, S.H. 1964
An Introduction to Islamic Cosmological Doctrines (Cambridge, Mass.: The Belknap Press of Harvard University Press)
Nasr, S.H. 1992
'Islam and Environmental Crisis', in S.C. Rockefeller and J.C. Elder (eds.) *Spirit and Nature: Why the Environment is a Religious Issue* (Boston, Mass.: Beacon Press)
Naumkin, V.V. 2005
Radical Islam in Central Asia: Between pen and rifle (Totowa: Rowman & Littlefield)
Newbigin, L.N. 1969
The Finality of Christ (London: SCM Press)

Newbigin, L.N. 1977
Christian Witness in a Plural Society (London: British Council of Churches)
Newbigin, LN. 1989
The Gospel in a Pluralist Society (Grand Rapids, Mich.: Eerdmans)
Newbigin, L.N. 1991
The Truth to Tell: The Gospel as Public Truth (Grand Rapids, Mich.: Eerdmans)
Newsom, C. 2006
'Baruch' in H. W. Attridge and W. C. Meeks (eds.) *Harper Collins Study Bible* rev. ed. (San Francisco, Calif.: HarperSanFrancisco) 1452-3.
Nicholson, R.A. 1914
The Mystics of Islam (London: Routledge)
Nolin, K.E. 1993
A Pilgrimage into Islam rev. ed. (Claysville, Pa.: unpublished typescript)
Norris, R.A. (ed. & trans.) 1980
The Christological Controversy (Philadelphia: Fortress Press).
Nyberg, H.S. 1919
'Ibn 'Arabi's *K.Insha'al-dawa'ir*' in *Kleinere Schriften des ibn 'Arab* (Leiden: Brill)
Osman, G. 2005
'Pre-Islamic Arab Converts to Christianity in Mecca & Medina: An investigation into the Arabic Sources' *The Muslim World,* 95 no. 1
Otis, G. 1991
The Last of the Giants (New York: Chosen Books)
Owens, H.D. 2005
'Nestorian Merchant Missionaries and Today's Unreached People Groups.' A paper presented at the National Meeting of the Evangelical Missiological Society, Minneapolis, September 22nd-24th.
Paret, R. 2001
'Translation of the Qur'an' in *The Encyclopaedia of Islam* CD-ROM Edition (Leiden: Brill)
Parshall, P. 1983/2007
Bridges to Islam (Atlanta, Ga.: Authentic & Grand Rapids, Mich.: Baker Book House)
Parsons, M. 2005
Unveiling God: Contextualizing Christology for Islamic Culture (Pasadena, Calif.: William Carey Library)
Peace TV 2010
Cited online at http://www.peacetv.tv/ accessed 6th March 2010.
Pearson J.D. 2001
'Translations [of the Qur'an] into Specific Languages' in *The Encyclopaedia of Islam* CD-ROM Edition (Leiden: Brill)
Peters, F.E. 1994
A Reader on Classical Islam (Princeton, N.J.: Princeton University Press)
Peters, F.E. 1994
Muhammad and the Origins of Islam (Albany, N.Y.: State University of New York Press)
Peyrouse, S. 2008
'The Partnership between Islam and Orthodox Christianity in Central Asia' in *Religion State and Society* 36, 4 December

Philadelphia
St Ignatius of Antioch, *Epistle to the Philadelphians* Roberts-Donaldson (trans.) Chapter VIII cited online at http://en.wikisource.org/wiki/Epistle_to_the_Philadelphians,_with_later_additions_%28Roberts-Donaldson_translation%29#Chapter_VIII.-The_Same_Continued., http://en.wikisource.org/wiki/Epistle_to_the_Philadelphians,_with_later_additions_%28Roberts-Donaldson_translation%29#Chapter_VIII.-The_Same_Continued accessed on 29.01.2010.

Pinault, D. 1992
The Shiites: Ritual and Popular Piety in a Muslim Community (New York: St Martin's Press)

Pinnock, C.H. 1996
Flame of Love: A Theology of the Holy Spirit (Downers Grove, Ill.: InterVarsity Press)

Platti, E. (ed.) 1987
Abū `Īsā al-Warrāq Ya'yā ibn `Adī De L'Incarnation CSCO v. 490-1 (Louvain: E. Peeters)

Powell, A. 1976
'Maulana Rahmat Allah Kairanawi and Muslim-Christian Controversy in India in the Mid-Nineteenth Century' *Journal of the Royal Asiatic Society* 1

Prestige, G.L. 1964
God in Patristic Thought (London: SPCK)

Pritchard, J.B. (ed.) 1969
Ancient Near Eastern Texts (Princeton. N.J.: Princeton University Press)

Protestant Episcopal Church in the United States of America 1977
Book of Common Prayer... According to the Use of the Episcopal Church (New York: Seabury Press)

Putman, H. 1975
L'Église et l'islam sous Timothée I (Beirut: Dar el-Machreq)

Al-Qāsim ibn Ibrāhīm. 1921-2
'Refutation of the Christians', in I. Di Matteo, (ed.) '*Confutazione contro I Christiani dello Zaydati al-Qāsim ibn Ibrāhīm*, Revista degli Studi Orientali, 9.

Qur'an 1946
Yusuf Ali (tr.) *The Holy Quran: Text, Translation, and Commentary* 2v. (Cambridge, Mass.: Murray Printing Company)

Qur'an 1975
A.Yusuf Ali (tr.) *The Meaning of the Glorious Qur'an* (London: Nadim & Co.)

Qur'an 2005
Muhammad A. S. Abdel Haleem (tr.) *The Qur'an: A New Translation* (London and New York: Oxford University Press)

Qur'an 2006
The Meaning of the Glorious Koran (tr.) Muhammad Marmaduke Pickthall (New York: Tahrike Tarsile Qur'an)

Radtke, B. 1989
'A Forerunner of Ibn al-'Arabi: Hakim Tirmidhi on Sainthood' in *the Journal of the Muhyiddin Ibn 'Arabi Society* VIII

Rahman, F. 1980 and 1994
Major Themes of the Qur'an (Chicago, Ill.: Bibliotheca Islamica)

Reisacher, E.A. 2001

'The Processes of Attachment between the Algerians and French within the Christian Community in France,' Ph.D. thesis submitted to Fuller Theological Seminary.

Rets, J. 2005

The Arabs in Antiquity: Their History from the Assyrians to the Umayyads (London: Routledge Curzon)

Richardson, A. & J. Bowden (eds.) 1983

A New Dictionary of Christian Theology (London: SCM Press)

Richardson, D. 2003

The Secrets of the Koran (Ventura, Calif.: Regal Books)

Rippen, A. 1986

'Sa'adya Gaon and Genesis 22: aspects of Jewish-Muslim interaction and polemic' in W.M. Brinner and S.D. Ricks (eds.) *Studies in Islamic and Judaic Traditions* (Atlanta, Ga.: Scholars Press)

Rissanen, S. 1993

Theological Encounters of Oriental Christians with Islam during Early Abbasid Rule (Åbo: Åbo Akademis)

Roberts, A. & J. Donaldson (eds.) 1885

The Ante-Nicene Fathers v. 1, *The Apostolic Fathers—Justin Martyr—Irenaeus* (Buffalo, N.Y.: The Christian Literature Publishing Company)

Robinson, S. 2003

Mosques and Miracles (Mt Gravatt: CityHarvest Publications)

Rogerson, J. & P. Davies 1989

The Old Testament World (Cambridge: Cambridge University Press)

Roy, A. 1982

The Islamic Syncretistic Tradition in Bengal (Princeton, N.J.: Princeton University Press)

Roy, O. 2007

The New Central Asia: The Creation of Nations (London: I.B.Tauris)

Saeed, A. 2002

'Economics' in J. D. McAulife (ed.) *Encyclopedia of the Qur'an* 6 v. (Leiden: Brill)

Saeed, A. 2004

'The Charge of Distortion of Jewish and Christian Scriptures' in *The Muslim World* 92, 3 and 4

Saliba, I.A. 1975

'The Bible in Arabic: The 19th-Century Protestant Translation' in *The Muslim World* 65 no. 4

Sakenfeld, K. D., S.E. Balentine & B.K. Blount (eds.) 2006

New Interpreters' Dictionary of the Bible 5 v. (Nashville, Tenn.: Abingdon Press)

Samartha, S.J. 1987

In S. Das (ed.) *Christian Faith and Multiform Culture in India* (Bangalore: UTC)

Samir, S.K. 1994

'The Earliest Arab Apology for Christianity (c. 750)' in S. K. Samir and J. S. Neilsen (eds.) *Christian Arabic Apologetics during the Abbasid Period (750-1258)* (Leiden: Brill)

Samir, S.K. & J. Nielsen (eds.). 1994

Christian Arabic Apologetics during the Abbasid Period (750-1258) (Leiden: Brill)

Sanneh, L. 1989
Translating the Message: The Missionary Impact on Culture (Maryknoll, N.Y.: Orbis Books)
Sawatsky, W. 1993
'Protestantism in the USSR' in P.S. Ramet (ed.) *Protestantism and Politics in Eastern Europe and Russia* (Durham, N.C.: Duke University Press)
Shamgunov, I. 2009
'Listening to the Voice of the Graduate: An Analysis of Professional Practice and Training for Ministry in Central Asia', Dissertation submitted to the University of Oxford for the degree of Doctor of Philosophy, Hilary Term.
Shariphzan, M. 2009
'Religious Intolerance Persists in Central Asia, Despite what Constitutions Say', Radio Free Europe, publ. 11th March 2009 cited online at http://www.rferl.org/Content/No_Matter_What_The_Constitutions_Say_Religious_Intolerance_Persists_In_Central_Asia/1508070.html.
Sheik, B. 1978
I Dared To Call Him Father (Grand Rapids, Mich.: Chosen Books)
Shenk, D. 2008
'The Bible, the Qur'an, and Mission' in R.G. Grams, I. Howard Marshall, P. Penner, R. Routledge (eds.) *The Bible and Mission* (Schwarzenfeld: Neufeld Verlag)
Shenker, S. 2009
Kyrgyz uprising 'no revolution'', BBC News, cited online at http://news.bbc.co.uk/2/hi/asia-pacific/4836916.stm accessed on 3rd March 2006.
Schaaf, Y. 1994
On Their Way Rejoicing: The History and Role of the Bible in Africa (Carlisle: Paternoster Press)
Schöck, C. 2003
'Moses' in J. D. McAulife (ed.) *Encyclopedia of the Qur'an* 6v. (Leiden: Brill)
Schore, A.N. 1994
Affect Regulation and the Origin of the Self: Neurobiology of Emotional Development (Hillsdale, N.J.: Lawrence Erlbaum Associates)
Schubel, V.J. 1993
Religious Performance in Contemporary Islam: Shi`i Devotional Rituals in South Asia (Columbia, S.C.: University of South Carolina Press)
Shahid, I. 1989
Byzantium and the Arabs in the Fifth Century (Washington, D.C.: Dumbarton Oaks)
Shahid, I. 1984
Byzantium and the Arabs in the Fourth Century (Washington, D.C.: Dumbarton Oaks)
Shahid, I. 2002
Byzantium and the Arabs in the Sixth Century (Washington, D.C.: Dumbarton Oaks)
Shahid, I. 1984
Rome and the Arabs (Washington D.C.: Dumbarton Oaks)
Sheik, B. 1978
I Dared To Call Him Father (Grand Rapids, Mich.: Chosen Books)
Siddiqui, A. 1997
Christian-Muslim Dialogue in the Twentieth century (New York: Palgrave Macmillan)

Singh, D.E. 1999
'Bases and Purposes of Christian-Muslim Relations' *Theological Book Trust Journal* 1, no. 1
Singh, D.E. 2001
'Radical Islamic Anthropology: Key to Christian Theologizing in the Context of Islam' in *Bangalore Theological Forum* 33 (1) June
Singh, D.E. 2002
'God, Jesus and Humanity in Islamic Mysticism: Promise for Dialogue between Christians and Muslims' in *Bangalore Theological Forum* 34 (2) December
Singh, D.E. 2008
'Muhammad, the Prophet like Moses?' in *Journal of Ecumenical Studies* 43.4, Fall
Singh, D.E. 2010
The Gujjars of the Rajaji National Park: Deobandi Islamization and the Gujjar Response (forthcoming)
Smith, B. 2009
'Critical Need in Central Asia' cited online at http://www.wycliffeassociates.org/news/articledetail.asp?id=349 accessed on 23 June 2008.
Smith, E. & C.V.A. Van Dyk, 1900
Brief Documentary History of the Translation of the Scriptures into the Arabic Language (Beirut: American Presbyterian Mission Press)
Smith, M. 2001
Muslim Women Mystics: The life and work of Rábi'a and other women mystics in Islam (Oxford: Oneworld)
Smith, P. 2008
The Age of the Reformation v.2 (Charleston, S.C.: BiblioBazar)
Snyder, J.C. 2002
After Empire: The Emerging Geopolitics of Central Asia (Honolulu: University Press of the Pacific)
Sookhdeo, P. 1996
'Kirche und Moschee in Zentralasien' in *Jahrbuch Mission 1996: Osteuropa Zentralasien* (Hamburg: Missionshilfe Verlag)
Sperber, J. 2000
Christians and Muslims: the Dialogue activities of the World Council of Churches (Berlin: Walter de Gruyter)
Stibbe, M.W.G. 1992
John as Storyteller: Narrative Criticism of the Fourth Gospel (Cambridge: Cambridge University Press)
Subhan, J.A. 2010
'Introduction' in D.E. Singh (ed.) *Sufism: Its Saints and Shrines* (Piscataway, N.J.: Georgias Press)
Swanson, M. 1993
'Some Considerations for the Dating of *fī tatlīt allāh al-wāḥid* (Sinai Ar. 154) and *al-gāmi` wugūh al-īmān* (London, British Library op. 4950)' in *Parole de L'Orient,* 18
Swanson, M. 1998
'Beyond Proof-Texting: Aproaches to the Qur'ān in Some Early Arabic Christian Apologies' *The Muslim World* 88
Sweetman, J.W. 1945-1955
Islam and Christian Theology 2v. (London: Lutterworth Press)

al-Tabari, Abū Ja'far Muhammad ibn Jarī, 1987
The Commentary on the Qur'ān (tr.) J. Cooper (Oxford: Oxford University Press)
Tabyshalieva, A. 2009
'Between Religious Freedom and Harassment: Christian Converts in Central Asia' *CACI Analyst*. Cited online http://www.cacianalyst.org/?q=node/3870 accessed 4th May 2006.
Tabyshalieva, A. 2008, 'Meet persecuted Christians in Central Asia' in *CACI Analyst* at http://www.opendoorsuk.org/search/ksearch.cgi?terms=meet+persecuted+christians&x=0&y=0 accessed on 19th February 2008.
'Textual Integrity of the Bible', 2008
'Islamic Awareness', cited online http://www.islamic-awareness.org/Bible/Text/ accessed on 24th September 2008.
Thomas Aquinas 1947
Summa Theologica tr. Fathers of the English Dominican Province 3v. (New York: Benziger Bros.)
Thomas, D. 2001
Syrian Christians under Islam: The First Thousand Years (Leiden: Brill)
Thomas, D. (ed.) 2002
Early Muslim Polemic against Christianity: Abū `Īsā al-Warrāq's 'Against the Incarnation' (Cambridge: Cambridge University Press)
Thomas, D. (ed.) 2003
Christians at the Heart of Islamic Rule: Church Life and Scholarship in 'Abassid Iraq (Leiden: Brill)
Thomas, D. (ed.) 2008
The Bible in Arab Christianity (Leiden: Brill)
Thompson, J.A. 1979
'Covenant (OT)' in G. Bromiley (ed.) *The International Standard Bible Encyclopedia* v.1 (Grand Rapids, Mich.: Eerdmans)
Thompson, M.M. 1993
The Incarnate Word: Perspectives on John in the Fourth Gospel (Peabody, Mass.: Hendrickson)
Thompson, M.M. 2001
The God of the Gospel of John (Grand Rapids, Mich.: Eerdmans)
Torrey, Charles C. 1919
'A New Edition of the Arabic Bible' *The American Journal of Theology* 23
Trimingham, J.S. 1968
The Influence of Islam upon Africa (London: Longmans)
Trimingham, J.S. 1979
Christianity among the Arabs in Pre-Islamic Times (New York: Longmans)
Troll, C.W., 1998
'Jesus Christ and Christianity in Abdullah Yusuf Ali's English Interpretation of the Qur'an,' in *Islamochristiana*, 24.
Uddin, Sufia M. 2006
Constructing Bangladesh: Religion, Ethnicity, and Language in an Islamic Nation (Chapel Hill, N.C.: University of North Carolina Press)
United Nations Development Progamme 2002
Arab Human Development Report 2002 (New York: United Nations Publications)

Van Gorder, C. 2008
Christian Muslim-Christian Relations in Central Asia (London: Routledge)
Vanier, J. 2004
Drawn into the mystery of Jesus through the Gospel of John (Ottawa: Novalis, Saint Paul University)
Walls, A.F. 1996
The Missionary Movement in Christian History: Studies in the Transmission of Faith (Maryknoll, N.Y.: Orbis Books and Edinburgh: T. & T. Clark)
Walls, A.F. 2000
'Eusebius Tries Again: Recovering the Study of Christian History' in *International Bulletin of Missionary Research* 24, 3 (July).
Walls, A.F. 2002
The Cross-Cultural Process in Christian History: Studies in the Transmission and Appropriation of Faith (New York: Orbis Books)
Watt, M. 1953
Muhammad at Mecca (Oxford: Oxford University Press)
Watt, M. 1956
Muhammad at Medina (Oxford: Oxford University Press)
Weber, M., T. Parsons & R.H. Tawney 2003
The Protestant Ethic and Spirit of Capitalism (Mineola, N.Y.: Dover)
Welcome to the United States: a Guide for new Immigrants (in Russian) 2005
United States, Dept. of Education, U.S. Citizenship and Immigration Services. (Washington: DIANE).
Wendell, C., 1972
'Pre-Islamic Period of Sîrat Al-Nabî' in *The Muslim World* 62
Wensinck, A.J. 2002
'Wahy' in *Encyclopedia of Islam* 2nd ed. v. 11 (Leiden: Brill)
Wessels, C. 1999
Early Jesuit Travelers in Central Asia 1603-1721 (Delhi: Low Price)
Westermarck, E. 1933
Pagan Survivals in Mohammedan Civilization (London: Macmillan)
Wheeler, B. M. 2002
Moses in the Quran and Islamic Exegesis (London: RoutledgeCurzon)
Wills, L. 2006
'Susanna' in H. W. Attridge and W. C. Meeks (eds.) *Harper Collins Study Bible* rev. ed. (San Francisco, Calif.: HarperSanFrancisco)
Woodberry, J.D. & R.G.Shubin 2001
'Why I chose Jesus' in *Mission Frontiers* March
Wright, N.T. 1996
Jesus and the Victory of God (Minneapolis, Minn.: Fortress Press)
Wylie, J.A. 2002
The History of Protestantism (Rapidan, Va.: Hartland)
Youngblood, R. 1998
The Heart of the Old Testament 2nd ed. (Grand Rapids, Mich.: Baker Books)
Yusuf, J.S. 2009,
'The Day of Ashura', cited online at http://archive.mumineen.org/awliya/panjatanpak/day_of_ashura.html accessed on 16th January 2009.

Yusuf Roni, A.M. 1979
Pembelaku Yang Agung (Jakarta, private publication)
Zahniser, A. H. M. 1997
'Sura as Guidance and Exhortation: The Composition of Surat al-Nisa'' in A. Afsaruddin and A. H. M. Zahniser (eds.) *Humanism, Culture, and Language in the Near East: Studies in Honor of Georg Krotkoff* (Winona Lake, Ind.: Eisenbrauns) 71-85.
Zahniser, A.H.M. 2009
'Wesleyan Synergism and the Dialogue with Muslims' in D. L. Whiteman and G. H. Anderson (eds.) *World Mission in the Wesleyan Spirit* (Franklin, Tenn.: Providence House) 227-34
Zaki, Y. 1991
'The Qur'an and Revelation' in D. Cohn-Sherbock (ed.) *Islam in a World of Diverse Faiths* (New York: St. Martin's Press)
Zugl, O.T. 2006
Die Herrnhuter in Russland: Ziel, Umfang und Ertrag ihrer Aktivitäten (Gottingen: Vandenhoeck & Ruprecht)
Zwemer, S.M. 1920
A Moslem Seeker after God: Showing Islam at its best in the Life and Teaching of Al-Ghazali, Mystic and Theologian of the Eleventh Century (New York: Fleming H. Revell)

General Index

REGNUM EDINBURGH CENTENARY SERIES

David A. Kerr, Kenneth R. Ross (Eds)
Mission Then and Now
2009 / 978-1-870345-73-6 / 343pp (paperback)
2009 / 978-1-870345-76-7 / 343pp (hardback)

No one can hope to fully understand the modern Christian missionary movement without engaging substantially with the World Missionary Conference, held at Edinburgh in 1910. This book is the first to systematically examine the eight Commissions which reported to Edinburgh 1910 and gave the conference much of its substance and enduring value. It will deepen and extend the reflection being stimulated by the upcoming centenary and will kindle the missionary imagination for 2010 and beyond.

Daryl M. Balia, Kirsteen Kim (Eds)
Witnessing to Christ Today
2010 / 978-1-870345-77-4 / 301pp (hardback)

This volume, the second in the Edinburgh 2010 series, includes reports of the nine main study groups working on different themes for the celebration of the centenary of the World Missionary Conference, Edinburgh 1910. Their collaborative work brings together perspectives that are as inclusive as possible of contemporary world Christianity and helps readers to grasp what it means in different contexts to be 'witnessing to Christ today'.

Claudia Währisch-Oblau, Fidon Mwombeki (Eds)
Mission Continues
Global Impulses for the 21st Century
2010 / 978-1-870345-82-8 / 271pp (hardback)

In May 2009, 35 theologians from Asia, Africa and Europe met in Wuppertal, Germany, for a consultation on mission theology organized by the United Evangelical Mission: Communion of 35 Churches in Three Continents. The aim was to participate in the 100th anniversary of the Edinburgh conference through a study process and reflect on the challenges for mission in the 21st century. This book brings together these papers written by experienced practitioners from around the world.

Brian Woolnough and Wonsuk Ma (Eds)
Holistic Mission
God's Plan for God's People
2010 / 978-1-870345-85-9 / 268pp (hardback)

Holistic mission, or integral mission, implies God is concerned with the whole person, the whole community, body, mind and spirit. This book discusses the meaning of the holistic gospel, how it has developed, and implications for the church. It takes a global, eclectic approach, with 19 writers, all of whom have much experience in, and commitment to, holistic mission. It addresses critically and honestly one of the most exciting, and challenging, issues facing the church today. To be part of God's plan for God's people, the church must take holistic mission to the world.

Kirsteen Kim and Andrew Anderson (Eds)
Mission Today and Tomorrow
2010 / 978-1-870345-91-0 / 450pp (hardback)

There are moments in our lives when we come to realise that we are participating in the triune God's mission. If we believe the church to be as sign and symbol of the reign of God in the world, then we are called to witness to Christ today by sharing in God's mission of love through the transforming power of the Holy Spirit. We can all participate in God's transforming and reconciling mission of love to the whole creation.

Tormod Engelsviken, Erling Lundeby and Dagfinn Solheim (Eds)
The Church Going Glocal
Mission and Globalisation
2011 / 978-1-870345-93-4 / 262pp (hardback)

The New Testament church is… universal and local at the same time. The universal, one and holy apostolic church appears in local manifestations. Missiologically speaking… the church can take courage as she faces the increasing impact of globalisation on local communities today. Being universal and concrete, the church is geared for the simultaneous challenges of the glocal and local.

Marina Ngurusangzeli Behera (Ed)
Interfaith Relations after One Hundred Years
Christian Mission among Other Faiths
2011 / 978-1-870345-96-5 / 338pp (hardback)

The essays of this book reflect not only the acceptance and celebration of pluralism within India but also by extension an acceptance as well as a need for unity among Indian Christians of different denominations. The essays were presented and studied at a preparatory consultation on Study Theme II: Christian Mission Among Other Faiths at the United Theological College, India July 2009.

Lalsangkima Pachuau and Knud Jørgensen (Eds)
Witnessing to Christ in a Pluralistic Age
Christian Mission among Other Faiths
2011 / 978-1-870345-95-8 / 277pp (hardback)

In a world where plurality of faiths is increasingly becoming a norm of life, insights on the theology of religious plurality are needed to strengthen our understanding of our own faith and the faith of others. Even though religious diversity is not new, we are seeing an upsurge in interest on the theologies of religion among all Christian confessional traditions. It can be claimed that no other issue in Christian mission is more important and more difficult than the theologies of religions.

Beth Snodderly and A Scott Moreau (Eds)
Evangelical Frontier Mission
Perspectives on the Global Progress of the Gospel
2011 / 978-1-870345-98-9 / 312pp (hardback)

This important volume demonstrates that 100 years after the World Missionary Conference in Edinburgh, Evangelism has become truly global. Twenty-first-century Evangelism continues to focus on frontier mission, but significantly, and in the spirit of Edinburgh 1910, it also has re-engaged social action.

Rolv Olsen (Ed)
Mission and Postmodernities
2011 / 978-1-870345-97-2 / 279pp (hardback)

This volume takes on meaning because its authors honestly struggle with and debate how we should relate to postmodernities. Should our response be accommodation, relativizing or counter-culture? How do we strike a balance between listening and understanding, and at the same time exploring how postmodernities influence the interpretation and application of the Bible as the normative story of God's mission in the world?

Cathy Ross (Ed)
Life-Widening Mission
2012 / 978-1-908355-00-3 / 163pp (hardback)

It is clear from the essays collected here that the experience of the 2010 World Mission Conference in Edinburgh was both affirming and frustrating for those taking part - affirming because of its recognition of how the centre of gravity has moved in global Christianity; frustrating because of the relative slowness of so many global Christian bodies to catch up with this and to embody it in the way they do business and in the way they represent themselves. These reflections will - or should - provide plenty of food for thought in the various councils of the Communion in the coming years.

Beate Fagerli, Knud Jørgensen, Rolv Olsen, Kari Storstein Haug and Knut Tveitereid (Eds)
A Learning Missional Church
Reflections from Young Missiologists
2012 / 978-1-908355-01-0 / 218pp (hardback)

Cross-cultural mission has always been a primary learning experience for the church. It pulls us out of a mono-cultural understanding and helps us discover a legitimate theological pluralism which opens up for new perspectives in the Gospel. Translating the Gospel into new languages and cultures is a human and divine means of making us learn new 'incarnations' of the Good News.

Emma Wild-Wood & Peniel Rajkumar (Eds)
Foundations for Mission
2012 / 978-1-908355-12-6 / 309pp (hardback)

This volume provides an important resource for those wishing to gain an overview of significant issues in contemporary missiology whilst understanding how they are applied in particular contexts.

Wonsuk Ma & Kenneth R Ross (Eds)
Mission Spirituality and Authentic Discipleship
2013 / 978-1-908355-24-9 / 248pp (hardback)

This book argues for the primacy of spirituality in the practice of mission. Since God is the primary agent of mission and God works through the power of the Holy Spirit, it is through openness to the Spirit that mission finds its true character and has its authentic impact.

Stephen B Bevans (Ed)
A Century of Catholic Mission
2013 / 978-1-908355-14-0 / 337pp (hardback)

A Century of Catholic Mission surveys the complex and rich history and theology of Roman Catholic Mission in the one hundred years since the 1910 Edinburgh World Mission Conference. Essays written by an international team of Catholic mission scholars focus on Catholic Mission in every region of the world, summarize church teaching on mission before and after the watershed event of the Second Vatican Council, and reflect on a wide variety of theological issues.

Robert Schreiter & Knud Jørgensen (Eds)
Mission as Ministry of Reconcilation
2013 / 978-1-908355-26-3 / 382pp (hardback)

There is hope – even if it is "Hope in a Fragile World", as the concluding chapter of Mission as Ministry of Reconciliation puts it. At the very heart of the gospel of Jesus Christ is a message of hope and reconciliation. Nothing could be more relevant and more necessary in a broken world than this Christian message of hope and reconciliation. ... I would like to congratulate the editors of Mission as Ministry of Reconciliation, for they listened carefully and planned with farsightedness. ... This rich book offers a valuable elucidation of the importance and the understanding of mission as ministry of reconciliation.

Petros Vassiliadis, Editor
Orthodox Perspectives on Mission
2013 / 978-1908355-25-6 / 262pp (hardback)

Orthodox Perspectives on Mission is both a humble tribute to some great Orthodox theologians, who in the past have provided substantial contribution to contemporary missiological and ecumenical discussions, and an Orthodox input to the upcoming 2013 Busan WCC General Assembly. The collected volume is divided into two parts: Part I: The Orthodox Heritage consists of Orthodox missiological contributions of the past, whereas Part II includes all the papers presented in the Plenary of the recent Edinburgh 2010 conference, as well as the short studies and contributions prepared, during the Edinburgh 2010 on going study process.

Pauline Hoggarth, Fergus MacDonald,
Bill Mitchell & Knud Jørgensen, Editors
Bible in Mission
2013 / 978-1908355-42-3 / 317pp (hardback)

To the authors of Bible in Mission, the Bible is the book of life, and mission is life in the Word. This core reality cuts across the diversity of contexts and hermeneutical strategies represented in these essays. The authors are committed to the boundary-crossings that characterize contemporary mission – and each sees the Bible as foundational to the missio Dei, to God's work in the world.

Wonsuk Ma, Veli-Matti Kärkkäinnen
& J Kwabena Asamoah
Pentecostal Mission and Global Christianity
2014 / 978-1908355-43-0 / 397pp (hardback)

Although Pentecostalism worldwide represent the most rapidly growing missionary movement in Christian history, only recently scholars from within and outside the movement have begun academic reflection on the mission. This volume represents the coming of age of emerging scholarship of various aspects of the Pentecostal mission, including theological, historical, strategic, and practical aspects.

Afe Adogame, Janice McLean & Anderson Jeremiah, Editors
Engaging the World
Christian Communities in Contemporary Global Societies
2014 / 978-1908355-21-8 / 235pp (hardback)

Engaging the World deals with the lived experiences and expressions of Christians in diverse communities across the globe. Christian communities do not live in a vacuum but in complex, diverse social-cultural contexts; within wider communities of different faith and social realities. Power, identity and community are key issues in considering Christian communities in contemporary contexts.

Peniel Jesudason Rufus Rajkumar, Joseph Prabhakar Dayam
& IP Asheervadham, Editors
Mission At and From the Margins
Patterns, Protagonists and Perspectives
2014 / 978-1908355-13-3 / 283pp (hardback)

Mission At and From the Margins: Patterns, Protagonists and Perspectives revisits the 'hi-stories' of Mission from the 'bottom up' paying critical attention to people, perspectives and patterns that have often been elided in the construction of mission history. Focusing on the mission story of Christian churches in the South Indian state of Abdhra Pradesh this collection of essays ushers its readers to re-shape their understanding of the landscape of mission history by drawing their attention to the silences and absences within pre-dominant historical accounts.

REGNUM STUDIES IN GLOBAL CHRISTIANITY

David Emmanuel Singh (Ed)
Jesus and the Cross
Reflections of Christians from Islamic Contexts
2008 / 978-1-870345-65-1 / 226pp

The Cross reminds us that the sins of the world are not borne through the exercise of power but through Jesus Christ's submission to the will of the Father. The papers in this volume are organised in three parts: scriptural, contextual and theological. The central question being addressed is: how do Christians living in contexts, where Islam is a majority or minority religion, experience, express or think of the Cross?

Sung-wook Hong
Naming God in Korea
The Case of Protestant Christianity
2008 / 978-1-870345-66-8 / 170pp (hardback)

Since Christianity was introduced to Korea more than a century ago, one of the most controversial issues has been the Korean term for the Christian 'God'. This issue is not merely about naming the Christian God in Korean language, but it relates to the question of theological contextualization - the relationship between the gospel and culture - and the question of Korean Christian identity. This book demonstrates the nature of the gospel in relation to cultures, i.e., the universality of the gospel expressed in all human cultures.

Hubert van Beek (Ed)
Revisioning Christian Unity
The Global Christian Forum
2009 / 978-1-870345-74-3 / 288pp (hardback)

This book contains the records of the Global Christian Forum gathering held in Limuru near Nairobi, Kenya, on 6 – 9 November 2007 as well as the papers presented at that historic event. Also included are a summary of the Global Christian Forum process from its inception until the 2007 gathering and the reports of the evaluation of the process that was carried out in 2008.

Young-hoon Lee

The Holy Spirit Movement in Korea

Its Historical and Theological Development

2009 / 978-1-870345-67-5 / 174pp (hardback)

This book traces the historical and theological development of the Holy Spirit Movement in Korea through six successive periods (from 1900 to the present time). These periods are characterized by repentance and revival (1900-20), persecution and suffering under Japanese occupation (1920-40), confusion and division (1940-60), explosive revival in which the Pentecostal movement played a major role in the rapid growth of Korean churches (1960-80), the movement reaching out to all denominations (1980-2000), and the new context demanding the Holy Spirit movement to open new horizons in its mission engagement (2000-).

Paul Hang-Sik Cho

Eschatology and Ecology

Experiences of the Korean Church

2010 / 978-1-870345-75-0 / 260pp (hardback)

This book raises the question of why Korean people, and Korean Protestant Christians in particular, pay so little attention to ecological issues. The author argues that there is an important connection (or elective affinity) between this lack of attention and the other-worldly eschatology that is so dominant within Korean Protestant Christianity.

Dietrich Werner, David Esterline, Namsoon Kang, Joshva Raja (Eds)

The Handbook of Theological Education in World Christianity

Theological Perspectives, Ecumenical Trends, Regional Surveys

2010 / 978-1-870345-80-0 / 759pp

This major reference work is the first ever comprehensive study of Theological Education in Christianity of its kind. With contributions from over 90 international scholars and church leaders, it aims to be easily accessible across denominational, cultural, educational, and geographic boundaries. The Handbook will aid international dialogue and networking among theological educators, institutions, and agencies.

David Emmanuel Singh & Bernard C Farr (Eds)

Christianity and Education

Shaping of Christian Context in Thinking

2010 / 978-1-870345-81-1 / 374pp

Christianity and Education is a collection of papers published in *Transformation: An International Journal of Holistic Mission Studies* over a period of 15 years. The articles represent a spectrum of Christian thinking addressing issues of institutional development for theological education, theological studies in the context of global mission, contextually aware/informed education, and academies which deliver such education, methodologies and personal reflections.

J.Andrew Kirk

Civilisations in Conflict?

Islam the West and Christian Faith

2011 / 978-1-870345-87-3 / 205pp

Samuel Huntington's thesis, which argues that there appear to be aspects of Islam that could be on a collision course with the politics and values of Western societies, has provoked much controversy. The purpose of this study is to offer a particular response to Huntington's thesis by making a comparison between the origins of Islam and Christianity.

David Emmanuel Singh (Ed)

Jesus and the Incarnation

Reflections of Christians from Islamic Contexts

2011 / 978-1-870345-90-3 / 245pp

In the dialogues of Christians with Muslims nothing is more fundamental than the Cross, the Incarnation and the Resurrection of Jesus. Building on the *Jesus and the Cross*, this book contains voices of Christians living in various 'Islamic contexts' and reflecting on the Incarnation of Jesus. The aim and hope of these reflections is that the papers weaved around the notion of 'the Word' will not only promote dialogue among Christians on the roles of the Person and the Book but, also, create a positive environment for their conversations with Muslim neighbours.

Ivan M Satyavrata

God Has Not left Himself Without Witness

2011 / 978-1-870345-79-8 / 264pp

Since its earliest inception the Christian Church has had to address the question of what common ground exits between Christian faiths and other religions. This issue is not merely of academic interest but one with critical existential and socio-political consequences. This study presents a case for the revitalization of the fulfillment tradition based on a recovery and assessment of the fulfillment approaches of Indian Christian converts in the pre-independence period.

Bal Krishna Sharma

From this World to the Next

Christian Identity and Funerary Rites in Nepal

2013 / 978-1-908355-08-9 / 238pp

This book explores and analyses funerary rite struggles in a nation where Christianity is a comparatively recent phenomenon, and many families have multi-faith, who go through traumatic experiences at the death of their family members. The author has used an applied theological approach to explore and analyse the findings in order to address the issue of funerary rites with which the Nepalese church is struggling.

J Kwabena Asamoah-Gyada

Contemporary Pentecostal Christianity

Interpretations from an African Context

2013 / 978-1-908355-07-2 / 194pp

Pentecostalism is the fastest growing stream of Christianity in the world. The real evidence for the significance of Pentecostalism lies in the actual churches they have built and the numbers they attract. This work interprets key theological and missiological themes in African Pentecostalism by using material from the live experiences of the movement itself.

David Emmanuel Singh and Bernard C Farr (Eds)

The Bible and Christian Ethics

2013 / 978-1-908355-20-1 / 217pp

This book contains papers from the Oxford Centre for Mission Studies' quarterly journal, Transformation, on the topic of Christian Ethics. Here, Mission Studies is understood in its widest sense to also encompass Christian Ethics. At the very hearts of it lies the Family as the basic unit of society. All the papers together seek to contribute to understanding how Christian thought is shaped in contexts each of which poses its own challenge to Christian living in family and in broader society.

Martin Allaby

Inequality, Corruption and the Church

Challenges & Opportunities in the Global Church

2013 / 978-1-908355-16-4 / 228pp

Why are economic inequalities greatest in the southern countries where most people are Christians? This book teases out the influences that have created this situation, and concludes that Christians could help reduce economic inequalities by opposing corruption. Interviews in the Philippines, Kenya, Zambia and Peru reveal opportunities and challenges for Christians as they face up to corruption.

Paul Alexander and Al Tizon (Eds)

Following Jesus

Journeys in Radical Discipleship – Essays in Honor of Ronald J Sider

2013 / 978-1-908355-27-0 / 228pp

Ronald J. Sider and the organization that he founded, *Evangelicals for Social Action*, are most respected for their pioneering work in the area of evangelical social concern. However, Sider's great contribution to social justice is but a part of a larger vision – namely, biblical discipleship. His works, which span more than four decades, have guided the faithful to be authentic gospel-bearers in ecclesial, cultural and political arenas. This book honors Ron Sider, by bringing together a group of scholar-activists, old and young, to reflect upon the gospel and its radical implications for the 21st century.

Cawley Bolt

Reluctant or Radical Revolutionaries?

Evangelical Missionaries and Afro-Jamaican Character, 1834-1870

2013 / 978-1-908355-18-8 / 287pp

This study is based on extensive research that challenges traditional ways of understanding some evangelical missionaries of nineteenth century Jamaica and calls for revision of those views. It highlights the strength and character of persons facing various challenges of life in their effort to be faithful to the guiding principles of their existence.

Isabel Apawo Phiri & Dietrich Werner (Eds)

Handbook of Theological Education in Africa

2013 / 978-1-908355-45-4 / 1110pp

The *Handbook of Theological Education in Africa* is a wake-up call for African churches to give proper prominence to theological education institutions and their programmes which serve them. It is unique, comprehensive and ambitious in its aim and scope.

Hope Antone, Wati Longchar, Hyunju Bae, Huang Po Ho, Dietrich Werner (Eds)

Asian Handbook for Theological Education and Ecumenism

2013 / 978-1-908355-30-0 / 675pp (hardback)

This impressive and comprehensive book focuses on key resources for teaching Christian unity and common witness in Asian contexts. It is a collection of articles that reflects the ongoing 'double wrestle' with the texts of biblical tradition as well as with contemporary contexts. It signals an investment towards the future of the ecumenical movement in Asia.

Bernhard Reitsma

The God of My Enemy

The Middle East and the Nature of God

2014 / 978-1-908355-50-8 / 206pp

The establishment of the State of Israel in 1948 for the Church in the West has been the starting point of a rediscovery of its own roots. In the Middle East the effect has been exactly the opposite: Christians have become estranged from their Old Testament roots, because they have been expelled from their land exactly because of an appeal to the Old Testament. The concept of Israel changed from a nation in the Bible, with which they could associate, to an economic, political and military power that was against them

REGNUM STUDIES IN MISSION

Kwame Bediako
Theology and Identity
The Impact of Culture upon Christian Thought in the Second Century and in Modern Africa
1992 / 978-1870345-10-1 / 507pp

The author examines the question of Christian identity in the context of the Graeco–Roman culture of the early Roman Empire. He then addresses the modern African predicament of quests for identity and integration.

Christopher Sugden
Seeking the Asian Face of Jesus
The Practice and Theology of Christian Social Witness in Indonesia and India 1974–1996
1997 / 1-870345-26-6 / 496pp

This study focuses on contemporary holistic mission with the poor in India and Indonesia combined with the call to transformation of all life in Christ with micro-credit enterprise schemes. 'The literature on contextual theology now has a new standard to rise to' – Lamin Sanneh (Yale University, USA).

Hwa Yung
Mangoes or Bananas?
The Quest for an Authentic Asian Christian Theology
1997 / 1-870345-25-5 / 274pp

Asian Christian thought remains largely captive to Greek dualism and Enlightenment rationalism because of the overwhelming dominance of Western culture. Authentic contextual Christian theologies will emerge within Asian Christianity with a dual recovery of confidence in culture and the gospel.

Keith E. Eitel
Paradigm Wars
The Southern Baptist International Mission Board Faces the Third Millennium
1999 / 1-870345-12-6 / 140pp

The International Mission Board of the Southern Baptist Convention is the largest denominational mission agency in North America. This volume chronicles the historic and contemporary forces that led to the IMB's recent extensive reorganization, providing the most comprehensive case study to date of a historic mission agency restructuring to continue its mission purpose into the twenty-first century more effectively.

Samuel Jayakumar

Dalit Consciousness and Christian Conversion

Historical Resources for a Contemporary Debate

1999 / 81-7214-497-0 / 434pp

(Published jointly with ISPCK)

The main focus of this historical study is social change and transformation among the Dalit Christian communities in India. Historiography tests the evidence in the light of the conclusions of the modern Dalit liberation theologians.

Vinay Samuel and Christopher Sugden (Eds)

Mission as Transformation

A Theology of the Whole Gospel

1999 / 978-18703455-13-2 / 522pp

This book brings together in one volume twenty five years of biblical reflection on mission practice with the poor from around the world. This volume helps anyone understand how evangelicals, struggling to unite evangelism and social action, found their way in the last twenty five years to the biblical view of mission in which God calls all human beings to love God and their neighbour; never creating a separation between the two.

Christopher Sugden

Gospel, Culture and Transformation

2000 / 1-870345-32-3 / 152pp

A Reprint, with a New Introduction,

of Part Two of Seeking the Asian Face of Jesus

Gospel, Culture and Transformation explores the practice of mission especially in relation to transforming cultures and communities. - 'Transformation is to enable God's vision of society to be actualised in all relationships: social, economic and spiritual, so that God's will may be reflected in human society and his love experienced by all communities, especially the poor.'

Bernhard Ott

Beyond Fragmentation: Integrating Mission and Theological Education

A Critical Assessment of some Recent Developments

in Evangelical Theological Education

2001 / 1-870345-14-9 / 382pp

Beyond Fragmentation is an enquiry into the development of Mission Studies in evangelical theological education in Germany and German-speaking Switzerland between 1960 and 1995. The author undertakes a detailed examination of the paradigm shifts which have taken place in recent years in both the theology of mission and the understanding of theological education.

Gideon Githiga

The Church as the Bulwark against Authoritarianism

Development of Church and State Relations in Kenya, with Particular Reference to the Years after Political Independence 1963-1992

2002 / 1-870345-38-x / 218pp

'All who care for love, peace and unity in Kenyan society will want to read this careful history by Bishop Githiga of how Kenyan Christians, drawing on the Bible, have sought to share the love of God, bring his peace and build up the unity of the nation, often in the face of great difficulties and opposition.' Canon Dr Chris Sugden, Oxford Centre for Mission Studies.

Myung Sung-Hoon, Hong Young-Gi (Eds)
Charis and Charisma
David Yonggi Cho and the Growth of Yoido Full Gospel Church
2003 / 978-1870345-45-3 / 218pp

This book discusses the factors responsible for the growth of the world's largest church. It expounds the role of the Holy Spirit, the leadership, prayer, preaching, cell groups and creativity in promoting church growth. It focuses on God's grace (charis) and inspiring leadership (charisma) as the two essential factors and the book's purpose is to present a model for church growth worldwide.

Samuel Jayakumar
Mission Reader
Historical Models for Wholistic Mission in the Indian Context
2003 / 1-870345-42-8 / 250pp
(Published jointly with ISPCK)

This book is written from an evangelical point of view revalidating and reaffirming the Christian commitment to wholistic mission. The roots of the 'wholistic mission' combining 'evangelism and social concerns' are to be located in the history and tradition of Christian evangelism in the past; and the civilizing purpose of evangelism is compatible with modernity as an instrument in nation building.

Bob Robinson
Christians Meeting Hindus
An Analysis and Theological Critique of the Hindu-Christian Encounter in India
2004 / 987-1870345-39-2 / 392pp

This book focuses on the Hindu-Christian encounter, especially the intentional meeting called dialogue, mainly during the last four decades of the twentieth century, and specifically in India itself.

Gene Early
Leadership Expectations
How Executive Expectations are Created and Used in a Non-Profit Setting
2005 / 1-870345-30-9 / 276pp

The author creates an Expectation Enactment Analysis to study the role of the Chancellor of the University of the Nations-Kona, Hawaii. This study is grounded in the field of managerial work, jobs, and behaviour and draws on symbolic interactionism, role theory, role identity theory and enactment theory. The result is a conceptual framework for developing an understanding of managerial roles.

Tharcisse Gatwa
The Churches and Ethnic Ideology in the Rwandan Crises 1900-1994
2005 / 978-1870345-24-8 / 300pp
(Reprinted 2011)

Since the early years of the twentieth century Christianity has become a new factor in Rwandan society. This book investigates the role Christian churches played in the formulation and development of the racial ideology that culminated in the 1994 genocide.

Julie Ma

Mission Possible

Biblical Strategies for Reaching the Lost

2005 / 978-1870345-37-8 / 142pp

This is a missiology book for the church which liberates missiology from the specialists for the benefit of every believer. It also serves as a textbook that is simple and friendly, and yet solid in biblical interpretation. This book links the biblical teaching to the actual and contemporary missiological settings with examples, making the Bible come alive to the reader.

I. Mark Beaumont

Christology in Dialogue with Muslims

A Critical Analysis of Christian Presentations of Christ for Muslims from the Ninth and Twentieth Centuries

2005 / 978-1870345-46-0 / 227pp

This book analyses Christian presentations of Christ for Muslims in the most creative periods of Christian-Muslim dialogue, the first half of the ninth century and the second half of the twentieth century. In these two periods, Christians made serious attempts to present their faith in Christ in terms that take into account Muslim perceptions of him, with a view to bridging the gap between Muslim and Christian convictions.

Thomas Czövek,

Three Seasons of Charismatic Leadership

A Literary-Critical and Theological Interpretation of the Narrative of Saul, David and Solomon

2006 / 978-1870345-48-4 / 272pp

This book investigates the charismatic leadership of Saul, David and Solomon. It suggests that charismatic leaders emerge in crisis situations in order to resolve the crisis by the charisma granted by God. Czovek argues that Saul proved himself as a charismatic leader as long as he acted resolutely and independently from his mentor Samuel. In the author's eyes, Saul's failure to establish himself as a charismatic leader is caused by his inability to step out from Samuel's shadow.

Richard Burgess

Nigeria's Christian Revolution

The Civil War Revival and Its Pentecostal Progeny (1967-2006)

2008 / 978-1-870345-63-7 / 347pp

This book describes the revival that occurred among the Igbo people of Eastern Nigeria and the new Pentecostal churches it generated, and documents the changes that have occurred as the movement has responded to global flows and local demands. As such, it explores the nature of revivalist and Pentecostal experience, but does so against the backdrop of local socio-political and economic developments, such as decolonisation and civil war, as well as broader processes, such as modernisation and globalisation.

David Emmanuel Singh & Bernard C Farr (Eds)

Christianity and Cultures

Shaping Christian Thinking in Context

2008 / 978-1-870345-69-9 / 271pp

This volume marks an important milestone, the 25th anniversary of the Oxford Centre for Mission Studies (OCMS). The papers here have been exclusively sourced from Transformation, a quarterly journal of OCMS, and seek to provide a tripartite view of

Christianity's engagement with cultures by focusing on the question: how is Christian thinking being formed or reformed through its interaction with the varied contexts it encounters? The subject matters include different strands of theological-missiological thinking, socio-political engagements and forms of family relationships in interaction with the host cultures.

Tormod Engelsviken, Ernst Harbakk, Rolv Olsen, Thor Strandenæs (Eds)
Mission to the World
Communicating the Gospel in the 21st Century:
Essays in Honour of Knud Jørgensen
2008 / 978-1-870345-64-4 / 472pp (hardback)

Knud Jørgensen is Director of Areopagos and Associate Professor of Missiology at MF Norwegian School of Theology. This book reflects on the main areas of Jørgensen's commitment to mission. At the same time it focuses on the main frontier of mission, the world, the content of mission, the Gospel, the fact that the Gospel has to be communicated, and the context of contemporary mission in the 21st century.

Al Tizon
Transformation after Lausanne
Radical Evangelical Mission in Global-Local Perspective
2008 / 978-1-870345-68-2 / 281pp

After Lausanne '74, a worldwide network of radical evangelical mission theologians and practitioners use the notion of "Mission as Transformation" to integrate evangelism and social concern together, thus lifting theological voices from the Two Thirds World to places of prominence. This book documents the definitive gatherings, theological tensions, and social forces within and without evangelicalism that led up to Mission as Transformation. And it does so through a global-local grid that points the way toward greater holistic mission in the 21st century.

Bambang Budijanto
Values and Participation
Development in Rural Indonesia
2009 / 978-1-870345-70-4 / 237pp

Socio-religious values and socio-economic development are inter-dependant, inter-related and are constantly changing in the context of macro political structures, economic policy, religious organizations and globalization; and micro influences such as local affinities, identity, politics, leadership and beliefs. The book argues that the comprehensive approach in understanding the socio-religious values of each of the three local Lopait communities in Central Java is essential to accurately describing their respective identity.

Alan R. Johnson
Leadership in a Slum
A Bangkok Case Study
2009 / 978-1-870345-71-2 / 238pp

This book looks at leadership in the social context of a slum in Bangkok from a different perspective than traditional studies which measure well educated Thais on leadership scales derived in the West. Using both systematic data collection and participant observation, it develops a culturally preferred model as well as a set of models based in Thai concepts that reflect on-the-ground realities. It concludes by looking at the implications of the anthropological approach for those who are involved in leadership training in Thai settings and beyond.

Titre Ande

Leadership and Authority

Bula Matari and Life - Community Ecclesiology in Congo

2010 / 978-1-870345-72-9 / 189pp

Christian theology in Africa can make significant development if a critical understanding of the socio-political context in contemporary Africa is taken seriously, particularly as Africa's post-colonial Christian leadership based its understanding and use of authority on the Bula Matari model. This has caused many problems and Titre proposes a Life-Community ecclesiology for liberating authority, here leadership is a function, not a status, and 'apostolic succession' belongs to all people of God.

Frank Kwesi Adams

Odwira and the Gospel

A Study of the Asante Odwira Festival and its Significance for Christianity in Ghana

2010 /978-1-870345-59-0 / 232pp

The study of the Odwira festival is the key to the understanding of Asante religious and political life in Ghana. The book explores the nature of the Odwira festival longitudinally - in pre-colonial, colonial and post-independence Ghana - and examines the Odwira ideology and its implications for understanding the Asante self-identity. Also discussed is how some elements of faith portrayed in the Odwira festival can provide a framework for Christianity to engage with Asante culture at a greater depth.

Bruce Carlton

Strategy Coordinator

Changing the Course of Southern Baptist Missions

2010 / 978-1-870345-78-1 / 273pp

This is an outstanding, one-of-a-kind work addressing the influence of the non-residential missionary/strategy coordinator's role in Southern Baptist missions. This scholarly text examines the twentieth century global missiological currents that influenced the leadership of the International Mission Board, resulting in a new paradigm to assist in taking the gospel to the nations.

Julie Ma & Wonsuk Ma

Mission in the Spirit:

Towards a Pentecostal/Charismatic Missiology

2010 / 978-1-870345-84-2 / 312pp

The book explores the unique contribution of Pentecostal/Charismatic mission from the beginning of the twentieth century. The first part considers the theological basis of Pentecostal/Charismatic mission thinking and practice. Special attention is paid to the Old Testament, which has been regularly overlooked by the modern Pentecostal/Charismatic movements. The second part discusses major mission topics with contributions and challenges unique to Pentecostal/Charismatic mission. The book concludes with a reflection on the future of this powerful missionary movement. As the authors served as Korean missionaries in Asia, often their missionary experiences in Asia are reflected in their discussions.

Allan Anderson, Edmond Tang (Eds)

Asian and Pentecostal

The Charismatic Face of Christianity in Asia

2011 / 978-1870345-94-1 / 500pp

(Revised Edition)

This book provides a thematic discussion and pioneering case studies on the history and development of Pentecostal and Charismatic churches in the countries of South Asia, South East Asia and East Asia.

S. Hun Kim & Wonsuk Ma (Eds)

Korean Diaspora and Christian Mission

2011 / 978-1-870345-89-7 / 301pp (hardback)

As a 'divine conspiracy' for Missio Dei, the global phenomenon of people on the move has shown itself to be invaluable. In 2004 two significant documents concerning Diaspora were introduced, one by the Filipino International Network and the other by the Lausanne Committee for World Evangelization. These have created awareness of the importance of people on the move for Christian mission. Since then, Korean Diaspora has conducted similar research among Korean missions, resulting in this book

Jin Huat Tan

Planting an Indigenous Church

The Case of the Borneo Evangelical Mission

2011 / 978-1-870345-99-6 / 343pp

Dr Jin Huat Tan has written a pioneering study of the origins and development of Malaysia's most significant indigenous church. This is an amazing story of revival, renewal and transformation of the entire region chronicling the powerful effect of it evident to date! What can we learn from this extensive and careful study of the Borneo Revival, so the global Christianity will become ever more dynamic?

Bill Prevette

Child, Church and Compassion

Towards Child Theology in Romania

2012 / 978-1-908355-03-4 / 382pp

Bill Prevett comments that ¨children are like 'canaries in a mine shaft'; they provide a focal point for discovery and encounter of perilous aspects of our world that are often ignored.¨ True, but miners also carried a lamp to see into the subterranean darkness. This book is such a lamp. It lights up the subterranean world of children and youth in danger of exploitation, and as it does so travels deep into their lives and also into the activities of those who seek to help them.

Samuel Cyuma

Picking up the Pieces

The Church and Conflict Resolution in South Africa and Rwanda

2012 / 978-1-908355-02-7 / 373pp

In the last ten years of the 20th century, the world was twice confronted with unbelievable news from Africa. First, there was the end of Apartheid in South Africa, without bloodshed, due to responsible political and Church leaders. The second was the mass killings in Rwanda, which soon escalated into real genocide. Political and Church leaders had been unable to prevents this crime against humanity. In this book, the question is raised: can we compare the situation in South Africa with that in Rwanda? Can Rwandan leaders draw lessons from the peace process in South Africa?

Peter Rowan

Proclaiming the Peacemaker

The Malaysian Church as an Agent of Reconciliation in a Multicultural Society

2012 / 978-1-908355-05-8 / 268pp

With a history of racial violence and in recent years, low-level ethnic tensions, the themes of peaceful coexistence and social harmony are recurring ones in the discourse of Malaysian society. In such a context, this book looks at the role of the church as a reconciling agent, arguing that a reconciling presence within a divided society necessitates an ethos of peacemaking.

Edward Ontita

Resources and Opportunity

The Architecture of Livelihoods in Rural Kenya

2012 / 978-1-908355-04-1 / 328pp

Poor people in most rural areas of developing countries often improvise resources in unique ways to enable them make a living. Resources and Opportunity takes the view that resources are dynamic and fluid, arguing that villagers co-produce them through redefinition and renaming in everyday practice and use them in diverse ways. The book focuses on ordinary social activities to bring out people's creativity in locating, redesigning and embracing livelihood opportunities in processes.

Kathryn Kraft

Searching for Heaven in the Real World

A Sociological Discussion of Conversion in the Arab World

2012 / 978-1-908355-15-7 / 142pp

Kathryn Kraft explores the breadth of psychological and social issues faced by Arab Muslims after making a decision to adopt a faith in Christ or Christianity, investigating some of the most surprising and significant challenges new believers face.

Wessley Lukose

Contextual Missiology of the Spirit

Pentecostalism in Rajasthan, India

2013 / 978-1-908355-09-6 / 256pp

This book explores the identity, context and features of Pentecostalism in Rajasthan, India as well as the internal and external issues facing Pentecostals. It aims to suggest 'a contextual missiology of the Spirit,' as a new model of contextual missiology from a Pentecostal perspective. It is presented as a glocal, ecumenical, transformational, and public missiology.

Paul M Miller

Evangelical Mission in Co-operation with Catholics

A Study of Evangelical Tensions

2013 / 978-1-908355-17-1 / 291pp

This book brings the first thorough examination of the discussions going on within Evangelicalism about the viability of a good conscience dialogue with Roman Catholics. Those who are interested in evangelical world missions and Roman Catholic views of world missions will find this informative.

Alemayehu Mekonnen

Culture Change in Ethiopia

An Evangelical Perspective

2013 / 978-1-908355-39-3 / 199pp

This book addresses the causes and consequences of culture change in Ethiopia, from Haile Selassie to the present, based on thorough academic research. Although written from an evangelical perspective, this book invites Ethiopians from all religions, ideological, and ethnic backgrounds to reflect on their past, to analyse their present and to engage in unity with diversity to face the future.

Godwin Lekundayo
The Cosmic Christ
Towards Effective Mission Among the Maasai
2013 / 978-1-908355-28- 7 / 259 pp

This book reveals a complex interaction between the Christian gospel brought by western missionaries and the nomadic Massai culture of Tanzania … an important insider's voice courageously questioning the approach to condemn some critical Maasai practices, particularly polygamy, and its missionary consequences. This is a rare study from a Maasai Christian leader.

Philippe Ouedraogo
Female Education and Mission
A Burkina Faso Experience
2014 / 978-1-908355-11-9 / 263pp

This volume is the result of six years research in 'Overcoming Obstacles to Female Education in Burkina Faso'. It narrates how Christians and religious groups can speed up female education and contribute to the socio-economic growth of Burkina Faso. Religious culture and traditions were seen as a problem to female education. However, the evidence from this research shows that Christianity is also part of the solution to a quality female education, thus a key factor of socio economic growth of the country.

Haw Yung
Mangoes or Bananas?
The Quest for an Authentic Asian Christian Theology
(Second Edition)
2014 / 978-1-908355-47-8 / 232pp

Over the past few decades there has been a growing awareness of the need for contextual theologies throughout Asia. But how genuinely contextual are these? Based on the premise that theology and mission are inseparable, the author applies four missiological criteria to representative examples of Protestant Asian writings to assess their adequacy or otherwise as contextual theologies.

Daniel Taichoul Yang
Called Out for Witness
The Missionary Journey of Grace Korean Church
2014 / 978-1-908355-49-2 / 167pp

This book investigates the theological motivation for GKC's missions: Reformed theology, Presbyterian theology, and mission theology. The book also shows the extent of the church's mission engagement by continents. Finally, the book turns its attention to the future with an evaluation of the church's missionary journey.

REGNUM RESOURCES FOR MISSION

Knud Jørgensen
Equipping for Service
Christian Leadership in Church and Society
2012 / 978-1-908355-06-5 / 150pp

This book is written out of decades of experience of leading churches and missions in Ethiopia, Geneva, Norway and Hong Kong. Combining the teaching of Scripture with the insights of contemporary management philosophy, Jørgensen writes in a way which is practical and applicable to anyone in Christian service. "The intention has been to challenge towards a leadership relevant for work in church and mission, and in public and civil society, with special attention to leadership in Church and organisation."

Mary Miller

What does Love have to do with Leadership?

2013 / 978-1-908355-10-2 / 100pp

Leadership is a performing art, not a science. It is the art of influencing others, not just to accomplish something together, but to want to accomplish great things together. Mary Miller captures the art of servant leadership in her powerful book. She understands that servant leaders challenge existing processes without manipulating or overpowering people.

Mary Miller (Ed)

Faces of Holistic Mission

Stories of the OCMS Family

2013 / 978-1-908355-32-4 / 104pp

There is a popular worship song that begins with the refrain, 'look what the Lord has done, look what the Lord has done'. This book does exactly that; it seeks to show what the Lord has done. Fifteen authors from five different continents identify what the Lord has indeed been doing, and continues to do, in their lives. These are their stories.

David Cranston and Ruth Padilla DeBorst (Eds)

Mission as Transformation

Learning from Catalysts

2013 / 978-1-908355-34-8 / 77pp

This book is the product of the first Stott-Bediako Forum, held in 2012 with the title *Portraits of Catalysts*. Its aim was to learn from the stories of Christian leaders whose lives and work have served as catalysts for transformation as each, in his or her particular way, facilitated the intersection between the Good News of Jesus Christ and the context in which they lived, in particular amongst people who are suffering.

Brian Woolnough (Ed)

Good News from Africa

Community Transformation Through the Church

2013 / 978-1-908355-33-1 / 123pp

This book discusses how sustainable, holistic, community development can be, and is being, achieved through the work of the local church. Leading African development practitioners describe different aspects of development through their own experience.

Makonen Getu (Ed)

Transforming Microfinance

A Christian Approach

2013 / 978-1-908355-31-7 / 264pp

"This book highlights the important role that Christian-based organisations bring to the delivery of financial services for the poor. It is times, significant and important and deserves a wide circulation".

Lord Carey of Clifton, former Archbishop of Canterbury

Jonathan Ingleby, Tan Kand San, Tan Loun Ling, (Eds)
Contextualisation & Mission Training
Engaging Asia's Religious Worlds
2013 / 978-1-908355-40-9 / 109pp

Contextualisation & Mission Training, offers "contextual frameworks" and "explorations" in order to enhance deeper engagement with the complexity of Asian social, cultural and religious systems.

On Eagle's Wings
Models in Mentoring
2013 / 978-1-908355-46-1 / 105pp

David Cranston writes unashamedly as a Christian for whom no account of mentoring would be complete without placing it in the biggest context of all – that of the relationship between humans and God.

John Lennox, Professor of Mathematics, University of Oxford
Fellow in Mathematics and Philosophy of Science

GENERAL REGNUM TITLES

Vinay Samuel, Chris Sugden (Eds)
The Church in Response to Human Need
1987 / 1870345045 / xii+268pp

Philip Sampson, Vinay Samuel, Chris Sugden (Eds)
Faith and Modernity
Essays in modernity and post-modernity
1994 / 1870345177 / 352pp

Klaus Fiedler
The Story of Faith Missions
1994 / 0745926878 / 428pp

Douglas Peterson
Not by Might nor by Power
A Pentecostal Theology of Social Concern in Latin America
1996 / 1870345207 / xvi+260pp

David Gitari
In Season and Out of Season
Sermons to a Nation
1996 / 1870345118 / 155pp

David. W. Virtue
A Vision of Hope
The Story of Samuel Habib
1996 / 1870345169 / xiv+137pp

Everett A Wilson
Strategy of the Spirit

J.Philip Hogan and the Growth of the Assemblies of God Worldwide, 1960 - 1990
1997 /1870345231/214

Murray Dempster, Byron Klaus, Douglas Petersen (Eds)
The Globalization of Pentecostalism
A Religion Made to Travel
1999 / 1870345290 / xvii+406pp

Peter Johnson, Chris Sugden (Eds)
Markets, Fair Trade and the Kingdom of God
Essays to Celebrate Traidcraft's 21st Birthday
2001 / 1870345193 / xii+155pp

Robert Hillman, Coral Chamberlain, Linda Harding
Healing & Wholeness
Reflections on the Healing Ministry
2002 / 978-1- 870345-35- 4 / xvii+283pp

David Bussau, Russell Mask
Christian Microenterprise Development
An Introduction
2003 / 1870345282 / xiii+142pp

David Singh
Sainthood and Revelatory Discourse
An Examination of the Basis for the Authority of Bayan in Mahdawi Islam
2003 / 8172147285 / xxiv+485pp

REGNUM AFRICA TITLES

Kwame Bediako
Jesus in Africa, The Christian Gospel in African History and Experience
(2000) (Theological Reflections from the South series)
SECOND EDITION FORTHCOMING 2013

Mercy Amba Oduyoye
Beads and Strands, Reflections of an African Woman on Christianity in Africa
(Theological Reflections from the South series)
2002 / 1-870345-41-X / 114pp

Kä Mana
Christians and Churches of Africa Envisioning the Future, Salvation in Christ and the Building of a new African Society
(Theological Reflections from the South series)
2002 / 1-870345-27-4 / 119pp

Ype Schaaf
On Their Way Rejoicing, The History and Role of the Bible in Africa
2002 / 1-870345-35-9 / 252pp

E.A.W. Engmann
Kpawo-Kpawo Toi Kpawo – Vol. 1, Adesai, Oboade, Lalai, Ajenui ke Shwemoi (Folklore of the Ga People)
(Gbotsui Series - Indigenous Sources of Knowledge in Ghanaian Languages)
2009 / 978-9988-1-2296-6 / 70pp

Philip Tetteh Laryea
Yesu Homowo Nuntso (Jesus, Lord of Homowo)
(Nyamedua series in Mother-tongue Theology)
(reprinted 2011) / 1-870345-54-1 / 176pp

E.A.W. Engmann
Kpawo-Kpawo Toi Kpawo – Vol. 2, Kusumii (Folklore of the Ga People)
(Gbotsui Series - Indigenous Sources of Knowledge in Ghanaian Languages)
2012 / 978-9988-1-2294-2, 186pp

Philip T. Laryea
Ephraim Amu: Nationalist, Poet and Theologian (1899–1995)
2012 / 978-9988-1-2293-5, 425pp

Jon P. Kirby
The Power and the Glory, Popular Christianity in Northern Ghana
(Trends in African Christianity Series)
2012 / 978-9988-1-2295-9, 350pp

For the up-to-date listing of the Regnum books visit www.ocms.ac.uk/regnum

Regnum Books International
Regnum is an Imprint of The Oxford Centre for Mission Studies
St. Philip and St. James Church
Woodstock Road
Oxford, OX2 6HR